AF479177

First published in Australia in 2016 by Power Publications

National Library of Australia Cataloguing-in-Publication data:

    Creator: Palmer, Sheridan, author.

    Title: Hegel's owl : the biography of Bernard Smith / Sheridan Palmer.

    ISBN: 9780994306425 (paperback)

    Notes: Includes bibliographical references and index.

    Subjects: Smith, Bernard, 1916-2011.

        Art historians--Australia--Biography.

        Art critics--Australia--Biography.

    Dewey Number: 709.2

Cover image: Helga Leunig, *Portrait of Bernard Smith*, 1990 (detail). © and courtesy the artist.

Cover design by Xou Creative

Internal design by Xou Creative

Typeset in Adobe Garamond Pro and Josefin Sans

Supported by:

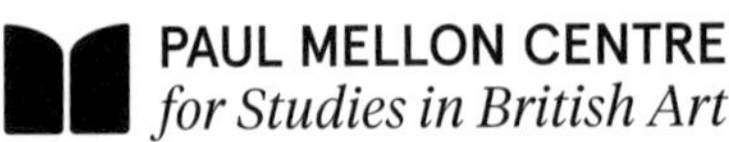

PAUL MELLON CENTRE
for Studies in British Art

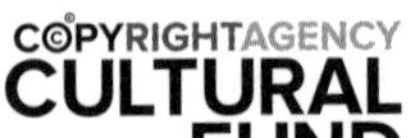

SIDNEY MYER FUND

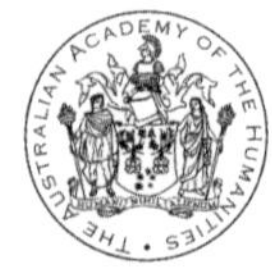

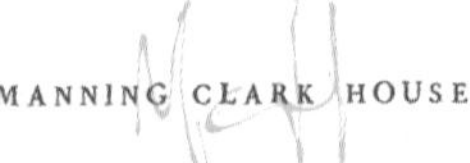

COPYRIGHTAGENCY
CULTURAL FUND

MANNING CLARK HOUSE

HEGEL'S OWL

The Life of
Bernard Smith

SHERIDAN PALMER

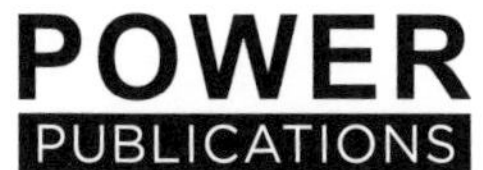

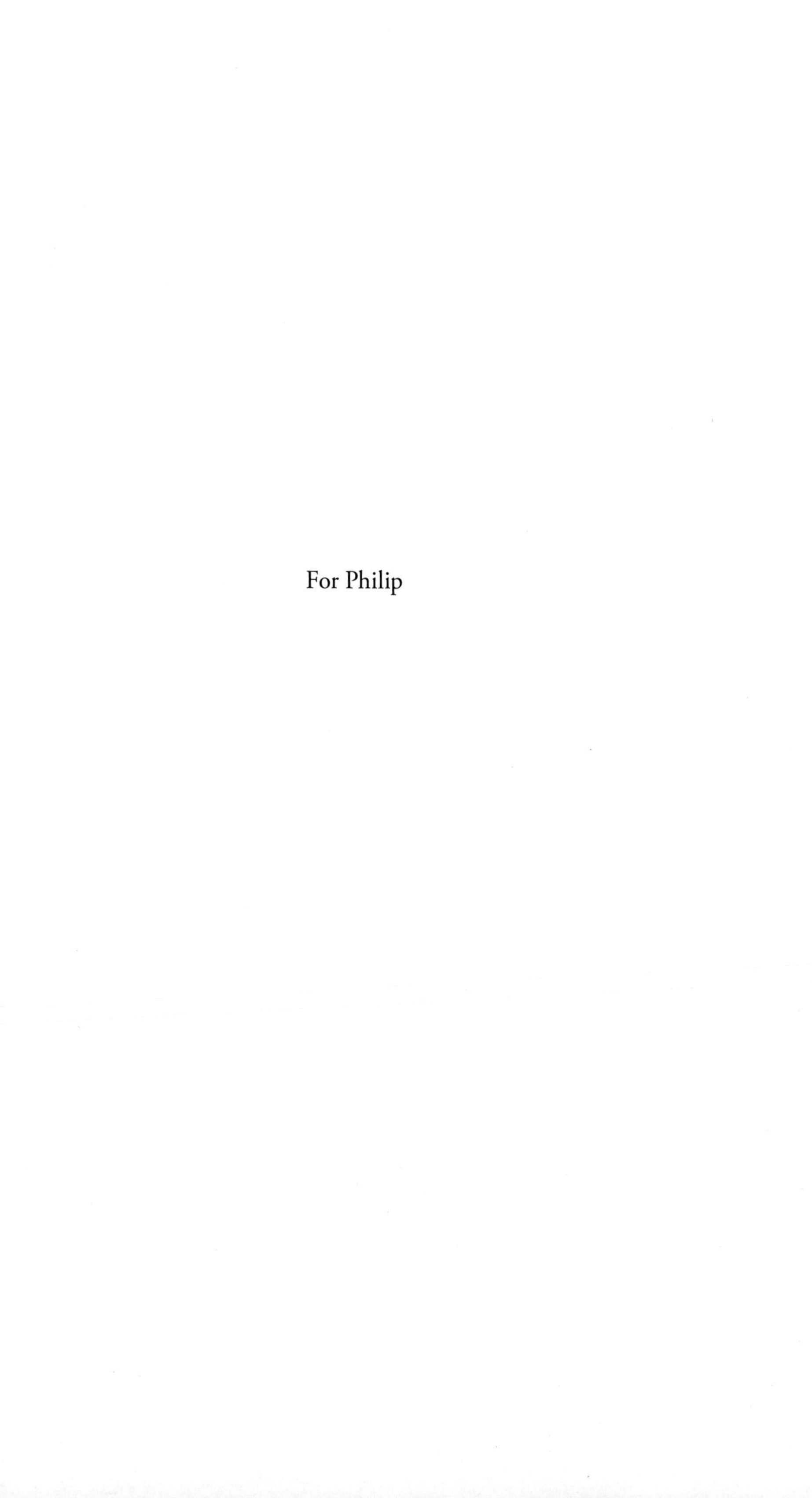

For Philip

CONTENTS

INTRODUCTION

Biographies of major intellectuals are ways of re-examining cultural landscapes, political entanglements and national histories. When a figure such as Australia's great art historian Bernard Smith (1916–2011) comes under the biographer's lens, an immense interdisciplinary world opens up, revealing a convergence of challenging relationships, compelling images and a man endowed with unwavering determination. To condense such a life requires an intricate understanding of the time and place in which he grew up and matured—interwar and postwar Australia—and the impact of tumultuous world events, but equally how his uncommon childhood, illegitimacy and identity as a ward of the State shaped him. From these he formed a complex relationship with society and an incisive vision of cultural inheritance. Always interested in the 'big picture' and how it served in defining Australia, Bernard Smith questioned and wrote from a fiercely antipodean viewpoint. His epic revision of Australia's modern cultural position and his theories of contact, exchange and identity, together with his ability to steer a critical course through vast historical terrains, mark him as one of Australia's most brilliant and pioneering intellectuals.

I came to know Bernard Smith late in his life, late enough to glimpse the hardened shell of a triumphant but battle-worn man, not unlike one of the old leather volumes in his well organised library. That library, collected over seventy-five years, filled more than four rooms with books that measured and marked his intellectual journey, and contained his favourite authors and apostles of knowledge—Darwin, Caudwell, Eliot, Forster, Hegel, Jack Lindsay, Marx, Poe, Toynbee, Vico, and the postmodernists Foster, Derrida, Bhabha, Bourdieu, Hassan, Rose, Said and Levinas. These book-ended his large trove of monographs and studies on Australian art and artists, from European settlement to his present.

I recall in particular one warm summer's evening in 2005 when Bernard and I independently emerged from a crowded exhibition at the National Gallery of Victoria, he inquiring—Bernard liked inquiring—whether I would walk with him to the tram. He would have been in his late eighties, but cut a distinguished figure with his long white hair, handsome in his cream linen suit. There was a virile quality to his easy, gentleman-like charm and conversation, and that short stroll to Flinders Street station and he to his tram, left a lingering impression of an old lion who had fought many intellectual battles and lived a fulfilling life—one that merited the title 'the father of Australian art history'. He had, after all, worked hard for success; it had not been handed to him nor had he inherited it, but he had been lucky, as he used to say. There was, however, a sense that he was not yet ready to fly off into the dusk of literary or scholastic oblivion.

When Bernard invited me to write his biography I felt much as Oskar Spate did when Sir Keith Hancock suggested he write a new *Australia*; he was extremely flattered—too flattered to decline. But like Spate, I was extremely anxious about such a massive task. Smith's reputation as a colossus in the world of art and cultural history, both antipodean and international, was without peer in Australia, and I knew that writing the life story of this man would be a weighty challenge.

A 'biography isn't a poem, it isn't a novel, it's a document', but in some ways Bernard Smith's life was all three genres.[1] He had written major historical works, biographies and autobiographies, had published his poems and criticisms, and left an archive of thousands of documents. So thoroughly visible had he left all his tracks, perhaps too visible for comfort, that the most gruelling aspect of this project was to find the hidden seams of his life, the secret closet of his mind and past. It therefore seemed sensible to work backwards until I found the origins of Smith's first moment of visibility; that, for a bastard boy, was not easy. Illegitimacy has a way of cloaking a child; and he was for the most part a *filius nullius*, but even there Bernard had been lucky and had escaped the usual destination of fostered children, many of whom were sent to farms that operated like nineteenth-century workhouses. Instead, he became a favoured ward in what was called a 'farming-out' house, the winsome child who flourished as best he could under the circumstances set by the State Welfare Department of New South Wales.

An exceptional life is determined by many factors and it cannot 'be entered by means of one key'.[2] Biography, as George Kubler wrote, 'shreds a frozen historic substance',[3] a block of time that, in Bernard Smith's life, covered two world wars, the Great Depression, radical political shifts, and the dramatic innovations of twentieth-century science and technology. Just as the industrial and French revolutions were major ruptures for Europe in the eighteenth century, so the Spanish Civil War was the turning point for the twentieth century, the harbinger of World War II and the source for Picasso's *Guernica* (1937). Bernard was drawn to historical ruptures, they helped define history's topography; as he said in *Place, Taste and Tradition* (1945), 'it is the business of history to . . . mark out the contours in time that renders the structure of our present intellectual and aesthetic landscape intelligible'.[4] He also held to the Hegelian notion that you cannot re-create the past, but only understand it.

Born with an innate sense of his boundary, imposed by his illegitimacy and state-ward rearing, the foundation to Bernard's character was determined by a deeply formed resilience—to society and to others, but not to himself. Ihab Hassan has written that it is one's 'sense of origins [that] haunts the critical mind' and Bernard Smith must be read in these terms.[5] In an essay written in 1956 on Coleridge's *The Rime of the Ancient Mariner* (1834), Bernard emphasised the importance of 'the feelings of childhood carried on into the powers of manhood', an admission or perhaps a glimpse into his own protected territory and primal hinterland. What is important is how he positioned himself in relation to everybody else and everywhere else.

For Bernard Smith words and the intellect were used to atone for the guilt of the flesh—that of his mother and father—and his own. Later he transferred his reliance on words for interrogating invasion, conquest, morality, dispossession, Indigenous genocide and national consciousness, and defining antipodeanism and modernism. Unlike many state wards,

Bernard experienced less ostracism due to the firm but affectionate family who fostered him. Nevertheless, his status as an institutional child made him develop an emotional distance, both from the polity and those who wielded power, and it instilled in him a Machiavellian attitude to the present and a preference for the past. Having inhabited a peripheral or decentralised position for the first part of his life, he grew to prefer marginality; it provided an objectivity that drove him to interrogate the centres and their fringes. As he matured and groomed himself on the seductive and coercive structures of Marx and Hegel, and the great art historians Winkelmann, Burckhardt, Gombrich and Pevsner, he gained the confidence to stride across cultural landscapes, whether colonial, postcolonial or his own modern antipodean world.

Robin Winks has suggested that a scholar's subject matter or academic discipline usually holds 'an autobiographical meaning, in that one is often attracted to a discipline that appears to reflect the world as one understands it, rather than using the discipline to order the world'.[6] If this were so, Bernard Smith used art and cultural history not only to understand what Oskar Spate called the 'the sociology of colonisation', but also the relations of exchange, the global present and his own 'position and position taking', even when he claimed that an historian needs 'distance from one's own time'.[7] It is important, therefore, to ask how he tracked and deciphered the cultural shifts associated with imperial colonisation, elitism, socialism, romanticism, and modernism, and established a cultural genealogy, a program of origins, traditions and transfigurations that situated Australia's cultural developments within the global and local conditions that had produced them.

Bernard wrote two memoirs covering the first half of his life. They reveal an obligation to truth, but memory is selective and, though he possessed an acutely sensitive and synthesising one, he wisely relied on contextual proof. A vigilant diarist who understood the importance of documenting events, he also used the diaries of others, for within such intimate documents are key emotions and the psychological knife. With those sources and his encyclopedic filing system where place, date and circumstantial evidence about those who mattered were recorded, Bernard validated his well-charted life. According to one colleague, he knew 'only too well that if one is being transformed into a myth in one's lifetime, it is sensible to take a hand in the process'.[8]

Bernard's large archive—held mainly at the National Library of Australia in Canberra—his two autobiographies, the exceptionally fine *The Boy Adeodatus: The Portrait of a Lucky Young Bastard* (1984) and *A Pavane for Another Time* (2002), and his extensively annotated private library housed at the State Library of Victoria, provided a rich index for understanding the scholar's mental processes, and they constitute the marrow of this biography. In accepting Bernard's offer to write his life story I also undertook a marathon in the history of ideas. Where his archive set my momentum, his scholarship drove my pace. Moreover, Bernard Smith was a 'participant historian', which is understandable for a man who had to build a vision of himself, his public profile and his career from scratch. He did not inherit any privileges and so, having had to make his own, he was fiercely proud and protective of his identity. The biographer has had to work with this as a driving force.

For Bernard culture was a complex synthesis of the traditional and the contemporary, which he investigated through visual, social, political and power relations; it is why he liked to call himself a pluralist. His intellectual legacy is remarkable—he stands as one of Australia's most important twentieth-century intellectuals, not only for his prodigious publications, but also for his often controversial and provocative motives—'the risk is worth taking if it is justifiable,' he said. Turning around notions of origins, identity and identification, expressed by the binary manifestations of Eurocentric values intersecting with southern regionalism, he believed that we must classify in order to understand the historical agencies and shifting paradigms that have shaped both art and Australia's modern identity. He also relied on the German philosopher G. W. F. Hegel's dictum: 'The teaching of a concept, which is also history's inescapable lesson, is that it is only when actuality is mature that the ideal first appears.'[9] Hegel was one of Bernard Smith's intellectual guides, a cicerone who provided him with the criterion of historical distance. That is why Minerva's owl is a metaphor for him as an historian: one who tries to see the complete picture and, in looking back, 'understands tradition better than it understands itself'.[10] It was one of Bernard's cardinal rules: events are clarified through time and distance, as the owl of Minerva looks back on the dying day. Biography as a literary genre also telescopes lives and events, and as the biographer, while painting the various shades of my subject's interior and exterior worlds, I have sought to hold on to the longer view.

CHAPTER ONE: ORIGINS

No matter how tenaciously a child works against the grain of illegitimacy a compromise is imprinted and a deep sense of the singular follows like a faithful dog—the more he tries to forget, the more it plagues him. Bernard Smith never forgot his blighted birth, nor the loss of status that accompanied it, and it helped him model and finely tune his path. Moreover, he positioned every player he encountered throughout his life in a chessboard of moves and counter-moves, a contest of survival in a world of 'unequal exchange'. Absent from that board, however, were the symbolic figures of the king and queen, his father and mother. While they acknowledged him as their own son and registered his birth, they abdicated their parental role and Bernard's state ward identity, his foster family and social marginality conditioned his childhood and adolescence. As he later said, 'If you are going to survive among the others—even among friendly others—you have to acquire some sense of yourself and your position in that institution we call the family.'[1] That institution, writ large, is called society.

On Tuesday evening, 3 October 1916, a 28-year-old, unmarried Irish woman gave birth in a rented basement room. Dr Hobbs and Nurse Thomson attended Rose Anne Tierney and present as a witness was the owner of the small, sandstone worker's cottage, Mrs Watson. The father of the child, Charles Smith, in whose room the birth took place, sat outside smoking his pipe. He had seduced Rose Anne when they had both been employed at a large house in Cairns, Queensland, owned by the Munroe family, where she had been a domestic servant and he had been the gardener. But at 30 years her senior, an itinerant worker and a peripatetic adventurer, the stark reality was Rose Anne was a pitiable casualty of the old man's lechery.

Charles Smith had a way with words and with women, but shortly after he had bedded Rose Anne he packed his bags and moved on. He did, however, leave his forwarding address in case any mail should arrive. Some months later, when a doctor confirmed her pregnancy, it was Rose Anne who wrote to him. Charles replied that he would do all he could and suggested she come to Sydney where he had found employment as a foundry worker at nearby Adamstown. As her pregnancy advanced she decided to accept his offer, booked a passage on the *Canberra* and sailed for Sydney. In a letter to Bernard 20 years later she wrote, 'Will I ever forget that trip. Going to where I did not know a living soul . . . only one who had deceived me'; she described her arrival at Circular Quay:

> As the boat pulled into the wharf, it never occurred to me that anyone would be there to meet me, so I just put my hand over my face and laid my head on the rail to hide it from my view. The sight of all those happy friends meeting but when I raised my eyes I recognised moving amongst the crowd below one familiar figure. So I breathed a little more freely.[2]

Rose Anne made her way down the gangplank and through the crowd towards the elderly looking man who took her by the arm and led her away. Charles stayed with her for a few days, showed her the sights of central Sydney and arranged accommodation for her with the Sisters of Mercy until he got a job at Morts Dock. Touched by his gentle consideration and surprised to find how much she enjoyed herself, she began to see why the Munroe sisters had been so enthusiastic about this man. As her condition advanced she also decided to put a cheap metal band on her wedding finger, temporarily change her name to Smith and move into Charles's rented room at number 197 Rowntree Street, Balmain.[3] This mockery of marriage may have been demeaning but even more sacrilegious to her Catholic faith was that Charles had a wife and three children, although that marriage had long fallen apart. His granddaughter Margaret Mattar has told how he had left the family to look for employment after a severe drought ruined his small property in rural New South Wales. When he wrote asking his wife to follow, she refused and returned to her parents in Sydney. After attempting a reconciliation of the marriage, she rejected him.[4]

Charles Smith decided his new son would be called William Patrick, but when Rose Anne looked down at her baby with his 'long black hair, the loveliest of dimples and large blue eyes', she was certain he should be called Joseph, after the patron saint of destitute children.[5] Several weeks after giving birth she received a letter from her family in Ireland telling of her brother Bernard's death in the freezing trenches of Flanders and, without hesitation, she decided that her baby would be called Bernard Joseph in memory of him. William Patrick was a transit name that would remain in the register of births, the first of many identity paradoxes for this illegitimate child.

The paradox of identity

Rose Anne knew it was impossible to stay with a man like Charles Smith, but whether she fully understood the difficulties that an unmarried woman with a new infant would face, especially with the tense moral climate of wartime and its stringent restrictions, her decision to leave him when she was in a new city without support seemed foolish. He tried to persuade her to stay but Rose Anne was prone to act impulsively; she packed her bags and walked away from the father of her child, returning to the nearby Irish Foundation, run by the Poor Clares of the Saint Clare's Convent at Waverley. While the sisters cared for her baby, Rose Anne searched for work, only finding a string of poorly paid jobs. Just as she began despairing for their future and thinking that she might have to give her baby up for adoption, she was told of a Protestant woman who took in orphans and state wards as part of the boarding-out enterprise. Fostering out her baby did not have the finality of adoption and at least she would know where he was and she might be able to visit him. After meeting Mrs Mary (Tottie) Keen, who lived with her family and a clutch of other state wards at 39 Esher Street, in the Sydney suburb of Burwood, it was arranged that Rose Anne would deliver her six-month-old baby the next day.

Fortunately, Rose Anne's separation from her child was not as abrupt as she expected because she found a domestic position nearby at Burwood Park and could visit her little boy every afternoon. Rose Anne also asserted her maternal control by renaming him Bernard Joseph William Smith, though not through any formal process.[6] Her baby soon became the charge of a stranger, who became the surrogate mother and renamed her new foster child Bennie Smith.

As life settled Rose Anne wrote to her parents in County Cavan informing them of her misfortune. Her mother's reply was of some comfort:

> I received your kind and ever-welcome letter and the lock of hair it is really nice. The poor little fellow is company for you although he give [*sic*] you a lot of trouble he may do you a good turn yet. It gives us a lot of grief to think of the hard time you had and you so far away from any person that you know but I hope your trouble is over.[7]

Ihab Hassan believes 'It is one's sense of origins [that] haunts the critical mind',[8] and Bernard's origins and illegitimacy tugged at him from a very early age. When he was two, his mother left Burwood and travelled to Queensland where her two brothers and sister lived. Why Rose Anne had not gone to them when she was pregnant is not known, although her deep shame may have affected her decision. Her oldest brother, Paddy, had emigrated from Ireland in 1910 and had been the catalyst for Rose Anne, Mary and Johnnie to follow in 1914, just before the outbreak of the Great War. Irish emigration, or the 'great diaspora', had been endemic well before the Great Famine of the late 1840s, and between 1801 and 1900 'more than seven million [Irish] people emigrated permanently' to various western countries, the majority being of 'the poorest rural dwellers'.[9] The Tierney siblings had hoped to find a better life in Australia and all apart from Rose Anne managed to establish themselves comfortably. This was probably why she decided to leave Sydney and make her way back to her family. Through them she hoped to find a better life for Bernard and herself, and she had fully expected to return to Sydney within a few months to collect her little boy. But six years passed before she could do so, by which time she had married and had a daughter, Marie. When she arrived at the Keen's house, Braeside, she could see Bernard was well cared for and adored and, after some discussion with Mrs Keen, it was decided that he would benefit by remaining with them in Sydney and completing his education. Moreover, it was a far better life than she and her husband could have given the boy, so she left her son once again. Bewildered by his mother's arrival and then her departure, Bernard nonetheless accepted the situation calmly and corresponded regularly with her, always signing his letters from the time he could write 'I remain your loving little son Bennie'.

Bernard only had a partial sense of his origins and did not discover more about his mother and Irish ancestors until 11 years later, when he spent the summer holidays of 1935 with Rose Anne, his two half-sisters and two half-brothers, uncles, aunts and cousins at Innisfail in northern Queensland. Ireland had always inhabited a nostalgic realm in his imagination, but there was one question that remained unanswered: who was his father, the old man he had met on several occasions as a little boy? When Bernard was 19 Rose Anne emotionally unburdened herself in her letters, which could only have made him feel the heavy load she had carried all those years. In March 1936 she wrote describing her encounter with Charles Smith at the Munroes' house in early 1916:

One morning on going out for to get the bread from the Baker, he [the baker] told me the terrible news of the declaration of war, [between] England and Germany. Of course we all taught [thought] rather lightly of it at first. Oh it would be nothing, couldn't possibly last longer than six weeks at the very most. We little taught [*sic*] then of what was in front of us, every second young man you met, he was going, Butcher, Baker etc all taught [*sic*] they were just going for a nice trip over the sea.

After I'd been at [the Munroes'] for perhaps three months or more I answered the doorbell one day. It was a middle-aged man, short, dark, moustache, asked if Miss Munroe was in. Miss

Marten, Miss Munroe's step-sister rushed out, poor me, Charlie Smith. She greeted him with such a hearty welcome. I wondered who could it be . . . afternoon tea was ordered and they must have talked for hours.

After he had gone she came and said, that is the best man ever we had working for us . . . After some days he came and worked there, the other chaps having left a week or so before. He seemed to think such a lot of the Munroes, they used to talk for hours together as he had worked for them while their brother was alive . . .

Charles Smith had been at sea for some years, before farming, but a drought left him penniless, then went prospecting at Kalgoolie [*sic*] used to tell me of all the times he had been to Ireland and of been [*sic*] shipwrecked just off the coast, was taught [*sic*] to be drowned for over 10 days but just managed to get in alive, and of the hospitality of the Irish people.[10]

Charlie Smith was a great raconteur, capable of charming spinsters, sailors and naive young women, but Bernard's most vivid memory of his father was when he was probably about four or five years old. After discovering where his son lived, Charles, then a man of 63 with a large moustache and shabby hat, unexpectedly called at 39 Esher Street (fig. 1). He had come to say goodbye to his son and gave Bennie a few tokens to remember him by: a book *Rivers of England* and a few old worn postcards depicting the windswept, barren hills of the English moors where Charles had grown up. He had also come to discuss the possibility of having his son adopted by a woman near to where he was then living, but this never eventuated. Bennie poured over those images of an unwelcoming, distant land with its 'strange intensity', so different to the Ireland from which his mother came. Charles also gave Bennie, or William as his father called him, an empty pipe case—an odd gift, but one that came to symbolise his father's absence. Whenever Bernard took the empty case from his drawer it triggered a memory of this enigmatic man—perhaps as Derrida wrote, 'I am my father's spirit . . . a blind submission to his secret, to the secret of his origin.'[11]

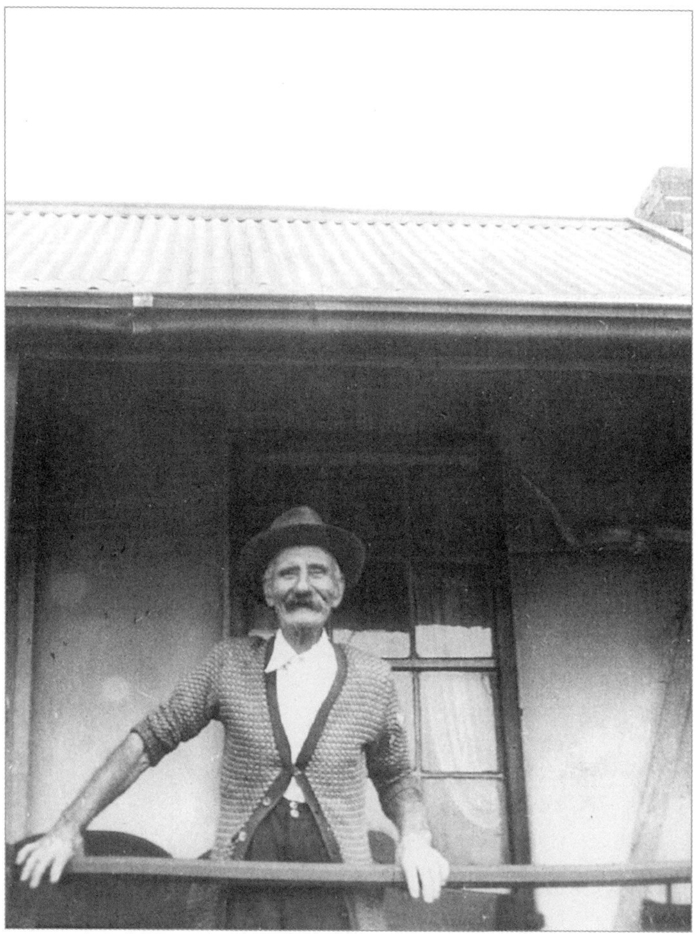

Fig. 1 Charles Smith, late 1930s

Events that occur in the first years of a child's life subconsciously manifest themselves in mysterious ways throughout their adult life. Bernard was a communal baby, and Rose Anne—called Mamma Parky by Bernard because in those early years she lived across the park—was an absent mother, while Mrs Keen became the managerial mother and her teenage daughter Bertha Keen a doting older sister. From the daily visitation there was a vague understanding of maternal love and security when Rose Anne arrived after finishing work at 4 pm. She would lavish her little son with affection, then leave him in the care of Tottie and Bertha Keen (fig. 2). Freud's concept of identification, 'the earliest and most original form of emotional tie . . . [and] the earliest stage in the process of ego-formation'[12] presents in Bernard's case as a complex triad. If the child takes the figure he most longs for as his model, the orphan or foster-child must then choose a replacement figure for his biological mother. During the first years of Bernard's life that choice oscillated between three providers. The sense of continual change and exchange between three females would not have unduly confused a young infant, but it would have set a pretext or expectation of his needs being satisfied by not one, but multiple women. It was a lesson in separation and mediating the self from the source of its primal needs; in other words, the initial stage of identification resulted in the tripartite structure of his 'otherness'. This was further compounded by the lack of a father figure and ontologically Bernard's beginning was an oedipal flurry of distinguishing emotional boundaries within multiple bonds and identity paradoxes.[13]

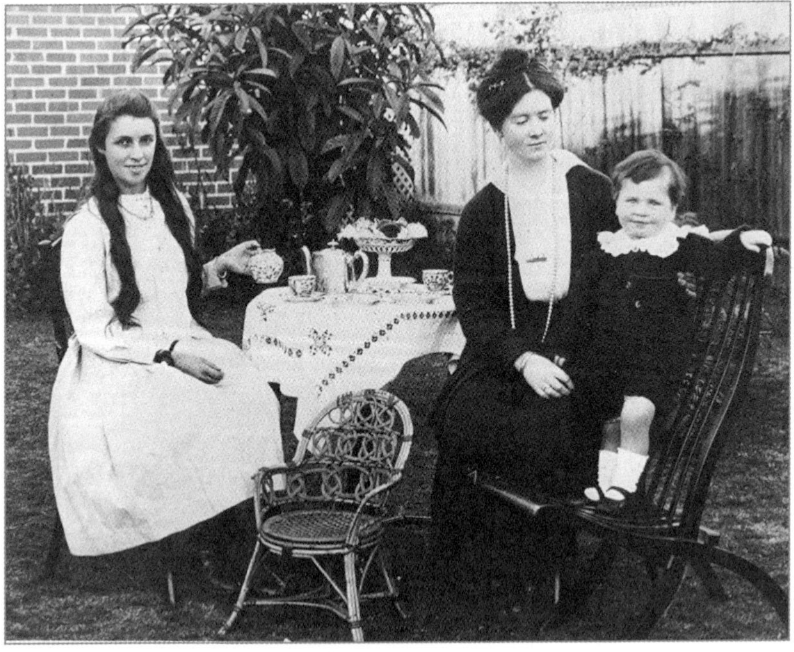

Fig. 2 Bertha Keen, Rose Anne and Bernard 'Bennie' Smith, at Braeside, 1918

The absence of a father figure also accounted for behavioural patterns that emerged as Bernard matured. His dominant community of women may explain his inability to develop close male friendships; his single-mindedness about work and career, a compensation for his father's failure to be there and to provide; and his promiscuity, perhaps subconsciously acquired—'I am my father's son'. Because Bernard did not have a strong bond with or image of his father, or for that matter any paternal figure, he was freer than most to construct his own masculine image.

Jacques Derrida considers origins especially important, particularly those blind and compulsive submissions that we make to our genealogical spirits.[14] Being illegitimate and a state ward meant Bernard was a socially anonymous child and this marked his passage through life, engendering a strong scrutinising vision with which he controlled his world. From childhood he learnt the lessons of economic, social and emotional distance; 'poverty is a hard teacher', and 'a state ward can't expect much' he said.[15] In a letter to Vincent Buckley in 1984 he wrote 'many illegitimate children who do not succumb to self-pity experience a kind of distancing from society. One sees oneself almost as a kind of witness figure.'[16] The legitimate child knows he is biologically, genealogically secure, whereas the illegitimate child is conditioned by the trauma of not knowing. Though Bernard had some knowledge of his parents—those brief afternoon visits from his mother or those fleeting occasions when his father appeared, only to disappear again—he felt keenly a sense of parental dispossession. Thus part of his survival strategy was to create his own hermetic world on the edge of society, answerable only to himself and to that institution called 'the State'. When it came to his obscure origins, that hinterland 'from whence he came', his sense of the 'other' would haunt and help him throughout his life; as he matured it underscored his attraction to outsiders or the underdogs of society.

The bench child

Bernard knew he did not truly belong to anyone, and that even his name obscured his identity. To Charles Smith he was William Patrick, to Rose Anne he was Bernard Joseph William and to his foster family he was simply little Ben or Bennie Smith. At the Keens' bungalow, Braeside, Bennie was the child at the centre, the favoured foster-child; 'such a nice little fellow,' Bertha Keen wrote of him, 'he is such a little darling I don't know how we are going to part with him' (fig. 3).[17] Even within this atmosphere of affection a temporisation pervaded his sense of home. Because of their favouritism towards him, Bernard ate his meals on a long brown bench situated directly behind the dinner table, while the other state wards ate out on the verandah or sat further aside. In the Keen household Bernard may have been a winsome little prince among other paupers, but he was also aware from the very beginning of his humble status. The German word for 'bastard' is *Bänkling*, meaning 'bench child', and alludes to conception occurring in a temporary location rather than the marital bed; ironically, Bennie's bench position could be seen to operate as a leitmotiv for his illegitimacy. Sitting quietly by himself on the bench, little Bernard witnessed a family's simple life, and a scene to which he could never truly belong.[18]

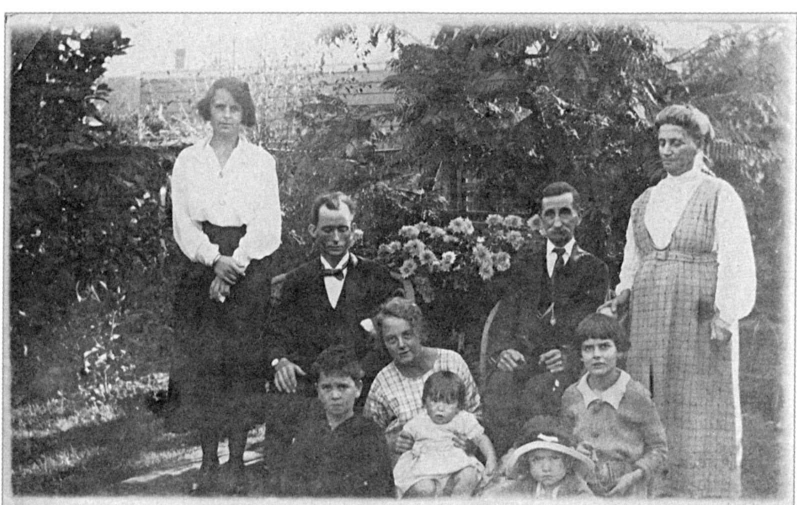

Fig. 3 The Keens with their state wards (Bernard at lower left), c. 1922

Outside the home it seemed normal to be an outsider, but when Bernard heard Bertha tell a door-to-door insurance salesman that he was not one of the family, to which the man replied 'Oh, he's one of those', he was shocked that his identity could be so bluntly handed across the threshold to a stranger.[19] The favoured bench child, the state ward treated affectionately within the family, felt a savage exclusion and an alienation that would haunt him for the rest of his life. Later he recalled, 'To know that was to know everything' (fig. 4).[20] Being biologically unfettered, however, had a positive side: it gave him a sense of freedom, of not being one of the tribe, but different. That blank space in his private history taught him emotional objectivity and how to stand apart and transit life's challenges. By default of his birth, the singular 'I' epitomised Bernard's detachment, but it also created a need in him to re-form himself, and gradually he developed into an ambitious, studious boy who admitted to being something of 'an intellectual prig'. While illegitimacy may have haunted him, it was also the harp song that motivated him to prove his existence.

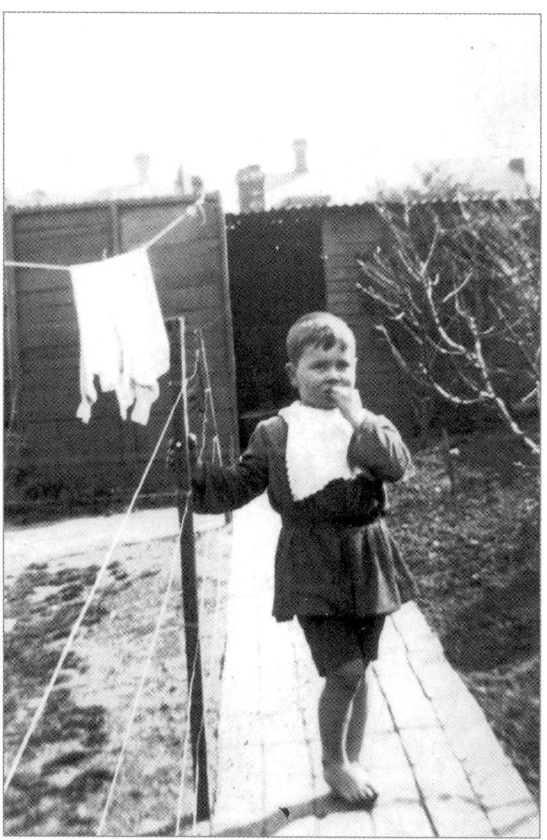

Fig. 4 Bernard 'Ben' Smith in garden, age five, winter 1921

A Darwinian conversion

Bernard understood the disadvantages of being poor. Self-reliance and frugality were essential conditions and when the Great Depression hit in 1929 the Keens merely adapted to a leaner world. Mrs Keen was a good, moral woman, a 'firm but friendly' Congregationalist who worked tirelessly bringing in state wards and washing to earn extra money. The house had only two bedrooms but it was part of Tottie Keen's economy to keep the beds full and board coming in, so there were often up to 10 people accommodated at Braeside, with the wards sleeping on the enclosed verandah. Tottie Keen's husband, Bert, was a quiet, Bible-reading man who never dominated his domain. He had retired from the New South Wales State Brickworks in Homebush Bay and retreated into himself, but the home was industry: a disciplined, communal environment where they grew vegetables and fruit, mended their own shoes and clothes, and bartered eggs for milk and other necessities. Poverty may have been a hard teacher, but in the Keens' household it was about cooperation, never competition—a good example of Christian socialism and Depression utilitarianism—and it left its mark on Bernard who considered labour a necessary component of a productive life. When he was older and he visited colleagues or friends he would 'bring as a gift not a bottle of wine or flowers, but a jar of chutney', a gesture of his belief in the simple usefulness of goods.[21]

As a boy Bernard's obsession with origins drove him to excel at history and geography, to interrogate and trace the great discoveries, triumphs and tragedies of the past. It had begun with the stories of the Bible, giving him a sense of the rise and the decline of civilisations, historical tragedy and pageantry, where origins, events and the deeds of men determined the fate of people's lives; but it was progress that fascinated him. Progress, 'subjectively conceived', meant that the 'self' can be recognised and cultivated and that things change, and that mattered to Bernard—'Progress and the storm "blowing from Paradise."'[22] From the time Bennie could read he memorised two chapters of his small, illustrated Bible every night for seven years. From this he forged his notion of the genesis of humankind, a world predicated upon good and evil, cataclysmic tensions, exiles, exotic cultures and fabled histories. Such stories were to be understood as the rule of law, as ethical and moral imprints of the adult world, and for Bernard they acted as 'the childhood twig [that] contrives to shape all our trees'.[23] The Bible was the panoramic backdrop against which his sense of history was formed, just like Walter Benjamin's image of 'history as an angel with its face turned to the past'.[24] As Bernard recalled, 'Out of the Bible I received a feeling of . . . drama at an extended sweep, and I suppose . . . of history working itself out.'[25]

Historical time linked with the present and stretched across into the hands of Burwood's civic missionaries. Bennie never wandered too far afield; the way state wards were seen by others in the community made friendships outside the Keens' extended family problematic; that early lesson in the principles of exclusion seared itself into his young identity. But he would cross Burwood Road to get to the local Salvation Army Sunday school, which he attended every week without fail. It was a routine that measured his week into days and his moral thoughts into 'goodness' and 'salvation'. Yet Sunday school was militant and Christianity was regulated by the word 'army' and sergeants in uniform; he thought there was not much room for progress. For six years he obtained his 'never absent, never late badge' that he proudly kept in a silk-lined box. In his seventh year, at the age of 15, he faltered. A schoolteacher had introduced him to Charles Darwin's *On the Origin of Species* (1859) and *The Descent of Man* (1871), books that radically changed his frame of mind, and in that common moment when a child questions and wants proof Bernard suddenly found the Bible 'absurd and preposterous nonsense'.[26]

On the Origin of Species was not only an exciting travel book, it was a revolutionary theory that questioned blind conformity and divine creation, and coupled with the burning high-mindedness that comes with youth, it broke the moral and theological spell under which Bernard had been living. As he embraced Darwinism and atheism, for the first time in his life he felt a deep sense of liberation. Natural selection positioned environmental forces as agents that determined mutations within species, changes that ultimately favoured survival and progress within organic units. Just as Darwin had observed the struggle for life as he watched great Galapagos marine lizards, giant tortoises, finches and other strange species of the Pacific manoeuvre for survival, so Bernard felt that his own passage in life had a certain fatalism. He saw natural selection as a biological levelling agent, an equaliser that, when applied to humans, gave uncontaminated dignity outside legitimacy, institutionalism or class. Further, Darwin taught him that the world was a vast museum in which visual variations occurred as a result of territorial and geographical conditions, and where animal, humans and nature were more often than not in disharmony; the combative instinct was a prerequisite for survival and change.

There was another magnetic quality to Darwin: he showed that the South Pacific and Antipodes were not only wonderful empirical theatres of evolution, but they were also where the dominating, civilised European and the primitive met. The clash of power relations captivated Bernard because it reflected a deep sense of injustice, something to which, as a state ward, he was sensitive. Many years later he developed this as a central argument in his pioneering thesis *European Vision and the South Pacific* (1960). It investigated the machinations of imperialism and how governing laws determined the centres of power and its peripheries. Consumed by the new scientific and biological theory, Bernard stopped attending the Salvation Army and never received his seventh 'never absent, never late' silver badge.

In his isolated but happy life at Braeside, survival often occupied his thoughts. Even before he had learnt of natural selection Bernard instinctively relied on his intelligence as a weapon in self-protection—for 'only those who have known discrimination have known its cruelty'.[27] Being a ward of the State, on the flipside of acceptability, placed him in a subordinate social position, or as he put it, 'after all a State ward . . . can't expect all that much'.[28] Being smart helped him rise above his station, particularly at school, where he regularly encountered bullying: 'Who's y'r father Ben?'[29] But when Mrs Featherstone, a middle-class, neighbourhood matron asked him to mow her tough, buffalo grass on a fiercely hot summer's day with an old hand-mower, he felt powerless in front of her authority. Not only did this 'large Leghorn hen', as Bernard described her, make him wait for more than an hour after he had finished, but she sent her daughter to pay him his threepence.[30] Mrs Featherstone's patronising attitude towards both 'Mum Keen' and him was humiliating and he felt the sharp distinction between the 'haves' and 'have-nots': as Julia Kristeva suggests, 'When others convey to you that you are of no [or little] account because . . . you are an orphan', then the weight of that obscurity crushes what fragile pride is left.[31] At school Bernard usually found ways to avoid conflict or bullying by using his wits and intelligence, but class structure was something else; as he later wrote, 'Australia possessed a class of people that dominated and a class that served.'[32] Just as his mother and foster mother were servers, he too fell into that dreaded category. Rarely did he succumb to self-pity, but Bernard never forgot nor forgave Mrs Featherstone and vowed he would never again be a 'server'.

Excelling at school improved Bernard's self-confidence and diminished his sense of social inferiority. Knowledge was one of his greatest pleasures but it was also a necessity. Being an institutional child and beholden to the Child Welfare Department meant that his educational achievement and good behaviour were values he dared not transgress for fear of punishment. The Child Welfare Department paid Mrs Keen a stipend to house, feed and care for him. It paid for his school uniform, educational expenses and dental treatment, and his performance was reviewed annually. Badly behaved or recalcitrant state wards were sent away to orphanages, farms, or homes for boys or girls that, from all accounts, were awful places of extreme discipline and brutal punishment. Thus, surveillance hovered over Bernard and persistently reminded him never to offend or to slacken at his schoolwork. A letter from the Child Welfare Department in January 1932 illustrates the passive pressures:

Dear Bernard,
I was very pleased to see that you obtained such a good pass in the Intermediate Examination, and now send you my congratulations. Always be a good boy, Bernard, and aim for the highest peak! Wishing you every future success
Y F A Thompson (secretary)

In a character reference of 7 September 1931 from the mayor of Burwood the institutional hand of accreditation is also evident:

I have pleasure in stating that I have known Master Bernard William Smith for some years and consider him suitable for entrance to the Public Service which I understand he is desirous of entering . . . He has resided with Mrs Keen of Burwood since infancy. I have known Mrs Keen for over forty (40) years and have pleasure in stating that she is a highly respected citizen of the district, and Master Smith has therefore had the benefit of a fine home training.

Another letter from the Child Welfare Boarding-Out Branch to Bertha, concerned Bernard's guardianship after Tottie Keen's death:

[Classifying] State Ward Patrick Smith as Adopted Boarder in your care for a period as from the 1st January 1934 to 3rd October 1934. Under the classification no further payment in his support will be made but he will be subject to the supervision of Officers of this Department.[33]

Nevertheless, Bernard was very grateful to 'Mum Keen', Bertha and the department, and cooperated in every way.

The enclosed garden

At Braeside life revolved mostly around the enclosed backyard where Bernard was content playing with his pet kookaburra and the other wards, Valerie Walsh and Jack Carns (fig. 5). Occasionally he would go on picnics with Bertha and her fiancé, Ralph Chivers, or for long rambling walks in the Blue Mountains. On special occasions he watched firework displays or went to the local fair, but his knowledge of the outside world was generally circumscribed by his social position. When his primary education finished, instead of being sent to work on farms like the other wards, Bernard was sent to Petersham Commercial Intermediate High School, a dull institution that focused on accountancy and business principles. This coincided with the Great Depression, a time he remembered as a 'spiritual malaise [that] accompanied the economic downturn' and which affected everyone's behaviour, including his own.[34] At school he joined a group of disruptive lads. It was a calculated risk but one he felt compelled to take, as his slight build, 'pretty girlish face' and state ward status made him easy prey. To prove his allegiance to the boys he drew comical sketches of the weakest students and the most dislikeable teachers,[35] and while he took pride in his drawings he flinched at the intended cruelty, but ultimately justified his actions as a necessary Darwinian lesson in survival.

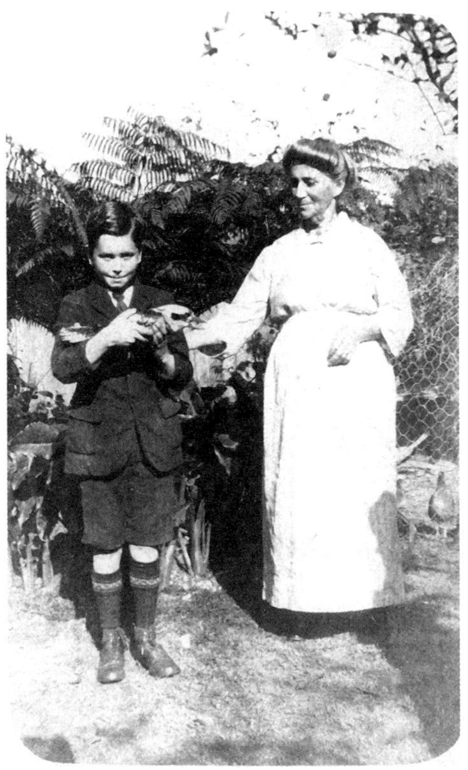

Fig. 5 Mary 'Tottie' Keen with Bernard and his pet kookaburra, Peter, 1927

By 1931 life at Braeside was changing. Tottie Keen was dying of heart disease, and the values of unity and productive hard work were beyond her. As the Depression tightened, her grip on life weakened, and when she died Bernard found that even then he was excluded from the family and was sent elsewhere while the funeral took place—'the privilege and duty of mourning was not his right'.[36] Though his relationship with Bertha remained close, tensions crept into his life at 39 Esher Street—a combination of pubescent sexual yearnings, the nihilism of the Depression and a growing yearning for autonomy. Life for Bernard at Braeside was unravelling and even the garden fell into decline.

In 1932 Bernard was transferred to Enmore High School, a temporary annexe that had been 'set up in an old trades school built at the turn of the century . . . the windows wired against vandals, the paint cracked and peeling . . . a tiny yard, asphalted and treeless, in which the sun made only a brief appearance'.[37] It was an adjunct of Sydney Technical High School and provided for the overflow of students who wanted to continue to senior levels—because of the Depression and the improbability of getting a job many students opted to continue their education. Bernard found value in study and the next two years at Enmore were intellectually and personally rewarding. As he recalled: '1933 was one of the most interesting years of my life. I was studying pretty hard but at the same time managed to meet a lot of interesting people and go about a lot.'[38] History excited him most because it 'gave him a sense of his place in the scheme of things . . . a sense of tradition . . . it was like standing between two mirrors, a mirror of the future and a mirror of the past, and seeing himself stretching away in both directions'.[39] He read Adam Smith and gained a basic understanding of Einstein's theory of relativity. T. H. Huxley's *Lectures on Evolution* (1876) and Darwin's theory of evolution further confirmed that men who made history were instruments of change and empiricism was a key to discovery. Logic and language were important tools in communicating and, with 'a clear visual memory', an inquisitive mind, broad study and an opinionated attitude, Bernard became dux of his class in 1933 and was awarded a two-year bursary to the Sydney Teachers' College.

The following years, however, were marred by uninspiring educational training, the product of a new breed of educationalists who believed that 'method' and 'technical efficiency' were superior to inquiry. The only positive experience for Bernard was studying art under the gifted May Marsden, a British-trained modernist who had been appointed lecturer in art at the Teachers' College in 1915. Though Bernard said he 'lacked a definite purpose [and] went through those years in a sort of . . . mental somnambulism', Marsden's inspired teaching more than compensated for the college's educational inadequacy. She transformed the 'cold, white corridors' of the college into galleries of old master reproductions, including paintings by Piero della Francesca, Bellini, Rembrandt, Vermeer, and the moderns Cézanne and Dalí. She also had original prints, drawings and paintings by the Sydney modernists Thea Proctor, Margaret Preston and Ethel Spowers on display and often conducted her classes in the corridors among the pictures. Though a champion of modernism, she believed in the continuum of tradition where 'composition, structure, form and the inter-relationship of shape' was, as Bernard recalled, ultimately all one needed to know.[40] James Gleeson, who was a student there with Bernard, remembered her as 'encouraging [them] to take risks, to experiment and to question everything about art that was generally taken for granted'.[41] While Marsden was a significant mentor for several generations of students, for Bernard her principles of modernism laid the basis for his approach to aesthetics and awakened his artistic soul and interest in the history of art.

Edge of the periphery

Towards the end of 1935 it was decided that Bernard would spend his Christmas holidays at Japoonvale and Innisfail in Queensland with his 'other family' (fig. 6). It was almost 12 years since he had seen Rose Anne, now a small, middle-aged woman with a short, blunt Depression-styled haircut. She met him at Silkwood Station and, with tears cascading down her face, all she could say was 'Oh Ben, Ben, you have come back to me.'[42] Highly protective of his autonomy and unused to such possessive talk, their reunion sent a shiver through Bernard and he recoiled in shame as she stroked his hands with her rough, gnarled ones—'but they are so smooth', she exclaimed. With the crude contrast between hard labour and the labour of the mind so blatantly obvious, the distance between them was never more sharply defined than at that moment.

Rose Anne had four children to Bob Kahl—Marie, Dermott, Isabel and Robert—but with her husband away for long periods with his bullocks and dray she had been left to raise the children largely alone in the tough, wet cane country of North Queensland. Bernard had written to

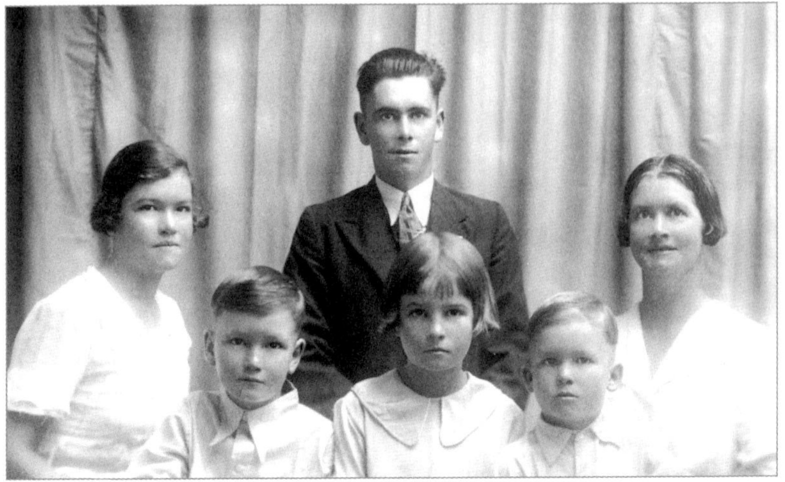

Fig. 6 Bernard with his mother, Rose Anne (far right), and
half-brothers and sisters, from left, Marie, Dermott, Isabel
and Robert, 1936, Japoonvale, Queensland

his mother assuring her not to worry about the state of her house, but
when they arrived at the jerry-built humpy he was shocked at their living
conditions. Quickly recovering his composure, he told his mother 'I have
never been used to anything elaborate and hope I never will'.[43] He had
long ago become accustomed to the fact that 'for those who are born
out of family the inner door of the house is closed and locked firmly'
and on seeing his mother's impoverished situation he had no intention
of opening this new door.[44] While Bernard was warmly accepted by his
new family and liked his half-siblings, he nevertheless felt awkward and
out of place, but he also desperately wanted to compensate in some way
for his mother's misfortune. To appease Rose Anne and his Irish relatives Bernard agreed to take religious instruction at their local Catholic
church, but this only further exposed the fault lines between his mother's
world and his secular, atheist one.

After several weeks Bernard was saved from further embarrassment
and boredom at the drab Catholic existence in Innisfail when a telegram
arrived from the New South Wales Education Department instructing
him to 'commence duties at Concord West', a public school less than a
mile from Braeside. At last his career as a primary school-teacher was to
begin, but no sooner had he commenced than another telegram arrived

instructing him to 'take up duties' at Murraguldrie Provisional School in remote rural New South Wales. This coincidently was the territory through which his father had wandered during the early 1900s as he mined for tin.

Just after Easter, Bernard arrived at Murraguldrie, a little outpost on Tumbarumba Road, situated on the fringe of a large pine forest. It was 300 miles (483 kilometres) south of Sydney and 80 miles (129 kilometres) from the large township of Wagga Wagga, and his duty as the sole teacher was to educate a clutch of primary students in a one-room, weatherboard school.[45] For all its isolation, Murraguldrie, which no longer exists, was a welcome relief after the enclosed, cramped conditions of Braeside and the recent memories of his mother and her extended family in North Queensland. It was a new beginning in which Bernard was able to separate himself from his past and re-evaluate his life. In his diary he wrote that he was pleased to be alone, it was exactly what he wanted and 'You could get lost in the country or get lost in yourself, and both were exciting to explore.'[46] Though it was at the edge of civilisation, Murraguldrie would prove to be an emancipating experience.

CHAPTER TWO:
NEW TREMORS

Bernard warmed to his new position as a teacher and learnt to handle the young students of varying ages and development who were all bundled together in one room; by keeping educational instruction straightforward the children remained attentive, a method he adhered to throughout his academic life (fig. 7). Outside his teaching duties country life was drab but, as he later told Vincent Buckley, 'so much life was drab during the depression, emotionally as well as objectively' and 'more importantly, [it] seemed drab to me because . . . of the image I had built up about myself'.[1] That image was of the 'lucky young bastard', a romantic, knowledge-seeking outsider who now analysed the world landscape from his hermetic isolation of Murraguldrie.

Rather than socialising with the locals, Bernard kept mostly to himself and turned towards the landscape. Wandering through the pine forest, along small creeks and over the steep hills, he sketched as the mood took him and painted competent but, as he said, 'insipid watercolours'. In his youth he had explored Berowra Creek, Govetts Leap near Blackheath, and Katoomba in the Blue Mountains, primal sanctuaries that goaded his young pagan imagination, but the bush around Murraguldrie was of a different type. Apart from the dark pine forest, a melancholic pastoralism stretched forever, yet he welcomed the immensity of space and was enthralled by the natural beauty. He remembered the writings of Charles Darwin, who recorded his observations on various landfall stops during the voyage on the *Beagle*: 'The elegance of the grasses . . . A most

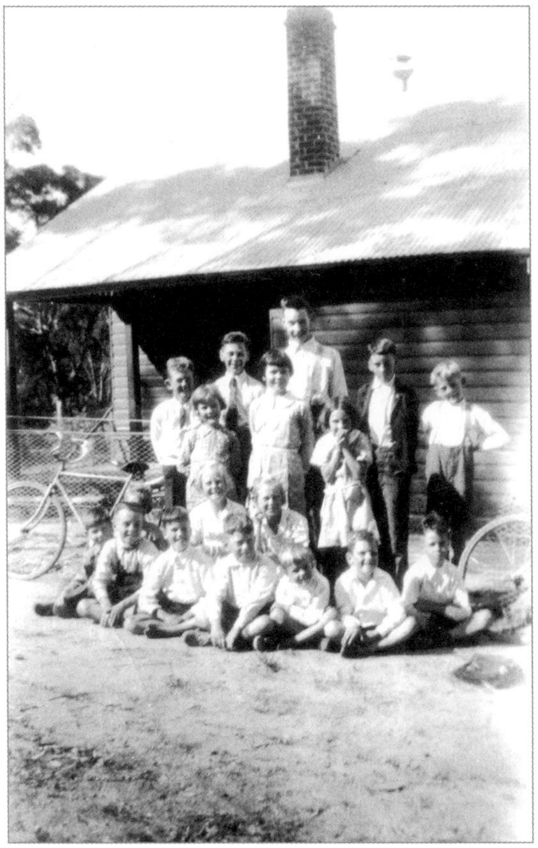

Fig. 7 Murraguldrie Provisional School and students, c. 1936

paradoxical mixture of sound and silence pervades . . . yet within the recesses of the forest a universal silence appears to reign.'[2] Occasionally Bernard lapsed into singing hymns, 'all things bright and beautiful, all creatures great and small . . . the good lord made them all'. He re-read John Ruskin's *The Elements of Drawing* (1857) and thought about May Marsden's teaching and how her modest cubism had influenced him. His landscape drawings had good perspective and his portraits of the students showed strong form and an engaged line, but during the long evenings it was poetry that he turned to:

I have listened to a creek at midnight
Murmur its tune

Walked down still aisles of pines
Of pine needles strewn
Heard the low moan of the westerly
Break in a wining croon.[3]

He also began a journal, which in his isolation helped to formalise his thoughts and emotions, but just as he was celebrating his independence a shadow began to creep across Europe and a mood of 'decadent defeatism' was cast over humanity. It was a critical moment in his ideological view of liberation, both individually and collectively.

The spectre of Guernica

'Those born in the struggle, the children of "Seventeen"', as Bernard called his generation, learnt resilience and resistance. Yet compared to Europe's 'doomed generation' that had played against the backdrop of World War I and matured during the rise of fascism, Bernard appeared to grow with each new crisis. In 1935 when he ceased to be a state ward and adjusted his civic identity, he emerged as a confident young man ready to engage with world issues. A defining moment in that transformation was the devastating air raid at Guernica in Spain on 26 April 1936. The atrocity awoke the political sleeper in Bernard and in his journal he declared 'I am a creature of the Spanish War', the act of violence providing him with an opportunity to reformulate the 'self'. Within a year Picasso's masterpiece *Guernica* (1937) had become an iconic visual protest against Franco's complicit deal with the Nazis and the return to savagery that would alter the concept of war forever.

As Bernard moved rapidly towards the left of the political centre he began reading as much literature as he could find about the historical causes behind the European crisis; Oswald Spengler's *The Decline of the West* (1918–23) warned of the Faustian forces that had led to civilisation's tragic demise, but it was his *Man and Technics: A Contribution to a Philosophy of Life* (1932) that appears to have impressed Bernard. The extensive annotations in his copy shows the young Marxist working with or against Spengler, 'the eye seeks out cause and effect, the hand works on the principle of means and end', and 'At last, with the twentieth, we have come to a century that is ripe enough to penetrate the . . . the totality [that] constitutes world history'; the words 'At last' heavily underlined.[4] Bernard also turned to the interwar generation of British writers and poets who were articulating the modern crisis. W. H. Auden's 'Spain', a lament for lost youth, especially moved him:

> To-morrow for the young the poets exploding like bombs,
> The walks by the lake, the winter of perfect communion;
> To-morrow the bicycle races
> Through the suburbs on summer evenings; but to-day the struggle.
> To-day the inevitable increase in the chances of death;
> The conscious acceptance of guilt in the face of murder;[5]

When societies are in decline art reflects the dynamics of decay and signals a utopian desire for rebirth, both of a new social order, a remaking of authority or power and, implicit in that, individual liberation.

Bernard learnt about what was happening in Europe by corresponding with a few friends in Sydney, reading out-of-date newspapers and listening to the crystal radio set in the evenings. In his diary entry of 3 April 1937 he recorded, 'War in Spain going strong', and 'Japan and China . . . at full-scale war with fierce fighting in Shanghai and Peking'. More reports predicted the likelihood of Russian intervention, followed in all probability by an escalation of conflict. He records this critical moment in history:

> The war continues in Spain. Riots in Yugoslavia over the Concordat . . . Palestine is still as troubled as ever [according] to a report of the Royal Commission on Palestine, signalling a partition of the country between Arabs and Jews . . . The Jew is dissatisfied because it leaves him with only a small portion of the land of his fathers, and the Arab says that he has been given the desert. A wireless speaker tonight suggests that a situation comparable to Ireland is inevitable, with a certain section of Palestine definitely Anti-British.[6]

Bernard counteracted the emotional strain of a world in crisis with an increasingly efficient and systematic approach to his personal arrangements, teaching and school duties. Conscientious by nature, and shaped by the emotional and institutional boundaries set during childhood, he established a strict modus operandi: 'I am going to get the maximum results from a minimum of time', he wrote in his diary. By his second year at Murraguldrie Provisional School—where his days were 'all routine . . . don the shorts and run a mile [1.6 km] around the pines, then wash and dress for breakfast. Thence to school'—his vigilant program of order and self-education continued. Apart from his evening meal with the Thompsons, in whose house he had a room, he spent his time reading and writing until midnight.

Tradition and history were fundamental to understanding the present, and Bernard ordered books on world cultures and their social histories from the travelling lending library. He covered architecture, philosophy, poetry and the arts—in other words, the entire grammar of the humanities—including Jacob Burckhardt's brilliant study on tyranny, humanism, society and culture, *The Civilization of the Renaissance in Italy* (1860). He also began intensively reading the social utopians Karl Marx and Friedrich Engels, and G. W. F. Hegel who set out a logical system of ethics, politics and aesthetics. Bernard also read Wilenski, Gascoigne, Freud and John Stuart Mill but still found time for local literature, praising Frank Dalby Davison's *Man-Shy* (1931) as a beautiful novel. Importantly, he bought a typewriter, an essential portable tool for any aspiring intellectual.

After his summer vacation in Queensland Bernard wrote regularly to his mother and, with distance between them, he felt their 'correspondence [was] becoming a living reality'.[7] In his diary he noted that he was 'learning to love her' and hoped he would one day be in a position to make her happy; even love had to be learnt. The poverty and hardship of her life had shocked him; he desperately wanted to redeem her situation and, implicit in that, himself. He bought a milk separator to help her with the cows and butter making and paid for her to take a holiday in Brisbane, but he detected something else in her letters, something that he had witnessed in Japoonvale that had 'frightened the hell out of him'.

Rose Anne could blow up like a 'terrible tempest of emotion'; indeed, he had never witnessed a woman so emotionally volatile. He attributed this to her difficult marriage, exhaustion and appalling living conditions and, from his reading of Freud, assumed it was hysteria. The Irish, however, would have attributed it to the banshee and he knew that folk from County Cavan, from where Rose Anne originated, still clung to these imaginary, malevolent little spirits that tampered with people's lives, causing tragedy or ill fortune. Though not superstitious, Bernard wondered whether it had jumped on board his mother's psychological cargo when she migrated to Australia in 1914.

Rose Anne's frank, intimate letters may also have been a way of explaining her guilt at having left him, the unwitting source of her downturn, or perhaps it was her way of eliciting a sense of duty from her son who had returned educated and with prospects of a good job. In any event Bernard's sense of obligation spurred him to want to succeed and he became so singularly focused that it affected almost everything he did. Consequently he began thinking about his future, whether it would be in the history of ideas or of literature, yet he also wanted to be an artist. Three words in his diary, 'ambition is sweet', reveal a young man looking beyond his provincial horizon.

In the absence of friends or a social life in Murraguldrie, Bernard's mother remained a central figure, both as maternal confidante and as a reminder of his origins. Ambition, though, could not be properly pursued until he resolved the major pillar of religion. Upholding the Roman Catholic faith of his mother was incompatible with his secular and increasingly politicised ambitions, and his hunger for historical facts, rather than a spiritual pathway to salvation, consumed him. To appease Rose Anne's anxiety about his religious unmooring he pressed on with his attempt to conform to the Roman Catholic Church, travelling regularly to the township of Wagga Wagga for meetings with the local priest. The process was neither enlightening nor gratifying. Bernard had been baptised at the church of St Augustine of Hippo in Balmain and his religious upbringing with the Keen family had been with the more liberal Congregational Church, which had put an emphasis on a rational approach to life that he considered significantly more satisfying. When Rose Anne sent him the 'The Thirty Days Prayer to the Blessed Virgin Mary', he capitulated:

> Mother of mercy, hope and comfort of dejected and desolate souls; through that sword of sorrow which pierced thy tender heart whilst thine only Son, Christ Jesus, our Lord, suffered death and ignominy on the Cross.

Bernard tried to pray, but he failed to see how prayer or confession could save lost souls and restore flagging faith. Moreover, his mother's 'despairing love and ceaseless battery of prayer bore down on him, stifling him with all the power of her ancient religion'.[8] He abhorred emotional indoctrination and the values of the Catholic Church posed insurmountable problems as well as advocating absurd moral paradoxes. Piety and pardon went hand-in-hand with what seemed like irreverence and indulgence. 'The Catholic religion seems alright', he mused in his journal, '[yet] you can go to Church in the morning and gamble at night; an unsatisfactory position.' Bernard had spent too much of his life in a state of dislocated suspension and that was what he felt the Catholic Church wanted. What he needed was a sense of unity, not the opium of the people, or to be subjected to the guilt of religion. More urgent issues were at stake—'the world was again becoming a dangerous place to live in'—and from his understanding 'the Catholic Church was not interested in change or finding real answers to the problems raised by social change'.[9] But what was the solution? 'If there were no satisfactory answers, then God was the satisfactory answer to all unsatisfactory things.'[10] Bernard could not embrace religion's paradoxes, spiritual abstraction, or the Church's dogma, any more than he could dance an Irish jig.

Sigmund Freud believed religion intimidated a person's intelligence and interfered with their options by reducing 'the value of life and distorting the real world by means of delusion'.[11] Added to that was Darwin's evolutionary theory that offered an infinitely more logical and superior scientific explanation for human behaviour and progress. Knowledge enlarged Bernard's view of the world while the Church and creationism narrowed it and chained his flight. As he attempted to navigate the maze he wrote 'The world is a great mass of interwoven dramas, each play an entity in itself, each play depending upon others for its existence. Such is life.'[12]

As a Darwinian convert who viewed history as an ocean of empirical variables, scientific logic and biological evolution, Bernard adopted other philosophical beliefs to help overcome the contradictions that he saw inherent in the religious, political and cultural dystopia of the world. Hegel's philosophy of ethics and aesthetics, and Marx's anti-capitalist and materialist theories enabled a clear understanding of people's machinations, yet as the rumblings of war persisted he agonised about his moral and spiritual dilemma:

> If ever a war does break out, I sincerely pray that God will give me sufficient courage to stand by the convictions I hold at present. . . . disbelieving in war itself there can only be one stand, under no condition can we partake in any war. We can only fight war by refusing to have anything to do with it . . . no matter what the consequences.[13]

Bernard's pacifism was a product of his upbringing with the Keens, whose disapproval of military aggression was in keeping with their non-conformist beliefs, but as the threat of war increased he began envisaging apocalyptic consequences.

Just days after the broadcast of the coronation of King George VI in Westminster Abbey in May 1937 he read a book that deeply disturbed him: 'Read Huxley . . . last night. I am still trying to fathom it all out. It was banned by the Commonwealth Government until recently. Just allowed in.'[14] He considered Aldous Huxley's futuristic satire *Brave New World* (1932) as 'completely destructive and offers nothing', yet its impact would exert itself and condition him for the creative emancipation that he was to experience with the surrealist movement and other unexpected detours in his life.

Brave New World was a dystopian tale about genetic manipulation and scientific totalitarianism in which social solidarity was achieved by a collective conditioning. Not only was the individual negated but nature and modern society were antipathetic, evolution de-historicised and God was replaced by the machine. Bernard naturally interpreted the book through his young political and scientific lens, and saw it as aborting Darwin's philosophy of natural selection, artificially removing class conflict, dismantling Marx's historical theories and transforming society into a static, non-regenerative body. The central character in the book was called Bernard Marx, an Alpha-Plus outsider who questioned the stability of the world and with whom Bernard most probably identified. While it was a fictional parody on modern political life, in particular American propaganda, mass production and Soviet communism, Huxley's cocktail of global obedience and drugged workers was unsettling.

By 1937 Bernard was obsessively dissecting his entire emotional and intellectual anatomy. Like Havelock Ellis, who some 50 years earlier had similarly taken a one-teacher post in remote rural New South Wales, Bernard attempted to reconcile aspects of his personality by feverishly relying on books. It was the only way to develop a 'philosophical justification for [his] actions', even though he admitted that 'I'm afraid I still live too much with words. They are still my master, I do not control them enough.'[15] Self-discipline and control were essential for the 'progress of his soul' and Murraguldrie was the perfect place to develop those instruments of will.

The absence of an intellectual and social life was frustrating for an atheist grooming himself in the ideas of the Enlightenment and Bernard's isolation began to pall, but he was determined to remain socially detached. Marx's dictum, 'It is not the consciousness of men that determines their being, but on the contrary, their social being that determines their consciousness' played on his mind.[16] In a frank letter to his mother he explained his position:

I am always selfish enough to think about what I am getting out of anything myself. During this year I have been able to settle down to my work and keep my mind on the future, instead of having to appease the natural hunger that insists in all of us for the company of the opposite sex, particularly at my age, and which people rather amusingly call 'having a good time'. Not that I have lived like a hermit of course, but at least the numerous acquaintances have not blossomed into endless flirtations . . . There is a girl twice as pretty as Evelyn in the closest house to here. Dances better too. I think she would just give the world for me to flirt with her. She is decent, respectable and very musical. But take all that away and there is nothing left; empty . . . I am no poor simpleton struck blind with cupid's darts. One day perhaps. For the present the brain and not the stomach predominates.[17]

Though he was interested in a couple of attractive girls, the fear of being trapped in a rural marriage was more than enough to hold serious romance at bay.

By 1938 Bernard was reading himself into politics. He had grafted Marx, Caudwell, Spengler, Lenin, Tolstoy, Sidney and Beatrice Webb, H. G. Wells and the poet T. S. Eliot onto his vision of a dying culture and, given the 'derangement and brutality of the struggle for existence' in Europe, he began synthesising many strands into a total perspective of a universal whole. It was Marx, as Wells said, 'who finally fettered the two ideas of Socialism and Democracy together', and which came to matter most to Bernard; moreover, '[Marx] sought in the resentment and discomfort of the disinherited a sufficient driving force for a revolutionary reconstruction of society.'[18] If the major nation-states of Europe were unstable and in decay, Bernard's own life also was also developing major contradictions in which reality and illusion were wedded yet pitted against the other, with each satisfying a different criteria. From politics to the human passions, from ecclesia to atheism, from the agonies of the individual to an eagerness for public participation, his journal reveals his anguish:

Newspapers, propaganda,
Wireless lies and slander,
And chaos, chaos, chaos,
Reason disembowelled
Distraught, deranged, defiled, deflowered.[19]

Bernard believed that the only position for the individual or intellectual in society was a political one, and to ease his acute frustrations he decided to return to Sydney as frequently as possible during his final teaching term. On arriving at Central Station he would walk to his old home Braeside, where Bertha and Ralph Chivers lived, but even there he felt estranged. 'Poor old Braeside, just the same and myself growing out of it like I did out of short trousers . . . Braeside, still pretty with flowers, still the same bed outside [on the verandah] and the chest of drawers of mine full up with rubbish.'[20] Distance and time had severed the ties to his adopted and once-beloved home, and that sense of not belonging cut deep.

South

As soon as the epidemic of infantile paralysis (poliomyelitis) in Melbourne had passed, Bernard decided to visit the southern city, particularly to see the great Felton Collection at the National Gallery of Victoria (NGV). He arrived in bleak weather, and the city's grey buildings and its people seemingly lacked warmth. He soon found himself infuriated by posters of General Franco with 'his head bathed in an aureole of golden light, a crusaders cross beside him', and was shocked to see the images 'canonise a brute; make blessed a military adventurer who had destroyed an elected government; this friend of Herr Hitler presented as a candidate for saint-hood'.[21] While the European collection at the NGV was magnificent and offered an exotic, foreign past, he also felt the poverty of his inheritance. As he roamed about the strange, cold city Bernard's bastardry haunted him; even Rembrandt's self-portrait looked melancholic. Having read William Moore's *The Story of Australian Art* (1932) he took a train to the outer suburb of Heidelberg where he hoped to glimpse where Australia's first impressionist painters had set up camp in the 1880s, but in the drizzling rain the semi-rural location did little to lift his mood and he returned to the city even more despondent. Melbourne, he decided, was depressing rather than enlightening, and as an acute sense of alienation came over him he took the train back to Sydney early.

The thought of returning to the closed, little world of Murraguldrie only exacerbated Bernard's pessimistic mood and in a letter to his mother, who had been complaining about her precarious financial situation, he wrote in anger:

> Let us hope things get better for you, particularly for the sake of the children. But you see I look at things differently from you. To you the family is all important, it is the centre around which the life of your children revolves . . . You grew up in a family and received their ideas and you cannot imagine a life without it as a central point. I missed all that. I lived with a family but they did not claim me . . .
>
> I write bitterly because the great curse of the world today has been the indifference and hesitancy of people who see only the shadows of things, because the reality is too cruel. Soon you will see the world plunged into a bloody hell that will make the last war seem like a cat fight . . . as though a cyclone had blown through the world and torn up civilisation by the roots and we have nothing to do with it. We have everything to do with it. We have tried to clothe ugliness and the law of the jungle in soft words and religious excuses, and now that we have nourished the monster we begin to wonder why it turns on us .[22]

His outrage was as much directed towards his mother, the Church and the world as it was about his social insularity, and that he did not belong anywhere or to anyone, and the termite in his foundation—his illegitimacy—denied him the one thing he yearned for: unconditional love. This reality of not belonging propelled him further towards politics.

A Marxist apprentice

There will be no future without Marx, without the memory and inheritance of Marx.
Jacques Derrida[23]

On a visit to Sydney in September 1938 Bernard joined the Left Book

Club, operated from the Anvil Bookshop at 191 Hay Street. It also doubled as a designation for the Workers Educational Association and the Communist Party of Australia, where political literature could be bought with 'a book a month at a price within reach of your pocket'. One of the first books he acquired was by the American communist Joseph Freeman, *An American Testament: A Narrative of Rebels and Romantics* (1936). The harrowing autobiography described the brutal lockouts and trade unionism of the 1920s and it convinced Bernard that communism was the correct political route to take in the current climate. His mother's views, however, concerned him. 'Communism,' she wrote, 'has the hiss of the serpent ever since I listened to the first on[e] speaking in Sydney years ago. I was astounded at the way he attacked religion, only the most ignorant could go on the way he did.'[24] But social change, cultural and artistic development, nationalism and Marxism now occupied Bernard, not religion. Heavily underlined in his copy of Mikhail Lifshitz's *The Philosophy of Art of Karl Marx* (1933) are the main features of Marx's economic standard for a democratic socialism and his alignment of political consciousness to the philosophies of art and literature. Marx argued that the abstract qualities of bourgeois romanticism and individuality be replaced with a communal truth in which 'freedom and material life must be united around a higher principle', and importantly, Marx chose 'Hegel's celebration of the guiding spirit of history into a materialist concern with the economic bases of life and culture'.[25] Bernard later said that Marxism gave him 'a dislike for any kind of elitist attitude to a subject'.[26] This was in keeping with his working-class origins and helps explain why he became attracted to the art of social realism.

If art were to be politically and morally driven, and the urgent issues facing humankind were to be addressed, the starting point for Bernard was to scour Sydney's second-hand bookshops for relevant literature. At The Ryecroft at 27 Rowe Street he bought a copy of Herbert Read's *Art Now* (1933) and *Surrealism* (1937), with an essay by André Breton dealing with the modern dilemma of artistic decadence and psychological re-awakening within an irrational world. Just up the street was Notanda Gallery, owned by the artist Carl Plate, where he bought Leo Tolstoy's *What is Art?* (1897), a compendium of important aestheticians including the founder of Aesthetics Alexander Baumgarten. Other literature furnishing Bernard's mind at the time included Trotsky's *Literature and Revolution* (1924); Jack Lindsay's *A Short History of Culture* (1939)—Lindsay considered culture a systematic interaction or fusion of ancient cultures; and Arnold Toynbee's first volume of *A Study of History* (1939). Clive Bell's *Since Cézanne* (1922), Christopher Caudwell's *Illusion and Reality* (1937), Stephen Spender's *The New Realism* (1939), and Cecil Day Lewis's *The Mind in Chains* (1937) were some of the other contemporary literature he bought. He found the symbolist poets Edgar Allan Poe and T. S. Eliot indispensable, while the mere names of the 'Prophets of Decadence', Lautréamont, Baudelaire, Mallarmé and Rimbaud, 'thrilled' and 'emancipated' him.[27] In acquiring a broad understanding of the anarchic romanticism of the modern movement, Bernard wholeheartedly agreed with T. E. Hulme that 'Romanticism is split religion', and this very dualism would characterise Bernard's intellectual development.

In the international best-seller *Man, the Unknown* (1935) by the Nobel Prize-winning surgeon Alexis Carrel, the author cautioned against the capitalist pressures that were jeopardising modern people's moral and physical survival. Carrel advocated that men and women could better themselves if they followed the guidance of an elite group of intellectuals, a superstructure of scientists that would lead and control human development. While tones of Aldous Huxley's novel were evident, Bernard believed that elite leaders were necessary to bring about social and political reform. With the world in crisis, it was only to be expected that a strange mix of scientific determinism would merge with a surreal form of decadence, but it was Carrel's manifesto for art in industry that really captivated Bernard. Its link to Marxian aesthetics and Carrel's idea of the artist as an important medium for expressing the spiritual and the simple realities of life reflected exactly how Bernard felt:

Aesthetic activity remains potential in most individuals . . . [but] we have been transformed into machines [and] the worker spends his life repeating the same gesture . . . He manufactures only single parts . . . never makes the complete objects. He is not allowed to use his intelligence. . . . In sacrificing mind to matter, modern civilization has perpetuated a momentous error . . . industry has deprived the worker of originality and beauty.[28]

This chimed with the English Socialist William Morris's famous slogan, 'I do not want art for a few, any more than education for a few, or freedom for a few',[29] a mantra that became a foundation for Bernard's humanism.

While Bernard was still living at Murraguldrie, a friend suggested that he organise an art club as part of the New South Wales Teachers Federation's cultural activities. By December, about the same time as the Contemporary Art Society (CAS) was being formed in Melbourne, Bernard was the moving force of the Teachers Federation Art Club and, though arduous to organise from his rural outpost, it connected him to a social unit. It also illustrated the enormous cultural gap between city and country—an experience he would find useful when he later came to work as an education officer at the National Art Gallery of New South Wales (renamed the Art Gallery of New South Wales in 1958), organising the *Art in the Country* travelling exhibitions in the mid-1940s. In 1938, however, his charge was the Teachers Federation art exhibition and its catalogue.

The inaugural exhibition was a small, amateur affair, consisting mostly of flower and vase paintings, landscape studies and a few portraits; Bernard submitted watercolours and several pencil sketches. He also wrote the catalogue essay, 'The Function of an Art Club', a manifesto-style critique of Australian art and education, offering a Marxist solution for improved cultural values:

Art in Australia, if an economic phrase is permissible in a question of aesthetics, suffers not from a lack of production, but a lack of consumption. Art still needs its patrons; but an art dependent upon the enthusiasm of a few collectors, and the whims of small dilettanti, can never be a national art . . . a reorientation of educational values is imperative if the appreciation of art in this country is to emerge from its present apathetic state.

Bernard's historical materialism and cultural politics were vigorously displayed:

> What we must realise above all is that the world of art and the world of education are mutually dependent. The facts of history are undebatable: Greece, the Renaissance and the Sung civilisation of the East all attained cultures wherein art and education were inextricably interwoven. The laws of sociology vary little; we must achieve this synthesis of art and education if we are to achieve a national culture and a national art.[30]

Apart from an emphasis on nationalism, those values would change little for Bernard, although the next year's exhibition was considerably more modernist. Rah Fizelle exhibited several of his schematised, cubist pictures and James Gleeson's paintings, with titles such as *The sky has many mouths*; *Sequence preceding the killing of lunatics* and *Usual things can be frightening*, revealed the influence of metaphysical surrealism. Gleeson also gave a talk during the exhibition, 'What is Surrealist Art?' Bernard exhibited six conventional watercolours of his own: his *The repressed chimney stacks praying to Prometheus*, an image of factories that had been closed down by the Depression, was a composition dominated by his social conscience, though the stirrings of surrealism was discernible. The 1939 exhibition catalogue iterated his commitment to cultural reform, but he had moderated his nationalist tone:

> To recognise as teachers that art comes into being as the expression of a continually changing society. To understand the needs and exigencies of our present-day modes of living . . . and having discovered the significance of art to our present-day society, to work toward educational forms that will give its members an aesthetic conscience.[31]

Tapping the contemporary mood and interpreting his world through an overarching Marxist political philosophy, Bernard connected the aesthetic and literary ideas of William Morris's social utopianism with John

Ruskin's paternalistic individualism and Herbert Read's organic and poetic socialism. As a major exponent of modernism, Read championed the role of the artist in society, insisting they must retain their freedom of expression—in the Hegelian sense of a genuine inner state—but channel it through their social consciousness. Having studied the art of many cultures and epochs when he worked as a curator at the Victoria and Albert Museum in London during the 1920s, Read attempted to find common cultural bases that he could synthesise with his philosophical approach to contemporary art. Tradition, he believed, was crucial to contemporary artists who 'could only come to maturity . . . by subsuming themselves within it in such a way that they became the end link in the long chain'.[32] This concept confirmed Bernard's admiration for Read, but he was equally attracted to other Marxist writers such as Caudwell, Toynbee and Lindsay.

Apocalyptic jitters

By the late 1930s, as the western world slid precipitously closer to war, sociologists and political humanists asserted a revolutionary approach to combat the evils of totalitarianism. The English futurist H. G. Wells was at the forefront of the salvation movement and toured Continental Europe and the USA before travelling to Australia to warn *Homo sapiens* of their fate. A few weeks before his arrival in Australia during the fiercely hot summer of 1938–39 to give public lectures in Adelaide, Melbourne, Canberra and Sydney, the American actor Orson Welles had broadcast over CBS radio readings of an alien invasion of New Jersey from Wells' science-fiction novel *War of the Worlds* (1897), 'alarm[ing] thousands on the eastern seaboard of the USA'.[33] As panic rippled across the oceans, Bernard was convinced that fascism had to be fought with whatever means were available, even though he still advocated pacifism. Melvin Rader's *No Compromise: The Conflict Between Two Worlds* (1939) pleaded with the new generation to wake up to the crisis and develop a 'new social mind', and after reading this book Bernard became noticeably more fanatical. Rader posed questions such as: 'Can there be a science of values?' 'Should the direction of society be placed in the hands of the elite?' 'Should individuals be subordinated to the State, or should the State be merely an instrument for the welfare of individuals?' And, the ultimate apocalyptic question, 'Can Western civilization survive, or is it doomed?'[34] The rhetoric affected Bernard so profoundly that he experienced what might be called an epiphany, writing in his diary:

> . . . there is a new light on an old changed personality . . . a bending of all changes toward a worthy achievement irrespective of the cost. Not a dissolute Bohemianism, but an ascetic invention. This day and the time calls for action and concerted action.[35]

As humans threatened to exterminate their own species, Bernard's agitation intensified and he fell victim to what he called the 'apocalyptic jitters'. While he saw how easily social Darwinism could be applied to the world crisis and understood how the theoretical basis of fascist policy could be mistaken for militant Marxism, he was convinced that a synthesis of Marxism and socialism could achieve effective change. He was not only prepared to join a political group, but believed that surrealism could provide answers to people's malcontent. He finished his 1938 diary with:

> 23 November. Still at Murraguldrie. Still in the same room in which I wrote the last page [a year ago]; but everything is different. I am older, I am 22. I have reached majority. I have founded an Art Society. This has taken most of my leisure time during the year, and I look at the world with greater confidence and with less desire to compromise with it. Surrealism recently has pointed out a new path to me in art. It is the thing for which I have been unconsciously waiting. I feel that I am going to find expression in the coming year [and] hope to produce some work which will be mine and only mine.

It was at that moment that Bernard crossed the threshold of social and political modernity, and his sense of his alienation lifted.

Surrealist impulses

*Art can do many things, but it cannot exist for long
upon the patronage of a lie.*
Bernard Smith[36]

Within a short time, Bernard had formed a deep interest in tradition, modernism, surrealism, communism and war, or as he put it, 'One has come under so many different influences during the time I left the writing of this diary last year that one hardly knows where to begin again.'[37] Art dominated his thoughts, not only because he was organising an art club, but also because he had been seduced by surrealism, linking as it did revolutionary romanticism with political activism. In a letter to his friend Lindsay Gordon he reflected:

> I am in favour of a bit of Surrealism, even if it does nothing more than clear the air. The values of this dream art may be questionable, but there is one thing certain, that the narrow representative conception of art is wrong.[38]

In contrast to surrealism's early phase, its later formulation encompassed 'the whole historic development of modern thought', from Hume to Hegel to Marx to Breton. The surrealists' debt to Hegel and Marx, particularly Hegel's dichotomies of actuality and abstraction, reality and alienation, were contradictions that Bernard understood, especially the contradiction between the State and the self, between institutionalism and individualism. In Hegel's *Philosophy of Right* (1820) a person exists only in relation to the external world, and only when he or she attains certain skills, erudition and ideas are they transfigured into a conceptualised character. Through social interaction and positioning ideas into the public or universal sphere, that person becomes accessible to others and acquires an 'identity'. By 1939 Bernard had established an art club, was convening public lectures on art and had become an art critic; the maze was beginning to recede and he was able to see a clear path ahead and his identity materialising.

The origins of surrealism go back to 1924, but by the mid-1930s the 'last wave of the romantic vibration', as Bernard called it, had embraced the cultural politics of communism. Surrealism's 'tandem components of words and images', its oppositional structures of individualism and collectivism, and its subversive and revelatory views of life were intended to destabilise capitalism and salvage humanity from imperialist fascism. Herbert Read's book *Surrealism* had introduced Bernard to the writings of André Breton, Paul Éluard and Georges Hugnet, and to the works of contemporary avant-garde artists such as Jean Arp, Edward Burra, Salvador Dalí, Max Ernst, Paul Klee, Rene Magritte, Joan Miró, Henry Moore, Paul Nash, Méret Oppenheim, Pablo Picasso, Man Ray and Yves Tanguy. Breton's political and aesthetic manifesto *What is Surrealism?* (1924) was about the liberation of humanity and was highly antagonistic towards conservative, regressive attitudes. Surrealism resolved conflict, not so much by synthesis, but by 'liquidating classicism' and challenging the 'old world' and its 'bankruptcy of art criticism . . . Cézannism, neo-academism, or machinism'.[39] According to Breton, surrealism 'deepen[ed] the foundations of the real', brought about a more passionate consciousness of the world perceived by the senses, and was not 'a refuge', but an organic process relying on material facts, and it investigated 'with eyes wide open' the realities of society.[40] As the surrealists fled Europe and spread their fantastic imagery like a magical virus into new cultural territories, such as Britain and the USA, Herbert Read evocatively captured their impact with the *International Surrealist Exhibition* in London in 1936:

> After a winter long drawn out into bitterness and petulance, a month of torrid heat, of sudden efflorescence, of clarifying storms. In the same month the international Surrealist Exhibition broke over London, electrifying the dry intellectual atmosphere, stirring our sluggish minds to wonder, enchantment and derision.[41]

Read also put it thus, 'There is a principle of life, of creation, of liberation, and that is the romantic spirit; there is a principle of order, of control and of repression and that is the classical spirit.'[42] Bernard was adamant that he wanted to belong to the former category and surrealism's countercultural thrust seemed the most appropriate platform for his re-entry into Sydney.

Being part of Sydney's avant-garde, at least in art and education, was important to Bernard, but it was precisely at this point that he began shifting back towards a traditional trope. He had been observing Gleeson's creative development, in particular his application of psychology to art. The two men had known each other since 1935 as students of May Marsden at the East Sydney Technical College, but Bernard differed from Gleeson in his belief that art was an act of wilful volition, even if its origins were exhumed from the pit of the subconscious. While he considered Gleeson an imaginative genius, he felt that he was too intrinsically bound to the nihilistic dream world of T. S. Eliot as a means of elucidating and rejuvenating reason. Bernard began to question whether surrealism's subjective, sensuous and primitive impulses, even if they were combined with a formal, historical rationalism, could successfully satisfy society's needs. He ultimately decided that 'Surrealism and its varied protean forms' was more of 'a parody of what was going on rather than the belief that there were psychological undercurrents stronger than ourselves'.[43] As the pendulum of insecurity carried the outsider back and forth, Bernard began to fall victim to contradictions. His rejection of surrealism and his realisation that it was more important to be part of society rather than a solitary, subjective artist, was a pivotal moment and one that was instrumental in renewing his belief in the politicisation of art as a method of social reform.[44]

The return

Travelling to Sydney most weekends to attend exhibitions, concerts, plays and the occasional ballet performance, Bernard's enjoyment of culture began to have a detrimental effect on his performance as a teacher. As he put it:

That is the trouble with the multiplication of goals . . . *One* must be followed . . . to follow both assures mediocrity. But in the correct place I will be a good teacher. I may be able to eventually affect the synthesis necessary between the work I do to live, and the work I do that will make life worth living.[45]

Despite his resolve to resist romance, Bernard fell for an attractive young woman he had known at the teachers' college. In 1935 Myrie Hannett had been unapproachable, 'so much the most beautiful girl in the place', but things changed when she became a foundation member of the art club in 1938, and during the following summer vacation they saw a lot of each other. At one of the first performances of *Petrouchka* by Colonel W. de Basil's Ballets Russes Company Bernard was overwhelmed by the spectacle of modern dance and also by his companion, 'a girl of high artistic sensibility . . . high intelligence and a well nigh perfection physically'.[46] As they watched the puppet Petrouchka come to life he felt a similar awakening, as if some coil inside him had been building up and was about to burst, no doubt the repressive conditions of Murraguldrie and the increasing drama and drums of war. Yet a nagging self-doubt still clung and he wondered how Myrie could be interested in a working-class lad like him. With one final term left at Murraguldrie the romance did not survive and the break up re-enforced Bernard's desire to get back to the world of culture and of women.

Finally, in April 1939, Bernard left his 'hamlet of daydreams' and returned to Sydney, taking a room in a boarding house in Llandaff Street, Bondi Junction. But after the quiet, simple country life he found himself overly sensitive to the city's bustle, noises and smells; even shadows seemed to follow him about. His nervous state was partly owing to the fascist gloom spreading across Europe and this, combined with his difficulty in acclimatising to the city, meant that he kept much to himself. At the risk of appearing conservative he took painting lessons at Julian Ashton's Art School in Argyle Street, The Rocks, noting 'it is hard to hear the sounds of the street in the studio . . . but the sounds are there; and there are drunken sailors, and drunken tenement houses bustling over one another on the water-side with long dark shadows.'[47] Surrealism's 'corridor of contradictions' still haunted him, which was why Ashton's, with its nineteenth-century atmosphere, provided a sense of security.

Even Henry Gibbons, Ashton's assistant, epitomised 'the clear, uncluttered art of the classical tradition'; qualities that Bernard felt were 'echoes of a saner age'.[48] Unlike the art being taught at Rah Fizelle's studio, which he considered more like the fractured climate of the times, Bernard felt that by applying a more traditional approach to his painting the negative implications of the world crisis could be minimised.

In the midst of Bernard's disorientation a young maid at his boarding house, an experienced girl called Annie, seduced him. The sexual encounter released a primal urge that Bernard appears to have previously kept under control and his response to the 'very purity of her lust' snapped him out of his emotional insularity. The irony of his sexual initiation was that it was a reversal of what had occurred between his mother, the maid, and his father, the gardener, in 1916; the end of his celibacy seemed a fitting celebration to begin this new phase of his life.[49]

During his adjustment to the city Bernard regularly visited his friend Lindsay Gordon, and the two men talked and listened to music for hours. Gordon was several years older, an accomplished musician and member of the Communist Party of Australia. It was through him that Bernard joined the party and met Vera McCafferty, another communist interested in music and drama (fig. 8). Communism, 'the great modern religion of the Not-Self' as Wyndham Lewis called it, aimed to integrate artistic growth within the working class and combine a utopian aesthetic with a Marxist approach to cultural production.[50] By the late 1930s the Communist Party of Australia, like that in Great Britain, was attracting writers, artists and intellectuals, and 'for the first time . . . Bernard could work within a community of like minds'.[51] They called him 'Bernie', and the teachers' branch of the party became 'his first university'.[52]

By May Bernard and Vera were involved not only in political and cultural issues but also in a relationship, and as that progressed so too did his enthusiasm for politics. Within a short time he was dominating her with overbearing attempts at party policy and Marxist doctrine, further aggravated by the philosophical and literary material on the tempestuous romantic movement he was reading for his Education Department thesis. All the negative forces of a decadent age had built up into an explosive mix and, with class and age differences, questions of his and Vera's

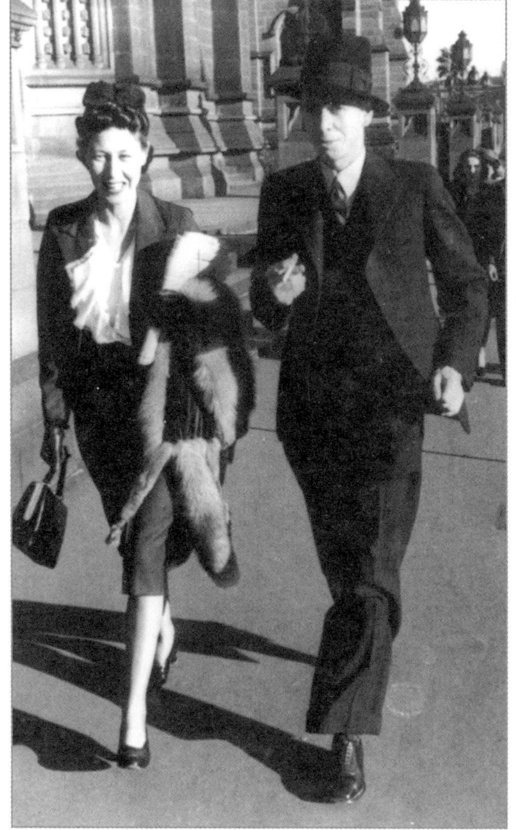

Fig. 8 Bernard Smith and Vera McCafferty, Sydney, 1939

compatibility arose. Hegel, Marx, Spengler, the party and the surrealists were not easy bedfellows for romance and Vera's doubts about their future were justified when Bernard's argumentative nature and political fervour intensified. Even he admitted:

I continued to interpret all situations in what I regarded as a truly positive manner, but found that instead of this producing positive results, the actual reverse has taken place and the contradictions in her attitude increased . . . This was evidence of the application of theoretical principles in a purely mechanical rather than a dialectical manner and . . . unless all the work of recent months was to be lost, had to change . . . I continued to assume that my influence was the most important single factor contributing to the development of her social consciousness, whereas the most important factor is the activising influence of the group itself. By maintaining the tactics used before she entered the [Communist] party I was actually denying that any change had taken place and thereby arousing instead nullifying contradictions.[53]

After Britain declared war on Germany on 3 September 1939 Bernard's anxiety increased still further and it was mutually decided that he alone would 'pursue in action and theoretical analysis' a role in the development of society and the working classes.[54] He and Vera parted.

One day Bernard was walking past the Prudential Assurance Company Building in Martin Place when he befriended a neatly dressed young man, though his tattered slippers revealed his destitution. Bernard took the penniless and hungry man for a meal at Wynyard Station and in the course of their conversation it emerged that Bill Robertson had been on the dole for five years. Contrary to common belief that the war was creating employment, serious unemployment was occurring in areas that had once thrived as hubs of labour. The boats were not coming into the harbour like they used to and it was difficult to get work at the wharves; 'they were putting men off everywhere instead of putting them on', Robertson told Bernard, creating a subclass of 'redundant poor'.[55] With barely enough money to cover the cost of his room, let alone feed himself, Robertson became one of its casualties. Hearing that stranger's story rekindled Bernard's civic conscience at a street level and illustrated that contact not only yielded understanding of individuals, but also of societies.

On Armistice Day November 1939, as Bernard passed through Martin Place on his way to Liverpool Junior Technical School where he was teaching, he noticed a couple of second-hand flags flapping idly in the morning air, but other than that there was little evidence of a war being on. As the school children assembled in the schoolyard gunfire was heard from the military camp across the river, and the headmaster spoke of the horrors of the last war—his only reference to the current one being that 'We must bring the war to a just conclusion, we are fighting for civilisation and a lasting piece [*sic*].'[56] When the children were dismissed and continued running around the schoolyard, Bernard was overcome with a sense of futility, of what T. S. Eliot called 'mankind's inane propensity' to repeat the mistakes of the past. Going home that evening to his boarding house he passed again through Martin Place, where the 'the poppy sellers were doing a roaring trade, and as the sun lowered in the sky he thought of the German troops amassing in Holland on the frontiers'.[57] There was no option but to fight for a new social order.

A few days later the *Herald Exhibition of French and British Contemporary Art* opened at the David Jones Gallery, Sydney, but Bernard's taste for European modernism had been soured by the declaration of war. The paintings appeared 'strangely unreal, if not surreal', and there were, of course, no examples of 'Russian constructivists, Italian futurists, German expressionists', only one purely surreal painting by Salvador Dalí.[58] Nor were there, as Richard Haese has since pointed out, 'examples of vorticism, dadaism, the more radical canvases and collages of Picasso's cubist work, or the abstracted fauvism of Matisse'.[59] Bernard believed that:

Despite the resplendent colour . . . the exhibition presented one aspect only of modernism, and even that aspect had been carefully sifted by the taste of Basil Burdett, Murdoch's critic, so that it would not unduly offend the hesitancies and the phobias that surrounded even the most 'advanced' Australian taste of that time.[60]

The hand-picked selection was unrepresentative and timid; what Bernard wanted was political modernism.

The Nazi–Soviet pact had been signed in August and as a newly conscripted communist Bernard had to somersault from support of the anti-fascist movement to that of condemning an 'imperialist' war. He justified Stalin's 'unpopular policy' because he felt there was no alternative to the politics of appeasement and it was 'easier to oppose an unjust war than to support a just one'.[61] The political adjustment coincided not only with his declining interest in surrealism and his reversion to a more socially representative art, but also to what would be a major turning point in his aesthetic ideology. Apart from the *Herald* exhibition, he visited another modernist show, *Exhibition I*, also at the David Jones Gallery. The semi-abstract paintings and sculptures by Grace Crowley, Ralph Balson, Rah Fizelle, Margel and Frank Hinder, Frank Medworth, Margo and Gerald Lewers, and the German sculptor and educator Eleonore Lange, who had organised the exhibition, may have stirred up the local art world, but Bernard's conflation of modernist abstraction with the political mayhem in Europe elicited from him a different response. For Bernard, a more comprehensible realist art was the only workable solution for addressing the horrendous humanitarian issues facing the world.

He thought of Russia's avant-garde political artists, those who had spawned an avalanche of twentieth-century movements—not the rigid formulaic socialist realism of the Zhdanov line, but the classical abstraction that had dismantled the old regime of feudalism and revivified modernism. Malevich's suprematist paintings *Black square* (1915) and *White on white* (1918) were 'a bridge between art and industry', a new art to reflect a new society, an art for the people and for change.[62] In those circumstances the impact of abstraction was twofold: not only was Russia the first country in which the working class had achieved power, but its artists had sought ideas outside prevailing aesthetic systems and institutions; they were the icebreakers who moved culture forward. Bernard was interested in how political ruptures marked cultural change, and from that point on he asked, 'What moved the movers?' He later claimed that 'the history of art is largely the history of the avant-garde'.[63] As 1939 drew to a close he noted in his diary that it had been a good but demanding year, 'full of history, full of change'.

The young historian

As part of the examination process for the New South Wales education system Bernard was required to write a thesis. He proposed 'The Surrealist Element in the Writings of William Blake' but the department decided 'Tendencies in Modern English Verse', a study of symbolism and the romantic movement, was a more satisfactory topic. This was Bernard's first ambitious piece of research in the history of ideas. It covered the revolutionary periods of protest and struggle of the late eighteenth century through to the early twentieth century—historical parameters that would occupy him for much of the next three decades, if not for the rest of his life.

The nineteenth century was instructive, but the eighteenth century was when individuals developed creeds; 'French materialist ideas blossomed into utilitarianism',[64] modern industrial workers emerged holding the Bible of Christian socialism, liberty stood at the barricades and politics developed democratic values. For art the period was defined by its dramatic, tragic and mystic qualities, with artists such as Goya, Hogarth, Millet, Delacroix, Daumier and Courbet helping to 'transform political space by replacing . . . the traditional vertical ordering of God, king and subject with a horizontal opposition' of liberty and egalitarianism.[65] Those were values that mattered to Bernard, for he had replaced God with Darwin, Marx and Hegel.

'Romanticism,' Bernard wrote, 'was both a protest against, and an escape from the social conditions ushered in by the industrial revolution'.[66] As capitalism and imperialism, both agents of possession, transformed the world through scientific and economic materialism, nature was eclipsed and a new mode of landscape painting emphasised open spaces and tempestuous nature, as seen in the work of William Constable and J. M. W. Turner.[67] Coinciding with imperial expansion and the opening up of the New World, the Antipodes began to lose its mythical status and, as W. J. T. Mitchell notes, 'Just as the landscape movement was at its height the islands of the South Pacific and the larger continental prize of Australia loomed to dislodge the Romantic pastoral.'[68]

As artistic production moved between *Sturm und Drang*, romanticism reflected the anarchic and utopian idealism that made way for the re-emergence of myth and symbolism. As Bernard noted, 'The Romantic revolt became the Pre-Raphaelite dream, the prophet became patronised', and just as primitive and early people had used symbols as social totems in order to deal with terror, so artists and thinkers in the nineteenth century used them to illuminate social isolation and fear.[69] Painters such as Fuseli, Goya, Caspar David Friedrich, Hogarth, Böcklin and William Blake were masters of the spiritual and social critique who employed symbolism to explain the nihilism of their *fin-de-siècle*. Of Blake, Bernard wrote '[he] was a symbolist who had to invent his own symbols. He was a man crying out for a mythology.'

Through an ambitious analysis of Christian socialism, Protestantism, neo-Hegelianism, the Oxford Movement, the Catholic revival, the Decadents and the Imagists of the late nineteenth and early twentieth century, Bernard believed he could show how modern society had evolved and how artists had helped to explain the creative function of history. By attempting to synthesise that large historical arc he came to the conclusion that the most 'important development in the thought of the nineteenth century [was] evolutionism . . . pioneered by Darwin as a biological theory [which] gradually influenced the whole realm of thought . . . add[ing] the principle of growth to the static philosophy of Utilitarianism without completely replacing it'.[70] In attempting to disentangle Darwin's theory from the development of the social unit, Bernard turned to Marx to better illustrate the impact of the industrialised capitalist world and its decadent materialism:

> The mode of production of the material means of life determines, in general, the social, political, and intellectual processes of life. It is not the consciousness of human beings which determines their existence, it is their social existence which determines their consciousness.[71]

With politics, poetry and painting so profoundly entwined during the romantic period Bernard looked to the poets Edgar Allan Poe (the first modern English Decadent), William Butler Yeats, William Blake and the 'modern magician' T. S. Eliot, whose 'allegorical scaffolding' best reflected their cultural periods. Whether it was Blake's 'dark satanic mills', Barron Field's fledgling city of Sydney in 1822, or Eliot's 'wasteland of the modern world', poetry embalmed the emotional psychology of human relationships within a capitalist society. By the twentieth century, existential symbolism was being used to great effect by the surrealists, poets and psychoanalysts:

> Here was not merely an ill-defined escape from the sneers of philistine society, it was a determined attempt to create a world of art

independent of the world of reality, possessing laws of its own, its own forms of development, its own private heaven and hell.[72]

Bernard's thesis was also a lesson in the craft of writing, and in one of his notebooks he copied Poe's 'Composition of Philosophy'; it would become a methodological benchmark for Bernard's literary style:

keep originality *always* in view . . . essays brief or long enough to hold the attention of the reader . . . better a succession of brief essays that make up the longer argument . . . [in which] intensity excites because all intense excitements are through physical necessity brief; the 'effect' or 'impression' must contain 'universal' elements and, importantly a single, emphasized word in rhyme, rhythm or verse could seal the impact of meaning.[73]

Yet it was Yeats' symbolic poetry and Celtic mythology that most impressed Bernard. Yeats brought the romantic myth of the past into the reality of the national present, threading symbolism into politics; Bernard would emulate this in his 1959 *Antipodean Manifesto*. Both Yeats and Poe illustrated that when society underwent a period of disintegration, art and poetry had the power to reflect the unfolding drama. In a letter to his mother Bernard revealed the impact his thesis was having on his perception of international events and on his own psychological state:

With a civilisation based on greed already tumbling into ruins and half the world sitting among the bricks either praying or moaning, it is necessary that some at least commence to build . . . We live in a period in which a few months may contain the normal happenings of ten years; such a period demands activity.[74]

To relieve the pressures building up in him Bernard began to paint. His first work, *The advance of Lot and his brethren* (1940) was influenced by El Greco's great stormy Toledo sky, the poetry and literature he had been reading and a study of Lot, Abraham's nephew, in Genesis 19. But the imagery also reaffirmed Bernard's allegiance to communism. Melvin

Rader's *No Compromise* (1939) emphasised that humans must adopt 'a new social mind' if civilisation and 'its treasures of inheritance' were to survive Mussolini and Hitler. That intense revolutionary faith is reflected in this painting as a requiem for a disintegrating society—Bernard's *Guernica*—in which the horrors of war evict humanity and an exodus of people pour forth from the crumbling mountain of civilisation as it collapses into a blood-red sea. It was, he wrote, an attempt to combine 'surrealist techniques with an emotional intensity greater than individuality'.[75] T. S. Eliot's poetic futility and 'fusing of things ancient and modern' further inspired Bernard to draw upon the biblical story of Lot, in which tragedy produces a visionary leader who guides his people out of decadence into a 'new world'. As an atheist, Bernard chose the figure of Marx as the 'political lever' who leads the whole proletariat and semi-proletariat mass forth, but Yeats' famous lines, also copied in his diary, helped lift the compositional pitch:

> Things fall apart; the centre cannot hold
> Mere anarchy is loosed upon the world
> The blood-dimmed tide is loosed, and everywhere
> The ceremony of innocence is drowned.[76]

This cathartic burst of creativity moved Bernard to write a poem about the decline and fall of social orders:

> Gird up thy loins Lot, take thy people hence,
> Up from Gomorrah . . . Let those that stumble lie,
> Those that linger die, but fly Lot, fly
> Out, out from this black doom into the day[77]

His concern about the state of the modern period was entirely in keeping with cultural critics of the time, but Bernard's accentuation of the world crisis was further dramatised by his attraction to the apocalyptic schools of the past. The northern Flemish artists Bosch, Grünewald and Bruegel, as well as Goya and the more contemporary German artists James Ensor, Emil Nolde, Otto Dix and George Grosz, all painted the decadence of their societies:

there were contradictions in th[eir] age too, so like our own . . . They expressed . . . its spirit . . . the sublime discontent . . . [El Greco's] pictures are the soul of the Spanish temperament, twisting flames and tortured fanaticism . . . the world is renounced by Spain whilst she conquers the world, and in the rising contradiction annihilates herself as a nation . . . The opposing rhythms which destroyed the Empire, for what shall it profit as a race if it shall conquer the world and lose its soul. And Spain lost her soul, not as did Italy in the material licentiousness of the dying Renaissance, but through the fanatical mysticism of her sons whose extremes led her to destroy the classes which gave her strength.[78]

Those artists had painted as witness and participant, and offered a historical reality that Bernard believed was fundamental to the art of his time.

With the 'phoney' war over and the whirlpool of events in Europe entering a critical phase Bernard began his second picture, the dystopian *Pompeii* (1940) (fig. 9). It was the first time he had experienced unbounded artistic inspiration, a rhythmic 'thumping beat', a primitive, instinctual pulse that pushed the composition to a crude, reductive level—'violent colours for violent emotions', as Ernst Gombrich might have put it.[79] Bernard used Hegel's allegorical three registers of the positive, the negative and the infinite to show how, at their lowest level, humans crawled along the rotting bowels of an internal purgatory where all 'the crimes against mankind' were invoked. In the centre a grotesque diva sings her siren call of destruction as humanity is buried under the conditions of war and 'its own contradictions'[80] It was, as Bernard reflected many years later, his most political and desolate work—'his judgment painting . . . [based] upon the illegitimate society that had produced him'.[81]

The advance of Lot and his brethren was shown in the 1940 CAS exhibitions at the NGV and David Jones Gallery. *Pompeii* was exhibited in the Teachers Federation Exhibition in October 1940 under the pseudonym 'Joseph Tierney', but both paintings were largely ignored; as Bernard said, 'It was like dropping a stone into a well and listening for the sound of a splash. Nothing but silence.'[82] There were many obstacles to being an artist, not least that 'one had to be passionate like Albert

Tucker or Gleeson' or have 'influential friends' as Sidney Nolan had.[83] Besides, Bernard had just met the woman he wanted to marry, and he knew how many of his artist friends led lives of extreme financial hardship. Moreover, Bernard conceitedly believed that his art 'was too far advanced both in form and content to be understood by an Australian audience', even asserting that *The advance of Lot and his brethren* was superior to Nolan's *Boy and the moon* (1939–40). His new friends, the recently arrived European refugee art historians, had similarly pointed out that 'there *was* no such audience for such art [in Australia]. It would have to be created'.[84] And so, laying down his brushes, Bernard decided to become an art critic, which meant he could remain in the art world but operate at the other end of the production line, at art's reception and evaluation.

Competing in that field, however, had its problems, and not just because of Bernard's dislike of the art critic Paul Haefliger, but also because Peter Bellew had recently moved to Sydney from Melbourne, where he had been appointed art critic to the *Sydney Morning Herald* and editor of *Art in Australia*, as well as establishing the New South Wales branch of the CAS. Though a figure of considerable presence, Bellew was widely disliked for his 'confrontational tactics', but it was his connections with the rich and powerful—he was a close friend of the newspaper baron Sir Warwick Fairfax and of John and Sunday Reed, hence his support of Sidney Nolan—that irritated Bernard. In Bernard's 1943 diary is written the line, 'The art of a class begins as a weapon and ends as a whip with a velvet thorn'; it may well have been intended for Bellew and his elite circle.

While the world crisis had led Bernard away from surrealism towards a politically conscious school of 'neo-realists', the CAS exhibition confirmed that the Melbourne artists Arthur Boyd, John Perceval, Albert Tucker and Yosl Bergner were at the 'storm centre' for art and ideas that engaged with social, moral and world issues. The Sydney scene, in particular the Merioola group, looked by comparison more like a charming tea party, 'flighty and breathless'. While the 1940 CAS exhibition was Bernard's swan song as an artist, he was committed to giving a paper on surrealism to the Federation Art Society with James Gleeson and

Albert Tucker. Tucker was one of the most articulate and intellectually engaged of the Melbourne modernists and took the role of the artist in society seriously. His understanding of the human condition, based on the increasing social evils of prostitution, capitalism and war, was just beginning to develop as a powerful ethical statement in his art. Bernard, however, while still supportive of surrealism's fundamental integrity, did not believe in its capacity to reform society on the scale needed: 'There are three forms of social organisations,' he said, 'which are active in the world today, the Democratic, the Communist and the Fascist.'[85] For him, it was communism that could best alleviate social inequalities and systematically treat the cultural and educational deficiencies evident among the 'lower ranks of life and commonplace men', not surrealism:

> If the Surrealist intends merely to use the galaxy of images conjured from the Hades, Pergatory [sic] and Paradise . . . I mean the Super-ego, Ego and Id of his mind . . . then the Surrealist seems to forget that if we have a subconscious mind then we certainly had it before Freud popularised it.[86]

Paraphrasing Marx, Bernard continued, 'Surrealists should remember that it is not the consciousness of men which determines their social being but their social being which determines their consciousness.' The lecture also flagged his new career direction, 'It is [the critic's] business to examine the past in the light of the present, to take up from the history of the past those aspects of art which have manifested themselves . . . in weighing . . . the direction and impetus of our contemporary culture.'[87] It was time to adopt a new generation of intellectuals, poets and artists—those who favoured a more positive approach and advocated social realism, as evoked in the words of the Irish poet Louis MacNeice:

> Not the twilight of the gods but a precise dawn
> Of sallow and grey bricks, and newsboys crying war.[88]

CHAPTER THREE: CULTURAL CROSSINGS

Every metamorphosis is to some extent a swan song,
to some extent the overture to a great new poem.
Karl Marx[1]

The provincial cultural climate of Sydney altered dramatically for Bernard between 1938 and 1948, a decade in which his transformation from a primary school-teacher into one of Australia's most brilliant young art historians and cultural critics was little short of spectacular. It was, he said, the happiest decade of his life. Not only had his political humanism been formed by the Spanish Civil War and 'all that led up to it; the Great Depression, the hunger marches, Sir Oswald Mosley's Fascist gangs . . . the Blum government in France and the Baldwin and Chamberlain governments in Britain [who] were more opposed to the communism of Russia than the rise of Fascism',[2] but his world greatly expanded through his meeting with exiled European scholars and his marriage to Kate Challis.

In Australia the political atmosphere was also profoundly affected by 'anti-Nazism, the Popular Front . . . the struggle between Stalin and Trotsky, between Marxism and anarchism'.[3] The Australian art historian Ian McLean perceptively wrote that Bernard preferred 'the dignity of struggle to the nihilism of bohemia' but that his ideology was equally 'geared to the pluralism and pragmatism of the popular front . . . which aimed at galvanising a broad alliance with liberal elements of the bourgeoisie in the fight against fascism'.[4] But as Fredric Jameson states, 'literature play[ed] a central role in the dialectical process'.[5] This suited Bernard's Marxist convictions and his need to be part of the great new political poem, one 'bound to the production of social futures'. As he put it:

> Why was it that so many of us became communists or communist sympathisers during the 1940s? . . . The 1930s alerted many of us to the profound vacuities of capitalism under stress. But it was the march to power of Hitler, the destruction of the Spanish republic and the programmed extermination of Europe's Jewish community and its political radicals which convinced us that the western capitalist democracies possessed neither the will or the capacity to defeat Hitler.[6]

The Communist Party of Australia had already emerged as a powerful political force, establishing the United Front Against Fascism and adopting a strong multicultural policy that openly supported immigrants and human rights. As Europe's refugees arrived, Australian cities became noticeably more European, but 'Sydney in 1940 was not Berlin in the 1920s', and the exiled newcomers had to negotiate their way carefully.[7] Louis MacNeice captures this in his poem 'Refugees':

> Into the hinterland of their own future
> Behind this excessive annunciation of towers,
> Tracking their future selves through a continent of strangeness.[8]

Ever sensitive to the principles of exclusion, Bernard gravitated towards these cultured refugees and invited several European Jewish scholars and artists to present lectures at the Teachers Federation Art Society, providing them with a venue to exhibit their intellectual credentials or to mark time until they returned to Europe. Though an aura of tragedy surrounded them they commanded an intellectual superiority in Sydney's cultural mediocrity and Bernard, intoxicated by their rich heritage and rigorous debates, 'was there to take it and I was excited by it all'. Importantly, they introduced an internationalism and inducted him into a sophisticated way of thinking that vigorously enlarged his knowledge of art history and the world.[9] Dr Stefan Palyak, for example, introduced him to Heinrich Wölfflin and confirmed Hegel's historical and temporal relevance, as well as teaching him about cultural diffusion, the centre and its peripheries. This started Bernard thinking about antipodal inversion—Europe was his Antipodes. Particularly advantageous was his meeting with the Viennese art historian Dr George Berger, who by 1941 was helping him develop the Federation Society's lecture series 'The Art of Today and Yesterday'.

Berger had studied at Vienna University under Josef Strzygowski, one of the first art historians to deflect attention away from the classical traditions of western art towards a study of cultures and peoples of the East and the Orient, and the Islamic and Jewish faiths. Strzygowski, Ernst Gombrich wrote, wanted a 'complete re-evaluation of art' and emphasised 'the importance of global art', not 'the art of the powers' but 'of the . . . steppes of the migrant population'.[10] Though a great rivalry had existed between Strzygowski and the scientific rationalism advocated by the New Vienna School of art historians, specifically Alois Riegl and Franz Wickhoff, Bernard could see from his talks with Berger that Strzygowski's method had a greater humanistic spread.[11]

The Europeans not only provided Bernard with more aesthetic space in which to mediate the 'hornet's nest' of modernism, but, as he said, 'We thought on a global scale from the beginning.'[12] They also gave him a first-hand insight into the totalitarian evils that had displaced them, thus enabling Bernard to see that nationalism had many faces and frontiers and that, through contact with strangers, he could establish new perceptive devices. He described the weight of those heavy political days:

How was it possible for a country that had such a magnificent tradition in art, literature and philosophy [and] had given us Dürer, Goethe and Beethoven, to trample its past under the heels of its storm troopers . . . Expressionist art which had flourished under the Weimar Republic was hung up in an exhibition of Degenerates . . . The Bauhaus of Walter Gropius became a Nazi drill hall. The writings of Thomas Mann burnt.[13]

Thomas Mann's belief that, 'in our own time the destiny of men presents itself in political terms' resonated with Bernard, but art also had to be part of that political destiny.[14]

Local adversaries

'Art endures, and outlasts War', wrote the scion of Australian art publishing Sydney Ure Smith in his 1939 foreword to the *Australian Art Annual*. As an elite cultural commodity art was serious business, especially with the establishment of Robert Menzies' Australian Academy of Art in Canberra in 1937. This 'pontifical authority' confirmed the values shared by many conservative bodies throughout Australian cities, but it ran into extreme opposition with modernists and those involved in the establishment of the CAS in Victoria in 1938.[15] Norman Macgeorge tackled the tensions between the inaugural exhibitions of the Academy on 5 April 1938 at the NGV and that of its rival CAS, held at the same institution some months later. The 'strange irony', Macgeorge claimed, was that the Academy's exhibition included some 'decidedly "modern"' paintings, yet its aim was to oppose 'the knavish tricks of modernity'. When the CAS exhibition opened it 'became apparent what the modernist could really do when in the mood of untrammelled creative frenzy'.[16]

Battlelines were drawn between the conservatives and the modernists, as well as within CAS, and some wondered whether art would outlast the war. Robert Menzies, Lionel Lindsay, J. S. MacDonald, Harold Herbert and Howard Ashton, with their preference for an 'ossified . . . pastoral academism', relentlessly inflamed the modernists, particularly Lindsay, who believed that only select individuals inherited their positions through a cultivated, dynastic hegemony. When Sir Keith Murdoch's *Herald Exhibition of French and British Contemporary Art* opened first in Melbourne, then at David Jones Gallery in Sydney in December 1939, Lindsay and MacDonald condemned the modernist works as 'imported and perverted art, germinated in the soil of affliction and squalor . . . and alien from Australian life'.[17] The following September Lindsay reviewed the CAS's first Sydney exhibition, held at the Teachers Federation Building, and attacked its lack of 'creative originality . . . where Europe has done [it] all' before:

> The Australian public is perhaps unaware that modernism was organised in Paris by the Jew dealers whose first care was to corrupt criticism, originate propaganda—in this infinitely superior to Goebbels, for it worked . . . One third of the Contemporary Art Society's exhibitors bear foreign names, which in view of the influx of refugees, is significant enough. These are: Hartog, Haefliger, Danciger, Dorn, Daniel Kohelhagen, Cardamatis, Cohen, Bellette, Lymburner, Orban, Herman, Thake, Rodriquez, Rubbo, Ebert and St. Nicholay . . . I find imitations of the works of the German degenerates, Baumeister, Max Ernst, Kandinsky, and of Feininger, Gleizes, Miro, Arp, Gris, Dalí, and even Picasso, present in the show.[18]

Lindsay cited these names to show the 'Germanic' intrusion into Australian art, claiming that 'true art grows like a tree from its native soil not from the sludge of decadent civilisations'; it was a prelude to his racist polemic *Addled Art* (1942).

Staunchly anti-elitist and horrified by the dehumanisation in Europe, Bernard replied:

> By the time Lindsay wrote his [review] many of the artists he named were already my personal friends. A small group of us had set up an art society within the NSW Teacher's [*sic*] Federation and from 1939 on had been organising regular fortnightly discussions on art history and modernism .[19]

Sam Lewis, the chairman of the Teachers Branch of the Communist Party, sympathised with Bernard's anger at Lindsay's anachronistic and xenophobic attitude and suggested he respond in a more creative, clever way. Lewis had observed that most of the lectures in the Federation Art Society series were about the art of other countries and asked why Bernard could not do something that would throw attention on the diversity of Australia's cultural influences. Rising to the challenge, Bernard began researching the origins of art in the new colony for a lecture titled 'The Development of Australian Painting'. As he unearthed material in the

Mitchell Library, a new historical landscape revealed itself; he traced the progress of capitalism from the early phase of European settlement, what he called 'the period of Colonial primitivism', where wealthy gentlemen-squatters were the arbiters of imported taste. And he saw how art was an important instrument in cultural change; from the discovery of gold, to the growth of an art market and the development of a new nationalism with an Australian school of painters whose art exemplified the heroic life of the working man. Linking the local story within a larger historical frame, he wrote: 'in the development of Australian culture we see, in certain aspects, a recapitulation of the origins of human culture'.[20] That lecture, he told Sir Keith Murdoch, formed the genesis of his first book *Place, Taste and Tradition: A Study of Australian Art Since 1788* (1945). It had sprung as much from his defence of the refugee scholars as from his objections to Menzies, MacDonald and Lindsay's crippling values and 'so-often parish pump aesthetics'.[21]

A modern world

While Bernard claimed that *Place, Taste and Tradition* was a Marxian 'wartime book', full of anger and hope, it taught him the importance of tracing things back to their source in order to understand the complexity of the modern world. 'Contingency is the guard dog of history', he would later write and, if taken in conjunction with T. J. Clark's statement that 'Politics is the form *par excellence* of the contingency that makes modernism what it is', Bernard then was both guard dog and a medium for cultural and political change during the late 1930s and 1940s.[22]

Modernism, or the modern movement as it was called, entered Sydney's 'well-fenced' cultural scene in 1919 with Roy De Maistre, Roland Wakelin, Adrian Feint, Margaret Preston and Thea Proctor championing new formal arrangements of line, colour and structure. Leon Gellert's *Burdekin House Exhibition* in 1929 and Alleyne Zander's *Exhibition of British Contemporary Art* in 1933 followed, but 'modernism in art remained a contentious, even political, subject'.[23] In 1937 the newly built Teachers Federation Building at 166 Phillip Street became the mecca of modern cultural activity. Its tenants included the Modern

Design Centre established by Dahl and Geoffrey Collings and their partner R. Haughton James who, with Richard Beck, began introducing principles of contemporary design into Australian industry. Ure Smith had his office in the building, as did the Journalists' Association, The Federation Players theatre group, the Music Club established by Lindsay Gordon, and a writers' club. Frank and Margel Hinder and Rah Fizelle chose Federation House to hold the inaugural meeting of the Sydney branch of the CAS in 1940 and the Teachers Federation occupied the seventh and eighth floors where Bernard held the Art Society lectures.[24]

As the Art Society's secretary, Bernard proclaimed, 'We are not coming to market to sell another brand of art, but rather would hope to create a market whereat ideas about art are exchanged.'[25] There were lectures on the history of art, and the Swiss artist Sali Herman spoke on 'Art and the Layman'; James Gleeson gave talks on 'Surrealism', 'Pieter Breugel' and 'Pablo Picasso'; and R. Haughton James spoke on 'The Practical Applications of Abstract Art'. Bernard lectured on the 'The Relation of Art Criticism to the Art of John Ruskin' and 'Art and Social Reflection: Goya, Courbet and Daumier'. The program was internationalist and broad: George Berger lectured on Mexican art, Hedy Spiegel on Chinese art, and A. D. Trendall, the newly appointed Professor of Classical Archaeology at the University of Sydney, presented lectures on the art of ancient Greece and Rome. Rah Fizelle, Arthur Fleischmann, Eleonore Lange and Margaret Preston delivered papers on child art, Balinese and Javanese art, Jacob Epstein, William Blake and Aboriginal art. While Melbourne benefited from exiled European artists, architects, scientists, photographers and scholars before and after World War II, the lecture series organised by Bernard and Berger was undoubtedly the seedbed of art history in Australia. As Bernard claimed, 'We believe that nothing quite like this has been offered to Sydney people before.'[26]

A civilising influence

Wartime romances were often swift, passionate liaisons, but Bernard's meeting with Kate Challis was one of those encounters when 'fate and character are commonly regarded as causally connected.'[27] Kate had left

England on a two-year teaching contract to work at Mrs Broinowski's Bellevue Hill preparatory school in Sydney, arriving first at Station Pier, Port Melbourne on 9 December 1938, where she stayed with her aunt Maggie and uncle Eric Adeney. She was also in search of a new life. Ruth Adeney, or Kate Challis as she preferred to be called—it was her birth name—came from a cultured English middle-class background or, as Bernard put it, 'what he had read in books she had experienced in life'.[28] When war broke out, rather than return to a claustral family situation, she chose to remain in Australia.

One cool July evening in 1940 Bernard arrived at Federation House to give a lecture on modern art at the Teachers Union Art Society— he was filling in for James Gleeson who had measles—and met Sali Herman and his Parisian wife, Paulette, who were accompanied by a young woman. As they caught the lift up to the seventh floor, Paulette spoke animatedly in French to her friend, who Bernard assumed was also foreign, but when he later heard her speaking perfect English, he immediately took an interest in her.

After the lecture Kate and Bernard went for coffee at a popular Sydney café, where they fell comfortably into conversation. Bernard's lecture, Kate told him, was very interesting, particularly his emphasis on William Morris's importance in the development of modern art—he had shown a slide of Morris's Honeysuckle chintz of which Kate owned fabric in the same design. She told him how her relatives had been closely associated with the Arts and Crafts Movement and the Fabian socialist tradition, and that she had known the sculptor and wood-engraver Eric Gill, whose Catholic Guild of St Joseph and St Dominic had attracted a following of artisans to Ditchling, the village in Sussex where she grew up.

They also told each other about their illegitimacy. The one significant difference was that Kate had been adopted and raised in a privileged manner. She was well-educated, fluent in several languages, an accomplished cellist and had a Diploma of Education. In contrast, Bernard was fostered into a working-class family and was bonded to the Education Department. Despite the class differences, and that Kate was, in Peter Craven's words, clearly of 'a higher mode of being',[29] her effortless charm put him remarkably at ease. Smitten, Bernard began courting Kate with flowers and invited her to a performance by Colonel de Basil's Ballets Russes with sets designed by Léon Bakst, Natalia Goncharova, Giorgio de Chirico and Joan Miró. Having discovered Kate's love of botany, he invited her on a walking weekend at Katoomba in the Blue Mountains, one of his favourite haunts. It was there that they consummated their new relationship.

Struck by Kate's lack of pretension Bernard wrote to his mother, 'with [her] perfect English accent . . . [she] possessed an intense dislike of snobbery, objected to wearing fine clothes and only used the faintest suspicion of makeup . . . [moreover, she was] never miserable or angry . . . one of those rare sparkling, happy natures'.[30] A sonnet he wrote expresses his infatuation:

I am bewitched of my love's artless charm,
Possessed by her spritely knavish spell
And wander powerless as those who dwell
In limbo, as those who, committing harm
To none, are damned.[31]

Within six months Bernard declared that 'his future was linked up with her' and 'commencing in the world equally we seemed to have travelled such widely divergent paths and yet gained such a strangely common feeling and outlook.' (fig. 10)[32]

By Christmas Bernard had been called up for mandatory military training and faced 70 days at camp with a company composed of teachers. It was a boring, banal experience, which he described to his mother: 'we rise at 5.30am, followed by physical training and marching, punctuated with talks on discipline and the penalties for absence without leave'. Writing to Kate he complained, 'We have been inoculated for typhoid, vaccinated for smallpox; powdered for tinea, paraded and drilled for co-ordination and military efficiency and inspected for syphilis.' He also told an officer in charge that he felt 'not much better than a packhorse living a mulish existence . . . pushed about all day until one hasn't the ego of an ant'.[33] Inevitably, he became unpopular with the army officials.

At one stage Kate spent three days with Bernard near Ingleburn, after

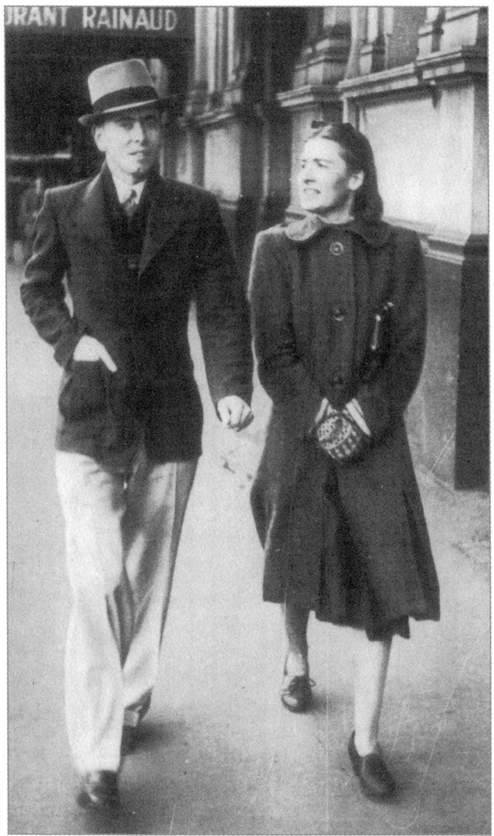

Fig. 10 Bernard Smith and Kate Challis, King Street, Sydney, 1940

which he wrote her a long, intense letter designed to persuade her not to return to her adoptive father in England, but to stay and marry him. Laden with metaphors and heavily inflected by T. S. Eliot's poetry, his assailable determination might easily have put her off:

I have all the languid indecision of a 'Prufrock' . . . Of course my problem is not identical with Prufrock's. You are much like your own, what is it? 'Prateacae' (of course I have spelt it incorrectly) as varied and as multiform for such an inexperienced gardener as myself to engage in your permanent cultivation . . . can a bud raised and tended so carefully in the mild climate of England expect to flower here in two short years? . . . A second transplantation to the original bed will probably mean the withering and dying of the whole [their relationship] plant.

Having learnt his mistake with Vera he was not about to repeat his heavy-handedness, yet his intensity continued:

> Was it not Kate who had to make a decision when she went up to the University. Did she not have to turn her face from a form of existence into which she could never fully mould herself. How little I know of either Kate or Ruth . . . Perhaps it was her origin that made it essential that she should grow out of the long adopted manner of living [with] the brilliant father . . . origins are strange things, and to be born outside of the conventions of a whole social structure . . . is to be critical forever.

Employing his knowledge of the divided self, the Freudian fever of possession and his skilful Marxist rhetoric, he tactically pursued her:

> Then came the second decision to leave your own country . . . There must have been the natural desire to go abroad, to see the world, to show one's independence of a family who had made Ruth Adeney . . . I do not want to simplify problems. You are neither Ruth or Kate. You are both Ruth and Kate . . . Not only our birth but our social heredity constitute our personality. One does not have to be born outside the social scheme to feel the conflicting gravities of two worlds . . . [but] bourgeois intellectuals realise that the day of their class is gathering to the twilight; they must summon all their energy to live on . . . through the long night of our present discontent when so many old things must perish and among them the very class which they represent . . . but classes have historical origins and exist for defined periods. They die, and the individual who once constituted those classes are merged in new social patterns. They experience a rebirth . . . It was Kate and not Ruth who made you come to Australia, but Ruth came also . . . Ruth who promised she would return again in 2 years.

Blaming William Blake for his evangelical tone, he assured her he would not impose his will on her 'sensibility and intellect':

> Would it be too much to suggest, am I too biased and prejudiced to even think of stating, that perhaps in Australia Kate Challis could develop more completely than in her own country, where the danger would be a continual reversion to Ruth Adeney.[34]

Bernard had offered Kate an escape and he was intellectually strong enough to pull her away from her English family. For Kate it was a leap of faith to stay with him, but her decision to do so was empowering. Moreover, there was something exciting about Bernard, something she could nurture without controlling.

Marriage

Kate was keen to establish a life away from her family in England where her relationship with her 'strange and sinister' father Cuthbert Adeney had been complex and often demoralising. Not only had Cuthbert sexually abused her when she was a child, but the prospect of raising his three young daughters, her step-sisters from a second marriage, implied a de facto–wife relationship with Cuthbert. With a war on, she felt even more that England had 'no real place for her'.[35]

To win Kate, Bernard had to commit to his part of an agreement. She wanted her own children; he wanted to rise in the system, a system that Kate understood. In accepting Bernard's offer of marriage she felt she could help him develop into a more worldly person and soften some of his political rigidity; moreover, he was highly intelligent, handsome, stimulating company and caring. On 16 May 1941 they were married at the Registrar General's Office in central Sydney, across from St Mary's Catholic Cathedral, with Lindsay Gordon as their witness. Their first home was a rented second-floor flat, 11 Ilan Court, 13 Wylde Street, in the lower, hilly part of Potts Point where they almost had a view of the harbour. It was known as the artists' quarter, with Sali and Paulette Herman living nearby. They eventually moved to the flat below them.

The artist Arthur Fleischmann, who was working on a large bas-relief panel for the doors of the newly built Mitchell Library, lived in the same street and William Dobell lived further up in Macleay Street. The government, however, had transformed the area into a noisy rumble of naval activity, captured in one of Bernard's poems published in the first edition of *Australian New Writing* in 1943:

> Dust over Potts Point, dry dock's dust at the road's end,
> Cranes, drills, dynamos, dredges drag the sea's bed,
> Rumbling down the tall flats, dry mud broken daywards . . .
> Noise on a snob's hill, drill's rhythm dinning a class dead;
> Dynamite blasts of our broken time, drumming each shift's end:[36]

Kate provides a snapshot of their newly married life in a letter to Clare Pepler, her adoptive mother's best friend:

> I am sitting on our back verandah—the harbour is bright blue as usual and the old ladies are wandering round their garden, they have lots of big sunflowers now and nice big lemons on their tree. Bernard is in his study deep in preparing next years [*sic*] Art Lecture series. The teachers are all out of camp again . . . its [*sic*] lovely for us though of course he may go again any time. The state schools are back again . . . Mrs B[roinowski] has decided to stay put though we have lost help at the school—many have evacuated to their country homes and learning through correspondence . . . we have a trench too, which pleases the parents. I have been shatter proofing all the windows and thinking that you must have done it too. B[ernard] has blacked-out very efficiently so we are already [*sic*] for when it starts—which may be any time now.[37]

Before Christmas 1941, Private B. W. Smith of the Sydney University Regiment D Company, was transferred to Bathurst where it was expected that mobilisation would be announced. Back in Sydney Kate seemed far more attuned to the dangers of attack, though Bernard assured her it was 'stupid to get panic stricken about the possible bombing of Sydney'. In 1942 and very close to where they lived in Potts Point, a Japanese submarine was bombed.

As their relationship deepened it became hemmed with a loving pragmatism and within a short time it also bore children. Marriage gave Bernard a dedicated partner, social elevation and, in ways not obvious to the outside world, enormous help with his cultural grooming and intellectual productivity. In her calm English manner, Kate transformed him into a cosmopolitan and provided him with an environment that sustained his intellectual labour. She taught him French and modified any remnants of his working-class habits and speech; she was, as Bernard said, his civilising influence.

For the previous five years Bernard had been in charge of his own life and the only woman who had ever had any real control over him had been the caring but strict Mrs Tottie Keen. His mother was a confiding but absent figure, a reminder of his origins. As he explained to Rose Anne, 'the other two girls I have known intimately, Evelyn and Vera McCafferty, admired me and thought I was clever, but they would never have really understood me'. Kate was different; she was a soul mate, a connection sealed by their illegitimacy, a Fabian and committed socialist whose love of the guild ethos of Arts and Crafts Bernard shared. Eric Gill's credo, 'An artist is not a special kind of man, but every man is a special kind of artist', is written in Bernard's 1943 diary.

Marriage, however, was not immune to Marxism or the politics of identity; it was a contractual document and Kate was Bernard's first legal possession. In his copy of Marx and Engels' *The German Ideology* (1846), he underlined 'The production of life, both of one's own in labour and of fresh life in procreation, now appears as a double relationship; on the one hand as natural, on the other as a social relationship.'[38] As fatherhood loomed, concepts of family, freedom and property took on a new significance, and Bernard re-read Hegel's *Philosophy of Right* and Lenin's *The Origin of the Family, Private Property and the State* (1884). Their first child, Elizabeth, was born in 1942 and Bernard wrote to Cuthbert Adeney with the news, enclosing a recent studio photograph of himself, as if to show Cuthbert that Kate's husband was not a rough-hewn colonial (fig. 11).

Cuthbert's reply was disarming but it also showed that he was keen to establish a position with his son-in-law:

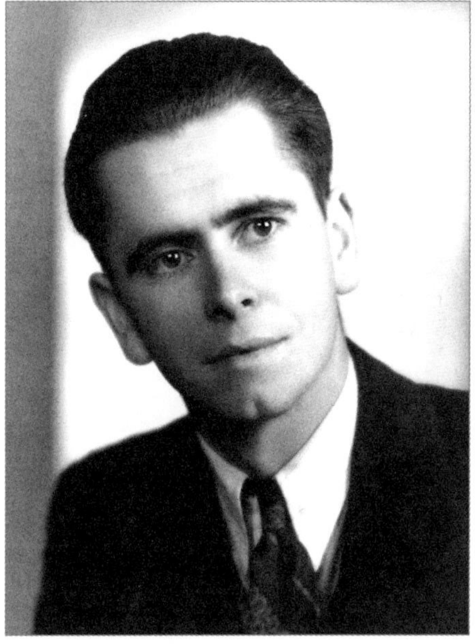

Fig. 11 Bernard Smith, 1942

The excellent photograph of yourself . . . arrived today; with its modest inscription. I must say that if you resemble it in any way I have no complaint to make about Ruth's choice; in fact taking into consideration such detail as the mid-chin impression, and the Tyrone eyebrow along with other physiognomic elements, without saying it outright other than handsome is handsome does, I might proceed to designate a parental attitude as that of a cheerful loser.[39]

If motherhood compromised Kate's autonomy, then Bernard considered fatherhood a regular after-work commitment, writing to Lindsay Gordon that 'paternity like other jobs is one that grows with tenure'.[40] John Challis Smith was born in August 1944, and the family unit was complete.

Within two years of their marriage, Bernard began the first of his extra marital affairs. Apart from his duties as a schoolteacher there were ample opportunities through his communist activities to deploy his charm and many women were attracted to him. In 1943 he met Deidre Cable at a three-day Workers' Educational Association conference at Newport, north of Sydney. She was a recent graduate of the University of Sydney and a member of the Communist Party of Australia, but as a married man, Bernard kept the affair discreet. They continued writing to each other for some time and a letter from Deidre describes their tryst:

> You are the only person to whom I can write the feeling, naked as it comes, onto the paper without faking anything. I don't do this all the time, of course, but I know that I could do it. It is because there is a strange deep intimacy between us, which comes so swiftly—remember—and I believe will last for a long time. It is wonderful of one to have it.[41]

Nietzsche had written 'A test of a good marriage . . . proves itself . . . by being able to endure an occasional "exception"',[42] but Bernard yielded to infidelity easily. Kate belonged to him; she was knowable, accessible and possess-able within the bounds of marriage, whereas submitting to the sexual impulse and seeking the conquest may well have been 'a male thing' as he called it, but it also gave him back his autonomy and satisfied his yearning for unbridled passion. As already suggested it was the primal release that subconsciously connected him to his father—'I am my father's spirit . . . a blind submission to his secret, to the secret of his origin.'

Cadre Smith

If it can be said that philosophy is a footnote to Plato, it might be said . . . that modern social theory is a footnote to Marx.
Bernard Smith[43]

In the booklet *The Communist Party and its Work* it is stressed that Marxist theory was not dogma, but a necessary guide to action for the working classes in their struggle for power. Each party branch organised and helped 'comrades in factories' to fight capitalism, but in the reform arena Bernard was interested in the broader cultural landscape. The slogan 'Today the Communist Party is the guardian of the Arts' reflected his role in the party's activities. Not only was he elected to the Social and Cultural Committee at Federation House where he wrote articles and developed study groups to raise the cultural awareness of its members, he was also active in Aid Russia meetings, was the secretary of the War Art Council between 1942 and 1945, and sat on the executive committee of the Encouragement of Art Movement (EAM), the Committee for the Encouragement of Music and Art (CEMA) and the Studio of Realist Art (SORA).

When Hitler advanced on the Soviet Union in 1941 Bernard declared his 'warm-hearted support' for the people of Russia as they resisted invasion. In November he presented a paper at the Cultural Conference in Sydney, his first public declaration on art and communism, but his pedagogic summary of the main developments of Russian art did little to fire his audience. It was more an act of loyalty to the party than a convincing response to political realism.[44] An earlier lecture for the Teachers Federation Art Society in May 1940, titled 'Art and Social Reflection: Goya, Courbet and Daumier' was significantly more coherent. It flagged his artistic heroes, men who painted with a street-level meaning that showed the theatre of the common man. If art were to be potent in times of upheaval it had to ask and answer questions of political and social urgency; it was Goya, Bernard argued, 'who went to the charnel-pits outside Madrid to record the truth of the Napoleonic invasion'[45]; it was Courbet the revolutionist who made the first departure from romanticism and painted the realism of nature and life. Those artists saw in the long march of history the lie, the social hoax, what Fredric Jameson calls '*the* administered world, *the* institutionalised society, *the* culture industry, *the* damaged subject—an image of our historical present'.[46] Like iconoclasts they were prepared to strip away the veil of bourgeois capitalism, mock imperial or elitist values and expose the struggle of the working class. It was why Bernard chose those artists as his culture heroes and why he used the pseudonyms 'Goya' and 'Courbet' to publish his literary criticism in the *Tribune*, especially after he began working at the National Gallery of New South Wales (later Art Gallery of New South Wales) in 1944.

By November 1941 the Germans had sunk HMAS *Sydney*; within a few weeks the Japanese had bombed Pearl Harbor and Australia had declared war on Japan. Those events galvanised artists against fascism and they were prepared to assist the government with the war effort in whatever way they could. Bernard felt that his contribution lay in literary criticism as a vehicle for political projection and public unity, and in late 1942 he approached the writer George Farwell and the novelist Katharine Susannah Prichard to help him establish a new literary journal *Australian New Writing*, or *The New Boomerang* as it was originally to be called.

Modelled on the British *New Writing* and the American *Left Review*, and published parallel to the official army magazine *SALT*, *Australian New Writing* was financially backed by the Communist Party of Australia. It offered the Australian and New Zealand working class, industry workers, soldiers, and allied servicemen and women the chance to be published. During the initial planning phase Bernard insisted on it having an explicit political component; 'In this country we still have to develop a consistent Marxist aesthetic, which will speak with authority and develop a tradition in active struggle with present existent aesthetic positions which, although they may appear small and unimportant, have their adherents.'[47] He also told the editorial board it should

> be prepared to go right in amongst the Lawlors, the Rex Ingamells, the Christesens and so on . . . if our editorials are going to convince the sceptics, they will have to shock people into realising that just in those spheres where they felt themselves specialists, 'New Writing', is speaking powerfully and with conviction.[48]

Hearing of the aggressive editorial approach, Clem Christesen of the literary journal *Meanjin* wrote to Bernard proffering a realistic overview of the difficulties that a new, small journal would encounter: 'The plain truth is that Australia cannot support a really high-class literary magazine. I knew that when I started *Meanjin* in 1939. But the problem is not only money . . . It is also lack of TIME.'[49] But *Australian New Writing* was never intended to be 'high-class'; its first edition of 10,000 copies sold out and a second run was printed, a remarkable achievement with wartime paper and printing restrictions. The editorial of the second volume noted, 'Fresh winds blow strong; does it matter if a few sober hats get knocked off?'[50] Christesen's prediction that magazines devoted entirely to literature lasted no longer than two years, however, proved correct, and only four issues of *Australian New Writing* were produced between 1943 and 1945.

One of the most politically committed artists concerned with cultural unity during the war was Noel Counihan. He had established the Artists Unity Congress in Melbourne and had organised an anti-fascist exhibition in December 1942, from which numerous cultural organisations, such as the Artists' Advisory Panel of Victoria, the Encouragement of Art Movement and the War Art Council of New South Wales, were spawned. In 1943 Counihan wrote to Bernard congratulating him on *Australian New Writing* and advising him 'For Christ's sake don't let "New Australian Writing" fall into the bogs of intellectualism, expressing the outlook only of a small, mutually-admiring clique, arty in its format. I hope all Australian publicists will learn from "Comment" and "Angry Penguins" just what must at all costs be avoided like the plague.'[51] While Counihan shared similar aesthetic and political ideas based on 'the working class, its struggle for decent living standards and a respect for its labour', Bernard found his hard-line and doctrinaire principles at times overbearing.[52] Perhaps Counihan reminded him of his earlier self.

As Bernard was finalising *Place, Taste and Tradition* in late 1944 he sent Counihan a section dealing with the contemporary period. Counihan praised him for devoting so much space to 'Aestheticism & Nationalism [and] the development of a pre-fascist mentality', but he also offered his view of Australia's cultural development:

As everyone is aware Australian literature has been marked from the beginning by its plebeian and strongly rebellious character— its intimate relationship to the labour movement and its reflection of militant democracy. All our major poets and writers were rebels, but look at Australian painting—what a contrast. Our 'eminent' artists have been the servants of the bourgeoisie.[53]

Artists who challenged middle-class or elitist values and promoted an emancipatory socialism were 'rare birds', Bernard said; it was why he would write the biography of Noel Counihan and begin one on Gustave Courbet, both fearless critics of society, even when they were victims of politicised discrimination.

In late 1943, another form of discrimination occurred. William Dobell's portrait of the artist Joshua Smith created unprecedented controversy when the trustees of the National Art Gallery of New South Wales awarded it the Archibald Prize. Action was brought against the trustees on the grounds that the painting was a caricature, and the furore that followed shattered both Dobell and his subject. Bernard admired Dobell because he painted 'the lower ranks of society', life's foibles and its Hogarthian parodies. He believed Dobell's art was brilliant, particularly in a country noted for its academic, drab portraiture, but in writing a critique of Dobell's painting he could have been describing one of Albert Tucker's *Images of modern evil*:

> Against the background of a classic column, the glare of neon lights and garages, and the mysterious depths of urban waterways, the emaciated yet defiant head rears itself out of the gloom and turbulence of the city night. It is not the face and body of Joshua Smith, but a symbol of the twentieth century artist living on in the last days of a dying culture.[54]

Bernard's dramatic prose reflected the anxiety of the wartime situation and the mood of social decline. The following year, however, Joshua Smith was awarded the Archibald Prize and Dobell was made a trustee of the gallery.

On loan

The war brought together a constellation of progressive modernists and influential individuals who gathered to advance Australian culture. In Sydney in 1943 Mary Alice Evatt was the first woman appointed a trustee of the art gallery; as the wife of the federal Attorney-General Herbert Vere Evatt and sister-in-law to the New South Wales Minister for Education

Clive Evatt, her interest in 'art education and public art projects' was well supported. Geoffrey Dutton considered her 'worth remembering . . . on the strength of her influence alone on Bernard Smith'.[55] The same could be said of her fellow trustee and chairman of the War Art Council, Sydney Ure Smith, who became Bernard's patron.[56]

Both Ure Smith and Bernard shared the belief that Australia's cultural future was a major investment and that 'art could improve and was an index of social change'.[57] In *The Society of Artists Book 1943*, Ure Smith stressed the importance of bringing art to the people—'Give them the chance to absorb [art], see it, understand it. Let it be part of their life.'[58] He also flagged the concept of regional travelling exhibitions and undoubtedly saw Bernard as capable of implementing such public programs.

With marriage and children came the responsibility to earn a better wage and, still classified at a second-level teacher's salary, Bernard needed to advance his position. In June 1944 he sat an examination at the Education Department at which he wrote an essay titled 'Adult Aesthetic Education'. Partly lifted from his manuscript *Place, Taste and Tradition*, it covered the impact of British and continental aesthetic structures on colonial Australia, the reorganisation and proliferation of academies and art museums, and illustrated the rise and decline of art as a social utility. The essay might well have been written with the proposed regional touring exhibition job at the gallery in mind.

Bernard argued that the system of art education as it presently stood in Australia needed a more unified approach to the production and consumption of art, its aesthetic impact and general benefits to society, and pointed out that CEMA, established in Britain at the beginning of World War II as part of the 'decentralisation of public appreciation of the arts', had been very successful in educating people about art and cultural activities. Bernard had also been reading the British *Museum Journal* articles about touring exhibitions to small British towns, factories, army and Royal Air Force centres.

Under W. J. McKell's New South Wales Labor Government a report had been drafted on the 'Plan for the Organisation of Travelling Art Exhibitions' and released to the trustees of the art gallery in May 1944. Bernard, however, had already pre-empted the report by writing to 'the

Art Gallery Board [and] asking that Mary Alice Evatt attend a meeting in connection with a proposal to establish a travelling art exhibition'.[59] When a subcommittee comprising Evatt, Ure Smith, Charles Lloyd Jones, Professor E. G. Waterhouse and Clive Evatt was established to act in association with the Education Department it was a foregone conclusion that Bernard would be asked to administer the scheme.[60]

In October 1944 he started as a seconded education officer at the Art Gallery, where he was to oversee the regional touring exhibitions. Bernard was shocked at how poorly the gallery functioned, due to a succession of conservative trustees who had treated it like an elite gentlemen's club, and over the decades the building and its collection had been badly neglected. There was no office for the director, nor were there any toilets, and with a shortage of space Bernard was expected to work from the Education Department in Pitt Street. He argued that it was completely impractical and insisted on working at the gallery, where eventually a tiny, custom-built cubicle was erected under the stairs. From there he assessed the collection and claimed to have originated the travelling exhibition program. Gwen Sherwood, the director's secretary, however, had already implemented it well in advance of Bernard's arrival.[61]

Drawn principally from the gallery's Australian collection, which possessed so few good modernist works, the travelling exhibitions had to be supplemented with works on loan from artists and private collectors. With Mary Alice Evatt's support, £500 was set aside to purchase recent Australian paintings. It was a clever way of getting good modernist works in through 'the back door' for the gallery's collection. Eric Wilson's *The kitchen stove* (1943) was one of the first semi-abstract paintings acquired and, as Bernard said, 'If we start at the beginning then we have to go to the end.'[62] Other artists acquired under this initiative included, among others, Ralph Balson, Grace Crowley, Douglas Dundas, Russell Drysdale, Rah Fizelle, Mary Webb, Grace Cossington Smith, Roland Wakelin, Thea Proctor, Margaret Preston and Frank Hinder. As Bernard gathered the artists' biographical details for the exhibition catalogues, the idea of a dictionary of Australian artists took shape, a project he would eventually see to fruition in 1962 with his book *Australian Painting: 1788–1960*.

Between 1944 and 1948 Bernard had organised 20 exhibitions held in

100 venues that were visited by over 150,000 people but, as he expressed in a letter, it was not always easy. There was often resistance from local authorities, with the mayor of Tamworth, 'Mr Collins, an ironmonger . . . point blank refus[ing] to open the show or have anything to do with it. He added that the people would agree with him for not wasting his time on such things.'[63] Bernard also encountered trouble with Peter Bellew who sabotaged his Wollongong program with an alternative exhibition that comprised much the same artists as he had selected. It was a reminder of Bellew's competitive and manipulative egotism, but fortunately Bernard was able to move his exhibition to Wagga Wagga at short notice.[64]

The travelling exhibitions were demanding projects for which Bernard had to prepare catalogues, publicity material, give talks to Rotary clubs and broadcasting stations, arrange insurance, dispatch the paintings, draft itineraries for the guide lecturers, prepare reports and supervise the movement from one venue to another—all with only a little help from the director's secretary Gwen Sherwood. He did, however, gain invaluable experience in exhibition management, public education, curating and art dealership, and it confirmed his commitment to art education in society.

In keeping with the War Arts Council policy, Bernard employed artists to give lectures—many being his friends, thereby providing them with a welcome income during the war. Paul Beadle, Rah Fizelle, Sali Herman, Mary Webb, James Cant, Roy Dalgarno, Jean Bellette, and Hayward Veal were among the speakers; even Mary Alice Evatt took her share in assisting, mounting and sweeping the floors of the Masonic Lodge in Canberra where she and Bernard hung the exhibition *Some Recent Australian Painting* in late 1944. This was his first encounter with the new national capital, 'white buildings in the planned wilderness . . . a city living in the future with its archives in the past'.[65]

From the outset Bernard's 'movement into the gallery' had been 'highly political in an art political sense', not only because he was a communist, but also because he was a modernist.[66] Paranoid that communism was infiltrating their hallowed institution, right-wing trustees such as Lionel Lindsay, John Maund and James McGregor were subversively antagonistic towards Bernard, but as he said, he 'developed strategies of sidestepping . . . the[ir] opposition' and 'never argued with any of them on aesthetic grounds but simply in liberal terms'.[67] With 'none of the redeeming lunacy' of his brother Norman, Lionel Lindsay, while appearing cordial enough to Bernard in the corridors, ranted to his friends and to his brother Daryl Lindsay 'may the Gods destroy him'. When Bernard, George Berger, Rah Fizelle, Sali Herman and Ian Fairweather applied for the position of director of the gallery in 1945 Lionel Lindsay wrote 'that commo Smith [and his] "reffo" friend the swine Dr. Berger' were nothing but 'political and racial vermin'.[68]

There were, however, some who appreciated Bernard; Gwen Sherwood, Hal Missingham, Sydney Ure Smith, Mary Alice Evatt, Charles Lloyd Jones and E. G. Waterhouse watched out for his survival at the gallery, though it was often a battle of wills. Forced to subvert his political activism he told Harry Gould at the Communist Party's headquarters that while he 'would endeavour to further the Party policy' he was obliged to hide under a pen name.[69] When Sydney Ure Smith published Bernard's *Place, Taste and Tradition* in 1945, a section was removed in which Bernard accused Lionel Lindsay, J. S. MacDonald and P. R. Stephenson of being pro-fascist nationalists and extreme retardants of Australian modernism. That censored chapter was finally published as 'The Fascist Mentality in Australian Art and Criticism', in the *Communist Review* in 1946 under the pseudonym 'Goya'. Another article Bernard wrote for the *Tribune* under the pseudonym 'Courbet' was a rallying call for social realism:

> True to form the capitalist press, chasing sensationalism, has written up the Contemporary Art Society's exhibition as a 'surrealist' show. This is quite false. Among the most vital painters, the death wishes, Oedipus complexes and skull-and-cross-bones salesmanship, are wearing thin. The trend towards realism that has grown up in face of strong opposition is today the most important factor.[70]

Such articles, Bernard said, provided a platform to 'further the Communist Party policy of encouraging art because these were important steps in our leadership of the cultural sphere'.[71]

Place, Taste and Tradition

By the time the 'shadow of Guernica' and World War II had engulfed the Australian psyche Bernard believed firmly that a more analytical and truthfully historical view of Australia's cultural heritage and its modern identity was needed. His notion of nationalism, cultural diffusion and antipodeanism had taken shape as a legacy of the exiled Europeans, and while Australia was a reflection in the imperial mirror, what mattered was how it had emerged from its colonial cradle and arrived at its own distinctive modern position. He was equally emphatic that he 'had to construct an alternative to Lindsay's model of Australian art as a vigorous young tree in danger of being blighted by an infestation of foreigners'.[72]

Place, Taste and Tradition was a remarkable book for an academically untrained young man. His reading of Australian art and culture was significantly more developed than anything previously attempted, such as William Moore's two-volume *The Story of Australian Art* (1934), and, though there are obvious flaws, it was only to be expected from such an oppositional Marxist intellect. By using distance as a disruptive force to the European matrix, together with an astute analysis of the rapid rise of capitalism in the 1880s, Bernard showed how historic and economic forces had shaped a new society and its cultural identity. By the late nineteenth century Australians were asserting themselves within an international context and their art had begun developing its own distinctive markings.[73]

Bernard's landmark book was based on his Teachers Federation lectures and material gathered in the Mitchell Library—he was astonished at how much was 'hidden away in those old books', telling his friend and comrade Lindsay Gordon 'we have to bring [them] into the light of the day and revaluate after the bourgeois myth has been blown away'.[74] His notebooks show a meticulous chronology, synopses of books, quotations and bibliographies, timelines that chart the arrival of artists in Australia and how the Europeans viewed the new land and transposed their traditions into their 'infant colony'. He compiled this under the sub-headings: 'Emigrant nostalgia', 'Morality', 'Romanticism', 'The pastoral', 'Patronage', 'Representation', 'Architectural styles', 'Colonial aristocracy', 'The public',

'Social relations', 'Criticism', 'Impressionism', 'Realism' and 'Nationalism', and made lists of reproductions and original artworks by pioneering artists that illustrated his episodic, cultural mapping.

At the time of writing the book, Bernard's Marxism had been further shaped by Arnold Toynbee's *The Impact of an Alien Civilisation*, Stalin's *The International Situation: Foundations of Leninism*, and Katharine Susannah Prichard's *Soviet Literature*, and naturally historical materialism inflected much of his writing. Indeed, he would always believe 'that economy and technology . . . provide in the long run the "superstructure" of culture, law, politics [and the] humanities'.[75] Margaret Preston's 1941 lecture on Aboriginal motifs in Australian art had interested him, but he was not convinced of her aesthetic symbolism and appropriated modernism. If anything he saw Preston's art as a form of antipodean palimpsest, later writing that 'There is a contradiction in her work, in its futuristic aspects it supported a Eurocentric industrialism, in its primitivistic aspects it was subversive of those values. That is the radical aspect of her work.'[76] He also dismissed Rex Ingamells' Jindyworobak group of poets and their journals as substituting Indigenous art and mythology for a new nationalism. One Jindyworobak publication, however, was of some benefit in that it mentioned how the English poets Keats and Shelley were 'able to see and think and speak in terms of their own north[ern] hemisphere conditions, their minds each with the aesthetic heritage that was rightly theirs'.[77] The notion of rights of possession helped Bernard define his theory of antipodeanism, later reflecting:

I was trying to define the business of what it is to be Australian, that is I was looking for what is typically Australian. But the only way you could logically define this, I thought, was to find out what is European, to distinguish what is European from what is Australian.[78]

One flaw was Bernard's treatment of modernism. Ure Smith had sent Bernard's manuscript to Russell Drysdale for comment, the latter writing to Bernard to commend the work, but also criticising his inadequate handling of the modern movement in Melbourne:

I should like very much to offer my congratulations on a work of real distinction. It comes at a time when such a book is very necessary … it is superfluous to say an exposition of the aims and tendencies of art in this country has never been seriously attempted before, and the value of your book will place art, and the approach to art, here in Australia, on its proper level of aesthetic appreciation.

Drysdale, who had just returned from London and Paris, had found a

growing movement among . . . younger painters to break away from the domination of the School of Paris . . . [George] Bell was very interested in this because he . . . felt . . . that we in Australia would only repeat our former 'isolation' as artists, by burying our heads in the sands of surrealism, and substitute for the shades of the plein-air school . . . another set of romantic symbols to obscure the path which was opening up to the younger painters of Australia.

Sufficient time has passed . . . to assess the valuable contribution that Bell and his school ha[ve] made to contemporary art.[79]

Drysdale's criticism was welcomed and addressed but, as Bernard wrote, 'New directions in art [were] notoriously difficult to observe during the first indications of their movement'.[80] In his later work, Bernard devoted considerable space to Drysdale as one of Australia's most significant modernist artists, showing his appreciation of the artist in numerous essays and especially in *Australian Painting: 1788–1960*.

Place, Taste and Tradition was unexpectedly successful and, even though a 'young man's book, researched and written quickly (most of it in six weeks)' as Bernard admitted to David Cunningham at Oxford University Press, it established him as a major critic and writer.[81] With 3000 copies printed at £1 a book, he reaped £200 in royalties within the first five months and by 1948 the book was out of print, having sold particularly well in Melbourne. The writer Nettie Palmer applauded his historical interpretation: 'We've both [Nettie and Vance Palmer] read your book carefully and with growing respect especially for its historical views. We were extremely interested in your interpretation of the grip the Eighteenth Century held on our art for so long; we have built all our theory of literary development on the same thing.'[82] Margaret Preston offered her congratulations—'It is so well constructed that it gives me much pleasure to read . . . May you live long and write more.'[83] The *Angry Penguins* editor and art patron John Reed wrote:

A. R. McClintock told me about your book on Australian Art and I am very glad to hear about it, as such a book is undoubtedly badly needed. I am only sorry that we did not have the opportunity of publishing it as I feel quite sure that with our interests centred in such matters as these, we would have been able to concentrate the maximum amount of enthusiasm and thought on it.[84]

One reviewer believed Bernard's 'process of revision and review in the light of contemporary findings [was] . . . most original . . . [developing] a new system of relationships to explore and to comment on.'[85] The American curator Edgar Kaufmann Jr, reviewing the book for the *Art Bulletin,* approved of it as 'well-condensed original research', but was critical of the poor illustrations and Bernard's 'perspective of art history' that had ignored certain artists and critics of the modern period, especially Haefliger, Bellew and Burdett. Bernard's partisan opinions and omissions of art forms like photography and stage design were regarded as further flaws, but those genres had not developed or attracted serious attention in Australia to the same extent as they had in Europe or in North America.

On the whole, Bernard was riding a wave of literary success and, keen to follow up with publicity for his book, travelled to Melbourne where he was met with favourable attention. One morning he caught a glimpse of *Place, Taste and Tradition* in a shop window and 'felt deliciously proud'. He noted in his diary that he had met Dr Ursula Hoff, Daryl Lindsay and Keith Murdoch; that Joan Lindsay and Mrs Allen Henderson, the wife of one of the NGV trustees had flattered him; and the head of the Council of Adult Education Colin Badger was eager to meet him. He met the *Argus* critic Alan McCulloch and *Meanjin's* Clem Christesen, and caught up with communist friends such as Victor O'Connor, from whom he bought his first painting, *The refugees* (1942), and Noel Counihan, whose 'mining' paintings he found extraordinarily powerful. Bernard wrote to Kate:

> if he develops in this manner he will become the most important painter in the country. These mining paintings are a complete vindication of what I have said about realism. In addition I found that he possesses an extremely keen and penetrating ability to criticise contemporary painting and with no mean knowledge of literature and music.

This letter also revealed Bernard's growing self-esteem:

> Down here . . . I find that I am as much as ever in love with the girl that I used to so look forward to visiting on Friday evenings. Your continuous subordination of your self and your largeness of heart, and what I suppose can only be called a genuine nobility that always stands in comparison with so many others. But I don't want you to subordinate yourself too much for my cause, or for my 'intellect'. I know my limitations well enough, however many books I write . . . But I should feel that our marriage had not been a success if I had taken one whom I have always considered a charming and intelligent woman, and made her a diligent, helpful and devoted wife to be mentioned with touching respect in the prefaces of my books.[86]

At a Melbourne CEMA branch meeting he encountered the young woman he had had an affair with in 1943. A delightful frisson still existed between them and Bernard wrote to Kate that 'Deidre Cable has been looking after me and introducing me to the CEMA group, writers etc. She's very bright and gay, but there is no need to be jealous. She is also very good', adding, 'Perhaps I should not speak for myself.'[87] Sensing he may have overstated his enthusiasm, he wrote a second letter to Kate:

> it is good, though selfish to get away for a little and do some mental

stocktaking . . . We are, I feel, passing through a difficult period of our lives. For you it is more difficult than for me, because you are so bound to a domestic routine and that is partly because of my own selfishness, but not completely. We must be careful not to allow ourselves to get into a domestic rut . . .

Another is the problem of sex, which we have often joked about . . . Physically I am as polygamous, I suppose, as any male, but rarely have I summoned the energy or the desire to transform vague feelings into action . . . there has been a few, a very few occasions, since marriage when this has occurred . . . but . . . these escapades have secured you more than ever in my own affections. That is the simple fact . . . as for the rest it must be like my forgetfulness, a physical attribute, but fortunately not as frequent.

I suppose a successful marriage is a continuous struggle like most things, and I do want ours to be successful. You have no real need to be jealous.[88]

Bernard's admission of adultery opened a wound in their marriage in which the seeds of Kate's sadness were sown; the distaste of deceit is evocatively captured in Ihab Hassan's words: 'There are wounds that fester at the very root of our being, so deep they neither hurt nor heal.'[89]

Art, society and the critic

During the war years Bernard felt that 'art was defending itself against its own death'; arguments were heated and position-taking divisive, 'people [had] the habit of advocating [those positions] strongly. We all felt that great issues were at stake.'[90] Albert Tucker was one of the more vociferous. In 1943 in his article 'Art, Myth and Society' in *Angry Penguins* he argued that art had become bankrupt under capitalism and that communism's cultural policy was inadequate to resolve the crisis. It sparked an avalanche of heated debate by artists and commentators, including John Reed, Herbert McClintock and Noel Counihan. Bernard weighed into this with his article 'The New Realism in Australian Art', published in *Meanjin* in 1944, but it was tame in comparison to his attack on Adrian Lawlor in the Australian

Quarterly two years earlier, in which he came very close to defamation. Linking Lawlor with the fascist mentality similar to that of Lionel Lindsay, he accused Lawlor of emotional self-indulgence, myth-making and a lack of social and creative responsibility. Bernard later reflected:

> It seemed to many of us at the time that the ancient centres of European high culture . . . had degenerated into a condition of psychotic imbecility. You had to live through those years to understand . . . what it was that drove the most serious art of that time, not only here in Australia but abroad also. What those dark years did was to make Australian art more international in its preoccupations.[91]

It was not long before Bernard came to the attention of Clinton Hartley Grattan, an American journalist and a keen observer of Australia, who invited him to write an essay for a book titled *Australia*, published by the University of California in 1947. Grattan's interest in Australia as 'a fascinating experiment in democracy' began in 1927 when he attempted to locate a 'characteristically Australian' cultural identity and published a booklet titled 'Australian Literature' in 1929.[92] It caught the attention of Miles Franklin, Nettie Palmer (who had suggested Smith to Grattan), Katharine Susannah Prichard, H. V. Evatt, Brian Fitzpatrick, Brian Penton and Sir Keith Hancock. Though Grattan was never a communist, Bernard was attracted to his far-left sympathies, pluralist approach to socio-cultural, political, economic and international relations, and his reputation for 'combative polemics'.[93] By the end of the war, with the USA asserting itself as the western world's watchdog, Bernard's essay, while drawing on *Place, Taste and Tradition*, denoted a new level of political articulation. It also marked his international debut as critic and historian.

In another article, 'Australian Art and the War', which Bernard was asked to write for the prominent American Marxist magazine *New Masses* in 1944, his grasp of the new globalism was further tested:

> The course of Australian art since the beginnings of settlement in 1788 offers a fine field of investigation for all interested in the

relations between art and social institutions of a young country. In this respect the art of Australia offers many parallels with the art of America.

Unlike the USA, however—which inherited many traditions of the British medieval period, including the guild mentality—the penal settlement of Australia

inherited neither craft traditions nor the Grand Style of Sir Joshua Reynolds. The convicts and the 'redundant poor', who constituted the early Australian community had been dispossessed of their cultural traditions almost as completely as they had been dispossessed of their land and their citizenship by the legal code of eighteenth century England. No country in the history of the world has begun the history of its art under more unpromising circumstances than Australia.[94]

The essays for Grattan and *New Masses* strengthened Bernard's profile as an up-and-coming intellectual and consolidated his interest in global imperialism, metropolitan centres and peripheral cultures.

In through the back door

As a 'latin-less' working-class boy, Bernard believed he would always be excluded from the portals of academia and would never attend university, but having done military training he was eligible for the Commonwealth Education Reconstruction Training program. In 1946 he enrolled in evening classes at the University of Sydney, taking Classical Archaeology, History and English. The Education Department permitted him only five hours a week on condition that he make up the time. Importantly, the university deflected his energies away from politics and towards the world of scholarship.

Professor A. D. Trendall's class was a revelation—'I got for the first time a feeling for the close examination of an art object, a sense of the empirical. And I got an approach that was distinct from that of taste', which Bernard equated with elitism. Trendall's training in the analysis and decoding of ancient civilisations and the piecing together of fragments of a world partially lost through time and empires greatly appealed to Bernard, but he was also a brilliant teacher who would remain an enduring influence and mentor for Bernard throughout his life.[95]

Short in stature, witty and Cambridge-educated, the New Zealand-born Trendall once remarked 'I have 20,000 loves, all of them vases.'[96] His studies began in 1933, the year Marxism hit the University of Cambridge and Hitler came to power, and after a period of research in Greece he took the position of librarian at the British School of Rome. There among baroque churches, classical temples and abundant collections of antiquities he might easily have ignored the increasing threat of Nazism and Mussolini's fascism, but he returned to Cambridge. In 1939 he was interviewed successfully for the Chair of Greek at the University of Sydney and was later appointed honorary curator of the Nicholson Museum from 1946 to 1951 before taking up his appointment as the Master of the newly built University House at the Australian National University (ANU) in Canberra in 1953 (fig. 12).[97]

Education was not the only additional activity in Bernard's heavy workload; the need to be part of the contemporary art world was still keenly felt. He noted in his diary that 'Realism is the objective portrayal of the significant of the contemporary.' What concerned him was that 'Art must reflect the society in which we live' and faced with a new threat of postwar cultural imperialism, he saw 'representational art bowing to formalism and abstraction, realism to aestheticism and artists who portrayed social themes or aspects of contemporary life being shunted into corners'. For Bernard, the 'centre of gravity' was shifting fast and he predicted that 'the academisation of the abstract is almost within view'.[98] Heated debates among realist artists and those who embraced 'with sublime disregard . . . the apparent impersonality of abstract art' provided the motive for a group, led by James Cant, to break away from the Sydney branch of the CAS and form a new society interested in realism.

Formed in Sydney in March 1945, the Studio of Realist Artists (SORA) and its aims were announced in a press statement:

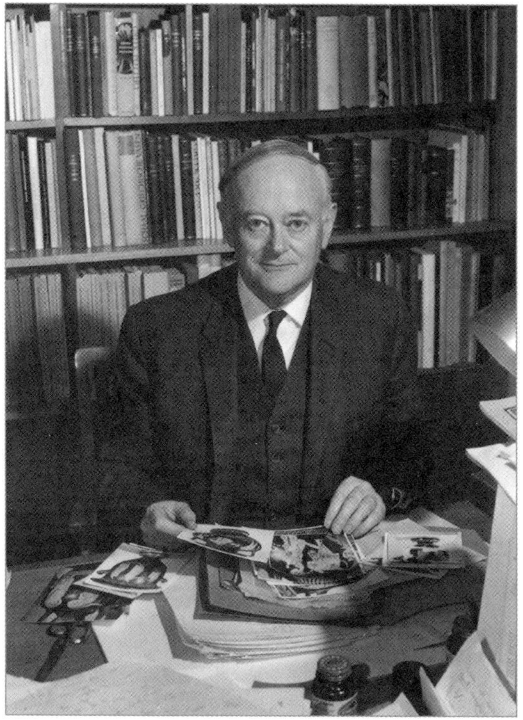

Fig. 12 Arthur Dale Trendall, c. 1950s

It is natural that such a group as ours should come into existence, in opposition to . . . art-for-arts sake that fills the walls of so many exhibitions—work that is an expression of decadence and puerility . . . People are showing in no uncertain fashion their dislike of the 'nostalgic' idea, the classical subject of the ivory tower complete with artists who 'look down on the world', by their support for such organisations as the Encouragement of Art Movement, C.E.M.A, and now the Studio of Realist Art. For art is no longer the prerogative of the few, but is rapidly becoming the concern of the many.[99]

SORA began in the basement of 171 Sussex Street but moved to the old *Bulletin* building at 236 George Street where it held regular art classes, fortnightly lectures, and offered members a monthly bulletin and the use of an art library. Its foundation members included James Cant, Dora Chapman, Roy Dalgarno, Adrian Galjaard, Herbert McClintock, John

Oldham, Roderick Shaw and Hal Missingham, with Bernard initially taking considerable interest in its development. He thought it one of the more vigorous contemporary art groups at the time. Lecturers included some of Sydney's major educationalists and artists such as Mary Alice Evatt, Desiderius Orban, Frank Medworth, Russell Drysdale, William Dobell, Sali Herman and Bernard. The casual, friendly atmosphere, small fees and good tutors attracted a large working-class following, including the young Charles Blackman. But SORA was not for everyone. Donald Friend claimed that one of its exhibitions was 'very bad indeed',[100] and Bernard's friend Lindsay Gordon felt that its idea of realism was 'sentimental and superficial', its patronising attitude to the worker 'a blokey kind' of condescension.[101] By the 1950s it was known as the 'wharfies art group', but during the late 1940s there were many members who were connected to the Communist Party of Australia as well as ex-servicemen, some of whom had been adversely affected by the war and were attracted to the group.[102]

By 1948, with increasingly virulent anti-communist campaigns, one writer commented:

The Studio of Realist Art, more familiarly known as SORA . . . brings the class war into the Art field . . . Star of the exhibition is the work of Noel Counihan, who earns a crust as a cartoonist for the *Guardian*, the Melbourne Commo paper . . . However, the intriguing thing about the exhibition is that it is being held at David Jones Gallery. One would not expect D. J's [David Jones] to be active in helping along the revolution, and surely, a firm like this could not be so short of chips it would let its Galleries to anybody, even pinkos

. . .

There is a complete lack of reality in dealing with the subject of Communists and Communism in this country, which of course, helps Comrades immensely. They are allowed to hide behind more aliases than a professional bigamist, and one of the thickest smoke screens they throw up is that of 'culture'.[103]

Bernard's association with SORA diminished as his work, study and a growing reputation in the professional art world increased, but his dedication to realism never subsided.

In 1946 Sir Keith Murdoch encouraged him to apply for the position of assistant director of the NGV and, though his qualifications were impressive, his application was unsuccessful because he had no active war service and was affiliated with the Communist Party. The position was offered to Robert Haines.[104] Others encouraged Bernard to study abroad, particularly Mary Alice Evatt of whom Lionel Lindsay quipped, 'Mrs Evatt is working for Bernard Smith and asked Dan [Daryl] if he didn't think it would be a good idea to send him [Bernard] to London for experience. To Hell would be better.'[105]

Though only part way through his undergraduate degree at the university, Bernard applied for a British Council scholarship to study at the Courtauld Institute of Art. His application stated:

I desire to study eighteenth and nineteenth century British art in relation to the beginnings of art in Australia. The object of my research would be to investigate the nature of the art produced in Australia between 1788 and 1833 with a view to ascertaining to what extent it was a continuance of, and a divergence from, the British art of the time. The main field of study would therefore embrace a comparative survey of Australian and British painting and architecture between 1788 and 1835.[106]

By June 1948 it was announced that he had been successful, and though the award was based largely on the merit of his book *Place Taste and Tradition*, strong references from A. D. Trendall, Daryl Lindsay, Joseph Burke and Sydney Ure Smith helped. In looking forward Bernard was not about to forget his past, and wrote to Clem Christesen, 'I hope not to break my association with *Meanjin*. There seems to be quite a colony of Australian artists in London now. An article on what some of them are doing, thinking and feeling, for the next summer issues might be worth while.'[107]

On 4 September the Smith family boarded the *Stratheden* at Sydney; Rose Anne, Bernard's half-brothers Bob and Dermott Kahl and a throng of friends were there to see them off. Robert Gollan, another Communist Party member who Bernard knew from the teachers' college, was also onboard; he had been awarded one of the ANU's first research scholarships. The ship sailed south around Wilsons Promontory to Port Melbourne where it docked for a day and the family disembarked; Bernard made straight for the NGV. The new Felton acquisitions were on display, including the fine Quattrocento head attributed to the Florentine School; the *Fountain of love*, attributed to the School of Pisanello (1395–1455); and the magnificent Nicolas Poussin painting *The crossing of the Red Sea* (1633–34). Next morning he visited Noel Counihan at his studio and bought one of the artist's print portfolios that was being sold to raise funds for Counihan's travel to England. Bernard also visited the newly appointed *Herald* Professor of Fine Arts at the University of Melbourne, Joseph Burke, who advised him about the Courtauld Institute and gave him letters of introduction.

When the *Stratheden* arrived at Fremantle Hal Missingham boarded with a wad of introductory letters, and a touching farewell note from Bernard's old friend Lindsay Gordon: 'Somewhere in the primitive deep of the mind and the ritual of fare-welling ships there is something of [the] birth image mixed up with the hint of Styx.' Where once the older man had been Bernard's mentor, now Lindsay felt the situation was reversed: 'If I have ever been a social conscience to you . . . you are fast becoming a literary and artistic conscience to me.'[108]

Life onboard was relaxing, but the 'incipient lethargy' irritated Bernard and he transferred his frustration into playing deck games. Aggressively competitive, his need to win at all costs caused great embarrassment to his children, yet the fear of failure stemming from his childhood was what drove him to succeed, and England would be a critical testing ground. Finally, after six weeks at sea, the ship arrived in England and the family went to Kate's adoptive father's cottage in the village of Ditchling on the South Sussex Downs. Bernard was impatient to start his research.

CHAPTER FOUR:
THE BLACK SWAN

To understand Australia one must look elsewhere.
Noel McLachlan[1]

Bernard and his family arrived in England in November 1948 for what was to be a one-year British Council research scholarship, but it was extended a further year when he was invited to collaborate on a major project on the art of James Cook's voyages. Those two years in England represented a major turning point in Bernard's life; it crystallised his scholarly development and gave him the 'distance' that he came to see as critical to his understanding of Australia. As he was launched into a school of international scholars, where his intellectual credentials were critically tested, he not only received encouragement and respect but also understood the necessity for a universalist approach to history. Reflecting on that period he would later write, 'I was looking for sources and the sources were northern European and still are.'[2]

Politically, Bernard gained an insight into the realities of the Cold War and engaged with both expatriate communists and those in British party branches, which, after his travel to Eastern Europe, culminated in his disillusionment with communism. In his personal life, being in England meant sharing his wife's origins and developing a new respect for her intellectual strengths, and recognising the challenges posed to his family by his academic commitments. On a trip to Ireland he was to find the house in which his mother had lived in the years before migrating to Australia just before World War I.

A steady stream of Australians, part of the postwar 'antipodean diaspora' as Barbara Blackman called it, were also leaving for Europe. The artists Mary Webb, Robert Klippel, James Gleeson, Grahame King and Albert Tucker, and the writers Patrick White and Alister Kershaw, were among the first wave in 1947, with Noel Counihan, Leonard French, James Wigley, Charles Bush, Roy Dalgarno, James Cant and his wife Dora Chapman leaving in 1949. Bernard knew many of them and he had admired them as artists, but during his time in England they became part of the wider context that helped him to develop a more acute sense of the differences between Europe and Australia, a distinction that was to become so conceptually important to him.

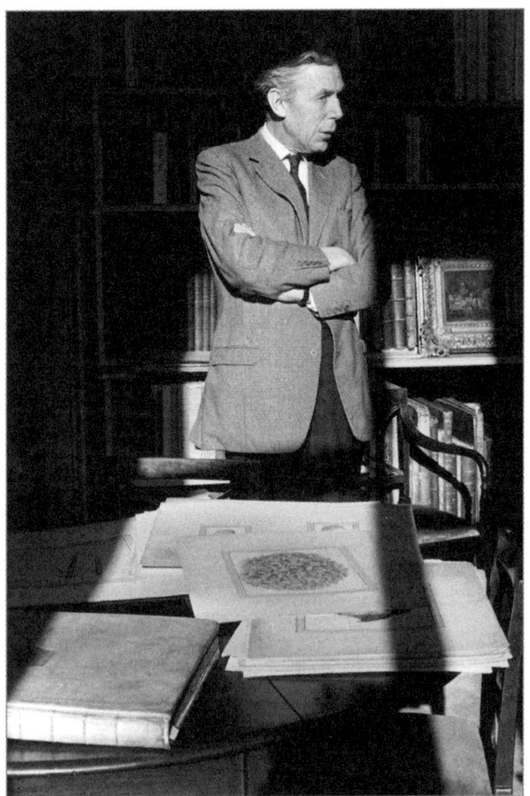

Fig. 13 Anthony Blunt, c. 1960s

In early November he arrived at the Courtauld Institute of Art, then situated at 20 Portland Square. Miranda Carter describes the Courtauld at the time as having a deceptive 'air of mild eccentricity. Behind the low-key chaotic façade, and the presence of nice young ladies . . . the Institute was intensely high-powered . . . [As] Peter Kidson discovered "Blunt, together with the Warburg Germans who were always on tap, operated at levels of scholarship . . . never before encountered."'[3] The registrar, confused by the arrival of a mature-age Australian without an undergraduate degree—Bernard being 32—alerted the institute's director, Anthony Blunt, who greeted him with impeccable, but somewhat aloof politeness (fig. 13). Keen to impress, Bernard gave him a copy of *Place, Taste and Tradition*, and after flicking through its pages, Blunt made the throwaway remark, 'I see you even have neo-Surrealist developments in Australia'.[4] Affronted by his comment, which suggested that Blunt saw Australia as culturally backward, Bernard defensively took the patrician Englishman to be lording it over a 'mere colonial, a modern Antipodean'. Bernard's reaction was not unfounded, as revealed in a letter Blunt wrote to the director of the Sir John Soane Museum, John Summerson, at Lincoln's Inn Fields;

> This is to introduce Mr. Bernard Smith from Australia, who has been working hitherto on the early phase of painting in and of Australia with remarkable results (contrary to the expectations aroused by the subject).[5]

What Bernard did not know was that Anthony Blunt's private life was in complete turmoil and his 'chilling elegance' was perhaps a wall hiding his personal and political alienation.

At the time Blunt was passing Foreign Office documents to Guy Burgess who was passing them on to Soviet intelligence officers, and it was not until late 1979 that the entire espionage affair was exposed, shocking colleagues, students and the world at large. If Blunt had access to secret intelligence files, of which there is a remote possibility, he may have learnt that Bernard was under surveillance, as the Australian Intelligence Bureau had informed MI5 of Bernard's communist affiliation. That might have made Blunt uncomfortable given his own undercover identity. At the end of the meeting he asked Bernard to return in a week's time while he decided where, and under whom, he should study.

A week later Bernard returned to see Blunt and was told he could not read a formal course at the Courtauld because of his incomplete honours degree. Instead he would move to the Warburg Institute and be supervised by Charles Mitchell. The Warburg, that 'republic of learning', had been closely affiliated with the Courtauld Institute since it relocated to London from Germany to escape the Nazis in 1933 and had played a crucial role in preserving European scholarship and encouraging intellectual reform in England.[6] Originally the private library of the revenant art historian Aby Warburg, the institute's massive collection of books, manuscripts and photographs offered scholars an extraordinary 'anthropology of images' and an iconology of symbols that opened avenues of inquiry into the classical tradition and cultural history. Warburg's emphasis on the collective value of the arts and the importance of images as records of human experience had created an unparalleled understanding of the 'absolute spirit' of humankind and, though unappreciated during his lifetime, renewed interest in him developed when Fritz Saxl, Ernst Cassirer and Erwin Panofsky became devoted followers of his interdisciplinary contextual methodology. It was largely through them that the Warburgian legacy of cultural inheritance as we know it today survived.[7] Under Saxl, Warburg's library was known as the Kulturhistorische Bibliothek Warburg and, after its arrival in London and the establishment of a successful arrangement with the Courtauld Institute, it became one of the most important scholarly research centres in Europe.

In many ways the Warburg Institute was a perfect place for Bernard, except for one problem: he did not have a foreign language. He felt this would greatly disadvantage him among such brilliant intellectuals, but things turned out far better than expected. This deficiency was perhaps seen as less important because of his subject matter but also, as the English art historian T. J. Clark suggests, the postwar atmosphere in Britain coincided with 'the long moment of "social democracy" [and] the time of Labour's insecure cultural hegemony.'[8]

In November Bernard met Rudolf Wittkower, the Warburg Institute's deputy director, at the Imperial Institute building in South Kensington, noting that he 'was a gentle and genial man . . . [who] greeted my project with enthusiasm . . . he the polymath and me the monoglot'.[9] Saxl, who had done so much to reinvigorate the tired cultural landscape of Britain and, according to John Pope Hennessy, had been largely responsible for 'transform[ing] Anthony Blunt from a *Jejeune* Marxist journalist into one of the most accomplished art historians of his day' had died in March.[10] But with scholars like Wittkower, L. D. Ettlinger, Ernst Gombrich, Gertrud Bing, Charles Mitchell, Otto Pächt, Joseph Trapp, Margaret Whinney and Frances Yates, the Warburg was as rigorous as ever.

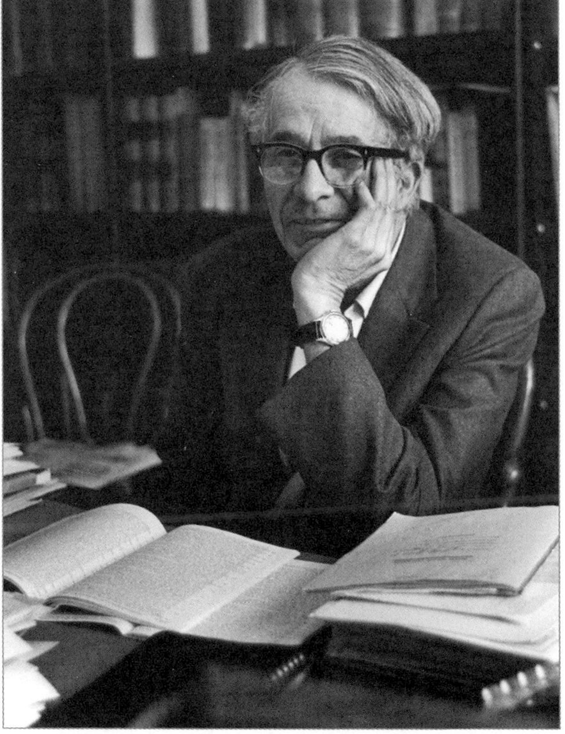

Fig. 14 Charles Mitchell, 1977

Charles Mitchell was an astute and imaginative Oxford-trained historian and one of the institute's core lecturers (fig. 14). When writing his thesis on Grünewald in 1934 he took private tutorials with Saxl who guided him on a micro-journey through the topography of Rembrandt's prints and drawings. The experience was profound and after Mitchell's discharge from the navy, having served in naval intelligence during World War II and acquiring a first-hand understanding of the heroism and dangers associated with sea voyages, he joined the Warburg Institute, where he lectured on Renaissance humanism and the history of the classical tradition. He had also worked at the National Maritime Museum at Greenwich from 1935 to 1939 and acquired a profound knowledge of eighteenth- and nineteenth-century British maritime and landscape paintings. The presence of British historians at the Warburg Institute was an important means of helping émigré scholars assimilate into the British academic system, as well as popularising continental art history. Blunt had been employed as a general editor for Warburg publications in 1937, partly for that reason.[11]

From the outset Bernard and Charles Mitchell made good progress, the latter directing his new student to material that opened up the imperial landscape and the penetration of the south seas by the British navy, their minds feeding off one another as they peeled back the layers of empire, colonialism and the perceptions of the South Pacific. Both men were of a similar disposition in that they liked 'to shape and form and not be formed' and, as Peter Craven rightly suggests, Mitchell was a Socratic figure for Bernard, teaching him how to ask questions that would provide answers.[12] Importantly, he gave Bernard confidence within an elite intellectual world where many scholars were caught up in their own gravitas.

Australia also interested Mitchell. During the 1930s he had been supportive of a number of young art historians at the Courtauld and Warburg institutes whose careers had taken them to Melbourne. In 1938, before migrating to Australia, Mitchell had procured a contract for Ursula Hoff's first book *Charles I: Patron of Artists*, published by William Collins in London in 1942. In 1947 Mitchell persuaded Joseph Burke, newly appointed to the *Herald* Chair of Fine Arts at the University of Melbourne, to publish his thesis on William Hogarth, writing to Burke, 'I have your MS of Hogarth's Analysis (why don't you publish it pretty well as it is and give us all a useful present?).'[13] He also became a valued contact for Hoff, Burke and, in particular, Bernard during the 1960s, when they sent several of their more outstanding Fine Arts students, such as Virginia Spate, Sister Margaret Manion and Jaynie Anderson, to be supervised by him at Bryn Mawr College in Pennsylvania. In 1977 Bernard repaid his debt to his old supervisor by inviting him to give the fourth Power Lecture at the University of Sydney.

Bernard had not waited for Blunt to place him academically before embarking on his research. He was not one to waste time and during that first week decided he would 'begin at the beginning' and look at the earliest perceptions of the Southern Hemisphere, the upside-down long view of historical reconstruction and how the Antipodes had first been conceived. It was a necessary precept to understanding how the European mind and artists in the eighteenth and nineteenth centuries interpreted the landscape and the inhabitants of the South Pacific. At the British Museum, Bernard read material on antiquity, medieval and Enlightenment concepts of the cosmos and the New World. Some of those sources included the Greek ethnographer Megasthenes (c. 350–290 BCE), who, as Bernard noted, had identified the Antipodes with a type of weird people whose feet pointed backwards. This peculiar perception developed into a fundamentally important concept of Antipodal inversion for Bernard, who later wrote:

> the epistemology of being Antipodean is relational. It is a relationship that is global. Derived from the Greek word antipous, meaning 'having the feet opposite', it requires the existence of two terms. As agents, places, persons or things, diametrically opposed to each other on the earth's surface . . . such positions are infinite. Any place on the globe can be antipodal to the other.[14]

He also read Isidore of Seville's *Etymologiae* (c. 560–636) and Magnetius Hrabanjus Maurus's *De Universe VII (De portentis)* (c. 842–847), listing 14 species of monsters; publications on Linnaeus; R. W. Frantz's *The English Traveller and the Movement of Ideas 1660–1732* (1934) and Francis Bacon's essay *Of Travel* (1625). As David Bindman's study of race and nationalism notes:

> Linnaeus offered a classification of humanity, based upon the

> Four Continents or Four Quarters of the Earth and the Four Temperaments associated with each . . . add[ing] a number of other categories, including the Wild Man and various forms of monster. The fourfold division was compatible with the idea of a lost primeval unity, the Judaeo-Christian Garden of Eden.[15]

This taxonomy and diversification of *geographica* led men of science, theology and exploration during the Enlightenment to expect in the New World 'human variety as on a scale of savagery to civilization, contingent on climate and environment'.[16] Francis Bacon's *New Atlantis*, published in 1627 when he was in semi-exile, was an imaginative construction of a new utopia in 'a remote part of the Pacific Ocean' and had influenced thinkers such as the French encyclopedists, Immanuel Kant and Karl Marx as a model for renovating scientific, moral and social laws. Bacon's fictional 'Salomon's House' became an institutional model for the Royal Society founded in 1660.[17] But Bernard found himself 'getting deeper and deeper into dark and unknown territory', writing to Lindsay Gordon 'I am becoming convinced that the conceptions of . . . Utopia, and "working man's paradise" in the Southern Land is one of the central historical ideas running through Australian literature, art and politics. It is perhaps the myth-making of the voyager and the emigrant . . . another aspect of *Illusion and Reality*.'[18] This 'myth-making' notion would run strongly through some of Bernard's more provocative concepts, especially the 1959 *Antipodean Manifesto*.

Not one to allow his human and social principles to be submerged by his research, and believing that intellectually those principles were fundamental to his development as a historian, Bernard was keen to see how social and political conditions in England differed from those at home and, in particular, how communism in the 'Mother Country' worked.

Politics and primitivism

It was not long before Bernard and Bob Gollan visited the British Communist Party's headquarters in Covent Garden where they inquired about party branch meetings. Unaware that Britain's secret intelligence body MI5 was monitoring their movements, it would be some time before Bernard realised the need to adopt a more shadowy political profile. He also wanted to meet Jack Lindsay, who had left Australia in 1926 to pursue a literary career in England. Lindsay had been closely associated with the British Communist Party, though his 'questioning [of] the Zhdanov line on Socialist Realism and his advocacy of a "dialogue with Sartre" had seen him almost expelled'.[19] What typified Lindsay's importance for Bernard was the writer's humanism and the notion of organic dislocation, political rupture and crisis; it is best expressed in Lindsay's words:

the creation and growth of Marxism must always involve a crisis of some sort. For each advance as well as each set back cannot but stir up new problems and set the past developments in a new focus, so the urgent issues of re-unification and redirection keep emerging.[20]

In late November Bernard was invited to Lindsay's home in St John's Wood where he met the Australian expatriate Vere Gordon Childe, Professor of Prehistoric European Archaeology and director of the Institute of Archaeology at the University of London. Though never a member of the Communist Party, Childe was a highly respected socialist with a 'passionate concern for a vital, integrated and just society', which appealed strongly to communists and left-wing organisations.[21] Marx and Engels had been major influences in his intellectual development and one of Childe's most popular books, *What Happened in History* (1942), calibrated human progress through a global, economic and Marxist framework. According to Childe, 'Marxism means effectively an approach to and a methodological device for the interpretation of historical and archaeological material'; a more contemporary view of his work sees it as 'a radical reconstruction of society in light of contemporary developments in Marxist thought'.[22] This was similar to Bernard's use of Marxism as a medium for crossing political and cultural boundaries. Childe's belief that the roots of European civilisation lay in the Near East, those of Mesopotamia and Egypt, rather than the Mediterranean, synchronised with what George Berger had taught Bernard in the early 1940s.[23] Moreover, Childe maintained that the only way of viewing human progress was by 'standing back' and using distance as a contextualising device, corroborating Hegel's notion of historical distance—the owl of Minerva looks back on the day as she flies off at the dusk of humanity.

Thrilled to have met Childe, Bernard also found him reserved—'a small man hidden behind bushy eyebrows and large spectacles' whose little 'withered hand' looked as if 'it had been embalmed for a thousand years'.[24] They talked of the importance of primitivism and the connection between modern and primitive art. That interested Bernard because of his research on European perceptions of the Pacific and the material concerning primitive and peripheral cultures. Childe's belief in artists reverting to older styles so as to create anew was something Bernard had tackled in a lecture he had given at the Teachers Federation Art Society in 1942 when he had discussed how the arts of primitive people became a fixation with certain artists. He cited Gauguin as a prime example of one who had 'rejected European Impressionism for a style . . . gathered promiscuously from Persian, Indian and Tahitian sources' and who was prepared to walk away from the cultural centre of Paris and live on civilisation's fringe. Furthermore, the artist's exotic modernism and aesthetic universalism was a product of cultural imperialism, his 'Pacific art [a] direct product of French colonial expansion'.[25] Art, Bernard believed, was usually politically driven, its representational value directly related to the laws of the State, taste and tradition, whether European or otherwise.

Within a month of having met Lindsay and Childe, Bernard saw the exhibition *40,000 Years of Modern Art: A Comparison of Primitive and Modern*, presented by the newly established Institute of Contemporary Art (ICA) at the Academy Hall in Oxford Street. Curated by Herbert Read and Roland Penrose, it brought together many of Europe's most famous avant-garde artists with rare ethnographic works from Europe, Africa, Australia and Oceania. Major institutions and private collectors had lent valuable artefacts, sculptures and paintings, including the British Museum, the Victoria and Albert Museum, the Tate Gallery, the Horniman Museum, the Ashmolean and Pitt Rivers museums in Oxford, the Musée de l'Homme in Paris, the Frobenius Institute in Frankfurt, and the Museum of Modern Art (MoMA) in New York. Of the modern works, Picasso's *Les demoiselles d'Avignon* (1906–07), on loan from MoMA, had never been seen in London and his *Weeping woman* (1937) was also on display. Other artists included Brancusi, Miró, Modigliani, Klee, Ernst, Gaudier-Brzeska, Henry Moore and Barbara Hepworth, while the oldest works in the exhibition were copies of prehistoric cave paintings from the Lascaux cave, a 'Venus' figurine carved in mammoth ivory from the Aurignacian area and copies of Indigenous Australian cave art from north-western Australia. Read wrote that the exhibition confirmed 'modern art is, without exaggeration, 40,000 years old' and 'we have merely discovered the timelessness of artistic magic and vision.'[26]

The pairing of the modern and the ancient, Bernard felt, could not be so simply reconciled. Read believed that by situating contemporary modern with primitive art the 'sources of inspiration in the most important trends in paintings and sculpture since the beginnings of this century' and the 'recurring phenomena' that is labelled 'modern' is powerfully illustrated.[27] What concerned Bernard about the trend in rehabilitating primitivism was not so much how 'ethnographic curiosities', as they were largely regarded, had been recast to the status of works of art, but that their historical and political associations had been overlooked. Eighteenth-century imperialism and the capitalist's purse had delivered antiquities, prehistoric objects, tribal and exotic specimens to Europe's wealthy collectors and colonial explorers, grand tourists, 'experimental gentlemen', or men of science and natural history who had avidly collected such objects, and they could not be ignored. The transactions and consequences of cultural exchange were complex and appropriation or assimilation of styles demanded intensive study. Once Indigenous people and their cultures were colonised, exterminated, or reduced by a dominating culture their art became an exotic collectable, or as Bernard pointed out, 'Primitivism sets in as a cult "The noble savage" living in his paradise is installed above civilised man.'[28] This did not contradict Childe's belief that cultures, rather than individuals, were determinants of change, but Bernard was adamant the policymakers and the aristocracy were responsible in the first instance and that every new conquest, every new colony meant a rebirth of art. Art might be timeless, but cultural convergence situated the work within a greater frame of appropriation and transference.

As an archaic return, primitivism often emerged in the wake of revolutions or new conceptual developments. In the late nineteenth century the Pre-Raphaelites and William Morris's utopianism entered the mainstream of contemporary art as a rejection of western society's bourgeois excesses and refined tastes. In the early twentieth century, the avant-garde shifts of Picasso, Derain and Vlaminck had introduced African masks and totemic forms into their paintings as an attempt to recover a purity of expression. In so doing, they formalised their radicalism. Psychoanalysts like Freud and Jung investigated taboos and primitive myths as a way of epistemologically understanding contemporary identity, personality disorders and sexual psychoses, while surrealism tapped the deep ancestral recesses and irrational margins of the mind where it hoped to harness 'the contentious issue of the relation between art and politics'.[29] During the 1930s the Nazis used primitivism as a political tool for censoring avant-garde art, its infamous 1937 *Entartete Kunst* exhibition, otherwise known as 'the Degenerate Art Exhibition', blatantly compared modernism with the primitive and the mentally deranged. On the opposite side, Hitler was being represented as an ape-like barbarian. The pairing of politics with primitivism had transformed avant-garde art into a persecuted subset of subhuman activity, yet as a censored object it became 'a desired, exotic collectable' to many western art collectors.

In January 1949 Bernard and Bob Gollan went to hear Childe lecture at the Horniman Museum on the transformation and progress of ancient societies through the communal needs and crafts of humankind. Afterwards Childe took them on a tour of the museum's collection—Bernard remembered it as a maze of spears, shields and tribal masks—but he felt under no obligation to remain with the art of the past and, with a letter of introduction from Joseph Burke, was driven in a British Council car to the village of Much Hadham in Hertfordshire to meet the sculptor Henry Moore.

Bernard had already seen Moore's work in March 1948 at the National Art Gallery in Sydney, where a small exhibition, one of the first postwar opportunities for Australians to see the work of an international artist, was enthusiastically received. Bernard had then been keen to establish lines of cultural difference and distance, writing in a review for the University of Sydney Union's journal *Hermes* that, 'In Australia we usually realise what is happening in the world of art later than everyone else . . . [and] that local criticism is often a system of echoes repeating what has already been said abroad, but more fitfully if not more faintly.'[30] Jousting from the fringe, he had attacked the promotional activities of curators and international critics as a 'softening-up' process, a political sweetener in the culture game; 'Words have grown about the works of Henry Moore, in a few years, like the tropical rain-forest which once grew about the Mexican sculptures he admires . . . But we must hack our way through all of it back to the stone, wood and lead of his sculptures before we can look at it with our own eyes.'[31]

Fixated with Australian identity, Bernard had already developed a Darwinian rhetoric and now that he was living in England it began taking on a heroic realism and an evolutionary separateness. Arriving at Moore's seventeenth-century studio, he found the artist repairing works that had been damaged during the exhibition's transportation from New York to Australia and New Zealand. As the leading exponent of the organic 'truth to material' style, their conversation turned to abstraction, with Moore telling Bernard how 'one carving grew out of another, so that they became a kind of continuous growth'.[32] Bernard, however, wondered whether Moore's sculpture was not more of an archaic reversion, rather than evolutionary aesthetics.

In March he met Herbert Read, the influential educationalist, art critic and the man whose anarchic socialism had sustained him during the past decade. Read and the anthropologist William Fagg were holding a discussion on the relation between primitive and modern art at the ICA and Bernard, anticipating an impressive figure, was 'disappointed at seeing Read in the flesh'.[33] Perhaps he detected something of what Wyndham Lewis had publically proclaimed, namely that 'Mr Read has the unenviable knack of providing, at a week's notice, almost any movement, or sub-movement, in the visuals arts.'[34] Through the coming years Bernard came to see the 'God of Modernism' very much as an 'alienating fadist'.[35]

Though 'ineluctably elitist', the ICA had been established as part of a vigorous postwar program aimed at reinstating the arts in people's lives and providing a centre for the isolated artist. Attracted by an excellent program of film evenings, discussions and forthcoming exhibitions, including *Traditional Art in the British Colonies* at the Anthropological Institute, Bernard joined as a member. At Read and Fagg's lecture he met the Australian artist Mary Webb whom he had known in Sydney. Webb was living at The Abbey Arts Centre, known as 'The Abbey', at New Barnet just north of London and invited Bernard to visit. A letter from James Gleeson to Bernard describes Webb at this time:

> Mary Webb had studied with Datillo [*sic*] Rubbo. I chanced to meet her again in London when I was looking for a place to paint. She suggested the Abbey where she had found a studio. Robert Klippel was already ensconced there—and I met him for the first time. Mary practiced [*sic*], at that time, a style that I can only describe as aggressive expressionistic—with heavy impasto and rough short-hand drawing. [36]

Bernard noted in his journal that he 'Went to Cockfosters and met Mary Webb, Graham [*sic*] King, Douglas [Green] also Peter Graham there. John [James] Wigley arriving soon. A queer large old early nineteenth century mansion with a church attached, a sort of Abbey for those who follow the Christian doctrine of the Patriarch of Antioch.'[37] While at The Abbey Bernard caught a glimpse of the extraordinary collection of antiquities owned by William Ohly, the art dealer and director of the Berkeley Galleries in Davies Street, London, and owner of the property.[38] He had just missed Gleeson and Klippel, and Webb would soon move to Paris where she found some success and was awarded a silver medal in a City of Paris art exhibition, but as with many women during the postwar period, she found making a living hard. According to Gleeson, Klippel claimed she died of starvation.[39]

Politics wove neatly into Bernard's weekly agenda during the first months of 1949, but a warning shot came from Sali Herman in Sydney. He had heard that Bernard's application for a Carnegie Foundation scholarship to visit the USA had been favourably received and he strongly advised him not to take part in politics, at least not for some time. But Bernard ignored Herman's advice and, with MI5 following him, his political activity undoubtedly cost him the award. In March Bernard, Gollan and Counihan, who had now arrived in London, attended a party meeting of artists at the Hampstead branch where they listened to Alick West, the author of *Crisis and Criticism*, discussing Christopher Caudwell's *Illusion and Reality* (both 1937). In his diary Bernard noted, 'Caudwell is being discussed continuously now, among party people here. Discussion very good, they talk better than they paint', but added 'the party artists of Sydney are much more mature than anything I saw around these walls'. Caudwell had been a major influence on Bernard in the late 1930s, and he rose to ask West a question, but when he was 'snapped down' Bernard interpreted this as another example of British patronising attitudes towards colonials. It was something that greatly disturbed him, but it also interested him.

By using 'culture' as a tool of analysis and a barometer of society's health, Bernard observed that Britain had been in decline for some time. After World War II it had forfeited its postwar autonomy in exchange for economic recovery under the Marshall Plan, and its economy was precarious. The Albion lion was a paradox: a society of patriots, elite class consciousness and small shopkeeper solidarity yet, in spite of those contradictions, it held together. The English historian Perry Anderson has described British cultural tradition as characterised by an 'absent centre' that 'may be defined as the European country which—uniquely—never produced either classical sociology or national Marxism . . . English society was never challenged as a whole from within.'[40]

After they heard West speak on Caudwell, Bernard and Counihan left the Hampstead branch to attend another branch party meeting, and the following morning they heard a paper given by Francis Klingender on 'Art and Capitalism'. Though he thought Klingender was 'a turgid and unconvincing speaker' Bernard was sympathetic to his *Marxism and Modern Art: An Approach to Social Realism* (1943), published the same year that Bernard began writing *Place, Taste and Tradition*. Klingender propounded a continuous tradition of realism that had begun with prehistoric art through to 'the age of non-objectivism', that is, abstraction. Other speakers gave excellent papers and despite being affronted by Alick West, Bernard found it 'a most stimulating and absorbing weekend'.[41]

Cold War tensions

In between burying himself in archives and participating in communist activities, Bernard met Counihan regularly. The artist's company was a welcome respite from his research: 'the dullness of some of the material I am treating worries me . . . [Am] read[ing] anonymous 18th C poetry on Tahite, Cook and Banks . . . getting tired of the subject matter.'[42] Letters from friends and comrades at home kept him up-to-date with political and cultural matters, with Rod Shaw writing that Drysdale's exhibition at Macquarie Gallery was disappointing and 'his formulae' looked tired, while at David Jones Gallery Sidney Nolan's show was a sell-out: 'Everyone agrees that "Nolan is novel"'.[43] Herman wrote that his portrait of Bernard was finished and Dobell's winning Archibald painting of Margaret Olley was 'well deserved' (fig. 15):

> You should have seen Dargie's painting hanging next to it. It was simply cruel. That was a good move of Hal . . . the Trustees bought Bill's painting for 600 gns [guineas]–that stopped immediately all stupid talk.

He added, 'Did you get news yet from America?'[44]

Two days later a letter arrived from the Carnegie Corporation of New York informing Bernard that his application for research in the USA was unsuccessful. With Cold War tensions rising anyone connected to the Communist Party would have automatically been disqualified. It would be another 12 years before Bernard gained entry to the USA and even then his communist past was to prove an obstacle. In Australia anti-communist sentiment was also reaching new heights, as Clem Christesen revealed, 'with the current witch-hunt rising to full cry, I might find myself in the jug! You know, no doubt, of the Royal Commission into Communistic activities. I've already struck trouble with the *Meanjin* printer, and there have also been other threats. All very unpleasant.'[45]

Politically, however, it was an exciting time to be in London. Bernard often accompanied Daphne Gollan and Harvey Clarkson to Kensington branch meetings and these contacts with hardline communists would have given Bernard vital information on the political climate and major developments in other western countries. Two days before the World Congress of Advocates for Peace Conference in Paris on 20 April, 30 people, including the communist journalist Rupert Lockwood, arrived at Gollan's flat to farewell Daphne and Noel Counihan. Counihan had been asked to join the Australian delegation in Paris, representing the Victorian Maritime Transport, Building Trades, Coal and Meat Workers unions and SORA. The American actor, singer and social activist Paul Robeson had also arrived in London and was providing the peace movement with a populist, dramatic edge. His rallying speeches and magnificent singing mounted pressure on the two great powers to resolve their major differences. Unknown at the time, the USA was preparing an atomic strike against the Soviet Union and the threat of a third world war was frighteningly real. Bernard noted in his diary, 'The struggle for peace is taking a sharp turn . . .'

New families

On their arrival in England the Smiths had made straight for Ashtree, Cuthbert Adeney's cottage in Ditchling. It was, as Bernard told Lindsay Gordon, 'an indescribably lovely village [that] the war has passed over' and Kate, or 'Ruth' as she was known in England, settled in with the children. At first Bernard thought he would be able to write well there, but he soon realised this was going to be unlikely. The peculiar house had few rooms and had been designed amateurishly by Cuthbert; the addition of four more people made life cramped and chaotic, and with postwar rationing milk and eggs were scarce and amenities in short supply. Moreover, Cuthbert Adeney was used to directing his life like a one-way street, his street.

Bernard described Cuthbert as a 'tall, slightly stooping figure, proud brow, high cheek bones . . . a clipped military moustache above mobile sensuous lips and eyes that wandered into an abyss when he looked at you'.[46] He was an intelligent man 'born of his class and culture', but he applied a tormented analysis to himself, others and the world generally. That made for strained company. His 'strange' personality could be partly attributable to the burden of guilt he carried from his first and second wives' deaths—Hilda had died from ovarian cancer at the age of 51 and his second wife, Rosita, a woman some 30 years his junior, died tragically when septicaemia set in following an abortion. It left him to raise three young daughters and had prompted him to pressure Kate to return from Australia to help him. Fortunately, she had already committed herself to Bernard and was able to escape Cuthbert's sexually complex and vengeful web. By the time Bernard met him in 1948 the retired physician was more subdued and kept much to himself, writing daily in his diary. It was not until after Cuthbert's death that Bernard obtained access to his diaries in the Royal College of Surgeons archive at Lincoln Fields Inn, enabling him to put together the puzzling pieces of Cuthbert Adeney's life.

Cuthbert's coldness may have been unpleasant for Bernard, but his hostility towards Kate was much more difficult to handle. He had always found Kate attractive and Bernard's presence exacerbated his desires for his adopted daughter. The atmosphere at Ashtree was often so disagreeable that Kate would retreat to her spiritual home on the common and Bernard to the fringes of the garden, usually with a book in hand. The children, however, were quite oblivious to those adult tensions. There had been some forewarning that things might be tense when, before their departure from Australia Kate had received a letter from Douglas Pepler, the father of her best friend, Susan, in which he had referred to Bernard's 'corrupting' political influence. Taking the matter into his own hands, Bernard replied to Pepler that neither he nor Kate would be intimidated:

I find it increasingly difficult to judge the personal worth of people by their political or religious convictions. I know several, avowed, or shall I say, devoted Communists who are, in my view, extraordinarily fine people. Fine you will possibly say, but misguided . . . I would not agree. Their communism is probably an aspect of their fineness. I also know several avowed or shall I say devoted Catholics, whom I consider fine people indeed. My mother is one . . . I have the highest opinion, indeed, of your Eric Gill. The Catholicism of such people is probably an aspect of their fineness.

. . . As to Ruth's politics, Dr Adeney may be right. He has had a
longer opportunity than I have . . . to know her, but I hardly agree
with him .[47]

Bernard may have saved Kate from Cuthbert, but she adored being home
among the people she loved, especially her sister Elizabeth and her closest
friend, Susan. Given how much Bernard annoyed Cuthbert and that he
had to commute daily to London, it was decided he would take weekly
lodgings in London.

Once the weather improved Kate wanted to show Bernard her favourite places in Sussex and with haversacks on their backs they set off
on a three-day trek around the countryside, walking to Devil's Dyke,
Chichester, Stonehenge, Wells and Glastonbury.[48] It was Kate's way of
introducing Bernard to her past as much as a lesson in acclimatising him
to the English landscape and its people. In villages they studied ecclesias-
tical and street architecture, and while she lingered inside parish churches
Bernard would settle on a tombstone to write. He teased her about need-
ing to reveal her Englishness to him, and argued about the two sides of
England, the pretty woods and fine traditional buildings, but also the
urban workers and city dwellers. At Warminster they made their way up a
three-mile (4.8-km) drive, passing a beautiful lake and gardens designed
by Capability Brown to the large country house Longleat, recently opened
to the public after being used as safe storage for important artworks
during the war. Restored to its original state, Bernard saw the opulence
of the wealthy ruling class and as he moved through grand rooms and
salons with swathes of Elizabethan portraits, masterpieces attributed to
Raphael, Titian and Holbein, and libraries rich in rare books, he was
overwhelmed by that elite world, one in which he could only enter as a
tourist or researcher.

When the Smiths visited Kate's Aunt Connie at the Welsh village
of Ystalyfera on the River Tawe, Bernard saw another side of class and
village life, one he described as having 'teeth'. The aunt's comfortable old
house and her cosy, merry life reminded him of a Rowlandson painting,
but once outside, the landscape was like an early L. S. Lowry industrial painting. Scarred from tin, iron and coal mining, the enormous

anthracite-filled hills and the great chimneys that had once billowed black, filthy smoke commemorated the industrialised world. While the village was rebuilding itself, Bernard thought of Alexis Carrel's manifesto on the poor, wretched workers reduced to diseased cogs in capitalism's wheel, and he was so moved by Ystalyfera that he wrote a poem; the lines, 'Istalyfera anthracitic and soggy/Caught like the Twyrch between the tors/Your oyster houses clinging to their streets/In the shallows of the choppy hills/. . . For they commemorate a tyranny/Their black barrows/ My Stone Age'.[49] It reveals Bernard's profound empathy with the misery and hardship of labourers.

London in 1949 was, as Doris Lessing described it, 'at its dingiest', its 'noisy sharp-faced children . . . a shock to a colonial, used to broad-faced, filled-in, sunburnt faces. It is a face not so much pale as drained, peaked rather than thin'.[50] Whether Bernard noticed the city's gaunt postwar visage is unclear, but he certainly noticed its buildings and signage, its history and architecture, which often seemed more important to him than its inhabitants. On one family outing he and Kate took Betsy, John and Rowena, Kate's little half-sister, on a boat down the Thames from Westminster to the Tower Bridge. They walked to Trafalgar Square to feed the pigeons and to the National Gallery, where a Botticelli caught the young ballet-dancing Betsy's eye. Strolling down Whitehall to the Horse Guards and up to Buckingham Palace before catching the train back to Ditchling, parenthood may have been life tenure for Bernard, but it remained very much a part-time job (fig. 16).

Bernard enjoyed wandering the streets of London, in particular its lanes; he liked reading a locality or the social spaces and absorbing the petit-points of a city's character, though he was not as analytic as the German philosopher Walter Benjamin. Newspaper vendors amused him, with one headline announcing the birth of Prince Charles—it was difficult to avoid the accompanying fanfare of crowds thronging towards the fountain at Trafalgar Square where the water had been dyed blue for the occasion. One evening on a break from his studies at the British Museum, he strolled towards the Royal Academy and Piccadilly Circus, where he noticed a group of prostitutes; 'one very sultry brunette's asking price was a mere £2', but he resisted her charms. The city, however, offered

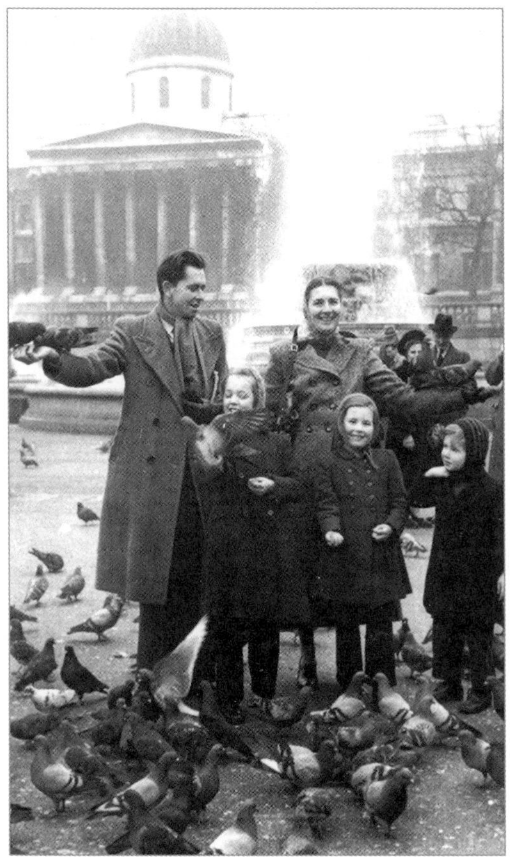

Fig. 16 Bernard and Kate Smith with their children John and Betsy and Kate's half-sister, Rowena Adeney (front left), London, 1949

other pleasures: eating at cafés and pubs, attending ballet and theatre performances—Bernard caught the Australian actor Robert Helpmann in *Hamlet* at The Old Vic and Sir Laurence Olivier and Vivien Leigh in *School for Scandal*. In short, life was very good.

Exhibitions also broke the intensity of his research. At the Leicester Galleries in March he saw Ivon Hitchens' recent works, and at Roland, Browse and Delbanco, *Aspects of English Romanticism*. In May he saw Picasso at the Hanover Gallery; Winifred Nicholson, Robert McBryde and Robert Colquhoun at the Lefevre Gallery; and Giorgio de Chirico at R.B.A. Galleries. When he arrived at the Victoria and Albert Museum to see *Art for All*, a London Transport poster exhibition, he noticed a small man trip and fall; it was Prime Minister Clement Attlee, who was opening the exhibition.

South of north

I had read in books that art is not easy
But no one warned that the mind repeats
In ignorance the vision of others. I am still
The black swan of trespass on alien waters
Ern Malley[51]

Bernard soon established a routine of moving between the Warburg Institute, the Natural History Museum, the Courtauld Institute, the British Museum and the National Maritime Museum at Greenwich, institutions where most of the visual and written records of the voyages of exploration in the Pacific regions were kept. Occasionally he stopped at the National Portrait Gallery or the National Gallery in Trafalgar Square to wander 'in a pleasant, desultory sort of way' among the masterpieces. He had once complained of his cultural poverty, writing 'I have not bowed among the Titians. I have not seen the greatest paintings of the world. That has been my misfortune', but now, moved by Europe's rich history, which had sustained its greatest artists, he felt that he was 'the subject' and Europe's traditions and 'spirits of the past' were sustaining him.[52] He might have thought of Karl Marx's Brumaire—'The tradition of all the dead generations weigh like a nightmare on the brain of the living'—but Europe's encounter with the New World was neither entirely a historic nightmare nor a heroic, idealised event; it was a convergence of cultures, even though imperial conquest and possession were the prize. Acutely aware that his reading of the past had to remain as disinterested as possible, he later wrote 'I am thinking of distance, or more precisely distancing as an intellectual tool both for aesthetic evaluation and for the writing of history.'[53]

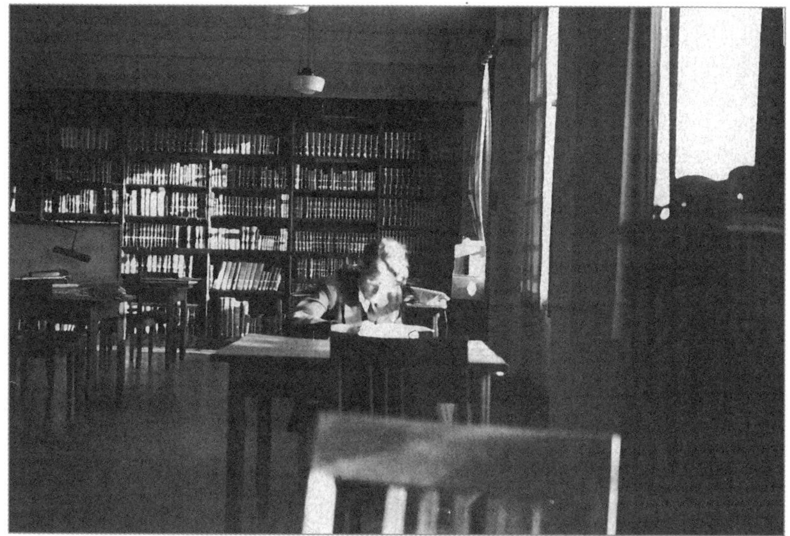

Fig. 17 Warburg Institute Library, London, c. 1940s

Under Charles Mitchell's supervision—'a fine fellow with none of the English reserve or high-browism that can be so tiring'—and occasional direction from Rudolf Wittkower, Bernard read widely in the Warburg Institute's library and attended lectures at the Courtauld Institute (fig. 17).[54] He heard Ernst Gombrich's brilliant paper titled 'The Renaissance Approach to Classical Sculpture', in which Gombrich emancipated the image and liberated Bernard's narrow iconographical vision with his now-famous phrase 'all art is conceptual'. Sir Kenneth Clark's paper on Piero Della Francesca was excellent and, as disagreeable as he found Anthony Blunt, Bernard could not dismiss his brilliance as a lecturer.[55] Frequently, Bernard could be found in the cold and empty Northern Library or the print room of the British Museum, or the Natural History Museum's archive library at South Kensington, going through pictorial and written records. In his diary he noted:

Had a satisfactory day reading Capt. Fitzroy's Account of the Voyage of the *Beagle*. Also Charles Darwin's 'Comments on Australia' in 1836 . . . Has a remarkable description of Australian vegetation . . . the best description of the Blue Mountains scenery I have read anywhere.

Through the art and descriptions of those early explorers, artists, naturalists and seamen who had accompanied Cook on his three voyages, or those of the First Fleet, Bernard found it was possible to gain a more accurate understanding of the procession of discovery, the encounters between nativism and imperialism, 'the colonised and the colonisers'. Many of the men were trained artists but a few were not, as he discovered in the Banks Collection. With 3000 drawings made 'of things never seen before by Europeans', those artists were critical witnesses in recording the moment of contact between the 'soft' and 'hard' primitivism of the 'Other'.

The sketch *First Contact* (1769) (fig. 18), was originally thought to be by Sir Joseph Banks, but has more recently been identified as by a young Ra'iatean called Tupaia who sailed on Cook's first voyage in 1768. It is an antipodal vision depicting the face of British imperialism as it engages with the exotic—a naval officer bartering a crayfish with a Maori. Cook, Bernard wrote, 'was the first of a new breed of explorers who made full use of visual and verbal records for conveying their observations.'[56] The focus on art as a recording tool of the Enlightenment's binary manifestations of science and nature, the empirical and the romantic, repositioned the role of the artist as a primary descriptor. The philosopher Emmanuel Levinas would later write, 'The Judgement of history is set forth in the visible. Historical events are the visible par excellence; their truth is produced in evidence.'[57]

Under Britain's spreading colonial power the 'the cultural impact' of the South Pacific was an important aspect of the romantic movement, and just as the Orient or the East had undermined the authority of classical Greece and Rome at a time when the neoclassical was being discovered and excavated, Bernard believed that the exploration of the South Pacific had profoundly affected European aesthetics and ideas. The artistic descriptions of unknown lands and strange people had created new systems of perception and visual devices from which a transformative arts program developed.[58] Yet as the Europeans sailed into the South Pacific and were confronted by their limitations in the spectacular 'unknown', they had to construct that 'unknown . . . in terms of the known'.[59] This, as far as Bernard was concerned, illustrated 'the insular British mind' and how it reacted 'to the vast ocean spaces' and 'free-love' arcadias of the South Sea Islands, in particular the Society Islands and Tahiti,[60] as well as a concept formed by northern traditions and the distance created between them and the southern periphery. What Bernard discovered were the interstices between reality and myth.

In a period of great visual excitement the opening up of the Pacific delivered images depicting antipodal contrariety and an extraordinary variation of species that 'gradually complete[d] the picture of the universe as a vast ordered chain of being'. This 'opened a new road to the science of man', of which Ernst Cassirer wrote:

> the motto, 'Back to Nature' [could] be heard everywhere, in inexhaustible variations. Descriptions of the customs of primitive peoples were eagerly snatched up; there was a mounting urge to acquire a wider view of primitive forms of life . . . Diderot made a report of Bougainville on his trip to the South Seas his starting point for celebrating with lyrical exaggeration the simplicity, the innocence, and the happiness of primitive peoples.[61]

It also brought the 'noble savage' to the drawing rooms of the genteel, in both flesh and in pictorial image, with the arrival of the young Ra'iatean Omai in 1774 being the most sensationalised (fig. 19). While anthropology was considered the handmaiden to colonisation and the study of humans precipitated the theory of evolution, the notion of the 'noble savage' and his sensual paradise resurrected a historical sentimentalism as well as potentially creating a new tourist trade. Omai was often depicted in the manner of a Roman patrician, while utopians, evangelical zealots and reformist societies saw 'the savage condition of our ancestors'. That instituted a wave of moral prudence aimed directly at transforming native cultures into controlled gardens of Eden or, as George Steiner put it, 'The *moraliste* uses "primitive" cultures, personally experienced or gathered second hand, as a tuning fork against which to test the discord of his own milieu.'[62]

Bernard's thesis demanded a comprehensive analysis of the 'epic colour of history', from scientific and botanical discoveries to philosophies of identity, politics, social and power relations, and he found that his 1939 thesis on the great reformative romantic period offered some useful material. As he assembled a cast of major and minor figures of the 'age of imperialism', policymakers who shaped the possession and reception of *Terra Australis Incognita*, he also drew up a systemic map of events in which the British Empire constructed the Pacific as a place and New Holland as a potential utopia and penal settlement, which simultaneously forged freedom and imprisonment, material wealth and reformism, and scientific progress with economic materialism.

One of the Warburg Institute's strengths was its emphasis on images as a seminal feature of intellectual and cultural history—'art as information', as Bernard would say. Three months after he had started his research in London Charles Mitchell approached him with an offer that he was unable to refuse. Mitchell's altruism in helping young scholars get a foothold in the world of scholarship was well-known and when the Pacific historians Dr James Wight Davidson and Dr J. C. Beaglehole, working on an edition of Captain Cook's journals for the Hakluyt Society, approached Mitchell about compiling a catalogue of the original drawings and paintings by artists on Cook's three voyages, he unhesitatingly thought of Bernard. Not only was Bernard the ideal man for the job, he was considerably more meticulous and infinitely better equipped than the artist and wood engraver Robert Gibbings who had been asked to write about the illustrations.

The Hakluyt Society had been planning an edition of Cook's journals for some time. Their objective was to 'elucidate the narratives as source material for Pacific history and for Cook's biography, and to illustrate every aspect of Cook's circumnavigations and his career'.[63] It would consist of three volumes with specialist essays and an additional fourth volume that contained the catalogue. Though already overwhelmed by the amount of work in front of him, Bernard could see that the catalogue was an integral part of the whole picture and accepted. Reflecting on this later, he wrote:

> none of us had the faintest idea of the scale of the task involved. What was to have been one essay in that 4th volume eventually

became three volumes (in four parts) published by Rüdiger Joppien and myself during the 1980s . . . That decision determined much of my subsequent scholarly life. Not only *The Art of Captain Cook's Voyages* with Joppien, it also directed my Warburg research.[64]

Anthony Blunt was equally adamant that Bernard take on the work—'*Catalogues Raisonnés* are excellent for art historians to assemble. They're good for their souls.'[65] So Bernard set aside one morning each week and, with expert assistance from R. A. Skelton, the Keeper in the Department of Maps at the British Museum, he began cataloguing Cook's coastal profiles. Some months later Beaglehole wrote to him:

Very interesting to me as we have been paddling around in NZ with the idea of the European trained eye impacted upon by Polynesian appearance and I should welcome extremely a treatment of the subject by one who has really made a study of it as you have. Also I am looking forward to your impressions of all the Cook stuff.[66]

This acknowledgement by one of the significant authorities on Cook may have been premature, but it certainly confirmed Bernard's profile as a presence among scholars of the Pacific.

For Bernard, 'The past itself is a chaos of fading memories; [but] the historic past is a human construction', and the settlement of Australia was without doubt a man-made construction of colonial expansion.[67] The group portrait by John Hamilton Mortimer may be seen as analogous to the concept of empire; it shows the architects of imperial exploration in relaxed conversation at Lord Sandwich's seaside property shortly after returning from their first voyage to the Pacific in 1771 (fig. 20). Moreover, it is the earliest known portrait of James Cook, who had just been elevated to Commanding Lieutenant. Joseph Banks, one of Britain's most influential philanthropists, botanists, and an insatiable collector of all aspects of the arts, commerce and sciences, is seated; the naturalist Daniel Solander, who had trained under Linnaeus, stands to Cook's right; John Hawkesworth, the writer and editor commissioned to publish Cook's account of the first voyage is to Cook's left; and their patron, John

Montagu, the Fourth Earl of Sandwich, recently appointed First Lord of the Admiralty, rests against a plinth with a statue of Echo atop.[68]

During the mid-eighteenth century Britain's burgeoning industrialisation and expanding population demanded new sources of economic wealth, food and mineral resources and, in establishing a neo-Europe, men of science and the arts were employed to advise on the suitability of new territories. The lands believed to exist in the Southern Hemisphere became an urgent concern and the wealthy 'experimental gentleman' and scientific virtuoso Joseph Banks was a central figure in that great enterprise. Having accompanied Cook on his first voyage in 1768, Banks helped to determine the future of New Holland; his testimonials to the House of Commons between 1778 and 1780 and again in 1785 were pivotal to colonisation. As Alan Frost points out, 'Banks viewed the Australian landscape not only "through the eyes of an English farmer" but also through a scientific filter that eventually enabled the First Fleet settlers to take with them a "portmanteau" of seeds and plants'. Banks' advice was heeded and *Terra Australis* became 'a food basket for both Great Britain's and Europe's immigrants, convicts and her "redundant poor"'.[69] Bernard, however, saw Banks as caught between 'the conflicting ideals of art and science', between the rules of taste and the demands of ethnographic accuracy, particularly marked by his appreciation of the picturesque for his own personal reasons.

In 1946 as a student in Professor Trendall's classical archaeology class at the University of Sydney, Bernard had been taught the Morellian method of attribution and connoisseurship—identification and classification—and he employed the method to establish the stylistic qualities of the early artists employed by the Admiralty and those working in Australia's early colonial settlements. One stylistic conundrum led him to

> call one cluster of drawings the work of 'The Port Jackson Painter'
> . . . [who] was probably Henry Brewer, provost-marshal on the First
> Fleet and a great friend of Governor Phillip. But this has never been
> proven . . . I called him the Port Jackson Painter in order to distin-
> guish his work from that of the others of his group . . . In such ways,
> a personal style is rescued from the abyss of anonymity.[70]

By naming the unknown artist or artists as the Port Jackson Painter Bernard was following Trendall's form of identification. Trendall had attributed thousands of Greek vases as the work of particular painters or collective groups, but was the term Bernard's invention? According to Alwyne Wheeler, formerly of the British Museum's Natural History department, the term had been around for a while, and it is possible that F. C. Sawyer, the zoology librarian who had been very helpful to Bernard in 1949, may have jointly coined it.[71] What distinguished the art of the Port Jackson Painter was what Bernard called the 'triumph of innocent vision . . . [pictures] drawn with clean, fragile and yet elegant line[s] and that feeling for space'.[72] Many years later the artist Eric Thake used the image of *Cygnus atratus*, the black swan by the Port Jackson Painter (fig. 21), for Bernard's *ex libris* bookplate (fig. 22). It was an appropriate metaphor for the 'Other', the dark trespasser of the Antipodes, the inverse of its northern white, European counterpart.

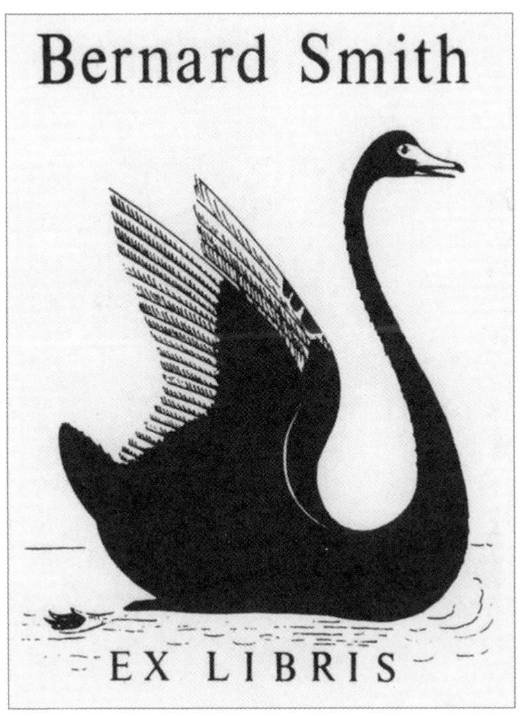

Fig. 22 *Ex libris* for Bernard Smith, designed by Eric Thake, c. 1980

In contrast to those beautiful, often naive pen-and-ink drawings, were engravings made by other hands, in which Bernard found discrepancies between the original sketch and the engraved image. These had been manipulated for propaganda and for profit as much as succumbing to the rules of eighteenth-century taste and the role of history painting. Bernard had previously noted this 'distortion of vision' in *Place, Taste and Tradition* and how the imperial gaze had transformed nature and natives into a noble imperial myth, and Hawkesworth's publication of Captain Cook's Voyage[73] was a prime example of 'concocting' values for a public market. Art as information had been romanticised or classicised by the engravers Giovanni Battista Cipriani, Francesco Bartolozzi and John Keyse Sherwin; even William Blake's engravings conformed to a stereotype of the 'noble savage'. While not all engravers had distorted the artist's original work, 'the imposition of European classical idealism [as] a piece of ostensible reportage of the South Seas' was, as David Bindman points out, 'a betrayal of observational principles to reinforce the banal pastoralism sought by fashionable London society'.[74] That included Joseph Banks and his circle of dilettante gentlemen.

Bernard found the artist William Hodges, who served under Cook on the *Resolution* between 1773 and 1776, a somewhat different case, not only because of the artist's creative capacity, but because Hodges was marginalised by the arbiter of taste, the Royal Academy. As Bernard wrote, 'I am interested in artists as failures . . . Hodges was a special kind of failure. The failure who is a forerunner we should, as art historians, pay more attention to . . . in seeking to understand the success of others.'[75] It was a prime example of the 'unequal exchange' that characterised Bernard's innate propensity in tracking historical outcomes. Hodges' importance lay in his innovative deconstruction of aesthetic space, a result of painting mostly from the large window of the great cabin, 'his mobile studio', under extremely difficult physical conditions at sea and from where he recorded atmospheric effects, terrifying oceanic phenomena and hemispheric and seasonal changes. When Cook sailed perilously close to the great southern ice cap of the Antarctic, Hodges had to work rapidly before fogs and Fata Morganas made all that was real dissolve into air, or the freezing conditions turned his ink and washes to ice. His sketches were more truthful than anything that had previously been attempted and his representation of the human presence in what was 'mere audience to the terrifying sublime of Nature' more powerful and more empirically real. As Bernard wrote:

> Hodges had to paint more broadly, and more directly, and gain an effect of atmospheric movement, that made his work . . . far closer to the later work of Constable and Turner . . . Indeed [it might be considered] the first stirrings of that naturalistic movement in landscape painting that led eventually to impressionism.[76]

In the tropical climes of Tahiti, where the Indigenous inhabitants called Hodges *Tuhituhi*, 'maker of pictures',[77] he painted the languorous sensuality of the islanders and the sublime scenery of towering mountains; in New Zealand he recorded the great waterfalls, gorges and forests, but he also captured the intensity of close encounters between the explorer and the native. Hodges understood the boundaries of territorialism and revealed the gaze of indigenous resistance that confronted the Europeans' invasive presence or, as Bernard put it, the colonial relation between 'civility' and 'savagery' (fig. 23).

Apart from William Hodges' important innovation of 'proto plein-airism,' his moral compass also appealed to Bernard's Marxist humanism and his anti-hierarchical leanings—'My pictures will constantly be lessons, sometimes of what results from the impolicy of nations, or sometimes from the vices and follies of particular classes of men.'[78] Truth and Hodges' painterly style did not accord with contemporary fashion and the artist became a victim of powerful individuals who controlled the rules of aesthetic taste and impeded certain careers while advancing others. Eventually Hodges gave up painting and, after personal tragedies and failing in other ventures, finally committed suicide. Such casualties, Bernard believed, needed to be recognised and investigated; that attraction to artists who suffered discrimination was replicated in his interest in William Blake, Gustave Courbet, Honoré Daumier, Noel Counihan and David Boyd.

After reading *Painting in Britain 1530–1790* (1953), in which the leading historian of British art Sir Ellis Waterhouse described Hodges as 'the most accomplished painter of fake Wilsons', Bernard was even more determined to rehabilitate the artist to a more prominent position. He wrote to Waterhouse asking for an explanation, but received no reply, concluding that 'For Waterhouse artists working beyond Europe in the field of science were largely ignored . . . topography [w]as the lowest category of art.'[79] In attempting to resituate William Hodges from an 'exotic footnote in the eighteenth century landscape tradition' to his rightful place in history Bernard took the matter to Sir Kenneth Clark:

> William Hodges calls for more attention. It seems to me that the empirical interpretation of nature championed by the Royal Society and the ideal interpretation championed by the Academy are first seen clearly in active conflict in his landscapes.[80]

While Hodges was important to Bernard, it was the Hakluyt Society's catalogue and his article 'Eighteenth Century Vision and Australasia' for the *Journal of the Warburg and Courtauld Institutes* that remained his foremost concern.

Locating major and minor works was time-consuming and Bernard had to travel throughout England to see paintings such as Joshua Reynolds' portrait of Omai, known as *The leper boy* (1776) at Queen Margaret's School at Castle Howard in York. Enormous collections of oceanic artefacts were in Cambridge and Oxford, not to mention what lay in drawers and cabinets at the Mitchell Library and the Nicholson Museum in Sydney, the Alexander Turnbull Library in Wellington, New Zealand, or in American collections. With so much material widely dispersed Bernard wrote to institutions asking them to compile lists of objects in their possession; he also sought and was granted an extension to his scholarship and enlisted Kate to help him with his research. That gave her a greater understanding of Bernard's work as well as forming an indispensable working partnership with her husband.

Antipodeans in London

'We are apparently engaged upon a somewhat similar production', wrote Rex Nan Kivell to Bernard in 1948.[81] The liaison officer for the Commonwealth National Library of Australia, C. A. Burmester, had told Bernard soon after his arrival in London about the expatriate New Zealand collector and modern art dealer Nan Kivell, who owned the Redfern Gallery in London and possessed an extraordinary collection of Oceanic art. Maie Casey, the wife of Australia's Minister of State, Richard Casey, had met Nan Kivell in 1937, and it was through this connection that his massive collection came to the attention of the Chief Librarian of the Commonwealth National Library, Harold White. Several months later Bernard met Nan Kivell at the Redfern Gallery in Cork Street (fig. 24). What ostensibly connected these two antipodeans was the art of the South Pacific, the naturalist's records, portraits and descriptions of the conditions of encounter, exchange and of two cultures clashing or merging.

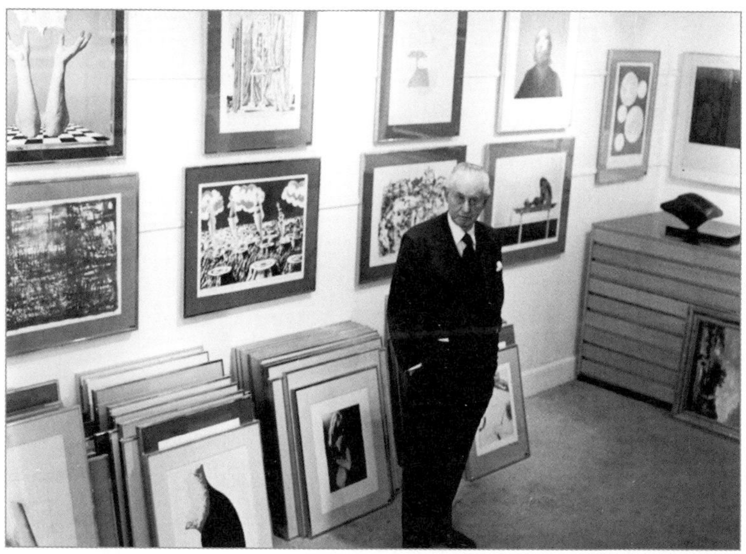

Fig. 24 Rex Nan Kivell, c. 1959

Like Bernard, Nan Kivell was illegitimate. Illegitimacy affected not only the way each man perceived themselves and the world, but how hard they worked towards making their lives successful. Raised Reginald Nankivell by his working-class grandparents as their own son on New

Zealand's South Island, he escaped his birthplace by joining the military corps at the outbreak of World War I and, after seeing some action in France, worked for the remainder of the war in a military hospital in Wiltshire, England. War provided Nankivell with the perfect theatre in which to reinvent himself and on demobilisation he emerged as Rex de Charambec Nan Kivell, a wealthy young cosmopolitan from the Antipodes.[82]

Through connections with wealthy people such as Arthur Knyvett-Lee, Anthony Maxtone Graham, Lord Alington and Earl Amherst—the original owners of the Redfern Gallery—and the Bloomsbury Group's Noel Coward, Cecil Beaton and Charles Laughton, Nan Kivell gained entry into London society and historic country homes. During the Depression he acquired, at exceedingly low prices, exotic memorabilia, and with the growth of Jewish art dealers in London, exiles from Hitler's Europe who knew of important collections on the Continent, Nan Kivell made 'daring dashes to rescue modern and traditional works of art' during the 1930s.[83] Though he had distanced himself from his past, the Antipodes remained Nan Kivell's paradise renounced and his decision to collect anything that referred to the South Pacific developed into such a major obsession that he admitted 'I have become almost of a one track mind now in collecting these Australian prints and pictures, and have almost forgotten that contemporary English paintings are being painted.'[84]

When Bernard visited Nan Kivell's apartment he saw a small portion of the collection. Many more works were stored in his country house in Wiltshire and a large consignment was on its way to the National Library of Australia. But Bernard realised that what he had found in one collector's hands were the visual resources and the vital evidence that would provide him with the aesthetic and material proof to define his thesis. Both men understood that by bringing together books, maps, art and ephemera of one of the most important programs of imperial colonisation ever recorded, a more accurate ecology of historical events could be made. In the mid-1950s, while Bernard was working on his doctoral thesis at the ANU, the reciprocal interests of these two antipodeans became evident: 'I want you to know . . . just how valuable your collection here [in

Canberra] is to me in pursuing this research' Bernard wrote and, a little later, 'You will also find how much the text of the book [*European Vision and the South Pacific*] owes to the existence of your collection.'[85]

At the Natural History Museum in South Kensington Bernard continued working on the 'Watling' and 'Forster Drawings' and discovered another 700 botanical and zoological drawings by Francis and Ferdinand Bauer. Only a handful of specialists had studied those meticulous illustrations of exotic flora and fauna, 'every one a masterpiece', and none had ever been published. Bernard contacted Wilfred Blunt, the botanical specialist and brother of Anthony Blunt, whom he found 'pleasant and congenial—quite a contrast to his formidable brother'.[86] Wilfred Blunt considered the Bauer brothers among the greatest botanical artists of all time and suggested that Bernard contact Sacheverell Sitwell, the editor of Batsford Colour Books about publishing the Bauer illustrations. Bernard also wrote to Nikolaus Pevsner, editor of King Penguin Books, but both men were emphatic that there was no commercial interest in either botanical art or Australiana (fig. 25).

One day, after working on the Bauer illustrations, Bernard made his way to the Cabinet Offices in Whitehall to meet the Australian historian Keith Hancock, whom he had heard, incorrectly as it turned out, would be appointed to a senior position at the new ANU in Canberra.[87] A polite and charming man with unruly white hair, Hancock apologised for keeping Bernard waiting, which was in contrast to Philip Jones, the director of the Fine Arts Section of the British Arts Council whom Bernard had met earlier that day, noting that he was 'the kind of Englishman I detest: a pompous civil servant type . . . [who] exudes the atmosphere that his time is precious and must not be wasted'.[88] Bernard's tendency to typecast people may have been his way of reclassifying himself within a country that half-expected 'unqualified' Australians to fail. On hearing his account of the Bauer drawings Hancock not only expressed an interest in seeing them, but showed a genuine interest in Bernard's research. This response was welcome at a time when Bernard felt overwhelmed by the immensity of his project.

The pressure of getting his article ready for Mitchell and an unexpected invitation to attend a UNESCO meeting in Paris in November

1949, however, delayed a meeting with Sir Kenneth Clark, but in a letter to Clark Bernard flagged his ambitions:

> I do feel that one of the things I should do before returning to Australia is to find out whether it is possible to arrange for a first-class exhibition of contemporary Australian painting in this country. I should like to talk this matter over with you . . . And do you think it will ever be possible for us to have a Constable, Turner or Gainsborough exhibition?[89]

He was capitalising on Clark's well-publicised excitement about his first visit to Australia where he had bought paintings by Sidney Nolan and Russell Drysdale. Clark, however, strongly advised against an exhibition of Australian contemporary art in London as it was not the right time, but the seed had been planted and would germinate. Several smaller exhibitions of Australian art would be shown in Britain in the early 1950s, such as *Twelve Australian Artists* in 1953, proposed by Clark to the Arts Council of Britain, in conjunction with the Commonwealth Art Advisory Board, and a number of other exhibitions organised by the Australian Artists Association. It would not be until 1959 that Bernard would broach the issue again with Clark, by which time he was convinced that a group of Australian artists called The Antipodeans could boldly take on the British art world.

Clark had heard that Bernard was in the country and had hoped to meet him towards the end of November, but Bernard became ill and the two men did not resume correspondence until March 1950. By that time Bernard had modified his assertive tone and sought a more intellectual footing with the English art historian:

> I would be interested to hear a few of your impressions of Australian art . . . I was particularly interested in your recently published Slade lectures, since during 1949 I was attempting to come to grips with the problem of European Vision in the South Pacific ca. 1765–1835 which became largely a matter of considering landscape painting as an expression of man's relation to nature . . . It surprised me

when reading your book how the different qualities of vision at the root of several categories of landscape painting were the very ones I had been seeking to track down in my piece of work. It was, indeed, the relation between the landscape of fact, the natural vision, and the ideal landscape, that I sought to elucidate.[90]

In late 1950 Bernard sent Clark a copy of his Warburg journal article 'European Vision and the South Pacific', suggesting it might be of 'some interest'.

The shock of poverty

Summer arrived and Bernard embarked on his first European tour in which he planned to see as many great monuments and works of art as he could. There was also another agenda: he wanted to see how Eastern European communism worked from the inside. The cultural attaché at the Czechoslovakian Embassy had arranged a program that would allow Bernard to see how art education, exhibitions and cultural activity were conducted in factories and schools but, in particular, he wanted to see what contemporary art had been produced since the war.

At Dover he and Bob Gollan caught a crowded ferry before transferring to an equally crowded train at Oostende, and they were soon passing through the beautiful Belgium countryside. As they entered Germany the ravages of war were painfully visible and all that was left of the Cologne station was an empty shell. The city was a graveyard; Cologne Cathedral had been badly battered and the once-glorious Romanesque Church of St Monica was destroyed. At Cologne Bernard and Gollan parted company, with Bernard travelling on to Nuremberg. It had also been obliterated by bombing, but he managed to find Albrecht Dürer's house, which was one of the first buildings to be repaired, indicating just how important the artist was to Germany's national spirit.[91] Having seen enough ruins, he travelled on to Prague where he had arranged to meet Stephen Murray-Smith and his Polish-born wife Nita. She was teaching English to union workers and Stephen was writing for various agencies, including the Ministry of Information. Bernard described the local culture and political environment in a letter to Kate: 'The Czechs are interested in Australian Literature . . . Henry Lawson is to be translated . . . Frank Dalby Davison's *Man-Shy* . . . and Murray-Smith wants them to translate my book [*Place, Taste and Tradition*].'[92] The thought of being read internationally and in a communist country added lustre to a 'truly wonderful and beautiful city' in which Gothic, Baroque and Renaissance architecture had been 'all thrown against each other in rich picturesque confusion'. The Castle of Prague was like a fortress town with tiny, doll-like houses overlooking a huge moat and unlike anything Bernard had ever seen, as were the city's 'minarets, towers and great blocks of apartments'. But Bernard found the Czech National Gallery of Modern Art disappointing, with only a few good Czech sculptures, a few fine Rodin and Bourdelle works and a small, but magnificent collection of French paintings by Pissaro, Monet, Derain, Cézanne, Picasso and Matisse, including 'the very lovely Henri Rousseau self-portrait . . . with palette and brush before a gaily be-flagged ship and bridge in the background'.[93]

Bernard had been given the names and addresses of artists and was provided with an attractive female translator who arranged meetings on his behalf. What he did not tell Kate in his letters was how shocked he was at the strict conditions and the lack of individual freedom, especially among the factory workers. This was 'the God that failed' and he decided that on his return to Australia he would resign from the Communist Party. After Prague he travelled by train through Austria to Vienna, passing quickly through the city, though not before experiencing confusion with officials in an area that was still Soviet-controlled. On showing a military officer his passport and visa he was asked, 'You are English?' Bernard replied that he was Australian, to which the officer said, 'It is the same thing.' 'No', Bernard replied, 'not quite.'[94]

He caught the train to Venice and awoke just as it crossed the long bridge that joins the city to the mainland; looking out of the window he saw the mudflats that Ruskin had written about in 1851. In the warmth of the summer sun, among the smell of good food, the stunning Venetian architecture and beautiful, lithe, tanned bodies, Bernard, who was usually vigilant with money, decided to indulge himself and drift in the Venetian dream. He took a gondola along the Grand Canal, visited San

Marco with its stupendous interior, and wandered through the Nationale Librario where Tintoretto's and Veronese's large fresco portraits of the great philosophers adorned the walls. He narrated his daily movements to Kate, relaying his excitement, though often within a marital code of affectionate reportage. Naturally, he refrained from telling her about his encounter with a prostitute.

A *flâneur*, as Walter Benjamin tells, instinctively feels no guilt and, like an addict, is compelled to seek out secret pleasures.[95] Desiring that which does not intimately belong was part of Bernard's fantasy of the forbidden. Jacques Lacan believed that 'desire seeks to win recognition of the "Other"'; but it was also an inheritance to seduce or be seduced that connected Bernard with his primal origins—'I am my father's spirit'. Being in the absolute present also acted as a foil to the intensity of his rigorous research that kept him incarcerated in the past; the future, he believed, 'would take care of itself'. Though he never told Kate about the Venetian prostitute, 13 years after her death he described his sexual encounter in his second autobiographical volume, *A Pavane for Another Time*, when confession could no longer hurt the woman he loved:

> I was finishing a glass of wine at a café near the Libraria Vecchio. She came quickly from the Piazzetta, her body silhouetted against the façade of St. Mark's, a slim girl affecting the confident hip sway twirl of her profession as she walked. Well, why not here if anywhere? For here it was, as Burkhardt [*sic*] had informed me many years ago, a most honoured Renaissance profession. So I rose, caught up with her among the evening promenaders, and took her by the arm as she walked. I said nothing. She said nothing, just walked me on through the Horologio into the Merciere where she was joined by two of her friends.[96]

After Venice Bernard travelled to Padua, Vicenza and Verona before arriving in Florence. He saw masterpieces that he had previously only seen in reproductions; Cimabue, Duccio and Giotto and magnificent Botticelli paintings, and the great Michelangelo and Donatello sculptures. Struck at the architectural differences between Italian cities, he described Venice as a glittering, sumptuous playground of eclectic styles, 'Florence [wa]s like a grey bed of oysters with all the pearls inside', whereas in Rome he was not prepared for the sight of poverty; 'People living in dirty little lanes . . . many cripples and nutrition disease everywhere . . . slum children clambering all over the exquisite fountains in the Piazza Navona . . . or their hair all shaven off and clambering around their priest like little grey mice.'[97] But Rome also offered a wealth of architectural antiquities, magnificent treasures and unsurpassed art collections and, in a letter to his mother, he described St Peter's as 'tremendously huge in every way', and said that his month in Italy was unparalleled in his 'training in visual experience'.[98]

The Abbey

While Bernard was travelling, Kate and the children moved to The Abbey Arts Centre, a rambling place set on three acres (1.2 ha) in the outer London suburb of New Barnet. Owned by the art dealer William Ohly, who had bought the property from a religious sect in 1946, it possessed a large three-storey house built in the late 1800s and numerous dilapidated outbuildings that had been turned into artists' studios. The Smiths rented a large, furnished room inside the house, but many young artists, including a succession of Australians, lived in studios where they paid peppercorn rents for basic facilities. Grahame King, Douglas Green, Peter Graham and James Wigley were named 'The Bush Boys' by Robert Klippel and James Gleeson, primarily because of their 'bushmen' skills repairing the dilapidated buildings and doing what needed to be done around the property.[99] Noel and Pat Counihan and their two young sons also lived in one of the outbuildings and in the evenings Bernard, after he had returned from Europe, would often walk over to Counihan's studio to discuss politics (fig. 26). After Noel's visit to Budapest and his intense survey of communism, the men had plenty to talk about and, as Inge King's studio was next door to Counihan's, their heated discussions could be overheard through the thin fibro-cement sheet walls, usually with Counihan 'instructing' Bernard.[100]

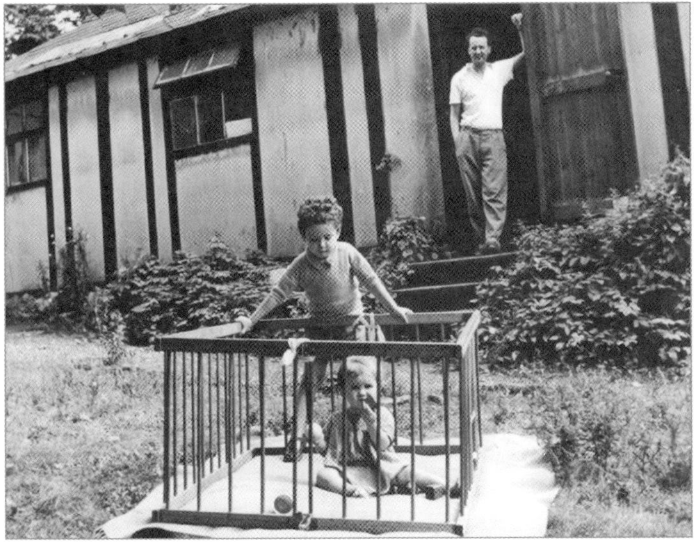

Fig. 26   Noel Counihan and his young sons outside his studio at The Abbey, 1950

A fourteenth-century timber-framed tithe barn, once a folk museum, had been transported to the property in the 1930s and contained an eclectic collection of religious and primitive artefacts from the Americas, Egypt, China, Melanesian islands and African secret societies, and a miscellany of religious and tribal art. When Ohly found that Bernard's research involved cataloguing works from the Oceanic region he gave him a separate room upstairs in the main house, next to his own large, relic-filled study where the two men discussed imperialism, anthropology and artefacts, Ohly owning a book of tapa cloth collected on one of Cook's voyages.[101]

Bernard was looking forward to the new academic year and studying under Rudolf Wittkower, one of the world's best architectural historians. He was planning to work on the beginnings of architecture in Australia, comparing early buildings with similar examples in Britain and ascertaining stylistic derivations and changes that occurred as the new colony acclimatised to its geographic conditions. Bernard liked Wittkower, writing of him, 'He is a very nice chap, and has already helped me considerably.'[102] His plans were interrupted, however, when he received an invitation to represent Australia at a meeting of 'art experts' at the UNESCO headquarters in Paris in November. As this was Bernard's first visit to Paris he took Kate with him, mainly because he had seen so little of her, but also because she was fluent in French. At the Gare du Nord they were met by a chauffeured Australian Embassy car and driven through the wide boulevards ablaze with autumnal colour. While Kate wandered around Paris, visiting churches and museums, Bernard spent four tedious days incarcerated in the UNESCO meetings where, much to his displeasure, he found his old *bête noir*, Peter Bellew, now head of the Arts Division of UNESCO, a post for which he had been recommended by Sir Kenneth Clark (fig. 27).[103]

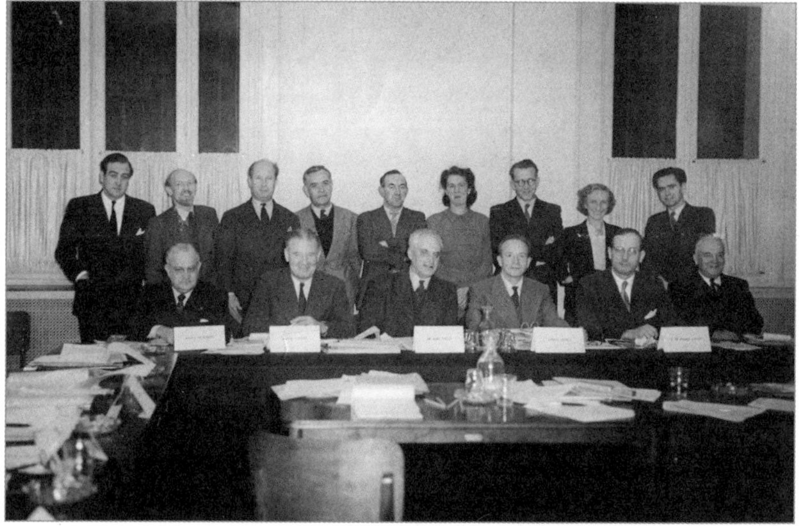

Fig. 27　Peter Bellew (far left), and Bernard Smith (far right), UNESCO Paris, 1949

They had not long returned to The Abbey when Bernard fell ill. That winter was notoriously bitter and Kate kept a roaring fire going in their room to combat the icy east winds blowing through the rattling windows, but Bernard's condition deteriorated and an ambulance was called. At St Stephen's Hospital in Barnet he was diagnosed with bronchial pneumonia and nephritis. That put an end to his studies with Wittkower and to his meeting with Sir Kenneth Clark. Elizabeth, or 'Betsy' as everyone called her, found her father's absence upsetting. The only other 'local male with the right accent' was the artist Grahame King, who had been living at The Abbey since 1947. King kept an eye on Kate and the children and regularly visited Bernard, and one afternoon invited Kate to his studio to see his latest paintings. With his canvases pinned to the walls, he explained how the beautiful colours in the stained glass windows of Chartres Cathedral had inspired him to brighten his palette (fig. 28). The paintings were for his final London exhibition, the sales from which he hoped would enable him and Inge, whom he had recently married, to buy their passages to Melbourne.[104]

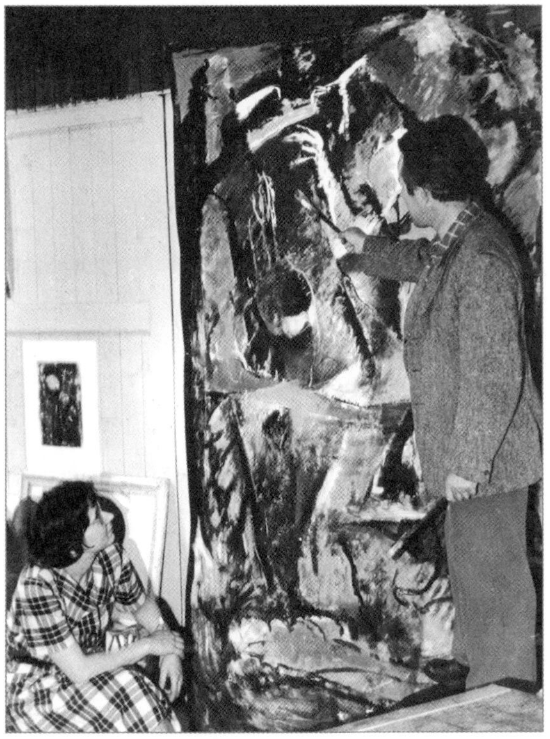

Fig. 28 Grahame and Inge King in their studio at The Abbey, 1950

Kate had seen so little of Bernard and with him convalescing in hospital, she wrote to make the point intimately—'I really need you back in bed these nights', as much, she said, for warmth as for marital comfort. Bernard was not the only one who had been hospitalised; Bob Gollan had been operated on for a duodenal ulcer and Noel Counihan, whose health was precarious at the best of times, came down with a 'ripe, gangrenous appendix'. While confined to their beds, Noel sent Bernard a petition, asking him to be a signatory to a peace congress that was to take place in Melbourne on 16 April. Its message was clear: the Cold War was escalating:

> The threat of the hydrogen bomb is the last detail needed to bring out the simplicity and finality of the issues that now face mankind. We the undersigned Australians in Britain, believe that it is the pressing duty of all intellectuals who feel the responsibility of their calling to take an uncompromising stand on the issues of peace.

Letters alleviated Bernard's hospital boredom: Sali Herman wrote that Elizabeth Vassilieff had 'had a crack' at Bernard in *Meanjin*; Hal Missingham's witty missals informed him that he had finally got rid of his troublesome, frequently intoxicated and rude secretary, whose meddling had become unendurable; and Rod Shaw wrote that Sidney Nolan's paintings of Central Australia had taken the art scene by storm.[105] Bernard also received a letter from Charles Mitchell, impatient for his article for the Warburg journal:

> Now, for your article. I have been, as you see, quite savage . . . but I have not . . . removed anything that is new and important. I'm not sure it doesn't improve with slimming. Once or twice I have had to put in a few phrases of my own, which I hope you will forgive.[106]

Mitchell emphasised that Bernard needed to determine the parameters and conditions of the Enlightenment and distinguish between dilettantes and professionals; was Sir Joseph Banks a scientific virtuoso or a quizzing 'Grand Tourist'? Bernard had been hesitant about Banks' role, but decided to classify him as a virtuoso, even if he were 'divided between the world of science and the world of taste'.[107] Banks' patronage and prestige, especially as the president of the Royal Society, had constructed a new genre of 'Art in the service to science', ultimately affecting the visual arts in the late eighteenth century.[108] Mitchell also took Bernard to task about his slack references and suggested that as he was laid up in hospital he should 'get his good wife to send [his] working notes to Miss F. Yates, the editor . . . [who] will then extract what information she can get from them'. He did, however, commend Bernard's article, especially the second half, which covered important new ground. By April proofs had been made; further amendments by Skelton and Beaglehole had been received, the former praising Bernard for 'throw[ing] a great deal of light on the pictorial records of Cook's voyages and admirably elucidate[ing] both what the artists took to the Pacific & what they learnt from it.'[109] For Bernard, he had made his scholarly mark.

After 12 weeks in hospital, Bernard returned to The Abbey, but within a week announced that he would squeeze in 10 days in Ireland before embarking on his second summer tour of Europe. His roles as father and husband, it seemed, were very much jobs in absentia.

Retracing origins

Ireland had always held a special interest for Bernard and he wanted to meet the remaining members of his mother's family and to discover 'his origins'—after all he was a Tierney. Gerald Dillon, an artist whom he had met at The Abbey, showed him around Dublin and they saw a brilliant production of Sean O'Casey's *The Shadow of a Gunman* at the Abbey Theatre. The famous theatre, he noted, was 'quite small and very 1890ish in black and white art nouveau style'; its long curving gallery, cast-iron pillars and long brackets, with 'seats a trifle hard' did not remain that way for much longer when fire destroyed the theatre in 1951.[110]

Bernard's trip to Bailieborough in County Cavan, where his mother was born and raised, was an experience unlike anything he had ever known.[111] Untouched by tourism and sparsely populated, he felt as though he was journeying 'into the middle ages'. He watched a boy cutting turf from the bog, a woman with seven or eight children spinning around her as she confusingly directed Bernard in every direction, and had long, rambling conversations with strangers. Half a day was taken getting seven miles (11 km) from Bailieborough to Derry, but finally he met a man walking along a road who, on hearing that Bernard was the son of Michael Tierney's sister from Australia, excitedly took him to a little cottage. It was where Rose Anne's father was born and where her mother died. With memories flooding back the old man told Bernard how he had visited the house the night before Rose Anne and her sister Mary sailed for Australia; he then took Bernard to meet his uncle, who was also cutting turf in the bog. That evening, as he listened to the men ceaselessly 'tale spinning, leg pulling and embroidering yarns', he felt that it was better than anything he had heard or had read from Synge or O'Casey and, though a complete stranger, Bernard had found his roots among the Irish peasants and felt no exclusion within that clan.[112]

Bernard's second European tour began in late August 1950 when he travelled to Bruges, Ghent, Brussels, Antwerp, Amsterdam, The Hague, Delft, Rotterdam and Paris, where Kate joined him. The Louvre was 'a veritable feast', but Versailles was without doubt a high point, especially Louis XIV's apartments and the spectacular Hall of Mirrors. But the real charm of the palace was its exterior and the exquisite parterre gardens with the mile-long (1.6 km) canal lined with avenues of great chestnut trees.

When Kate arrived they caught the train to Venice in time to catch 'the greatest of the early post-war Biennales'. In the Salon of the Fauves, Bernard saw Braque, Derain, Matisse and Vlaminck; in the Cubism Salon he found Picasso's *Uomo con violini* (1913) from Roland Penrose's private collection and *Il Poeta* (1911) and *Construzione* (1914), which Peggy Guggenheim owned. Heavily underlined in his catalogue were the artists Giacomo Balla, Umberto Boccioni and Carlo Carrà from the Futurist Salon, several abstractionists and, in the German pavilion, a strong display of Wassily Kandinsky, Paul Klee, Franz Marc, Ernst Barlach, Max Beckmann and Emil Nolde, artists who had been dismissed as 'Degenerates' in 1937, but who were now reinstated in modernism's pantheon. There were José Clemente Orozco, Diego Rivera and David Alfaro Siqueiros in the Mexican pavilion and a salon devoted to Henri (Douanier) Rousseau, whose rich colours and primal emotions caught Bernard's attention. He saw a major retrospective of the landscape painter John Marin in the American pavilion; as well works by Arshile Gorky, Jackson Pollock and Willem de Kooning. The Pollock, Bernard thought, 'was like Alan Davie' the Scottish artist living at The

Abbey, but Davie had been influenced by Pollock. Bernard, however, was unimpressed by the artist's 'dribble technique', or what he called 'the glamorous wallpaper of his own alienation',[113] and in the margin of his catalogue he wrote 'What crimes are committed in the name of Liberty!'[114]

Another crime was the absence of Australian artists, and Bernard decided that when he got back to Sydney he would try to rectify that, but before returning to England he had one final journey to make; to the Lascaux cave in the valley of Vézère.

Cave of origins

To our distant ancestors
Fernand Windels[115]

The Lascaux cave was discovered in 1940, but excitement was still circulating in the archaeological and art historical world when Bernard and Kate visited it in August 1950. Accompanied by two young men who had found the ancient cavern, they descended into the dark 'little subway' before entering the Great Hall of the Bulls. Chalked onto the walls was a 13-foot (3.9-m) bull in black charcoal and red ochre, a magnificent beast drawn in a program of divining an image that affirmed human presence. Unicorns, friezes of horses, bison, deer and other strange animals also adorned the walls, and all so exceptionally well-preserved that anthropologists had thought them to be fake.

Bernard had recently bought Fernand Windels' large illustrated book *The Lascaux Cave Paintings* (1949) (fig. 29), which suggested that realism 'whether intellectual or visual, covers . . . that of perspective, for to observe the laws of perspective is to reproduce things as they are seen, while to ignore them is to represent things as they are known to be'.[116] Thus the cave drawings implied that the artists were imaginatively and technically advanced, even though the images were thought to be 17,000 years old. Painted on high ceilings and in treacherously deep and undulating passages, there was a kinaesthetic, three-dimensional modern

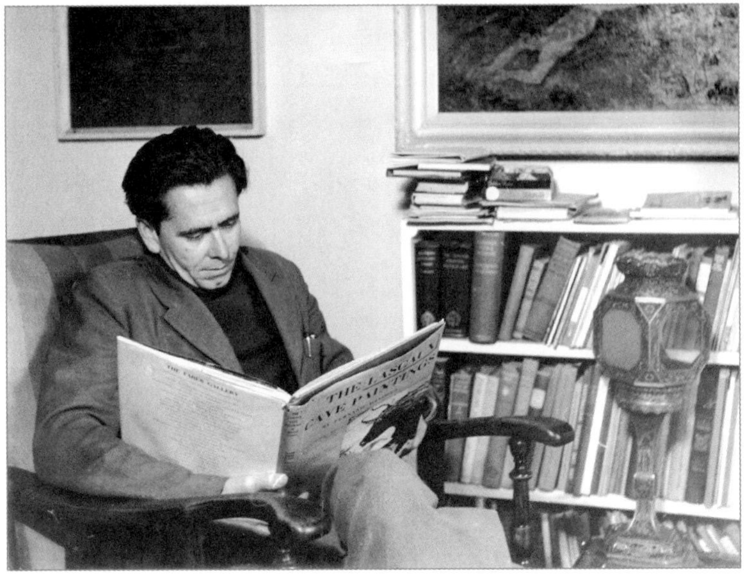

Fig. 29 Bernard Smith reading in his room at The Abbey, 1950

quality to them; at a shamanistic level this banquet of prehistoric drawings linked with and across time to function as historical consciousness
and collective memory.

Reappraising the role of primitivism within the canon of modern aesthetics was, as Bernard had already reasoned, problematic; the drawings
had served the needs of hunter-gatherers and where one beast was super-
imposed over another they represent fertility rites. Aby Warburg had
postulated something similar after living with Pueblo Indians in 1896.
The cave art may have been the cradle of humanity from which all other
visual styles bloomed, but in the pall of the Cold War, some saw them
as representing humankind's incessant thirst as a murderous hunter. The
French avant-garde intellectual Georges Bataille had also visited the cave
and wrote that 'light is being shed on our birth at the very moment when
the notion of death appears to us'.[117] Bernard understood that the will
to dominate was inherent, as was the will to murder, especially during
wartime; as Thomas Hobbes succinctly put it, '*Homo homini lupus*, man
is wolf to man.'[118]

From the time of his arrival in England primitivism, that 'aesthetic
other . . . art as practised beyond the dominance of European taste and

value', had preoccupied Bernard.[119] He had discussed it with Gordon Childe, had seen the 1949 ICA exhibition *40,000 Years of Modern Art* and anthropological and ethnographic collections from the Pacific at Oxford, Cambridge and London, including the collections of Nan Kivell and William Ohly. Picasso's early cubist works used a form of aesthetic tribalism that showed how the primeval was 'part of ourselves', and though Bernard recognised prehistory and the sap of myths as 'the key to history', a great lacuna had covered it. Though the origins of aesthetics were once cave-bound and a universe of virile dreams where the great horn of death was always present, the bridge to understanding humankind's earliest art remained, for him, largely undecipherable. Art, no matter how old or new was nevertheless an authentic response to the laws of existence.

Years later, when he lectured on prehistoric cave art to his undergraduate students, Bernard approached the subject as a lesson in chronological dating as well as the earliest lessons in material evolution. The paradoxes of pre-history and anthropology were, he said, not his field, yet the cave paintings showed a unity of style, which inferred a tradition, of which modern humans were the inheritors.

Visibility

Bernard spent his remaining months in London mostly promoting himself. When Melbourne University Press rejected his manuscript 'Dobell's Art and Other Essays' he approached the publishers William Collins and Heinemann in London, but neither could muster interest, nor could Routledge & Kegan Paul where Herbert Read worked. Only his Warburg article proved a winner. Writing to Gwen Sherwood, Hal Missingham's former secretary at the National Gallery of New South Wales, he said that he had stayed too long in London and the gloss had worn off. Sir Kenneth Clark had shown interest in him and faintly nodded about his suggestions for exhibitions, but not even the brilliant Bauer drawings were of enough significance. Anthony Blunt, however, finally recognised Bernard's achievements:

Dear Smith,

I only got your letter on reaching London yesterday or I should . . . have mentioned it to you when I saw you in Paris [Blunt regularly lectured at the Louvre, and they had briefly met during Bernard's UNESCO trip]. I wish we could fit in a lecture of yours here during the coming term, but . . . our time-table is made up and extremely full, and further, that your particular subjects do not fit in naturally to the curriculum of the first term. I am sorry about this, but it is at any rate good to know that our students can read a good many of your results in the new number of the Journal . . . I rely on you to come and see us before you finally go back to Australia.[120]

Quite simply, there was not enough interest in the Antipodes as a historical or cultural entity; geographical distance and British principles of exclusion still hampered contemporary Australia almost as much as it had 150 years before. Though unable to get his Australian essays published or to present a paper at the Courtauld Institute, Bernard managed to give several Broadcast Talks at the BBC on 'Australian Landscape Painting' and 'The Artist's Vision of Australia'. From the discovery by Cook and the importance of Sir Joseph Banks and Charles Darwin, he led the listener through the unique qualities of the Australian landscape and how it created a distinct type of painting. From the colonial, picturesque, romantic and impressionist genres he finally arrived at Russell Drysdale, who painted the landscape within its own terms of reference, as though 'half in love and half in fear of his subject . . . because the Australian landscape is . . . a wilful capricious thing, half-wild, half-tame, half-myth and half reality'.[121] It was also a useful reference for Drysdale, whose exhibition was due to open at the Leicester Galleries the following week.

Bernard's two years in Britain had significantly broadened his knowledge; he had made valuable contacts and his two summer journeys through Europe had given him a real sense of the cultural past and the global present. But he knew he could never feel comfortable in England; he *was* antipodean. In a letter to his mother he assured her he would not be staying on as he felt he could do much more important work back home.

In late November, with their European odyssey over, the Smiths sailed on the *Otranto*, arriving in Sydney on New Year's Day 1951. It was 'a cold homecoming' with a Menzies government in power, the Communist Party in decline, and his position at the art gallery under a cloud.

CHAPTER FIVE: THE LONE ANTIPODEAN

What appears at first sight to be isolation often turns out, it seems to me, to be a process of selection and rejection.
Bernard Smith[1]

Disillusioned by communism and aware of the increasingly tense political situations at home and abroad, by 1950 Bernard's political activism had drawn to a close. One of the first things he did on returning to Sydney was to hand in his Communist Party ticket. Severing ties with the political community to which he had belonged for more than a decade was hard—it had been his clan. His confidence had, however, now been bolstered by his scholarly achievements and his rewarding international experiences. His focus would be on establishing himself professionally and having a tangible effect on the wider Australian art world. The former he would achieve very significantly, though with some delay; his record in the latter would prove more problematic.

Shortly before returning to work at the Art Gallery of New South Wales (AGNSW) he was distracted by a letter in the *Sydney Morning Herald* about a local proposal to mount a major exhibition of Australian art in London. Having taken to heart what Sir Kenneth Clark had recently told him he immediately wrote to Sir Charles Lloyd Jones, the author of the letter, advising him that it would be foolish to place Australian art in the mouth of the Albion lion:

> I am firmly of the opinion that any . . . exhibition of Australian art held in London in the near future will not promote . . . our best painters . . . [nor be] recognised by responsible critical opinion. I discussed Australian art with a wide circle of critics, art historians and painters in London, and elsewhere, while abroad. I found there is almost complete ignorance . . . among all but a few. I think I am right in saying that there has not been a large exhibition of Australian art in London since 1923. That exhibition, I think I am right in saying again, met with unfavourable, almost hostile critical reception. The exhibition held at Australia House some years ago, also . . . misfired badly.

And he warned:

> If the Londoner of taste and judgment, the dealer, critics, historians and buyers, dislike what they see, then it won't be possible to talk of another exhibition for another decade . . . I take pride in the achievement of contemporary Australian painting. I believe that it has considerably more vitality than contemporary English painting . . . [but the English] distrust big shows from countries which have not attained a long tradition of critical excellence . . . London critical opinion will not temper its wind to the shorn lamb even if it is a pure Australian merino . . . as a matter of fact I discussed the question with Sir Kenneth Clark shortly before I left, and . . . in his opinion a large exhibition at the present would do more harm than good.[2]

Even though Bernard's information had come from one of the most reliable sources in the 'Mother Country', numerous Australian committees, including the CAS continued to push for overseas exhibitions, although most efforts proved fruitless.[3]

Back at the AGNSW little had changed, except that Lionel Lindsay had resigned, Sydney Ure Smith had died and Bernard's guardian angel Mary Alice Evatt was often absent overseas; moreover, Hal Missingham had appointed Tony Tuckson as his assistant, a position that Bernard had thought might go to him. He was adamant, however, that he should not return to organising the travelling exhibitions and wrote to the trustee B. J. Waterhouse proposing that 'the field of Gallery activities' in which he could 'most contribute' would be to catalogue the prints and drawings, which had grown considerably since 1928 when the last catalogue had been made. But without a defined position and convinced that pressure was mounting to get rid of him, Bernard began looking for employment elsewhere. He wrote to Joseph Burke about compiling a dictionary of Australian artists and architects; applied for the job of director of the Art Gallery of South Australia; and eagerly resumed his university degree. He also began organising the gallery's modest library and print collection along the British National Gallery's Martin Davies' model, a method which set a new cataloguing standard that included more extensive provenance details and contextual literature. The only other person working in Australia in this manner was Ursula Hoff at the NGV. By March Bernard had started cataloguing the Australian paintings. Daniel Thomas, a curator at the AGNSW from 1958, considered those catalogues to be Bernard's greatest legacy to the gallery and after Bernard left in 1953, both Thomas and Tony Tuckson continued updating what Bernard had started with annual acquisition catalogues.

To counteract his professional marginalisation Bernard projected himself as a critical voice within the broader cultural scene. On the fiftieth anniversary of Federation in 1951, he gave a talk titled 'Development of Australian Painting and Sculpture over the Past Fifty Years', broadcast on the ABC to all the states in April for the Commonwealth Jubilee Celebrations. His opening remarks denounced 'the English way of looking at things here', suggesting that to appreciate the real development of art in Australia, it had to be replaced by 'an Australian way of looking'. Written in a racy, journalistic manner and pitched at the broader population, he encapsulated the main contours of Australian art:

In March 1906 Holman Hunt's painting 'The Light of the World' burst upon the country with the force of a religious revival. Fifteen thousand people fought their way to see it in three hours at the Melbourne Gallery . . . The next year, Norman Lindsay, grandson of a missionary, began to exhibit with the Society of Artists. From his pen and brush there poured tumultuous mobs of hairy satyrs, Spanish dwarfs, lusting gods, and an inexhaustible flood of naked and buxom ladies . . . The crowds that had adored the 'Light of the World' as high art were horrified and denounced the new paganism. 'Art', said Norman Lindsay, 'was creative energy' as he rode into battle against the wowsers of the whole world.

He was also critical of selling out the shorn lamb to international stylism:

the great promise that gleamed for a moment in the late eighties and early nineties was not realised; within a decade the painters of the Australian school were mainly concerned in gaining recognition at the Royal Academy and the Paris Salon, more than producing original art. Their desire for sales and success hardened the arteries of their sensibility and their imagination.[4]

But Bernard's sight was fixed further afield, and in response to continued suggestions about Australian artists exhibiting at the Royal Academy in Burlington House, he wrote to the *Sydney Morning Herald*:

It seems to me that the place where Australian art should be represented in 1952 is Venice, at the 26th Biennale . . . When I was visiting the 25th Biennale in October last an English friend expressed his surprise that whilst such countries as South Africa, Ireland, Egypt, Columbia and Israel were represented, nothing was to be seen from Australia. But I was not surprised . . . Is it that the Biennale Committee has never invited Australia to exhibit, or is it that we have not been interested? . . . If we want our best artists to be better known abroad some of them, at least, should be shown in Venice in 1952.[5]

Typically, he contacted the Italian Consul General about the biennale's procedures and Australia's future representation, and received a prompt reply and assurance that 'the road to Australia's participation is open and you can rely on our most cordial cooperation'.[6]

Spurred on by this response he wrote to the gallery trustee James McGregor pressing for Australia's representation at the next biennale, and also suggested that a pavilion could be erected in memory of Sydney Ure Smith, 'surely . . . a gesture worthy of the Federal Government and worthy of the man'.[7] This would honour his patron and memorialise the pioneer of Australian modernism but he had also heard that Peter Bellew had asked the Commonwealth Government for financial assistance to the cost of £15,000 to publish a print portfolio of Indigenous Australian engravings and paintings for UNESCO, and in a game of one-upmanship Bernard suggested to McGregor:

If the Com[monwealth] Treasurer should insist on an either or between an Australian pavilion at Venice where original works by our best artists could be shown every two years, and a portfolio, which good as it may be, will be out of date within five years, I know which I should choose.[8]

Although his campaign failed, and Bellew's succeeded with the publication of a book containing 'the first large-scale tribute paid to aboriginal art and culture in the medium of modern colour reproduction',[9] Bernard continued to press for Ure Smith's acknowledgement. He raised the idea of a memorial lecture with Prime Minister R. G. Menzies and prominent members of the Australian Academy of Humanities, but this too came to nothing. Eventually he dedicated *The Antipodean Manifesto: Essays in Art and History* (1976) to Sydney Ure Smith.[10]

During Hal Missingham's leave of absence in 1951 Bernard was asked to take over as acting director of the gallery, a bridging position that he had similarly filled in 1945 when awaiting Missingham's appointment. Hal's good-humoured letters from Europe, of time spent with Margaret Olley 'who is working quietly away and blossoming (or bosoming?) into quite a character' and with Moya Dyring in her Paris apartment on the Left Bank and her convivial reunions of Australian expatriates, only reminded him of his own recent halcyon time in Europe. Paris was pleasure, whereas Sydney was stifling.

The rest of the year tumbled along with old friends welcoming Bernard back. Muir Holburn had revived the literary soiree meetings along much the same lines as the *Australian New Writing* gatherings of 1943, and new art groups had sprung up, all hoping for Bernard's blessing and participation. He joined the Opposition to the Rearmament of Japan and the Citizen's Movement in Defence of Australian Art and Culture, and petitioned against the Frank Hardy libel charge, but generally he kept a low profile, juggling his studies at the university and work at the gallery consuming most of his spare time. At weekends he began to spend more time with the children, taking them to the gallery, or picnics and long walks through the botanical gardens, swimming and playing cricket, or camping in national parks. When he did take time off with the family he could be playful, silly and affectionate, but in all these activities Bernard instructed his children as a teacher might. He taught them the art of survival—how to make a camp fire, how to boil a billy, navigate by the star map of the south—and Kate would teach them to identify flora; the rules of the game were important and everything had a reason and an explanation.

When Clem Christesen invited Bernard onto the editorial board of the literary journal *Meanjin* he was pleased, but Christesen was notoriously sensitive and depressive in equal measure about the journal's survival and Bernard's association was at times tested. Alan McCulloch had taken over the 'Art Pages' and when he challenged Bernard's meaning of 'expressionism' in an article he had written on Dobell and Drysdale, Bernard, who was intolerant of anyone 'tinkering' with his critical judgement and authorial autonomy, sent him an uncharacteristically aggressive letter:

You will appreciate that words such as expressionism, impressionism, classicism, mannerism etc. are not strictly matters of fact but matters of critical opinion. The difficulty is that they masquerade as facts. So the position simply is that we differ in opinion concerning Dobell and Drysdale's art, and probably, in what we mean by expressionism . . . If you intend to edit critical opinion the art section will degenerate into a vehicle for your own ideas . . .

Pardon my frankness, but I have studied expressionism too, and think about words carefully before I use them. So may I make a suggestion. Publish my talk as it stands. Then follow up in your next issue with a criticism of my use of expressionism. Hit me as hard as you like, I enjoy it. Then let me reply later. Then you can have your last little editorial reply and we'll call it a day! Remember *Meanjin* should be a forum. Keep it that way and you will keep an audience. In criticism there is no last word about anything, not even in defining of expressionism. I am sure we can be excellent friends really if you don't attempt to turn matters of opinion into matters of fact.[11]

This not only demonstrated Bernard's feisty, critical attributes, but also typified his need of a kicking boy when things were not going well, in this case, reflecting the anxiety about his precarious position at the gallery. While McCulloch may have been lacking in historical knowledge, Bernard warned Christesen 'Watch his prose, watch his prose.'

For much of 1952, still seconded to the AGNSW, Bernard worked on the catalogue of oil paintings while finishing his arts degree. If his career were on hold, in October it looked close to disintegrating when the Department of Education wrote that he was to take up general teaching duties the following year. That meant returning to a primary or secondary school, possibly in a regional centre, and after all he had recently achieved he considered that preposterous. In desperation, he began searching for a lifeline, writing to the director of Tutorial Classes at the University of Sydney, contacting Sam Ure Smith, now the head of his late father's publishing company about re-issuing a second edition of *Place, Taste and Tradition* or publishing a new history of Australian art and architecture. A letter from Noel Counihan, still in London and preparing for his return to Melbourne, did little to lift Bernard's mood. Worried about Australia's postwar economy and the 'foreboding' inflationary prices 'in the era of Ming the Merciless' Counihan wondered just 'where do mere artists fit in to all this?'[12] Bernard also wondered where he fitted in. A reprieve came when his secondment to the gallery was renewed, but only until the end of June.

Bernard had first met Joseph Burke in late December 1946 when the English art historian arrived in Sydney from the USA *en route* to take up the *Herald* Chair of Fine Arts at the University of Melbourne. Sydney Ure Smith had sent Burke to the AGNSW to meet Bernard, who took him on a tour of the collection. Apologising for the superfluity of mid-nineteenth- and early twentieth-century British Academy pictures and the conservative Australian section that lacked good modernist paintings, Burke replied, 'Oh please don't worry about that. I am an art historian . . . I take the bad ones with the good ones'; a useful line he had picked up from the Warburg scholars in London during the 1930s and that he often used when visiting Australian provincial cities and art galleries.

It is most probable that the two men discussed the present 'degenerated standards' of cultural institutions, as Bernard's article 'The Art Museum Today' had recently been published in *Meanjin*. Impressed with the education officer, Burke may have seen Bernard as potentially useful to his civilising plans, later claiming that 'In spite of his youth Smith is . . . a man of quite exceptional ability.'[13] They kept in contact and within a year Burke had provided a reference for Bernard's application for a British Council scholarship and letters of introduction to some of Britain's most important scholars, artists and museum people. In 1953, however, their correspondence took a serious turn when Bernard wrote to Burke:

Despite my work abroad I have absolutely no formal recognition at all from the Education Department of N.S.W. . . . I have served the Gallery . . . for nearly ten years without any kind of real promotion . . . Unless I am prepared to allow the present unsatisfactory position to continue indefinitely I must seek an appointment in a Teachers College next year as an art lecturer. This may possibly mean some years in a country college—which from a research point of view are years largely wasted. The main trouble is that the consideration of art in a humane, scholarly and objective sort of way is non-existent in Sydney—with the notable exception of Trendall's work.

He added:

> You will appreciate, therefore, that I frequently find things here in Sydney extremely frustrating. There is so much that could be done to improve the situation, but I am not in a position to make my opinions carry weight.[14]

Bernard's plea for intellectual asylum came just as Burke's small Department of Fine Arts had reached breaking point. The need for another full-time staff member was a matter of urgency and Smith, it was felt, could bridge the histories of European and Australian art, as well as introduce Australian art history as an academic subject. Burke and his colleagues Franz Philipp and Ursula Hoff had all read Bernard's article 'European Vision and the South Pacific' in the *Journal of the Warburg and Courtauld Institutes*, and felt his scholarship was sound. More importantly, there were few, if any, qualified art historians in Australia who could match their high scholarly standards as well as Bernard. Though he was the obvious choice, Burke warned the path ahead would not be strewn with roses:

> I greatly appreciate your taking me into your confidence about your personal position. If there is any chance of securing your services in my department I should be prepared to move heaven and earth at this end. Philipp is as keen as I am about the idea. My main difficulty at the moment is that . . . there is an atmosphere of financial stringency .[15]

The last detail was to prove a factor in Bernard devising the *Antipodeans* exhibition in 1959, a plan aimed at highlighting the importance of contemporary Australian art and communicating its role within society, as well as popularising Fine Arts at the university.

The conferring of his degree from the University of Sydney in April opened up the next phase of Bernard's career and he applied for a research scholarship in the School of Pacific Studies at the Australian National University (ANU). His proposed thesis topic was 'a study . . . assess[ing] the Pacific "contribution" to Primitivism in European art' and extending to Australian colonial art from 1788 to 1851. On his 37th birthday Bernard wrote to his mother that things were finally brightening up. His application for the scholarship had been successful; he had delivered lectures at the University of Melbourne's Fine Arts Department and the NGV; and Joseph Burke was anxious for him to join his department on a part-time basis, to be made permanent when he had completed his doctorate.

Age of the mandarins

The capital of Australia is a sort of permanent gesture,
Scratched on the earth with a large compass.
Bernard Smith[16]

The eminent geographer Oskar Spate, appointed to the School of Pacific Studies at the ANU in 1951, described the campus as a 'collection of weatherboard and tin roofs surrounded by rickety decking' where 'physicists and historians, lawyers and geographers (one of each) were all packed into the little tearoom of the Old Hospital Building'.[17] Coming from the London School of Economics to a raw country town with a population of 27,000 had been a culture shock for Spate; 'Bottled milk, which had been promised in 1938 for 1939 didn't arrive until 1954, so one had to put the billy out.' But the community had 'an unsophisticated gaiety' and the university, established primarily as a research centre for postgraduate training, was keen to 'lure back to Australia sons and one or two daughters who had attained academic eminence overseas'.[18] J. W. Davidson, who in 1949 had induced Bernard to catalogue the art of Cook's voyages, was also at the School of Pacific Studies and believed Bernard's intellectual tenacity and ambitious nature was exactly the sort of recruiting stock the ANU was looking for; it had been on his suggestion that Bernard apply for the research scholarship. As a new door opened Bernard could leave the agonies of the AGNSW and the Department of Education behind, the trustee E. G. Waterhouse attesting to the difficult times he had experienced:

I know that often you must have felt insecure from year to year, not knowing whether you would be transferred elsewhere by the Department. But now with your work and experience in Canberra I feel sure you will be able to establish yourself and lay claim to something better.[19]

Certainly, the exciting development gave Bernard a much-needed boost of confidence.

In 1954 Bernard's workload increased. Part of his arrangement with the University of Melbourne was that he spend two fortnightly blocks a year teaching at the university. Philipp proposed his lecture program: 'What we had in mind was something like "A contemporary evaluation of Classical Art" . . . [or] as a former Trendall student . . . a stronger focus on Late Antiquity, eg. Roman illusionism and archaising-orientalising tendencies or . . . the Cretan-Minoan and archaic phases.'[20] There was no indication of Australian art, though Burke had claimed on numerous occasions that 'It will be Smith's main task to encourage and train young Australians to do research in the art history of their own country.'[21] On top of his already compressed postgraduate studies, Bernard had batches of essays to mark and, if he were to strengthen his chances of starting with a senior lectureship in 1956, Burke suggested he organise a UNESCO conference at the Women's College in Melbourne in June. His participation in the Paris UNESCO meeting in 1949 left him with little option but to accept the additional responsibility. By late May Bernard was formally offered a lecturership in Fine Arts, effective from April 1954, but with leave of absence until January 1956. In the meantime he received a salary of £200 per annum as a part-time lecturer.

With only a few months to organise the UNESCO seminar to stimulate discussion about the role of art education and the community, Bernard pitched his aim bluntly:

Secondary school education in Australia was probably the most backward in the world . . . because our educational system did not separate intellect from sensibility, it tended to produce 'Philistines'.

Not surprisingly all the speakers were male. They included Joseph Burke, Desiderius Orban, Ludwig Hirschfeld-Mack, Daryl Lindsay, Hal Missingham, John Dabron, John A. Campbell, Gordon Thomson, Colin Badger and the University of Melbourne's Professor of Psychology O. A. Oeser. The absence of women educators as guest speakers was symptomatic of the male-dominated professionalism of postwar Australia, but Bernard had the grace to acknowledge May Marsden and Frances Derham in his introduction to the conference's published proceedings, writing that as 'teachers [they] had been courageous and indefatigable pioneers of creative education in New South Wales and Victoria'.

With the conference finished, Bernard shifted his attention to his thesis and Australia's colonial phase. His supervisor, J. W. Davidson, left him largely to himself, primarily because Bernard was capable of setting his own pace and direction, but Davidson did introduce him to the term 'multicultural'. That provided an integral conceptual device in Bernard's thinking about colonial cultural traffic or, as he put it, 'melancholy flows from the migrant nostalgia'.[22]

In his 1952 English BA Honours thesis titled 'The Interpretation of Nature During the Nineteenth Century', Bernard had looked at antipodal contrariety and how melancholic perceptions of the Australian landscape by new settlers had established a visual process aimed to inspire or to induce a sense of hope; 'Hope was the great mover that kept men active and free of despair.' From that visual and emotional shift emerged a response to the realities of the continent—what Bernard termed 'Ideographic Prophecy'—and it formed the conceptual basis for interpreting a new language of vision:

For Australian nature was not merely something to be seen, but something to be revealed, something hidden from vulgar eyes and still unknown. The mystery of the bush could inspire not only fear but also hope . . . and the hopeful and melancholic conventions fused into a complex unity capable of reflecting the finest shades of experience and emotion. They are therefore landmarks in the emotional maturity . . . and . . . Australian identity.[23]

Traditional Australian art was an aesthetic that possessed specific characteristics. The country's Indigenous inhabitants had a unique culture and artistic heritage that had remained intact well after European settlement, but it was a race in transition and in translation, one that had been dramatically reduced by disease, neglect and brutal attrition. Together with the continent's strange vegetation, fauna and geographic oddities, exploration of Australia was contiguous to the emergence of evolutionary thought. Similarly, colonial art was parenthesised by an interest in the pastoral as well as tourism or 'the prospective migrant', and was therefore not Australian art, but rather European art made in Australia, 'a kind of brand name', as Bernard put it. Such artists as John Glover, Augustus Earle, Conrad Martens or Eugene von Guérard entered the canon of Australian art once their work constituted an Australian tradition, but essentially they were 'the messengers who transplanted the styles and institutions based upon the European art systems as they knew them'.[24]

Bernard's postgraduate thesis 'European Vision and the South Pacific' was a sophisticated pioneering study on imperial colonisation and cultural convergence between a dominant power and the peripheral cultures of the Pacific region. It showcased his formidable grasp of historical material and the interdisciplinary methods he had consolidated at the Warburg Institute. Formed around the double dialogues of art and science, its structure and narrative interweaved between historical events, ideas and images, and was a major evaluation of recovered criticism, literature, empirical observation, visual perception and Enlightenment values. It was also an exceptional work on territorialism, possession and ownership as seen through the dramatic acquisition of the exotic as a potential commodity. Put together, these constructed a new optic into the eighteenth and nineteenth centuries and established parameters for a concept of identity that was both antipodean and European. As Peter Beilharz says of Bernard's work, 'The logic of discovery, or seeing afresh is . . . one of disruption as well as of confirmation.'[25] As Bernard scrutinised the imperial gaze and the textural and pictorial evidence provided by people of taste and science, or artists both trained and untrained, he showed how the European imagination, as it came in contact with the unknown world of the exotic, affected the future of *Terra Australis Incognita*, and how the colonial diaspora gradually transformed the exile into the pioneer. The complexity and composite vision of the thesis, in which a phenomenal range of material was held mostly in dynamic tension, was a watershed in the study of geopolitical imperialism and the Pacific, and is why many contemporary historians recognise this as Bernard's magnum opus. Not only does he predate Edward Said's highly acclaimed *Orientalism* (1978) by a decade, but Said acknowledges Bernard's *European Vision and the South Pacific* in his *Culture and Imperialism* (1993) as 'perhaps the most extended analys[i]s of the practice available'; it also is why Ihab Hassan saluted him as the 'global antipodean'.[26]

In April Bernard's family joined him in Canberra and they moved into one of the Forrest Flats that the university had provided. With his study, academic demands and professional networking consuming most of his time, the children saw little of him, except at mealtimes. One evening his son, John, remarked about his absence, to which Bernard snapped 'Who needs a father.'[27] This cruel reaction was not so much about being absent, but rather revealed a deep emotional scar about his own fatherless childhood. The greater the pressure he was under, the more volatile and more difficult Bernard became, and while he usually apologised for such outbursts, parenting often took the brunt of his frustrations.[28] For Betsy and John it was often a lesson in hard love.

Fortunately Canberra was a close-knit community and their neighbour and Bernard's fellow student Russel Ward often took the children on outings. J. W. Davidson, Bernard's supervisor, also occasionally drove the family to the Murrumbidgee River on weekends for a swim, and Betsy and John could stroll just along the road to play with Dymphna and Manning Clark's children at their newly built modernist house designed by the architect Robin Boyd. Kate alleviated her isolation by teaching Latin and French at the Canberra Grammar School, but there was very little else to do in what was a small city for mandarins, politicians, diplomats, militia and a handful of scholars.

As Bernard's academic career developed, egotism, the brash mask of 'self value' was scaled upwards, perhaps in part to meet the small corpus of Canberra's intellectual elite or to prepare himself psychologically for Melbourne's cultural elite. That precocity to justify his intellectual credentials was partly well deserved—his book *Place, Taste and Tradition* was being widely used in Victorian schools and universities. The historian Manning Clark had been instructing history students to read it since 1948, and in addition Bernard's article on Samuel Coleridge and the astronomer William Wales had also been accepted by the Warburg journal committee for publication. The digression into literary criticism, based upon his discovery of Wales' journal in the Mitchell Library, was greeted by a small group of scholars as a stimulating piece that 'threw new light' on the genesis of Coleridge's famous poem *The Rime of the Ancient Mariner*. Much to Bernard's annoyance it never received the attention he felt it deserved, though he considered it one of his most original pieces of research. The lack of recognition by northern critics of anything emanating from the south was Bernard's albatross.

William Wales had accompanied James Cook on his first voyage of exploration in 1767, after which he taught mathematics at Christ's Hospital School in London where Coleridge was a pupil. Bernard's conjecture that Wales had influenced his young student with his dramatic sea-voyaging stories was, in Bernard's view, a clear 'transmission process', and there are distinct similarities between Wales' journal and Coleridge's poem. The English poet and critic Edmund Blunden also considered this a distinct possibility: 'I sometimes wonder whether, germinally, the Ancient Mariner is not one of his Christ's Hospital poems.'[29] But Bernard's old supervisor Charles Mitchell had been more critical:

I'm disposed to like this essay because I respect the writer and admire his attention to detail. On the other hand I'm always a bit worried by his tendency to try to fit his hunches into a Procrustean bed of proof . . . In any case, I think the argumentative approach should be toned down. Hammering away at unclenched possibilities makes a less positive impression than juxtaposition of Wales' argument with Coleridge's. I suspect the value of the essay is that it deepens our awareness, because it sharpens the context of Coleridge's interest in sea voyages. All the world had Hawkesworth and Byron and Shelvoke: Coleridge had personal contact with Wales. The mere parallel is suggestive.

Mitchell then captured the crux of Bernard's character:

> PS. It also . . . fails to note the way Coleridge lifts the whole thing
> from the level of marine curiosity to that of mental experience. But
> that's not in Smith's line. He's a facts man.[30]

Bernard's obsession for factual proof may have characterised his research as historiographically reliable, but his article convincingly testifies to his extensive knowledge of the conditions of Cook's voyage as well as significant literary criticism. Not only did he illuminate the relationship between the 'youthful Coleridge', and the 'old mariner home from the seas . . . [as] a most likely person to fertilize the young poet's mind with a remarkable repertoire of images drawn from the sea and sky', but he beautifully encapsulates his interdisciplinary approach; 'All who have felt the haunting and dreamlike power of the poem know well enough that the *Ancient Mariner* is not a room to be entered by means of one key.'[31] Aside from Mitchell's report, Gertrud Bing wrote saying; 'We are all glad to hear that you are continuing the studies which you began with such great success at this Institute.'[32]

The art historian Erwin Panofsky believed that 'The humanities are not faced by the task of arresting what would otherwise slip away, but enlivening what would otherwise remain dead.'[33] When J. A. La Nauze, R. M. Crawford and Kathleen Fitzpatrick nominated Bernard as an inaugural member of the newly established Australian Humanities Research Council in 1956, Bernard joined the ranks of Australia's intellectual elite.[34] Though his publication record was slight in comparison to many of the other members, such as Archibald Grenfell Price, John Passmore or T. G. H. Strehlow, his recently completed dissertation, regarded as brilliant, legitimated him as Australia's foremost art historian. Importantly, the membership gave him access to some of Canberra's most powerful policymakers, such as H. C. Coombs and Harold White, at a time when economic thought, cultural management and bureaucratic professionalism extended well beyond departmental boundaries.

The concrete grid of Melbourne

From Sydney's 'pluralist pessimism' and 'modernist shiftings', via Canberra's close scholarly community, Bernard arrived in 'the concrete grid of Melbourne'[35] at the beginning of 1956. The city was in the grip of Olympic fever and the fanfare of internationalism and a new national cultural vision was being vigorously debated. The *Herald* announced Bernard's arrival: 'Australian Art expert for our University—A leading authority on the history of Australian art has been appointed . . . Professor Burke said Mr Smith was the "finest capture" the University could make to direct studies in Australian art.'[36] A letter from Bob Gollan suggests:

> Your influence will be good because you have those things rarely found in combination in academic circles—great ability, interest-ing and a deep sense of responsibility towards what you believe to be worthwhile values in art.[37]

But Bernard was astute enough to realise that it was better to tread cautiously in Melbourne's cultural and academic circles, especially during the Cold War.

According to Peter Bellew, Melbourne was a closed city 'in every way, not only in the art world'.[38] Socially and morally its character remained as firmly fixed as it had always been. Manning Clark summed it up as a mixture of patriarchal conservatism, elitist capitalism and cultural chauvinism, but it also possessed a humanism based on neoclassical and European standards, evident in its intellectual tradition as well as its grand Victorian buildings and institutions. Sir Kenneth Clark was more critical on his visit in 1949, 'Compared to Sydney, Melbourne is rather staid and conventional . . . It has one fine street, a magnificent botanical garden, and some attractive nineteenth-century ironwork.'[39] The city's affluence and stern qualities are captured by the poet Chris Wallace-Crabbe:

> From Scottish rigour/And Victorian gold/They built an icon,/
> Something solid/You could touch and hold,/While at the angles/
> Of spacious/Dove-grey city/They would stand/Honing razor of/
> A radical mistrust,/A cutting-edge of reason/Something to have

in hand,/Something to show/That in the balmiest season/A conscience of cold steel/Endured below[40]

Comprising a mixture of liberal Protestants, right-wing Catholics and cultural and political cosmopolitans of the far and middle left, Melbourne's artists and intellectuals used its paradoxical spirit as grist for their creative and polemical mills. But it was also a city that was quick to expel unsuitable intruders or wayward sons. The eccentric prankster Barry Humphries, who vented his comic spleen and subversive public performances indiscriminately on conservative Melburnians, had left for the more fluid cultural world of Sydney by 1958. Brian Fitzpatrick also suffered at the hands of Melbourne's intellectual and political conservatives, and the new director of the NGV, the urbane modernist Eric Westbrook, was greeted apprehensively by Melbourne's cultural elites. Bernard must have wondered how he would fit in among that new league of men, but having learnt how to deal with some of Sydney's conservative philistines and Canberra's formidable mandarins, he felt reasonably confident he could offset any smug snobbery or political moralising.

Bernard and Kate bought their first house, a run-down, roomy weatherboard on Beach Road, Sandringham, and the family settled into the pleasures of bayside living (fig. 30). If not required at the university he rose early and retreated to his study, breaking briefly for lunch and resuming until 4 pm, whereupon he would take a walk or a swim and let his intellectual labours settle. Kate, who had always nurtured his work ethic, made sure she was home by that hour. If Bernard went to the university to lecture he rarely joined his colleagues after work at the Swanston Family pub, or the more academic watering hole of Jimmy Watson's Wine Bar in Carlton. Instead he preferred the company of his wife or the artists Arthur Boyd, David and Hermia Boyd, John Perceval and Len French at the Red Bluff Hotel in Sandringham. But there were other reasons for staying away from the university; it was a well-known site of ASIO surveillance and for conscripting young spies. Chris Wallace-Crabbe recalls being followed and observed as potential recruit material[41] and, while Bernard had put his communism to bed and was ostensibly apolitical, it was one more reason to keep his distance.

Normally, Bernard never bothered much with men's clubs but he joined the newly established Twenty Club, a group 'of not more than 20 men', formed in 1957 when Vance Palmer, Frank Dalby Davison and Leonard Mann decided they needed a venue for dining and conversation. The group included Hume Dow, Brian Fitzpatrick, Sydney Rubbo, Alan Marshall, Geoffrey Serle, Eric Westbrook, Ian Turner and Cameron Jackson to name a few, and met on a monthly basis to discuss current affairs. In 1959 Bernard chaired the evening's discussion on 'Camp David and the World Tomorrow' and a later topic was on the withdrawal of South Africa from the Commonwealth.[42]

The Twenty Club was a considerably low-key affair compared to the elite gentlemen's club The Society of Collectors, established by Joseph Burke in 1953. It met annually at University House to discuss connoisseurship and patronage and to 'promote the cause of collecting in Australia and specifically to help the University of Melbourne add to its collection'.[43] Bernard not only 'shunned luxury' and 'status symbols', but felt that 'wealth or its pursuit . . . corrupted',[44] but he may also have felt that Burke had a conflict of interest, given he was a member of the NGV's Felton Bequest and the Melbourne Club in which he and Daryl Lindsay were actively establishing an art collection. But few ever questioned Burke's motives; he was to all appearances beyond reproach. When he asked Bernard to collect a pair of silver candelabras from one of the Society of Collectors' homes as an item for discussion, Bernard felt this to be demeaning and refused to be an errand boy. He told Burke 'he was not here at the University to collect valuable artefacts from his friends'.[45] Perhaps it stirred unpleasant childhood memories of the middle-class Mrs Featherstone when he swore he would never again be a 'server' or 'a tool of the ruling class'.

Nor was Bernard a team player. He enjoyed cultivating contacts, but not making close friendships; it was not in his nature, nor was there time. When he did, it usually involved a double motive or was due to a genuine appreciation of his work, and it often occurred with women. Of the few close relationships Bernard developed in Melbourne, his friendship with the art historian and curator Ursula Hoff was the most professionally productive and personally piquant. He had first met her at the NGV in 1945 where, as the only qualified art historian working in a state gallery, she provided a depth of scholarship never before experienced in Australia. Bernard held the highest respect for her, but he also detected in her reserved manner the mark of an exile, a trait he had noted with several of the Sydney refugee art historians. When they met again in England in 1950, a new dimension developed in their friendship. Hoff appeared more confident because her professional profile at the NGV had risen considerably, especially concerning her curatorial influence and her quiet transformation of the gallery's collections—Sir Kenneth Clark, several trustees, including Sir Keith Murdoch and the gallery's director, Daryl Lindsay, ranked her 'with the sibyl of Delphi'—but also because the Warburg and Courtauld scholars thought she was a changed woman and showed a new respect for her.[46]

Hoff had been in London settling family business, but she had also been buying prints and works on paper for the NGV. Having trained during the 1930s in the iconography of high northern European art under the tutelage of Erwin Panofsky and Fritz Saxl in Hamburg, she exemplified the rigorous continental scholarship Bernard was then encountering at the Warburg and Courtauld institutes. Having fled with her parents from Hamburg to England in 1933 after Hitler came to power, she continued her postgraduate studies at the Courtauld Institute while maintaining close connections with the exiled German scholars at the newly relocated Warburg Institute.[47]

Though well connected and familiar with English culture, Hoff was perceived as a German refugee, and that sense of being an eternal foreigner, no matter where she lived, persisted throughout her life. With Bernard it was different; there was an ease being in his company where she did not have to pretend to be someone other than herself. While their backgrounds could not have differed more—Hoff came from a culturally sophisticated and, at one time, very wealthy Jewish family—both shared similar experiences of having to work their way up as art historians through difficult social and economic conditions. Later, a strong intellectual rapport and personal warmth developed between them, where each watched out for the other.

In 1948 Ursula Hoff had been engaged on a part-time basis as one of the inaugural lecturers in Joseph Burke's Department of Fine Arts, and with Bernard's appointment in 1956 they became colleagues. Both were interested in similar art-historical trends, particularly the effect European culture had on Australia, and they often relied on one another for advice and assistance. When Hoff was researching Charles Conder it was Bernard who assisted her with contacts and locating works; he also steered her small monograph on the artist to publication in 1960. Similarly, Hoff read the proofs of two of Bernard's books, his magnum opus *European Vision and the South Pacific* and *Australian Painting* (1962), and arranged reproduction permissions for paintings held in private and public collections. In the small curatorial and art-historical world of Australia during the 1950s and 1960s their collegial friendship was free of intellectual jealousies and, as Bernard said, 'it was an intellectual affair', one that endured—intimately—for 60 years.

Lady Grimwade and Lady Bassett, both friends of Hoff, were other acquaintances of Bernard's. Lady Bassett was a pioneer in women's history and appreciated Bernard's Coleridge article: 'I thoroughly enjoyed the paper, a grand bit of analysis, a sort of through the looking glass into a country unrealised where, thanks to your clues, real people become visible and one can watch them think!' Clarity of expression was characteristic of his writing and his congenial accessibility was appreciated by colleagues, students, peers and the lay reader alike.[48]

Bernard also engaged several women to help him collect material for his large survey project *Australian Painting: 1788–1960*. The arts librarian at the Public Library of Victoria, Joyce McGrath, gave generously of her time and helped him revise his bibliographic notes; she also put him in touch with the art collector Margaret Carnegie whose private collection of post-1950 contemporary Australian art was considered one of the best in Australia. At Bernard's request Carnegie collected catalogues and biographical material on many of the artists she had acquired.[49] But not all women found him agreeable. The sculptor Anita Aarons, who knew Bernard from the Sydney branch of the CAS, thought him a changed man when she attended a lecture by him at the National Gallery Society, writing:

In sorrow (and in anger) I tell you frankly I believe your recent lecture at the gallery, to be a great disservice to art. Parading under 'scholarship' you criticised work in a manner that distressed me and many others. Certainly, in a slow beginning an odd gleam of sincerity and knowledge flashed. It appeared you 'know what you like' but when your appetite was not tempted you eschewed scholarship and settled for clever invective. To invite artists to . . . attend the delivery of your 'arduous' effort and then treat them to two hours of mainly bad taste, was a shocking display of intellectual rudeness . . . One remedy . . . would be for you to face the same audience for a joint survey of good contemporary works. I challenge you .[50]

Bernard's pithy mien, what some called 'pomposity', may have been a response to Melbourne's cultural elitism, though when the impeccable and imposing June Stewart, Joseph Burke's secretary, first met him in 1953 she described him as 'socially inept and unpolished' and wondered how he would fit in. In her view 'Franz [Philipp] had a brilliant teaching vision, Ursula Hoff was a curator' and 'Bernard's vision as a teacher had to be built. While his ego was good, his manner was school-masterish.'[51]

University and the community

The 'depressing conditions and poverty' of the university sector in Australia during the 1950s was, in one academic's view, a result of neglect and 'forlorn politics'.[52] Yet Wallace-Crabbe remembers the University of Melbourne as 'mercifully lacking in managerialism, a wonderful Oxfordian beehive of polymaths in an intellectual parkland'.[53] Both versions were correct, and Bernard's first full year in the department was not especially difficult. He already had several lectures prepared, which he had previously given at the University of Sydney under the title 'The Australian Scene' in 1953. Most were on ancient art—Egyptian, the Orient, Greek, Early Christian and Byzantine—and he took special pleasure lecturing on Palaeolithic cave painting and 'Lascaux: The Beginnings of History'. Proud of having seen 'the double helix of human imagination' and of being a bona fide witness, he could legitimately say that 'knowledge is conditioned by seeing'.[54] It would not be until late 1958, when the Department of Fine Arts was in need of revitalisation, that he began lecturing on Australian art. As Helen Brack has suggested, the 'weak courses ran the risk of being weeded out—they had to have a practical usage and value to the community'.[55]

Raising the importance of art history within the university and the community was part of Joseph Burke's brief as the *Herald* Professor, and when Bernard began in 1956 Burke encouraged him to take on extramural duties. In 1957 he gave 10 lectures on Australian art and architecture for the Centre for Adult Education, and held discussions with the director of the National Gallery of Victoria Eric Westbrook about an Australian dictionary of painters. The university was in 'acute financial crisis' and applying pressure on Burke's department to prove its value meant something more substantial was needed than judging suburban art prizes or opening art exhibitions. According to June Stewart, it had to 'get out and sell itself'.[56] Bernard decided it was time to upgrade and expand *Place, Taste and Tradition*, which he retrospectively admitted was 'a sort of wild oat'. Moreover, his knowledge of colonial settlement had considerably developed since 1944 and he was also in a position to develop a fresher feel for Melbourne's contemporary art scene, having befriended artists through the Melbourne branch of the CAS. Compiling material on the contemporary Sydney scene was made easier with Elwyn Lynn's recent appointment as the secretary of Sydney's CAS and editor of its broadsheet. Lynn sent regular dispatches and updates—'just ask me for any other information you may need'—his letters and articles always a mix of highly attuned art criticism, 'theoretical positioning' and private musings.[57]

Bernard was an excellent teacher and his lectures to the students in fine arts were well received. Ruth Zubans found him extremely approachable; his capacity to communicate ideas in a well-structured way and his analysis of paintings gave her a real understanding of the Australian landscape, and to an immigrant this was especially valued. Quiet and courteous with large, framed glasses, Rosalie Horner found him bookish, quite the contrast to the elegant, patrician Joseph Burke who 'looked as if he had stepped out of a Gainsborough portrait'. (fig. 31)[58] Similarly, Patrick McCaughey found Bernard 'a relaxed figure',[59] particularly compared to the erudite Germanic Franz Philipp or the austere Ursula Hoff, and while Bernard was regarded as a distinguished 'force in Melbourne art', he never quite captivated students to the same extent as Burke or Philipp. Mostly he lectured on the classical or romantic periods, though Lucy Ellem thought his lectures on colonialism, drawn from *European Vision and the South Pacific*, fascinating, but it was his down-to-earth treatment of art from the pyramids to Picasso that she also considered pedagogically reliable.[60] The young historian and anthropologist John Mulvaney found him friendly and helpful when establishing his course on Indigenous pre-history at the university in 1956; Bernard lent him his thesis 'European Vision and the South Pacific', at that time unpublished, which profoundly influenced Mulvaney's own work, as well as shaping his subject.[61]

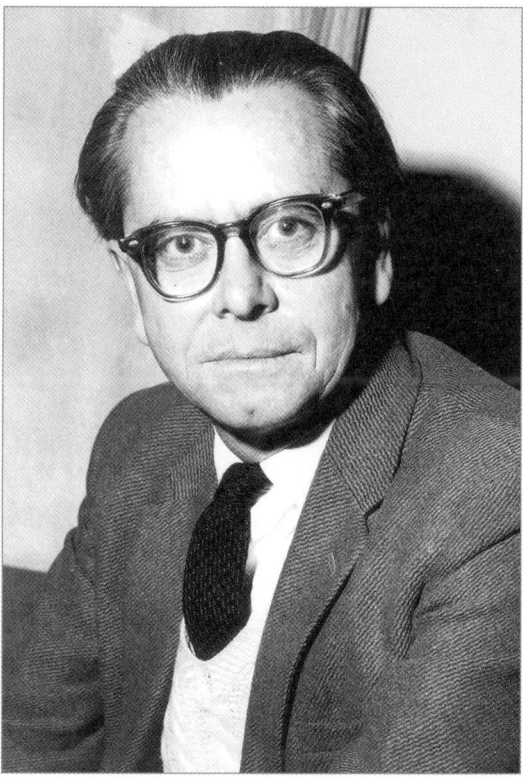

Fig. 31 Bernard Smith, c. 1957

Bernard's brotherhood

In the early 1940s Bernard had recognised the originality of contemporary Australian art, but by the 1950s he wondered whether international perceptions of it had reached any kind of maturity. The answer to that he found depressingly negative. Moreover, there was an increasing danger to the distinctiveness of Australia's art with the incursion of abstraction, which he saw as politically inspired and in ways just as imperial in its assumptions as British sentiment and colonial presumptions. Since returning to Australia in 1951 he had been frustrated by those issues and sought to prevent local art from being fed into the vortex of British prejudice and the prevailing international cultural forces.

For Bernard 1959 was a critical and important year: his thesis 'European Vision and the South Pacific' was accepted for publication; he was busy writing his large survey on Australian art; and early in the year he convened a group of seven artists for whom the image was a vital aesthetic. He had wanted to mount an exhibition showcasing the best of contemporary Australian figurative art with the aim of touring it nationally and internationally for some time, and had raised the issue with Sir Kenneth Clark in 1949. When he attended a lecture by Robin Boyd at the Institute of Architects in 1957, his idea for an exhibition was revived. Boyd's paper was an elegy for Australia's deculturalisation, a lament on the 'featurist' and 'Austerica' banality of urban design and architecture, and Bernard excitedly wrote to Boyd:

> I cannot tell you how much I admired and enjoyed your lecture . . . I am right behind you—but can anything really be done about it? Like yourself I'm not anti-communist, anti-migrant, Jindyworobak-chauvinist, or Communist fellow-sundowner. But I should dearly love to think that one or two of our artists and architects were standing up squarely on their own feet and thinking out their own problems before an Australian and a world audience. Of course the waters of nationalism have always been treacherous ones to fish in—but at least they're deep.

The genesis of 'the Antipodeans' had evolved, as the letter shows:

Can anything be done? . . . What is needed is a small compact group of artists (architects, painters, perhaps a sculptor), about 6 or 7 would be enough with a common purpose . . . one thinks of The Impressionists, de Stijl, The Pre-Raphaelite Brotherhood . . . they did something. Better to make history than write about it. What is needed is a brotherhood of some kind, compact, devoted, with a colourful title . . . The artists I can think of . . . who would qualify for what I have in mind are Sid Nolan, Arthur Boyd, John Brack . . . If some sort of Antipodean Brotherhood did somehow crawl upsidedownedly into existence its birth would have to be veiled in mysteries . . . I can assure you I rarely write letters like this—but this is what you have brought me to . . . Meanwhile my congratulations on your magisterial stand against the . . . hands of Austerica .[62]

Sixteen months later, on a warm February day, David and Hermia Boyd joined Bernard and Kate for afternoon drinks. The discussion revolved around John Perceval, Charles Blackman and Clifton Pugh, who regularly painted together at Pugh's rural property Dunmoochin, and their idea of holding an exhibition that showed a connective spirit of place and subject. It resonated with Bernard's mission of a uniquely Australian show.[63] A meeting was organised with five more artists the following week and the Antipodeans were born.

John Brack, Charles Blackman, Arthur and David Boyd, John Perceval and Clifton Pugh—the Sydney artist Robert Dickerson was also invited—were all 'distinctively Australian, without being self-consciously nationalistic'.[64] And while they rejected Bernard's proposed name 'Antipodean Brotherhood', with its connotations of a guild mentality, they accepted his idea of a manifesto. Art had to communicate as 'a recognisable shape, a meaningful symbol' and as a reflection of society, but the exhibition was also an opportunity to convert artists and audiences away from the 'vacuous geometric patterning' of abstract expressionism. Abstraction reduced paintings to an atomised mix and disregarded historical variables that made up an individualised world, and Bernard was emphatic that Australian artists had to retain their autonomy, their difference. But as he told the Adelaide art dealer Kym Bonython, he was not entirely against abstract art:

> Whilst I like some local abstract and semi-abstract work here . . . Gleghorn for instance—I am quite sure that . . . for the great bulk of it simply cannot compare with the best work of this kind done in England and America—and they are looking for something original from the Antipodes anyway—not pale reflections of the things they are familiar with.[65]

Evaluating the importance of an artist's work was made much easier if there were less derivation of international styles, which reduced the extent of comparison—far better and safer to be unique, was how Bernard saw it.

In his copy of Friedrich Nietzsche's *The Birth of Tragedy* (1872) the following is underlined:

> let us consider abstract man stripped of myth, abstract education, abstract mores, abstract laws, abstract government; the random vagaries of the artistic imagination unchannelled by any native myth; a culture without any fixed and consecrated place of origin . . . Man today, stripped of myth, stands famished among all the pasts and must dig frantically for roots . . . What does our great historical hunger signify . . . our clutching about us of countless other cultures, our consuming desire for knowledge, if not the loss of myth, of a mythic home.[66]

Mythic identity was important, especially to Indigenous Australians and those framed by the Antipodes, but with Australia's cultural identity at risk of the new international abstraction, Bernard decided to refashion the mythic past with the political present, something he had learnt from the poet Yeats. His promotion of antipodeanism could assert a more distinctive aesthetic, and to avoid being tagged nationalistic, the group decided not to use the word Australian, but adopt 'Antipodean'. Europeans, Bernard explained, 'have used [it] in connection with this part of the world ever since the Greeks and there is no reason at all why we should sneer at it . . .

no reason why painters . . . should not be able to find something worth saying both to their community and to the world at large.'[67] The correlation between the antipodean exhibition poster by Blackman (fig. 32) and the weird antipode creatures depicted in the 1493 *Nuremburg Chronicle* (fig. 33) suggests that Bernard may have directed Blackman to look at the medieval book in the public library; as the manifesto states, 'For Europeans this country has always been a primordial and curious land. To the ancients the antipodes was a kind of nether world, to the people of the Middle Ages its forms of life were monstrous, and for us Europeans by heritage (but not by birth) much of this strangeness lingers.'[68]

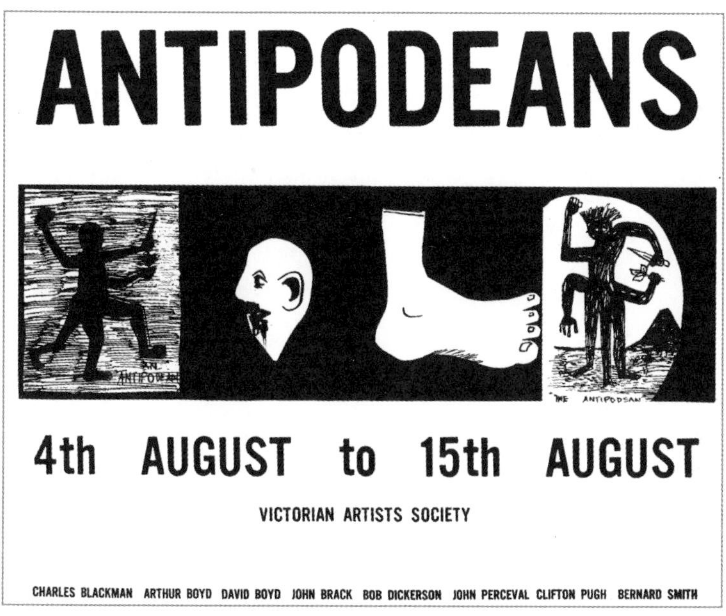

Fig. 32 Charles Blackman, poster for the *Antipodeans* exhibition, 1959

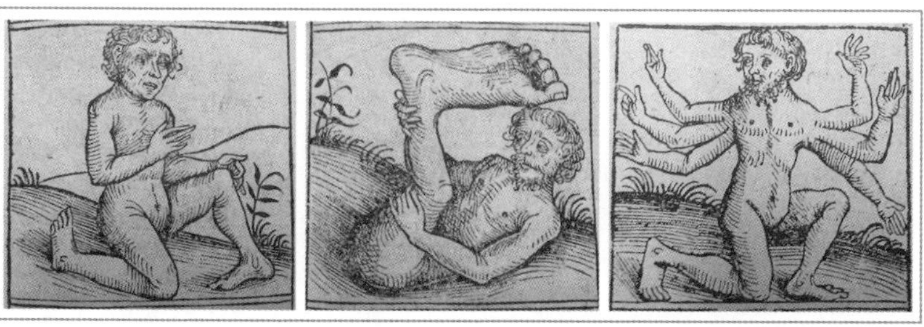

Fig. 33 *Liber Chronicarum* (*Nuremburg Chronicle*), 1493

Peter Beilharz considers that Bernard was neither nativist nor Australianist, but 'pure hybridity' and his nationalism was 'cryptic'.[69] But cultural imperialism, which Bernard qualified as 'a study in inequality', was political and therefore 'what is vital and native to our tradition' needed protection. Australian artists, he said, had to 'battle for survival in the post-war years against powerful and at times overwhelming cosmopolitan tendencies, at times stimulating and vitalising, at times devitalising'.[70]

While the seven artists were unanimous that the exhibition be bound by a figural 'solidarity', they also stressed it had to be 'neutral in art politics'.[71] Noel Counihan, one of the finest figurative artists working in Melbourne, was not invited because of his hard-line communism, and while Bernard had learnt to control his political spirit he managed to coax the artists towards seeing that the new international abstraction was symptomatic of the USA's increasing cultural monopoly. It had been evident at the 1950 Venice Biennale and he also knew that major American exhibitions touring Europe since the beginning of the Cold War had been funded by the CIA and MoMA; but he did not entirely disclose that information to the artists.

Bernard's politicised 'program' brought together the major historical and contemporary themes that had preoccupied him since the 1940s, specifically cultural imperialism and the tensions of the Cold War. By establishing a regionalist style—Bernard preferred calling it 'being oneself [or] standing on one's feet'—in opposition to the largely dominant New York school of international abstraction, Australian art might have a chance of being noticed internationally. 'It is natural that we should see and experience nature differently in some degree from artists of the northern hemisphere,' he wrote.[72]

For the manifesto Bernard asked the artists to write a statement about their aesthetic beliefs. Brack wrote:

The older I get, the more difficult it seems to set out a statement of artistic belief. In 1945 when I was . . . begin[ning], the direction that ought to be taken seemed quite clear. The road represented by abstraction was unattractive, because to me it signified a withdrawal from life, whereas I considered what was needed was an immersion.

He continued:

I want to ask questions. The poets have asked questions, and I think the painters may too, in their own language . . . So it seemed that the image had to be restored. Picasso asked questions of course, but I wanted mine to be more direct, more lucid . . . at no time did I think in terms of a national style. Those who influenced me were not Streeton or George Bell, but the Flemish Primitives, George De La Tour, Seurat, Sickert and later on Buffet. Yet always I felt the necessity to paint the life I saw and knew. The Australian flavour was, and is, enough to come as a by-product from this activity.[73]

Brack distilled his thoughts into something less personal for the manifesto; 'We take cognisance of all that has happened in art during the last fifty years—not to do so would be folly.' David Boyd stressed that the artist is a moralist; Pugh was more interested with people's fate in an unstable world, writing 'the very powers that threaten us can also bear us to new heights'. The Blackmans wanted affirmation, not refutation, while Perceval asked Tim Burstall to formulate the following statement for him:

We . . . believe modern art has taken a wrong turning . . . now the Tachists say 'We paint paint' . . . But whatever the causes, tachist, action painters, abstract expressionists and their followers dom- inate the scene in New York, London, San Francisco, Paris and Sydney . . . We believe that painting is a humanist art. It deals with man and nature using as its language the recognisable image .[74]

Bernard's contribution was unmistakable:

Art is willed. No matter how much the artist may draw upon the instinctive and unconscious levels of his experience . . . a work of art is a purposive act . . . Take the great black bull of Lascaux, for example, an old beast and a powerful one, who has watched over the birth of many arts and many mythologies . . . Destroy the living power of the image and you have humbled and humiliated the artist, have made him a blind and powerless Samson fit only to grind the corn of the Philistines.[75]

After a lot of fratricidal arguing it was left to Bernard to shuffle the artists' statements into the *Antipodean Manifesto*, which under his imprimatur fell well short of any political neutrality. At the time its reception was more mocked than taken seriously: 'The age of manifestos had largely by-passed Australia. Are the Antipodeans trying to catch up?' wrote Franz Philipp.[76] Retrospectively, Bernard explained that the *Antipodeans* exhibition was 'not at bottom an attack on abstract art; it [wa]s an attack on the policy of the State Department of the USA to use abstract art as a political instrument in opposition to the Soviet Union's use of socialist realism as a political instrument.'[77] In other words Bernard had misused the Antipodeans for his own political purpose, all the while maintaining 'we still have to interrogate images for their validity and intention'. David Boyd later qualified this by saying that 'Smith was a politician of the arts . . . [who] had another agenda which he did not lay on our table at the time.'[78]

Despite the *Antipodeans* exhibition's success—it drew a large crowd of 700 on opening night at the Victorian Artists Society and more than 2000 visitors in two weeks—the event became one of the most divisive moments in the history of modern Australian art. While it consolidated the artists' rising reputations, it created rivalry between the 'abs' and the 'figs' and reignited antagonism between Melbourne and Sydney artists, with John Reed claiming 'Nearly all Sydney painting is mere playing with paint.'[79] Georges Mora, the president of Melbourne's CAS, and a respected cultural mediator, believed the 'cult of the informal' was a 'symbol of a new spirit and a great ally in the fight for freedom from anguish and fear'.[80]

Inevitably Bernard bore the brunt of the criticism and David Boyd was made the scapegoat. By derailing abstraction and tying figurative art to the tracks and holding it ransom, many thought Bernard's attempt was damaging the very cause he was fighting for. Sali Herman thought the Boyds' and Perceval's paintings were 'over-rated', 'crude, bad in drawing and concocted in ideas' and told Bernard 'it seems to me you are already a subjective-Melbournian', warning him to 'just beware for your own and the sake of art.'[81] Helen Brack objected to the hegemony of the group and the 'genius' factor that positioned one artist above another or, more specifically, one group above all others.[82] Barbara Blackman, however, considered it 'an irrefutable landmark in Australian art':

> Where tradition is wanting, certain prejudices and preconceptions may also be lacking. The Antipodeans made their gesture from necessity and out of direct experience and so have helped to shape the present particular contours of our art, a distinctive and virile growth alongside the modern art of other countries.[83]

Though a critical and respected voice in the contemporary art world, Bernard had upset Melbourne's restrained art community, and by positioning himself at the political and cultural barricades risked the very expulsion he had initially sensed on his arrival in 1956. Shortly after the exhibition at a dinner speech to the Fellowship of Australian Writers in September 1959 he told the guests:

> We are taking up a position in opposition to the extreme forms of abstract art . . . What we are opposing is not so much abstract art in itself but the overweening arrogance of its champions who maintain that it is the only form of contemporary art, that it is a new pictorial language, and that there is no longer any need to draw upon the art of the past. It is avant gardism run mad with all the intolerances that is associated with it.[84]

A number of the guests also tore into him about his 'Fellowship of the Antipodeans'. Afterwards Stephen Murray-Smith wrote expressing his admiration at how he had held his ground with 'effective argument' and his 'serenity and urbanity under heavy fire . . . A very good show—though you might have been warned!'[85]

Undeterred by the opposition, or perhaps emboldened by it, Bernard forged ahead with the proposed London exhibition and invited Jon

Molvig, Fred Williams, Sidney Nolan and Albert Tucker to join the Antipodeans. He had not seen Tucker for many years; 'A good deal of water has passed under Princes Bridge and the Ponte Vecchio since James Gleeson, yourself and myself sought to explain the mysteries of surrealism to some odd Sydney culture gatherers at 166 Phillip Street. And then I missed you in Paris in 1948'.[86] But neither Nolan, Tucker nor the other artists were interested in Bernard's plan and Brack dismissed himself from the group as soon as the *Antipodeans* exhibition finished.

Bernard would never have said he failed; on the contrary he believed everything he did, wrote and said was a responsible act, aimed at opening up the dialogue about art and cultural matters. Later he wrote, 'Melbourne resists change, but when change does take place there is considerable disputation associated with it.'[87] The *Antipodeans* and their polemical document was as historically significant as that argued by Conder, Roberts and Streeton during their *9 x 5 Impressions Exhibition* in 1889, or the Angry Penguins of the 1940s and the Ern Malley hoax of 1952.[88] Originality and individuality had proclaimed itself within its own locality and globally, not as a measure of exclusivity, but as a protest against the cultural authorities emanating from metropolitan centres. Bernard also claimed that the 'clamour' surrounding the Antipodeans, especially about Fred Williams' exclusion from the group, ultimately benefited Williams' art, suggesting that it had 'opened out a space between abstraction and figuration that he [Fred] was able to explore in his own way'.[89]

Shortly after the group's formation in early 1959, and convinced that Australian art was ready to take on the British art world, Bernard had written to Sir Kenneth Clark. He wrote again in August and September, but received no replies. Clark had deferred to Bryan Robertson, the debonair director of the Whitechapel Gallery and one of Clark's protégés who was working on his 'New Generation' series. Taking the best of young artists in the USA and Britain, he had his own agenda for Australia's contemporary artists. His exhibitions at the Whitechapel Gallery between 1952 and 1969 attest to his ambitious curatorial program. In 1956 he mounted *This is Tomorrow*, which included some of America's most avant-garde artists and the iconic Richard Hamilton collage *Just what is it that makes today's homes so different, so appealing* (1956), an image that flagged the new-age comforts of American consumerism. In 1957 he put on a Sidney Nolan exhibition followed by a Jackson Pollock retrospective; a Roy De Maistre exhibition in 1960; and Mark Rothko's retrospective followed Robertson's *Recent Australian Painting* exhibition in 1961.

In late 1959 Ursula Hoff was in London and wrote to Bernard after hearing about Robertson's proposed visit to Australia to select paintings for a large Australian exhibition in which he 'hop[ed] the Antipodeans would be willing to contribute'. Bernard replied:

The information you gave me concerning Whitechapel . . . makes things somewhat difficult, doesn't it? . . . But then, who are the sponsors? A private patron or our gallery directors? My request may have placed him in a dilemma. I think that small shows, say an exhibition of abstract painting, and a separate exhibition of figurative painting from Australia would do much more to make Australian art known in London than a big national show in which I think bad money would drive out the good. It will be most interesting if you can find out anything more about the situation from Sir Kenneth Clark when he comes back.[90]

He wrote again to Clark; 'This cuts across our original plans in a rather unfortunate way', but then, modifying his tone, he continued, 'I am sure the group', referring to the Antipodeans, 'will be delighted to assist a general Australian show in any way possible. At the same time, we are keen to present our work, not so much as the work of an Australian group, but as a group with a specific point of view outlined in the Manifesto.'[91] Audaciously, he suggested that the Antipodeans could hold an exhibition at some other gallery before Robertson's show. There was silence. Robertson had stolen Bernard's thunder and marginalised him. What Bernard did not know was that Robertson's Whitechapel exhibition had taken root as early as 1957 when the Australian art writer John Henshaw raised the idea with Hal Missingham who, in turn, raised it with Bryan Robertson in early 1958, well before Bernard and the Antipodeans had come together.[92]

The myth of isolation

There is of course some core truth at the heart of any myth.
Bernard Smith[93]

When Bernard first proposed presenting contemporary Australian art to Sir Kenneth Clark in 1949 he had been dissuaded; his second attempt in 1959 fell on barren ground, Bryan Robertson later dismissing his *Antipodeans* exhibition as there was not 'room for two shows at the same time' (fig. 34). But there was more to it than overcrowding; as Robertson later said, 'Bernard was too narrow and self-conscious [in his] selection of art . . . a tough vantage point [that] ruled out anything that contradicted it.'[94] Moreover, Australian artists saw Robertson as an exciting alternative to Bernard's restrictive aesthetics, which had the potential to alienate them as artists. Robertson also looked to the USA 'where . . . informed taste [was] more energetic and *in the present*'.[95] The final insult for Bernard came when Robertson appointed 22-year-old Sydney architecture undergraduate Robert Hughes as the catalogue essayist (fig. 35).

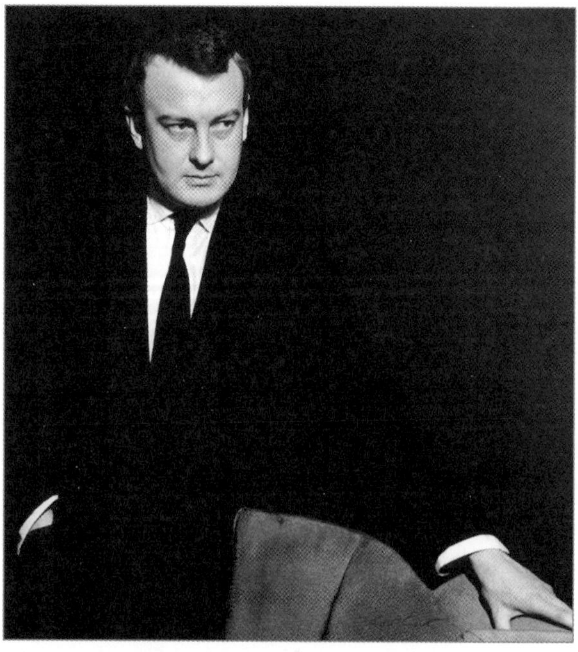

Fig. 34 Bryan Robertson, 1958

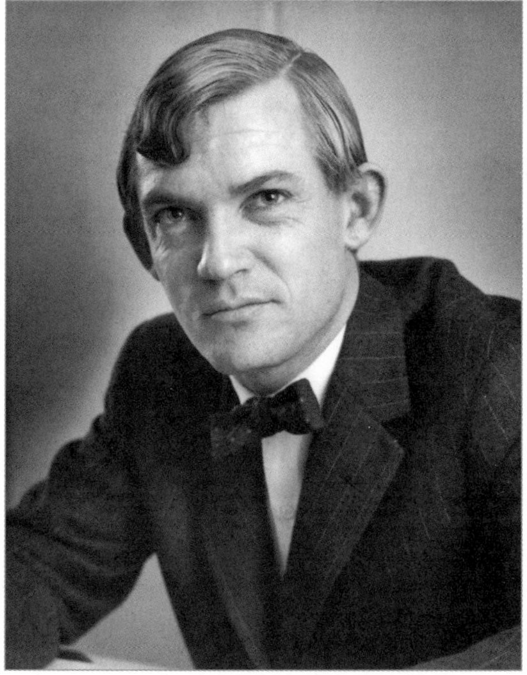

Fig. 35 Robert Hughes, 1963

In a letter to Hal Missingham, Robertson conveyed his excitement at the phenomenal success of his *Recent Australian Painting* exhibition: 'the Gallery is very crowded from morning till night . . . the presentation is impeccable . . . [and] it makes a great spectacle. We have got enormous tropical plants and trees in the Gallery, some of them Australian, and the place blazes with light and colour.'[96] Further, the Tate Gallery had acquired a triptych by Godfrey Miller and a large abstract painting by Brett Whiteley; Allen Lane of Penguin bought a Leonard French work; and Clifton Pugh's *Self Portrait* (1960) had been acquired by Magdalen College in Oxford. Robertson also told Missingham 'A formidable list of one-man shows is now lined up . . . Dickerson, Olsen, Hessing, Pugh, Blackman, Whiteley'. Enlivened by royal visitors and celebrities, and Australia's enfant terrible, the golden-haired 'Shirley Temple of modern art' Brett Whiteley, the exhibition was unequivocally a brilliant success.[97]

In the introductory essays by Sir Kenneth Clark and Robertson, Australian culture is described as having been moulded by its isolation and by being a major food bowl producer in which the 'redundant poor' had been replaced by 'sun bronzed sheep farmers'. While things were changing, Robertson wrote, and modernism had gradually induced a 'fresh cultural identity', Australians on the whole were still a conservative, anti-authoritarian, often rowdy, unruly mob of folk from a 'mildly dull kind of suburbia', who kept their women in the background. The spinning of the myth was simply too irresistible, but it was the country's vast landscapes and immense distances, he said, that created a sense of real isolation:

> A friction in the air itself finds expression in the edge and bite which underlies [its] art. A fierce, tough, often rather slangy imagery is invariably described in the most tender and loving manner . . . [but] the imagery itself, cut off from our European environment, is highly inventive and has one unifying factor: an unremitting sense of the drama of the isolated moment.[98]

Robertson was not going to let Bernard off either; having obviously read *Place, Taste and Tradition*, and probably *European Vision and the South Pacific*, he claimed 'A nation based on an idea rather than on blood needs some transcendent image to reveal itself' and, more pertinently:

> Power politics have made nationalism a dirty word . . . Australian artists . . . are at once passionately interested in *what is* Australian art and highly suspicious of the answer. At the same time, these problems do not concern the painters as much as critics and interpreters for who the painters feel mostly a proper and essential distrust.[99]

Hughes also attacked Bernard, writing, 'some things I am told, can only be seen clearly from a considerable distance' and 'exoticism depends on where you stand'. With his superb cast of phrase, Hughes continued, 'The first convict settlement was made here [Australia] in 1788. In the next few years, a cultural transplantation took place. But though you can ship works of art, you cannot put a climate of thought in a crate'.[100] As he proceeded to decipher the past, uproot its traditions and uncover

Bernard's political mask, referring to him as a 'critic' who had 'evolved' an Australian mythology, Hughes took aim:

> Recently an 'opposition group' was formed in Melbourne under the leadership of the distinguished art historian Bernard Smith. His programmic intent was clear. Australia he argued lacks a tradition of art but possesses strong social traditions. It has acquired its own myths, heroes and white man's folklore. If the artist, then, is to function as an effective social unit his art must reflect this and draw its inspiration from it . . . The Antipodean notion of an image seems to concern a pressure point for a number of beliefs . . . which need have nothing to do with aesthetic sensation or the existence of the object itself. It is an art of association. Under this aspect, an image is the firing pin and not the grenade.[101]

Being admonished by a dilettante was one thing, but Bernard felt Hughes, Robertson and Clark's ill-informed and 'pre-conceived' reading of Australia's historical and modernist position was unacceptable. Just months after the Whitechapel exhibition had opened Bernard retaliated when he gave the John Murtagh Macrossan Memorial Lectures at the University of Queensland. While those lectures reached only a small audience, they were a brilliant riposte to British perceptions of Australia's cultural isolation, which he saw as their way of maintaining imperial distance and cultural elitism. The lectures also reflected his unwavering concern with metropolitan centres and hostility to anything that subordinated ideas or relations of exchange, whether of a national or individual kind.

In 'The Myth of Isolation' lecture Bernard argued that Australia had never suffered from cultural isolation, neither from Europe's renaissance, nor its modernist movement. As a young pastoral society its cultural identity had been formed upon a Eurocentric philosophical and cultural inheritance and what had been brought to the colony was adapted, modified or changed by the geographic, climatic and developing social conditions, not formed under cultural isolation. Its distinctive cultural character had been carved out from its dominant European beginnings.

But a culture on the periphery—and this was Bernard's important *coup de grâce*—was able to develop in a more vital way because it was less hampered by the ever-prevalent 'graveyard of memory' or the heavy hand of European cultural traditions evident in major northern centres such as Paris, London and New York. Australian cultural identity, he insisted, was not inferior or forged through provincial isolation, but lay in its democratic difference.

The only time Australia had experienced anything close to isolation, or 'isolationism' as Bernard called it, was following World War I and then because its undernourished modernism was a by-product of conservative managerialism, led by nationalist Anglophile philistines such as Robert Menzies, J. S. MacDonald and Lionel Lindsay. Thirty-seven years after the Whitechapel event, and still prickling with indignation, Bernard wrote:

> For there lingered a strong belief in Britain that since Australia was only a cultural colony of Britain we could not, as critics of our own art, represent ourselves, so we had to be represented. But the British representation of Australian art, as masterminded by Mr Bryan Robertson . . . was a myopic vision that disastrously misrepresented modern Australian artists. They were presented as white noble savages who possessed no knowledge whatever of the Renaissance tradition from which in fact our art had sprung.[102]

The London critic John Douglas Pringle, who had lived and worked in Sydney, understood how Britons tended to misread Australia as a distant, inhospitable land of mythological proportions, and he began his review of the Whitechapel exhibition with tongue firmly in cheek:

> Many people in this country must imagine that contemporary Australian painting is a rather exotic art form discovered by Sidney Nolan in a cave near Alice Springs, round about the year 1940, and since handed on—under oath of secrecy sealed in wallaby blood—to Albert Tucker and Arthur Boyd.[103]

Bernard articulated this further in his second Queensland lecture, 'The Rebirth of Australian Painting', outlining how the assimilation of international modernism from the 1930s to 1960s had produced its own innovative originality within local traditions: 'Today, the creative artist in Australia retains the freedom of choice to work in the mode [he] prefers.'[104] It was this willingness to 'stand alone' and question cultural hegemony in the challenging manner that Bernard did which made him one of the most exciting and important intellectuals operating in the middle decades of the twentieth century.

In 1988 the art historian and curator Daniel Thomas wrote 'The Margins Fight Back', an article evaluating Australian art from the late 1960s to the late 1980s within an international context.[105] Bernard, however, had fought from the margins with his Antipodeans, but had been stymied by local antagonism and British cultural elites. Not only had he engaged in combat with a double-headed goliath of two dominant international cultures, the USA and Britain, but he had been penalised for it, even before his contemporaries realised the full impact of his intentions. Yet Bernard's incisive antipodean discourse, though seen as inhibiting, was nevertheless important for artists who were in the process of aesthetically defining themselves. He later wrote 'Distance is our *longue durée*, the near-constant factor in our history, that does so much to transform our art—and if we are creative and intelligent we can put it to our advantage.'[106] He had been shaken by the failure of the Antipodeans and his lack of recognition, later admitting to Vincent Buckley that the decade of the 1950s had been 'a low time . . . when I kept mostly out of sight, except for the Antipodean affair . . . and buried myself in work'.[107] But he had established a fertile platform from which future generations of art historians, critics, sociologists and artists developed critiques of reception, provincialism and their new art histories. For this alone, he was eventually acknowledged as the father of Australian art history.

CHAPTER SIX: THE 1960S

During the 1960s Bernard continually adopted new positions and directions. He remained acutely attuned to the slightest flutters of the art and academic worlds, which at times were full of pitfalls and unexpected rewards, and despite adopting a lower profile after the attacks following the *Antipodeans* exhibition, his reputation continued to rise. He delivered important lectures in Newcastle and Brisbane, and in late 1960 won a major prize for *European Vision and the South Pacific.* That year the Ernest Scott Prize was awarded jointly to Bernard and J. C. Beaglehole, with Bernard's book considered a masterpiece. Beaglehole expressed great gratification at sharing the prize: 'I think you should have had the whole thing. I really can't feel that Cook's second voyage had much to do with the history of colonisation, while your book is bang on the subject'.[1] Though Bernard's intellectual labours had been rewarded, there was little time to reflect as his next major project, *Australian Painting: 1788–1960*, now demanded most of his attention.

The new history of Australian art, he told William Dobell, was to 'replace my former book *Place, Taste and Tradition*'.[2] He made it clear that it was 'in no way' a revision or 'a second edition of his first book', but a new work he had begun in 1951 as a concept for a dictionary of painters, insisting that the 'final chapter' would be written 'as disinterested and detached as I can hope to make it'.[3] He had learnt his lesson about politicising the contemporary in *Place, Taste and Tradition*, and moreover, from the late 1950s there had been a national swing towards an interest in Australian art of all periods. With the rise of commercial art galleries, dealers and Eric Westbrook's pro-modernist approach at the NGV, where the *Survey* shows were institutionalising the 'new', the divisional lines between the traditional and the contemporary were beginning to diminish and modernism had become fashionable. Elwyn Lynn remained a crucial contact for Bernard in preparing his research on the developments that had occurred in Sydney in the preceding decade, while Bernard contacted and visited many artists for their updated biographies. Often he found himself acting as an adviser or de facto art dealer, as when he bought a painting from Grace Cossington Smith for himself and contacted Daniel Thomas at the AGNSW, suggesting that:

> as the Sydney Gallery seems to be in the process of buying paintings by the early Sydney moderns it might well consider Miss Grace Cossington Smith's The Sock Mender which was shown in the Royal Art Society Annual exhibition of 1915, and is still in her possession. It is an exquisite painting revealing, I think a direct Matisse influence, and it would make a fine acquisition. I bought The Reader (R.A.S 1916) of hers myself and would love to own the The Sock Mender too, but I really think that it should be in a public collection. If you people don't want it I shall mention it to the Melbourne Gallery, but I think the Sydney Gallery is the place where it should be.[4]

The second major work the AGNSW acquired on Bernard's recommendation was Spencer Gore's *The Icknield Way* (1912) in 1962, and in 1983 he lobbied the Premier of New South Wales, Neville Wran, to acquire John Webber's 1782 portrait of Captain Cook. Webber had travelled with Cook on his last voyage, and had been 'in an unrivalled position to assess [Cook's] character and temperament'; the magnificent portrait was, in Bernard's view, superior to the 'much more official portrait of Cook by Nathaniel Dance'.[5] It now hangs in the National Portrait Gallery of Australia in Canberra.

Australian Painting: 1788–1960 was published in late 1962 and Ursula Hoff praised it as 'the first important history of Australian painting written by "a man of our time" with the training and the outlook of a professional art historian'. She also stressed that, unlike European art historians who had at their disposal copious histories and 'specialised treatises' on their own cultural and artistic heritage, 'Dr Smith . . . had to uproot the trees, burn the weeds, break the hard soil, plough and harrow before he could sow. . . [to] show a consistent view of history.' He was a great pioneer historian, but Hoff also had some criticisms of her friend:

> I am inclined to think that Dr Smith places too great an emphasis on the relation of the artist to his place of birth and over-estimates the effects of expatriation. Meldrum, Streeton and Lionel Lindsay may have become tyrannical after their return from abroad, but there is no saying that they might not have done so even if they stayed here.[6]

She further berated him for turning his favourite contemporary artists into 'culture heroes', particularly William Dobell and Russell Drysdale. Elwyn Lynn, writing in *Meanjin*, considered his exclusion of major artists who lived outside the Sydney–Melbourne axis unforgivable, criticised his theatrical distortions of the postwar period in which abstract expression-ism reigned as a 'factitious fantasy' and thought his understanding of the contemporary international art scene was 'ill-informed and distorted'.[7] Lynn was justifiably angry, for Bernard had ignored a great deal of infor-mation he had sent him on the Sydney scene, asserting 'his account is disconnected and inaccurate'. It was as though a veil had fallen from Lynn's eyes and he could see how Bernard harvested and discarded or bent things to fit his own 'loaded rhetoric'. Other critics felt Bernard's 'deep seated bias' on the contemporary had 'tarnish[ed] the gloss of his achieve-ment'. Wallace Thornton admonished him on the same point that Sali Herman had made about the 'Antipodean' spectacle, that his 'Melbourne insularity' had obfuscated his vision, while John Brack was critical about his conflicting roles as a critic and historian and considered his handling of landscape painting, in particular the Heidelberg School artists, was insufficient and 'carelessly exasperating'.[8] Bernard's lack of 'image analy-sis' was a point that art historians in the 1980s, such as Ian Burn, would take up with gusto. In spite of those faults, *Australian Painting* remained the authoritative text on Australian art for five decades, furnishing the minds of generations of art critics, artists and art historians. Despite more recent art surveys, it still retains its value.

It also won acclaim with London critics who went 'Smith in hand' as they viewed the large 1963 Tate Gallery exhibition *Australian Painting: Colonial, Impressionist, Contemporary*, the 250 copies on sale at the Tate selling out quickly.[9] The large, conservative exhibition with its cargo of 221 pictures, had been badly organised by the Commonwealth Art Advisory Board and, according to Alan McCulloch, perpetuated 'the stigma of provincialism from which we have struggled so hard, for so long, to escape'.[10] Bernard had warned the audience at the opening of the *Antipodeans* exhibition in 1959 that 'a big Australian show in London . . . would be absolutely disastrous for the reputation of Australian art abroad . . . a mixed bag selected by a committee in which each member was pushing his own fancies'.[11] John Brack described it as a 'mess' and wrote 'screams have been echoing round the country . . . on the one hand a very unpleasant display of clawing, biting and snatching, and on the other an incredible exhibition of stupidity, inefficiency and cowardice. Why are all the public affairs of art so squalid?'[12]

The reviews were either punitive or tongue-in-cheek, calling the exhibition 'Kangaroo tail-brush' or as Geoffrey Grigson put it, '*their* [Australia's] political corroboree'. According to Quentin Bell:

> the provincial artist is the natural victim of the received image, and despite all the new-found and quite justifiable enthusiasm for Australian painting, despite the fact that Mr Bernard Smith in his admirable study calls our attention to painters who deserve to be far better known in this country . . . the hard truth remains that until recently . . . the art of Australia, like the art of America and the mother country, has been overshadowed by the too impressive eminence of foreigners.[13]

Nigel Gosling of the *Observer* raised the issue of nationalism in his review, 'The Struggle for Australianism', declaring the exhibition had attempted to find an answer to that ongoing question. But Gosling settled for the easy way out, deciding it was premature to expect maturity from a country with such a young history. George Butcher of the *Guardian* found the contemporary artists exciting: 'Perhaps the answer to regionalism is that the success of one's fellow artists breeds the confidence to be oneself. The landscape remains distinct: but . . . convictions about art itself . . . become denationalised.'[14] Fifty years after the Tate blockbuster, an equally large 'definitive survey' at the Royal Academy titled *Australia* was excitedly embraced by the general public, in particular the contemporary Indigenous Australian art, but the exhibition overall received a similar reception from British art critics. Like its 1963 predecessor, it elicited several scathing reviews that repeated the same timeworn role of the British as arbiters of taste and values.[15]

In Melbourne architectural modernism was the topic of concern, with plans underway for the redevelopment of the new art gallery and cultural centre in St Kilda Road. Premier Henry Bolte invited Bernard to join the General Committee and Art Subcommittee in which he was to advise on education, students' needs and the art school. As he worked through the details of Roy Grounds' design Bernard's meticulous eight-page report reflected his years of experience at the AGNSW, his extensive observations of major galleries and museums throughout Europe, and his ongoing concern with the role of art in education. The design, he wrote, should 'assist students, scholars and cataloguers . . . [with] benches or desks on castors or wheels . . . no "architecturesque" notions about pleasant vistas and "spatial flow" [should] sweep all seats away', but his primary concern was the issue of lighting. The furore over Eric Westbrook's explanation of Roy Grounds' lighting feature was anything but 'sweetness and light'; neither was the architect's proposed 'five foot [1.5-m] gap'.[16]

In January 1960 two William Constable paintings had been vandalised and Eric Westbrook used this as an excuse to pave the way for Grounds' revolutionary design features, or fissures, that would separate works of art from visitors. Westbrook told the press 'it might be necessary to design the new gallery so that vandals could not get near the paintings', but the aim was also:

To allow natural light to filter down the walls of the gallery to illuminate works of art, the first, second and third floors will not extend the full 50-foot [20 m] width of the galleries. Instead they will be cantilevered 'floating' platforms. The gallery will be the first in the world to use these 'floating' floors and it will solve a natural lighting problem that has defied experts throughout the world. Many of the works of art will be illuminated by a combination of daylight and artificial lighting.[17]

Bernard could not have agreed more with Westbrook that the new gallery should be a leading cultural beacon for Australians, designed for the people and not for the 'highbrow and elite'. Though Westbrook's 'funfair' approach seemed at odds with Grounds' austere bluestone building with its heavy, reductivist monumentality, and more in keeping with the Cultural Centre's 'gilded rocket needle' spire, concerns remained in many circles about the architect's influence.

When the presentation plans of the Cultural Centre were released to the public in late 1960 with no indication of the proposed '5ft gap', suspicions were raised that Grounds was going to push through his design. Anyone critical of Grounds, including the *Herald*'s art critic Alan McCulloch, had had their opinions suppressed, which led David Saunders, Franz Philipp and Bernard to write to the *Nation* and *Meanjin* to express their deep concern. It was not so much 'a problem of lighting, but one of principle regarding the display of paintings . . . We ask the Committee to issue at once a statement assuring the public that the ultimate form of the project will not include ten foot [3 m] ceilings or a gap between picture and spectator.'[18] Signatures were collected but Grounds, well-known for his 'bull-dozing' arrogance, was heard to say that he had 'got it all tied up . . . [the public and critic] can't do a thing'.[19]

Elitism was bad enough, but conspiratorial managerialism was unforgivable, and in his *Nation* article Bernard argued that the 'chasm' would alienate the spectator, reduce visual intimacy, create museum fatigue, inadequately light the paintings and potentially invite vandalism, not to mention the dangers of visitors falling 20 metres if they toppled over the balustrade. With further pressure mounting on Grounds, the architect finally backed down and George Bell wrote to Bernard thanking him for helping to save the building from the 'fiasco of the 5' gap and the 10' ceiling'.

Opposite directions

Bernard was convinced that the 'only way art history can ever come to anything in Australia' was for art historians to get away once a year to reinvigorate their research and consolidate their professional connections. On 3 January 1962 Basil Gilbert, Margaret Crawford and Ruth Zubans, all students of Bernard's, stood at Port Melbourne pier to see him and Kate off on the *Oriana*. It was his sabbatical year and instead of heading to the USA for five months on a Carnegie grant, which he had just been awarded, they were sailing for England. His research trip had been thrown into disarray when the United States Department of Immigration denied him visa entry and he was forced to reverse his itinerary. Daniel Thomas, hearing of the change, wrote 'you sailed off in the opposite direction to the one intended. I am sure there is a moral to this.'[20] The moral was no less a political tale.

With his history as a communist on file and numerous recent references to Cold War tensions between the USA and the Soviet Union, Bernard was blocked. He contacted Joseph Burke and Max Crawford at the university to help sort out the problem and Franz Philipp sympathetically mused, 'I thought the Americans were a little more reasonable now.'[21] Even with Burke's impressive American connections—he was a member of the Committee of Cultural Freedom—and his writing to the Foreign Service, the green light for Bernard's visit to the USA was not granted until September. While his proposed study was to be on romantic and early nineteenth-century painting in relation to the scientific thought of the day, 'a sensible continuation' of his *European Vision and the South Pacific*, there was, as usual, a double motive involved. Just as Bernard's visit to Eastern Europe in 1949 had been to see how communism worked from the inside, Bernard wanted to see what the contemporary art climate was like in the USA.

Arriving in London, he began studying Victorian paintings and the works of Gainsborough and Constable at the Victoria and Albert

Museum. When Kate joined him they went to lunchtime concerts, on one occasion catching a magnificent Purcell, *Expostulation for the Virgin*. Part of his research program was to prepare bibliographies and visit art collections, historical houses and monuments. The couple travelled as far north as York and Durham, west to Birmingham and Coventry, and to Norwich in the east. Bernard arranged meetings with Ernst Gombrich, Joseph Trapp, Rudolf Wittkower and L. D. Ettlinger at the Warburg Institute and asked Nikolaus Pevsner if he could sit in on his classes and lectures at the Courtauld Institute. He heard Margaret Whinney lecture on Flaxman and Alan Bowness on Gauguin, symbolism and the Nabis, but it was Pevsner's class on Boullée and Ledoux that he found revelatory. The correlation between Roy Grounds' design for the new NGV and Boullée's 'Temple of Reason', with its compelling domed arch and colossal façade, was striking, the former an unmistakable appropriation of the latter.

Many of Bernard's artist friends had decamped to London and he spent the following months between research and imbibing in the contemporary art world. The Blackmans, Boyds and Nolans, Jean Langley, Roy and Betty Dalgarno, Barry and Rosalind Humphries, Francis Lymburner, as well as Peter Upward, Lawrence Daws and the Whiteleys—Brett had an exhibition scheduled at the Matthiesen Gallery in March—were all busy establishing themselves. John and Mary Perceval in Australia were anxious to join their fellow expatriates, and John wrote to Bernard asking him to 'please send me some news of my old mates. They are all so cagey about what they are painting and how they are getting "on", on the "London scene".'[22] There were also the established expatriate Australians such as Roy de Maistre, Charles Osborne, Alannah Coleman, Clytie Jessop, Harry Tatlock Miller and Loudon Sainthill. At Rex Nan Kivell's Redfern Gallery in London Bernard saw the Spencer Gore exhibition, from which he recommended *The Icknield Way* to the AGNSW. They bought it for £1200.

On visiting Arthur Boyd in Highgate, Bernard found preparations well underway for Boyd's retrospective at the Whitechapel Gallery in April. Several hundred paintings were stacked in the front room awaiting Bryan Robertson's selection, but Bernard found Arthur's new work from his *Diana and Actaeon* series disappointing. Influenced by the great mythological masterpieces in the National Gallery in London, Arthur was understandably abandoning some of his antipodean imagery, but Bernard may not have allowed for this expatriate transition. The paintings were also poignant metaphors for Arthur's infidelity; the faithful dog that watches over the tragic lover's death a reference to the end of his long affair with Jean Langley. Ursula Hoff better understood the works and how Piero di Cosimo was one of the vital sources for Arthur's inspiration; the 'wildness' and 'streak of primitivism, the slightly macabre association of eroticism and death' operated at a perfect pitch for Boyd's emotional state.[23] Franz Philipp, who had agreed to write the Georgian House monograph on Boyd—later published with Thames and Hudson in 1967 as a large, groundbreaking study—also confirmed Piero di Cosimo's *Death of Procris* (c. 1495) as the visual touchstone that inspired Arthur's 'recumbent nudes' a 'persistent symbol of desire in Renaissance and post Renaissance Western art'.[24]

In mid-February Bernard met Sidney Nolan to discuss the monograph he had agreed to write for the Georgian House series. After Cynthia Nolan gave her approval, numerous meetings and discussions followed, in which Bernard made two tape recordings and was privy to Nolan's 'working' of the contemporary art scene. He also got an insight into the artist's instinctual relation with reality, and he reversed his earlier derision of the artist's *Boy and the moon*, exhibited at the 1940 CAS exhibition. Accompanying Nolan to a rehearsal of Kenneth MacMillan's production of Stravinsky's *The Rite of Spring* at Covent Garden, he found Nolan's stage design visually electrifying. The ambiguous imagery appeared to dissolve form and its poetic abstraction offer multiple shades of meaning, and yet somehow it seemed accidental. What were the dancers worshipping?

The rising sun, the tree of knowledge and death, or a great Bacchic phallus arrogantly asserting the rights of man? Is it the atomic cloud which dominated the dance or that wandering moon which for an older generation of romantics was such a symbol of hope and constancy in a changing world?[25]

Impressed by Nolan's genius, Bernard quickly drafted an article on his 'iconomorphic form' and recorded 'Image and Meaning in Recent Painting' for the BBC's Third Programme, also published in the *Listener* to coincide with Nolan's exhibition at the Institute of Contemporary Art. Bernard published a further article, 'Nolan's Image', in the September issue of the *London Magazine* and suggested giving a lecture on Nolan in the USA later in the year.[26] Like many before and after him, Bernard had succumbed to Nolan's charisma and was enthralled by the artist's prodigious talent and productivity, but he was equally aware that Nolan was like a big-game hunter after the best trophies and that he continually orchestrated his career.[27]

Usually Bernard's research was meticulously honed, but by spreading himself across such a broad spectrum his work on the nineteenth century began to slip. He dined with the Pevsners at their home in Hampstead and with T. S. R. Boase at the Travellers Club, attended lectures at the Courtauld and Warburg institutes, and saw a large number of exhibitions. Some of these included the Spanish paintings and the École de Paris at the Tate Gallery; the Karel Appel exhibition at Gimpel Fils; an Armitage exhibition at the New London Gallery; and a very fine Mark Tobey exhibition at the Whitechapel Gallery. He saw a Keith Vaughan exhibition and *Vanguard American Painting* at the American Embassy, noting 'the Pollocks looked pleasantly decorative, the rest poor'. Larry Rivers' talk at the ICA in May was, according to Bernard, also 'very poor'.[28]

When a letter arrived from L. J. Ray of the Department of Anatomy at the University of Melbourne to say that the original busts of Truganini and Woureddy might be in the Musée de l'Homme in Paris, Bernard felt relief.[29] Locating the original busts, if that were possible, would be exciting, but more gratifying was the thought of visiting France, the cradle of modernism and where the emancipation of the working class had been at its most heroic. Having failed to carry the Antipodeans further, he decided to pursue a different line of investigation, one that linked his commitment to the working class and figurative realism of the nineteenth-century's most dissenting spirit, Gustave Courbet. His interest in this undervalued artist, who had chosen the new realism of social relations to address political change, was the perfect conduit for

Bernard's political and aesthetic beliefs; as he wrote 'the egg of realism came from this nest'.[30]

But just as Bernard's plans for France were taking shape a letter arrived from the deputy vice-chancellor of the University of Sydney, A. G. Mitchell, asking for his views on the new Power Bequest and the proposed directorship. Bernard had known Mitchell during the 1940s when Mitchell was the McCaughey Professor of Early English Literature at the University of Sydney and later at the Australian Academy of Humanities in Canberra, and they had remained on friendly terms. As the Power Bequest had only recently been publicly announced Mitchell enclosed some particulars about its key features, but Bernard also wrote to Joseph Burke asking for any information he had seen in the press, adding that he was personally interested in the position. Burke was 'deeply grateful' for being taken into Bernard's confidence and assured him that should he be consulted about applicants for the Power job his advice would be unequivocal; it 'could only point to one man' and 'Sydney could not do better than to approach you'.[31] Burke was also forthcoming with advice on what he saw as the 'the very elastic terms of the Bequest':

A Million pounds is a lot of money, and a lot of things can be done with it. Amongst these a very high priority is the Department of Fine Arts or Art History. The occupant of the Chair will have to be a specialist in the art of the nineteenth & twentieth centuries—to isolate the C20 from the C19 could be completely unacademic. The Museum of Modern Art has always stressed the historical background, especially the C19, hence the high standard of its publications on Picasso etc. . . . . Sydney would then become the main centre of research into the art of the modern period. Finally the whole point of the testator's intention will be missed if these studies are not linked with the study of Australian art.

Returning to Bernard's interest in the position, Burke told him:

You have long been entitled to a Chair . . . If you went, a lot of things you are doing would not be done at all, but you have laid splendid foundations.

There is evidence that Burke was happy to let Bernard go, particularly as there had been criticism about his preference for working away from the university, rather than being involved in the department; others saw it as Burke giving in to Bernard's ambitious nature.[32]

With Sydney interested in him, Bernard realised he would have to engage more fully with the contemporary and he restructured his program for the USA accordingly. There remained one problem: 'the trouble with the contemporary', he insisted, 'is that it hasn't formed. Hegel said you have to look backwards to understand what had taken place.' Turning his thoughts to Australia's most successful expatriate contemporary artist, he recalled what Sidney Nolan had said about his early, albeit brief, art training at the NGV's Art School in Melbourne. One of Nolan's fellow students had put him onto a book about 'study and form'—most probably *The Art and Craft of Drawing*, by Vernon Blake—which had fundamentally changed the way he saw and drew; 'What a painter sees is the spaces between the trees, not the trees.' Nolan's own poetry and writing also helped him express himself 'in the form of imagery'.[33] That, Bernard decided, was how he would approach his research in the USA, by looking at the image and form in American contemporary art.

Again Joseph Burke came to his assistance and wrote to Alfred H. Barr Jr, inquiring 'whether there would be any facilities for [Bernard] to study "Image and Form in Contemporary painting" at the Museum of Modern Art as a holder of a Carnegie Fellowship'. Burke effusively praised Bernard as 'our leading scholar in the field of modern art . . . as a critic and as a champion of avant-garde movements' and noted that he was being consulted by the University of Sydney about the new Power Bequest for contemporary art.[34] Barr replied that Smith was welcome and would be given the title of Research Fellow, adding that he knew 'something of him . . . especially his valuable 1945 book on Australian art'.[35]

Before sailing to the USA, there was still Bernard's visit to France, the country whose nationalism he regarded as 'the most powerful collective emotion during the course of modern history'.[36] In Paris he and Kate were met by the Australian expatriate artist Moya Dyring who had organised a room with a fine view of the Seine just a few doors from her own apartment at 39 Quai d'Anjou. On their first day they wandered around Paris looking at cathedrals and churches, including Kate's favourite L'Eglise Madeleine, flanked by its massive classical columns, and the more humble St Eustache at Les Halles. The inscription on the façade of Notre Dame, *Le vrai mystique a la passion*, may have captured the French spirit, but Bernard realised that if he were to write a biography and catalogue raisonné of Gustave Courbet he would have to be more fluent with the spoken language. He had been learning French for 20 years, but was simply not a linguist and besides, he could always depend on Kate for help; however, he enrolled in advanced lessons for foreigners at the Alliance Francaise and by the end of June was taking classes at the Institut de Linguistique et Phonétique. In between lessons he and Kate visited galleries and museums, with Bernard discovering paintings of Australia's lost expatriate John Peter Russell hanging in the dining room of Auguste Rodin's old house in the Parisian suburb of Meudon. Three years later the Australian Government bought them, their destination being the National Gallery in Canberra.[37] After Kate returned to England, Bernard toured Burgundy with Dyring, where they met up with Cynthia and Sidney Nolan at the village of Noyes.

On his last day in Paris Bernard made a pilgrimage to the Pére Lachaise Cemetery to visit the tombs of David, Daubigny, Gericault and Corot, before catching the night ferry to London. Ahead lay a hectic week of appointments: meetings with Nolan, who was about to leave for Kenya; and with Arthur Boyd and the Blackmans; and he had a final meeting with Oxford University Press who were taking great pains with the publicity for *Australian Painting*. A newsy letter from Hoff alerted him to Robert Hughes having 'talked Allen Lane into letting him do a penguin on Australian art, to be ready next year! A few months work', but she had further news that confirmed Bernard's opinion of the young upstart:

There was a very funny article in *Honi Soit*, the University of Sydney Magazine by a man called Lehmann, who proved, verse by verse that Hughes, some years ago won the Henry Lawson prize with a poem which he had copied, with very slight re-arrangements of words from a poem by the Greek modern poet George Seferis, plus a line from Dylan Thomas . . . *The Daily Mirror* took the matter up and also printed a drawing by Hughes which was an obvious piece of plagiarism of one by Leonard Baskin. Hughes, the self-styled 'Coming young man in the arts', refused to comment.

Hoff also informed him that:

Hughes wrote a very independent article about the Power Bequest in which E. W. [Eric Westbrook] is quoted as the only man in Australia fit to be director of the Power Bequest Gallery etc. etc. The trouble with him is that the whole irrational, emotional outpourings which characterize most of the writing in the Angry Penguins years ago, is coming again . . . and, what is more, is taking everybody in.[38]

Bernard took this news about the Power Bequest as a signal that it would most likely become a highly contentious issue.

On his final day in London Bernard met Professor John White, a late medieval and Renaissance specialist from the University of Manchester, who had been approached to make a report on the implementation of the Power Bequest. Their conversation was about the interpretation of J. W. Power's will. By late afternoon, he and Kate were on the train to Folkestone in Kent where they were met by Sir Kenneth Clark; it was ironic that Bernard, who had so recently felt alienated by Clark and Bryan Robertson, was now a welcomed guest at Clark's large old Gothic home Saltwood Castle. On arrival they found Victor Pasmore, one of Clark's early protégés, and his wife as guests. Clark's propensity to promote young artists or, as Bernard put it, his legendary 'genius spotting', hence his adoption of Sidney Nolan, was well-known. They undoubtedly discussed Bernard's recent BBC broadcast and his proposed monograph on Nolan, but Bernard was also interested in Pasmore who had recently renounced figurative painting in favour of objective abstraction—he was considered Britain's pioneering abstractionist; such transformations were intriguing. The privilege of seeing Clark's art collection, with its 'very fine Henry Moore sculpture and drawings, Pasmores, a Degas, a splendid late Turner, a Millet and a magnificent Constable of Hampstead', capped the evening off.[39] The next day Bernard and Kate were at sea.

The USA

Ship travel gave Bernard time to relax, order his thoughts and indulge in literature. On board the *Sylvania* he read Bertrand Russell's *Has Man a Future?* and Patrick White's *Riders in the Chariot* (both 1961), and as primers for his encounter with the United States, Galbraith's *The Affluent Society* (1958) and Nabokov's *Lolita* (1955). As the ship entered New York harbour on 11 September, 'the Statue of Liberty looking a wonderful green . . . the city shimmering and dreamlike against the sky', Bernard was unusually excited, but as the afternoon dragged on getting through customs and waiting for their landing cards, their enthusiasm evaporated.[40]

Bernard kept much to his original itinerary, meeting directors, curators and academics of major American museums and fine art departments, with everyone keen to make his acquaintance. At the Metropolitan Museum he was taken aback by the magnificent Greek and Roman antiquities and, on Ursula Hoff's behalf, inquired whether the museum employed interns or trainees in the field of display. The NGV was focusing on temporary exhibition spaces and its director Eric Westbrook wanted the young exhibition officer, John Stringer, to study abroad; Bernard also made similar inquiries at MoMA.[41] At the Guggenheim Museum he was critical of the architecture, noting it was 'not as advanced in gallery design despite some arresting features'. From Princeton University they travelled to Philadelphia and then Pennsylvania, where he visited his supervisor Charles Mitchell at Bryn Mawr College and caught up with Virginia Spate, who had won a prestigious scholarship to that university. Returning to New York he met Bernard Karpel, MoMA's chief librarian, and began working each morning in the library on postwar American art. The afternoons were spent looking at the collections with Kate. In a letter to Clem Christesen, Bernard admitted:

with the paintings all around one it is possible to feel something of the vigour and excitement that grew up around the abstract expressionist 'movement' during the late 40s & early 50s. I can see now what I failed to see in Pollock and de Kooning's work when I first saw their paintings in Venice in 1950. And I have come to have great respect for the criticisms of Clement Greenberg. But the tone of criticism here is harsh, ill-mannered and emotional, with its eye firmly on the object.[42]

This recapitulation would soon pass, but in the open-air cafés, with their fine examples of Moore, Rodin, Maillol, Despiau, Archipenko, Lipschitz, Matisse, Renoir, Calder and Lachaise, Bernard was unashamedly embracing the spectacle of contemporary art.

At Yale he met Joseph Burke's former supervisor, Theodore Sizer, and at Boston he was delighted to meet Professor W. G. Constable, the former director of the Courtauld Institute, who had been Hoff's supervisor in 1934. Then another letter arrived from Alex Mitchell, informing him that while they were still some way off determining how the Power Bequest would be used, he wondered if Bernard would inquire about buying modern art and obtain any information on the American approach to the study of contemporary art. Another letter from Hoff told him that she had met a number of professors from the University of Sydney who endorsed Robert Hughes's article in the *Nation* on the Power Bequest, adding 'We saw the Power pictures which are a bit stale, and also Dobell's magnificent portrait of Prof. Anderson, and . . . Eric Westbrook was making arrangements to have Power's pictures shown in Melbourne.'[43] Bernard had not seen Hughes's piece on the bequest and replied:

but I cannot believe that Syd. Univ. would give much weight to his opinions. They have a wonderful opportunity . . . if they concentrate this money on building a first-class library of books and photographic material, and seek out a thoroughly qualified staff of art-historians; and the past will have to be taught, with the present in the top research brackets . . . there is not enough money to build a first-class collection of paintings at an international level. So I hope that will not [be] given first priority. That is how it appears to me at any rate. Perhaps I should tell you that I am not at all sure in my own mind whether I should want to have a hand in establishing a department in Sydney. When I first heard of it I was quite excited, but the more I think about the Power Bequest the less attractive the idea of leaving Melbourne appears.[44]

His response to applying for the Power Institute position would continue to oscillate during the next five years.

In early October Bernard met Alfred H. Barr Jr, the founding director of MoMA, and they talked at length about abstract expressionism, the revival of the image in painting and collecting contemporary art. According to Barr's biographer, who wrote 'the potent combination of art and money, whether in the marketplace, with the patron, or in the functioning of the Museum presents an inherently explosive situation' and that satisfying benefactors while building an outstanding collection was, as Bernard could see, a minefield.[45] Barr, the author of *Cubism and Abstract Art* (1936), also admitted to him, 'I just can't bear to look at another abstract expressionist picture', which thoroughly amused Bernard.[46]

Resuming their travels, Bernard and Kate visited museums and institutes in Detroit, Chicago, St Louis and Baltimore. As they laced their way through the USA the drums of the Cold War intensified as the Soviet leader, Khrushchev, began erecting missile sites in Cuba. This would give the Soviets strategic nuclear power to destroy most of the eastern seaboard of the USA and in confronting that hostile act President Kennedy publicly accused Khrushchev of making a 'clandestine, reckless and provocative threat to world peace'.[47] For several days the world teetered on the brink of nuclear war and, though he was terribly alarmed, Bernard thought of his clarion call in the *Antipodean Manifesto* and how little things had really changed since H. G. Wells warned the world in the late 1930s of a similar apocalypse.

Fortunately a copy of *Australian Painting* arrived just as Bernard was to give lectures at Ohio University titled 'Image and Form in Contemporary

Art' in which he discussed the works of Francis Bacon, Sidney Nolan and Arthur Boyd. At the University of Texas in Austin he showed the Nolan documentary on the Ned Kelly series and the Arthur Boyd film *The Black Man and his Bride* (1960). Hoff wrote congratulating Bernard on his book, though she warned him, 'You can be a proud man . . . and so being a wise man you will anticipate a certain unpopularity among colleagues.'[48] She also told him that he had been elected secretary of the Australian Humanities Research Council, a position he thought he could not refuse, but it took him completely by surprise that such a duty and 'honour' had been thrust upon him so soon:

> the one thing I would like to do in that post would be to see whether we can obtain much greater freedom . . . of movement to and from Europe & America for Australian academics and scholars whose teaching and research requires it. I am concerned that this is one form of 'isolation' that we must try to break down if Australian scholarship is ever going to compete fairly with scholarship overseas. And it is a job for the council.[49]

While he believed Australian artists could flourish within their geographic isolation and could develop a vital cultural autonomy, intellectual 'isolation' remained a serious problem—he implicitly understood the necessity of international study, having reaped enormous benefits from his own scholarly European immersion.

From Dallas the Smiths flew to New Mexico and Santa Fé, through Arizona and on to Los Angeles and San Francisco, their travels checked only by Bernard's meticulous schedule and his seemingly endless appetite for viewing art. At the University of California in Berkeley they dined with Herschel B. Chipp and by the end of December, exhausted, they boarded their ship for their homeward journey to Australia. As Bernard settled down to read Dostoyevsky's *The Possessed* (1872), a novel about the political chaos of nineteenth-century imperialist Russia, he reflected on his successful and satisfying excursion into the heartland of American culture.

Intermission

Back in Melbourne Bernard continued with his French lessons, gave talks to the NGV Art School students on contemporary art in Britain and closely monitored the developments of the Power Bequest. In March he had a long discussion with Tony Tuckson in Sydney on what the Power Bequest represented and how it could be implemented, but the contemporary was never going to be easy. The Georgian House publications reminded him of this only too well; Sidney Nolan was becoming evasive, John Olsen had changed illustrations at the eleventh hour and refused to answer letters, and Albert Tucker disliked Alan McCulloch's manuscript and was equally unreliable.

From Sydney he caught the train to Canberra for a meeting of the Australian Academy of the Humanities, which coincided with the opening of the Menzies Library at the ANU. It was now almost a decade since the Duke of Edinburgh had opened 'Professor Lewis's immortal masterpiece', as Franz Philipp called University House, designed by the Melbourne architect Brian Lewis. Bernard enjoyed Canberra's intellectual community with its collegial goodwill and where one could always hear reliable news about important cultural developments or academic opportunities. Learning of the generous research fellowships being offered by the Nuffield Foundation for the Warburg Institute, Bernard wrote to Ernst Gombrich about applying. His proposed topic, 'A study of the survival of classicism and the rise of primitivism in French and British art, c. 1850 to c. 1914', would be another extension of his previous research. He also sent Gombrich his Macrossan lectures, adding that he thought 'the first lecture [was] in the spirit of the Institute's emblem *Mundus Anus Homo*', but his application was unsuccessful and he turned his mind to the contemporary again.

At the CAS general meeting in late April he was reminded once again what a hornet's nest the contemporary art world was. For years there had been waves of bickering and ineptitude and finally, under Albert Tucker's presidency, complete discord erupted. Both Tucker and John Gooday 'were accused of redrawing art history to place Tucker in a favourable light . . . and they were forced to resign their memberships'.[50] The acting chairman, Peter Burns, vacated the chair and Bernard was asked to take over, further upsetting those who regarded him as an adversary, especially after the Antipodean affair. The division between the older generation and the 'new generation' and a lack of '*esprit de corps*' progressively eroded the CAS as a unifying body for contemporary art and gradually it faded into oblivion.

An academic art critic

In January 1963 the young art critic Robert Hughes asked the rhetorical question, 'Art criticism in Australia: what does it amount to?' The cultural climate in Australia, he answered, was a failure, an apathetic landscape with no backbone, logical structure or framework of historical inquiry. For Hughes, there were only three critics in recent times, excluding himself, who approached their duty seriously; those included the Angry Penguins critics, Bernard Smith and Elwyn Lynn, but 'generally, the vocabulary of Australian criticism feeds on the desiccated carcase of Clive Bell's theory of significant form'.[51]

The first meeting of the Australian division of the Association Internationale des Critiques d'Art (AICA) took place on 7 May 1963 in Eric Westbrook's office at the NGV. Alan McCulloch was in the Chair, with Robert Hughes, Daniel Thomas, Alan Warren, Arnold Shore, Jean Battersby, Gertrude Langer from Brisbane, Earle Hackett from Adelaide deputising for Geoffrey Dutton, Elwyn Lynn, Wallace Thornton and Bernard Smith present. Westbrook had made an earlier attempt to hold an informal discussion on 'Critics and Criticism' in September 1957 and now, six years later, they gathered to discuss improved conditions for the art critic. No sooner had the Australian division been formed than Arnold Shore died and Bernard was asked to replace him as the *Age* critic. He explained to Ursula Hoff:

> Yes I have taken on the *Age* job. Joe [Burke] suggested it . . . At first I thought it quite impossible, then realised it would be a wonderful chance to see the shows. I had only seen 4 this year! Yes I am enjoying it. Walking or tramming around Melbourne on Monday morning feels like playing truant.[52]

Art criticism meant that Bernard could re-engage with society at a critical level and in particular reveal how the art community might better understand itself. 'Criticism . . . begins as a dialogue between the artist and his work', but 'the most the critic does is to initiate a public discussion', he wrote. If artists exhibited their work in the public domain then they should welcome criticism, for silence or apathy was to be feared. Being an art critic not only kept Bernard on the trail of the contemporary, but it was a relief from the tensions in the Department of Fine Arts, where friction between Joseph Burke and Franz Philipp over course restructuring, teaching loads and appointments was taking its toll, especially on Philipp. Philipp's efforts to expand the paradigms of art history were continually frustrated by Burke's appointment of school teachers to the department—some felt that Philipp had set the bar too high—as well as Burke being distracted by his demanding extramural activities. The undergraduate course and lecture program had not changed since 1947 and it was generally felt that the department had ossified.[53]

Bernard was also adamant that the critic's and the historian's work was not conterminous with the artist's work, and that clear parameters and structures were necessary to understand the artistic process of production, reception and distribution—as he said, the 'critic and historian begin where the artist leaves off'. His first review for the *Age* in July was 'Recent British Sculpture' at the NGV, in which he wrote: 'For many centuries British sculpture has been a provincial art looking to the great metropolitan schools of Europe. Only this century has it acquired an international reputation' and particularly since 1945 when the threat of the Cold War had seen artists producing work imbued with the terror of annihilation, especially the sculpture of Henry Moore, Eduardo Paolozzi, Kenneth Armitage and Reg Butler.[54] In the following six months Bernard saw many exhibitions, including Sam Atyeo and Joy Hester's at John Reed's Museum of Modern Art (MOMA), Heide; Helen Maudsley at the Leveson Gallery; Robert Rooney at the South Yarra Gallery; Norma Redpath's 'outstanding' exhibition at Gallery A in Melbourne; and Moya Dyring's exhibition at South Yarra Gallery.

Bernard believed art criticism had to be taken seriously and he began collecting contemporary criticism from distinguished international art critics like John Berger, Lawrence Alloway, Quentin Bell, John Pope-Hennessy, Bernard Berenson, Edgar Wind, L. D. Ettlinger and Nikolaus Pevsner, most of whom wrote for the *Times Literary Supplement* and the *Listener*. This helped him stay in touch with international exhibitions and current art movements; his intention to remain objectively disinterested, however, did not always hold, especially if the artist swayed towards abstraction or an overly romantic interpretation of the world. Though Bernard had praised Hans Hartung's work in the 1953 *French Art Exhibition* as effective calligraphic strokes—the 'loaded brush is drawn across dry canvas' and 'reduces painting to the purity of its initial acts'[55]—he castigated the young Peter Upward's 'zen-like paintings' or 'intuitive automatism' as lyrically decorative derivations of Franz Kline, concluding that 'much has been lost between master and disciple'.[56] His disdain for action painting, which he saw as 'expression reduced to its limits, a kind of vestigial romanticism . . . shorn of any . . . references to the outside world'—and, in Upward's case, which he associated with Jackson Pollock's painterly process—revealed that his bias against abstraction had not changed.[57] Bernard, however, was one of the first art critics in Australia to combine historical training with an extensive knowledge of major national and international art collections, as well as having an intimate awareness of local artists' work. Art history and art criticism, in his view, were indissolubly linked:

> operat[ing] in and across time . . . History is a modality of criticism.
> Art history interprets values past, events as they reveal themselves
> in temporal sequences, art criticism interprets and values works of
> art in order to establish their particularity, the specificity of their
> forms and meanings.[58]

Linked, but with clear parameters, which was characteristic of Bernard's innate sense of boundaries in life, art and business.

After attending Shore's funeral Bernard flew to Canberra to introduce Sir Herbert Read at the opening of the UNESCO Art Seminar at Bruce Hall. Read spoke on his educational theories and afterwards the two men discussed the Power Bequest. Their divergent interpretations of

Power's will became apparent when Read's article 'Art in an Australian University' was published in the November issue of *Art and Australia*. Incensed by the ageing 'alienating faddist' who 'attempt[ed] to read into [Power's will] his own highly contentious educational theories', Bernard felt that Read's anarchic idealism and polarising polemics not only unduly separated the intellect from the imagination, but the academic from the artist. Furthermore, his suggestion of disposing with artworks once their 'contemporaneity' had passed would create nightmares for artists, dealers and collectors. Then there was Read's idea of an experimental studio in which artists could be observed from an elevated window by the lecturer and audience; this was an invasion of creative privacy and a perverted form of surveillance, a kind of residual twist of Britain's Mass Observation campaign or, at worst, something out of Aldous Huxley's *Brave New World*. Read also made the fatal mistake that other Englishmen like Anthony Blunt, Sir Kenneth Clark and Bryan Robertson had made, claiming Australia's cultural life was derivative, immured in its 'Australian Ugliness' and in urgent need of elevation and of transformation. Yet Read's 'crazy' concepts pressed Bernard to define what he thought the Power Institute should become and by the end of the year, though not intending to make a public comment on the Power Bequest because of his interest in the job, Bernard drafted his reply.

The Senate of the University of Sydney was 'proceeding with utmost [legal] care in its realisation of the terms of Power's will' and it was going to be a protracted affair; therefore Bernard felt it was important to set Herbert Read straight.[59] Before sending his article to *Meanjin*, however, he had further discussions with Alex Mitchell and decided to find out more about J. W. Power as a person and an artist.

John Joseph Wardell Power (fig. 36) was born in Sydney in 1881, and after graduating with a Bachelor of Medicine from the University of Sydney left Australia in 1904 for England, later writing to his friend the British art critic Anthony Bertram, 'that he had found "life unendurable in my native land"'.[60] The grandson of William Wardell, the architect of St Patrick's Cathedral in Melbourne and the son of a distinguished surgeon and founder of MLC Insurance Company, Power was, by inheritance, a wealthy man. By the end of World War I, and at a time when radical political and cultural changes were occurring throughout Europe, he had abandoned medicine and was devoting his life to art. As a restless cosmopolitan Power settled comfortably into that milieu and gravitated towards avant-garde cohorts and ateliers in London, Paris and other active European centres, amassing along the way an art collection that included Léger, Ozenfant, Gris, Gleizes, Picasso and Diego Rivera. He died at Mont à L'Abbé on the island of Jersey in 1943 during the German Occupation of the Channel Islands.

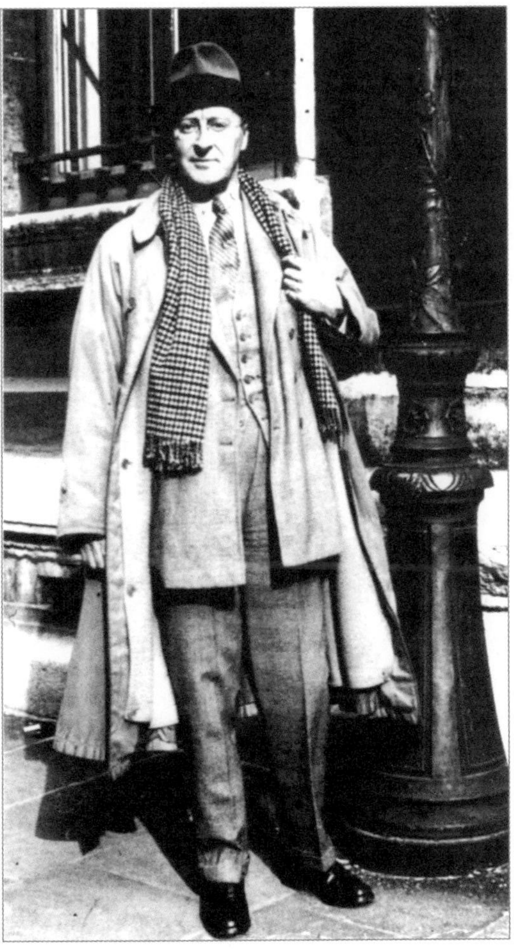

Fig. 36   J. W. Power in Paris, c. 1935

At the University of Sydney's Fisher Library, Bernard read Power's *Éléments de la Construction Pictorale*, a theoretical treatise on art and cubism written in 1933—Power had inscribed a copy and gifted it to the university in 1934. As Bernice Murphy claims, this was the first autonomous theoretical text by an Australian artist abroad.[61] Bernard also discovered that Power had been a member of the London Group of artists, the CAS of England, exhibited with the Abstraction-Création group and that Sir Samuel Courtauld owned several of his paintings. Power's ideas appealed to Bernard, particularly his concept of tradition and the sense of what ought to be recovered and what deserved to be preserved; it accorded with Bernard's own historical preferences.

In writing his reply to Herbert Read Bernard realised how problematic the proposed Power Institute would be and decided that when the position of the director was advertised he would not apply; as he put it to Ralph Farrell:

When the news of the bequest was made public I was keenly interested in the possibilities it opened up, and had . . . the position . . . been advertised during 1962–63 I should certainly have been an applicant . . . As public discussion about the Bequest developed, its tenor (tone!) distressed me considerably . . . I felt that the tremendously long-term goals which the Bequest made possible might be sacrificed for rather flashy kinds of pedagogical experiment. Things came to a head when Sir Herbert Read came out here in 1963 [and when] many people discussed the Power Bequest with him . . . The article . . . which he wrote for *Art in Aust.* raised in my mind the strong possibility that Sydney Univ. might be led to conceive of the Bequest more as a cultural novelty directed to the public at large than a (Dept., Faculty, Institute?) freely integrated within the academic structure. So I decided to write a reply to Read in *Meanjin*. In writing the article I decided not to apply.[62]

By June Bernard's resistance to the idea of the Power directorship had moderated and he wrote to John White confirming that 'After considering the matter carefully since we met [in London] I have decided . . . I will be available for consideration for the position of Head of the new Department or faculty.'[63] But Bernard's enthusiasm again waned as legal and bureaucratic problems continued to plague the process.

Back on the critic's trail, he reviewed the 'controlled vocabulary' and 'splendid visual metaphors' of the master Japanese woodcut printmaker Shiko Munakata at the Argus Gallery on the corner of Elizabeth and Latrobe streets, Melbourne. In contrast, the exhibition *Australian Painting Today* at the NGV in 1963–64 was 'a lamentable affair'. Put together by the Queensland Art Gallery's director Laurie Thomas, with assistance from the Commonwealth Art Advisory Board to tour nationally and internationally, the choice of works, according to Bernard, distorted Australia's contemporary artistic reputation. Not only had Robert Hughes written the catalogue introduction, but there was an 'acreage' of Peter Upward's 'Klein duplicates'. When Mike Brown's *Mary Lou as Miss Universe* (the second version) was removed from the exhibition on aesthetic and moral grounds—'it contained over 150 photographic images of nude and semi-nude pin-up girls cut from magazines'[64]—Bernard was furious. *Mary Lou*, a composition of junk and collage, epitomised the modern, synthetic 'machine woman' or, as Elwyn Lynn said, it was 'refreshingly and crudely vulgar'. In a later review of Mike Brown's work at John Reed's MOMA, Bernard commended Brown as 'an articulate voice in the wilderness', a true radical whose avant-garde, anti-elitism and pictorial perversity challenged the smug conformity of middle-class values and the art market. 'Originality', Bernard wrote, 'is an elusive and capricious virtue, and harder than ever to find today . . . but I would say without hesitation that Michael Brown's show [is] active and alive . . . [a]nd he has had the courage to write an introduction to his catalogue . . . without ambiguity, mystification or paradox.'[65] Anyone prepared to write a manifesto deserved credit and Bernard showed his support by buying one of Brown's paintings. He also reviewed Herbert Read's *Art and Education* (1964), essays based on discussions that took place at the 1963 UNESCO seminar in Canberra, at which Bernard labelled the eloquent art educational philosopher as a stimulating but 'useful irritant'.

As Bernard continued working on the Nolan book for the Georgian House series he was unaware that Cynthia and Sidney's friendship with

Elwyn and Lily Lynn had been flourishing. Lynn's perceptive writing on Nolan's art made Bernard's prose look prosaic and the monograph, begun with such paean, faded to a whimper. Within a year it had been shelved and Lynn had replaced Bernard. Like a jilted lover, Bernard would later write a scathing review of Lynn's *Sidney Nolan: Myth and Imagery* (1967), destroying both Nolan and Lynn's trust of him. In 1964, however, believing his own Nolan monograph was nearing completion, Bernard contacted the Melbourne art collector Joseph Brown to see the Nolan paintings in his possession.

The two men shared common interests; both were passionate about Australian art and enjoyed rehabilitating marginalised artists, particularly the 'lost' Australian impressionist painter John Peter Russell, who Brown claims to have rediscovered. Other expatriate artists such as Hilda Rix Nicholas, Percy Leason, Horace Brodzky and Peter Purves Smith were also given renewed attention.[66] Bernard and Brown shared an enthusiasm for colonial art in which they could trace the historical fabric and fascinating records of Australia's social origins and urban progress. Brown said he felt comfortable in Bernard's company and there was an obvious admiration and acknowledgement that both were pioneers in bringing Australian art into a more prominent and historical position.[67]

Joseph Brown also belonged to the 'outsider' realm—born Josef Braun, he anglicised his name soon after arriving with his Polish Jewish family in Australia in 1933, part of the refugee diaspora. Bernard, as noted, was drawn to European exiles, and he found in Brown what he found in Ursula Hoff and the refugee art historians in Sydney in 1940, the ability to stand at the edge of society and see it for what it was (fig. 37).

Of things to come

As the Power Bequest continued to make ripples in the press, Bernard and Elwyn Lynn engaged in a public forum in early June 1964 to discuss the ongoing confusion about its configuration, educational potential and public accessibility. The art collector Oscar Edwards was in the audience and commented:

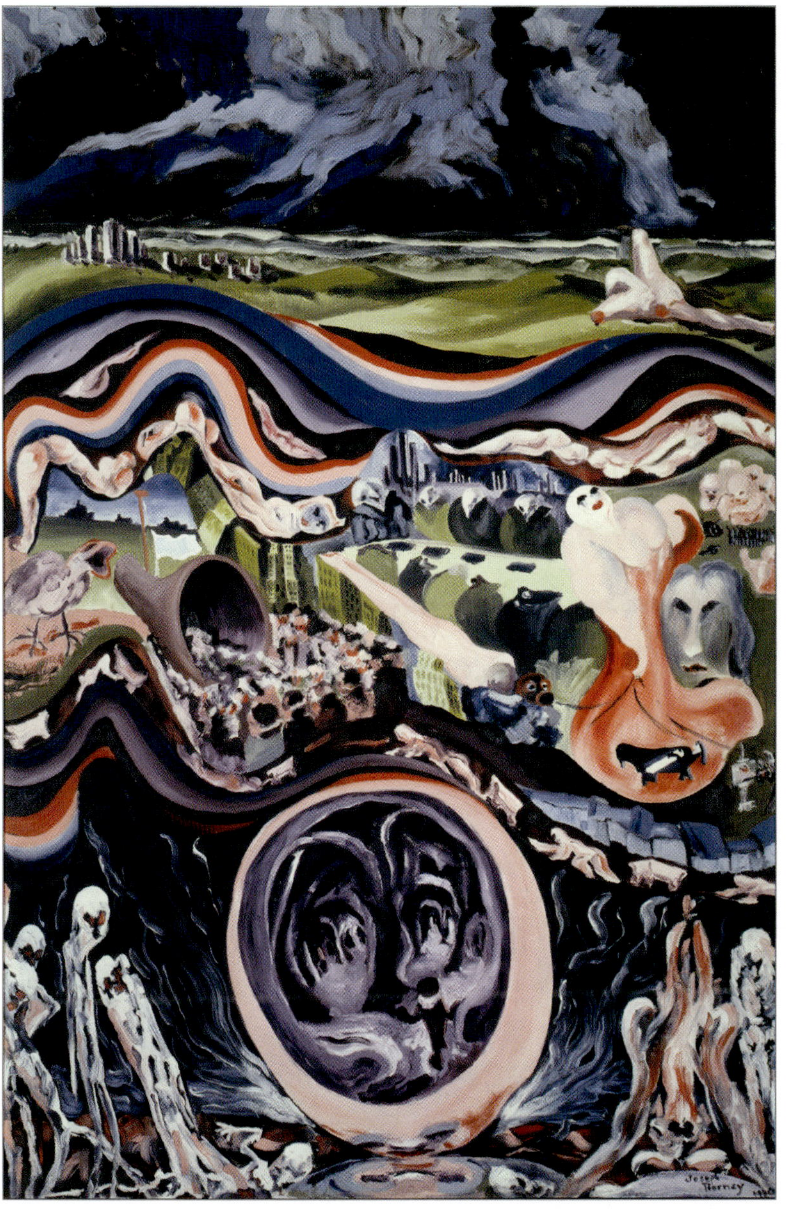

Fig. 9 Joseph Tierney, *Pompeii*, 1940

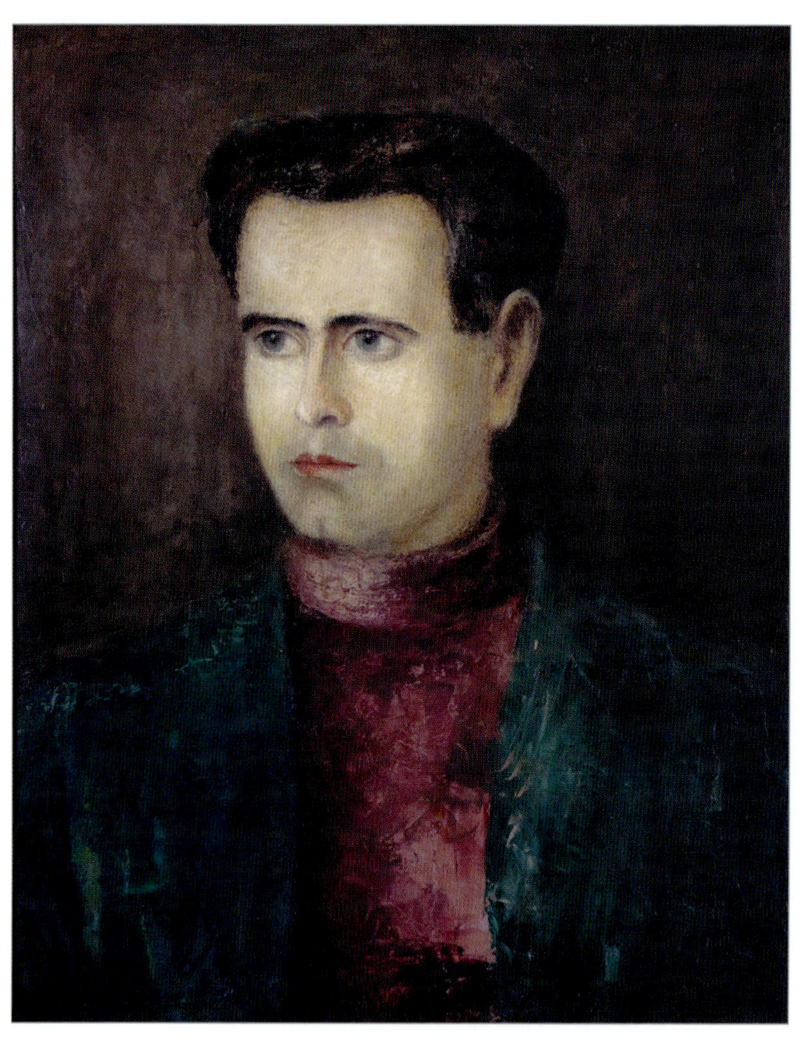

Fig. 15 Sali Herman, *Portrait of Bernard Smith*, 1949

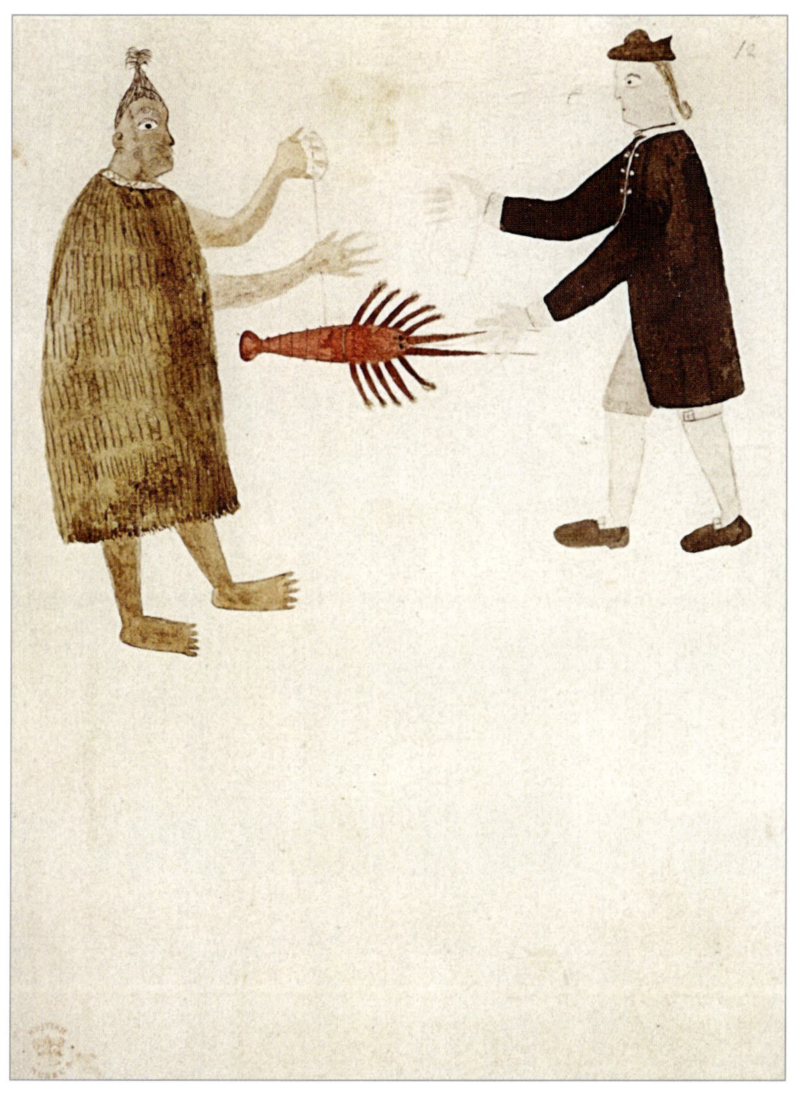

Fig. 18 Tupaia, *First contact*, 1769

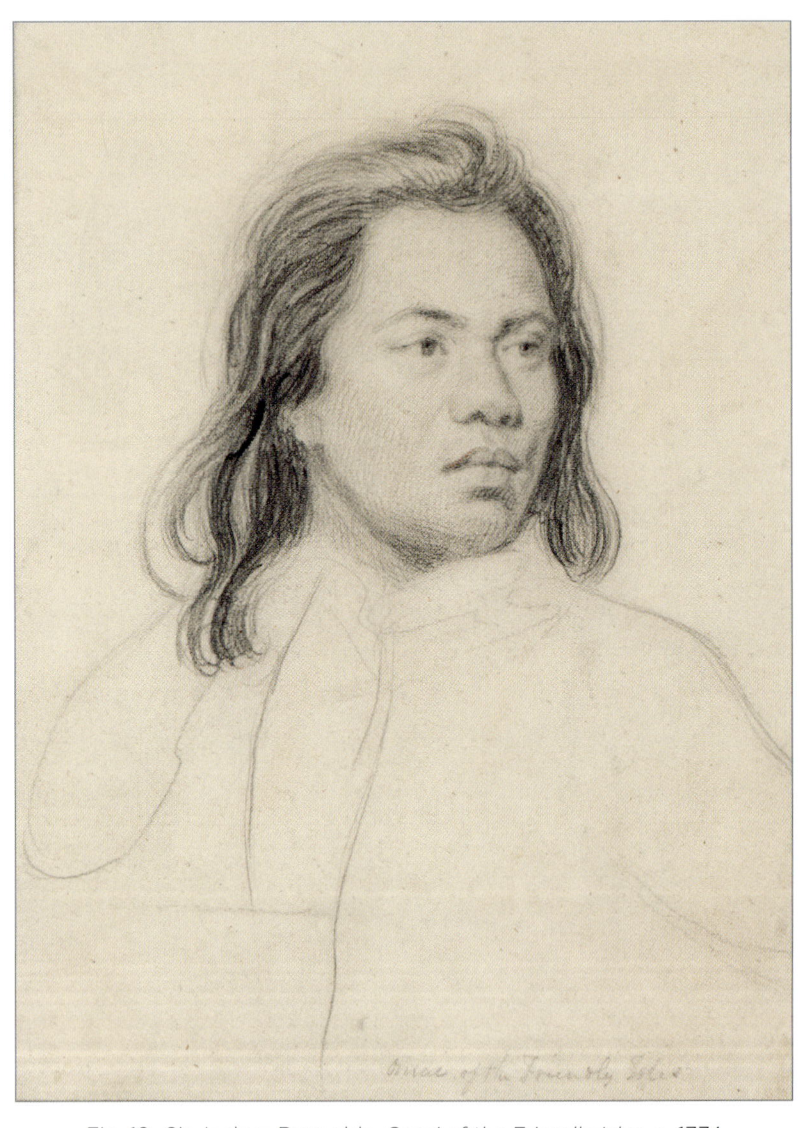

Fig. 19 Sir Joshua Reynolds, *Omai of the Friendly Isles*, c. 1774

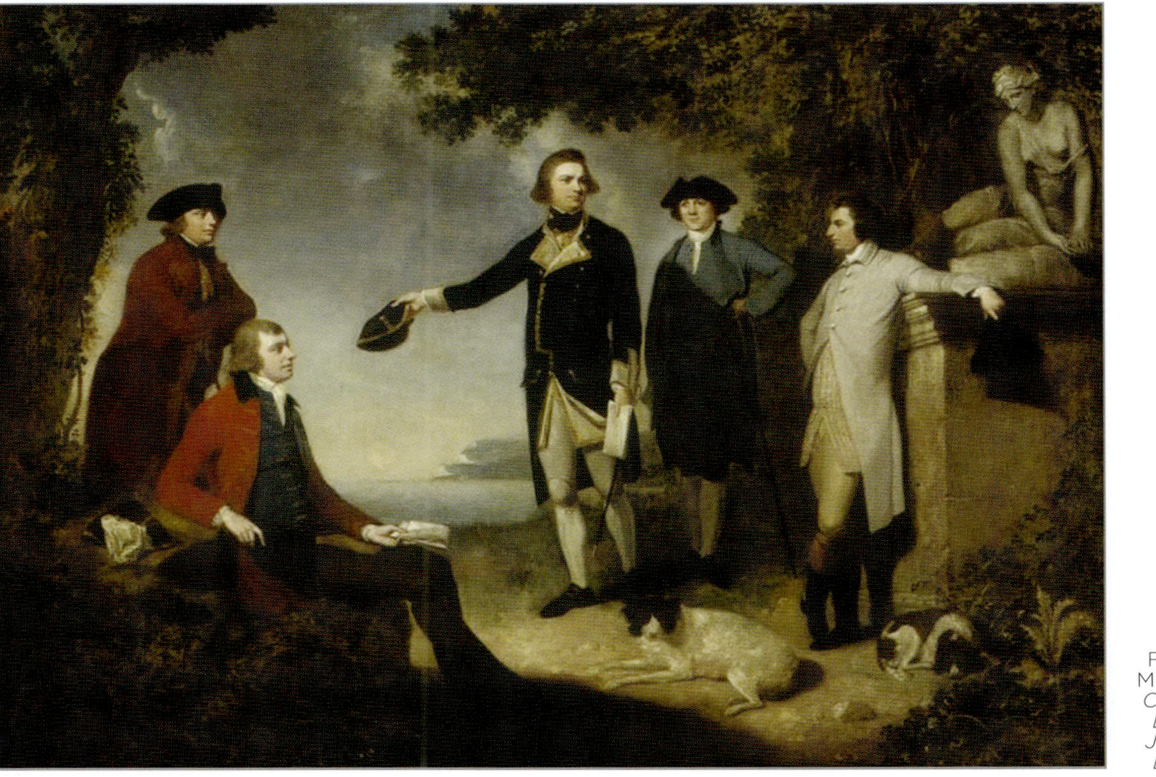

Fig. 20 John Hamilton Mortimer, *Captain James Cook, Sir Joseph Banks, Dr Daniel Solander, Dr John Hawkesworth and Lord Sandwich*, c. 1771

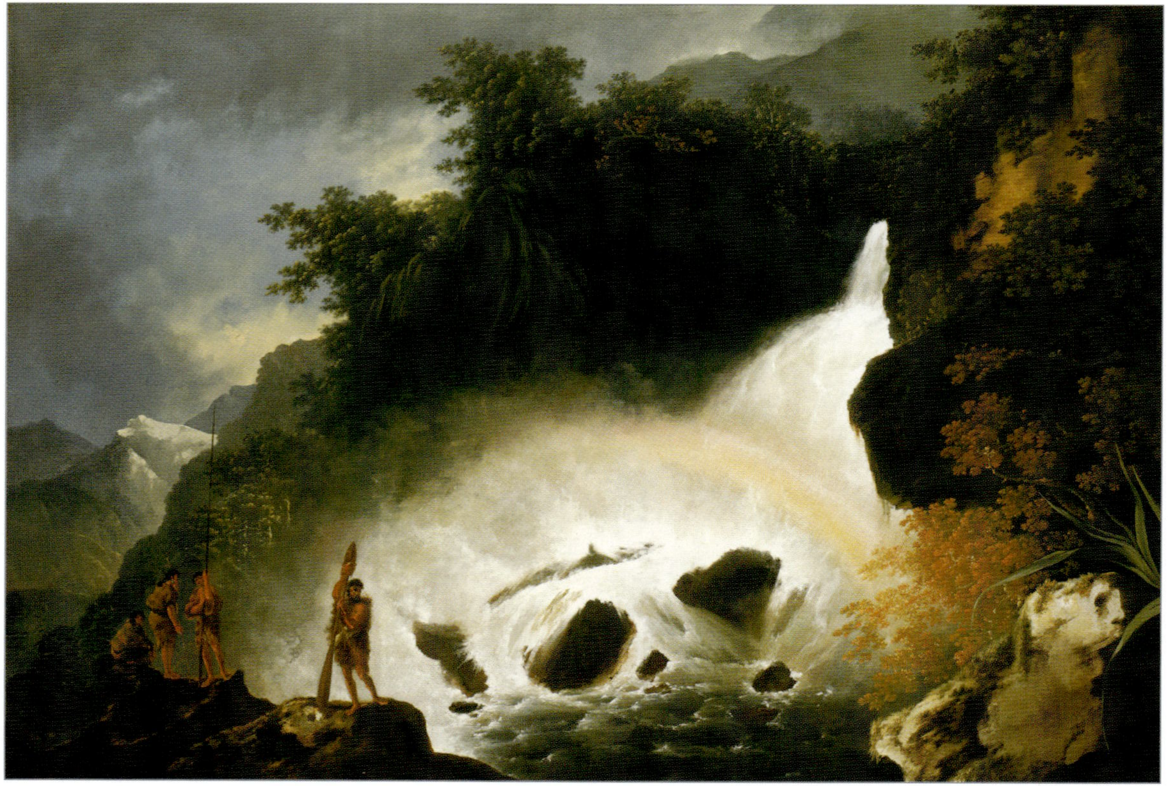

Fig. 23 William Hodges, *Cascade Cove, Dusky Bay, New Zealand*, 1775

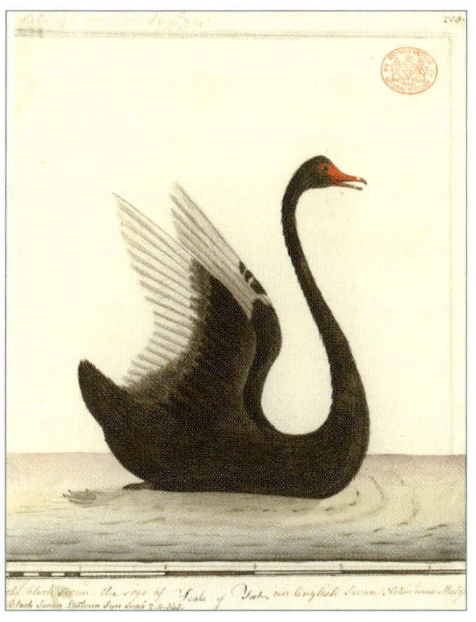

Fig. 21 Port Jackson Painter, *Cygnus atratus* (black swan), c. 1788 to 1792

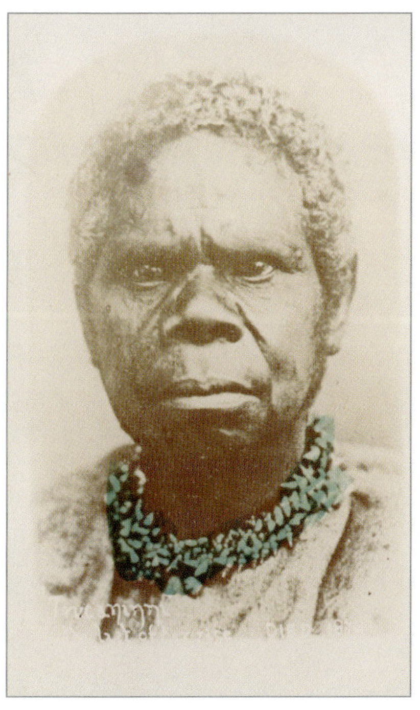

Fig. 49 C. A. Woolley, *Truganini*, 1866

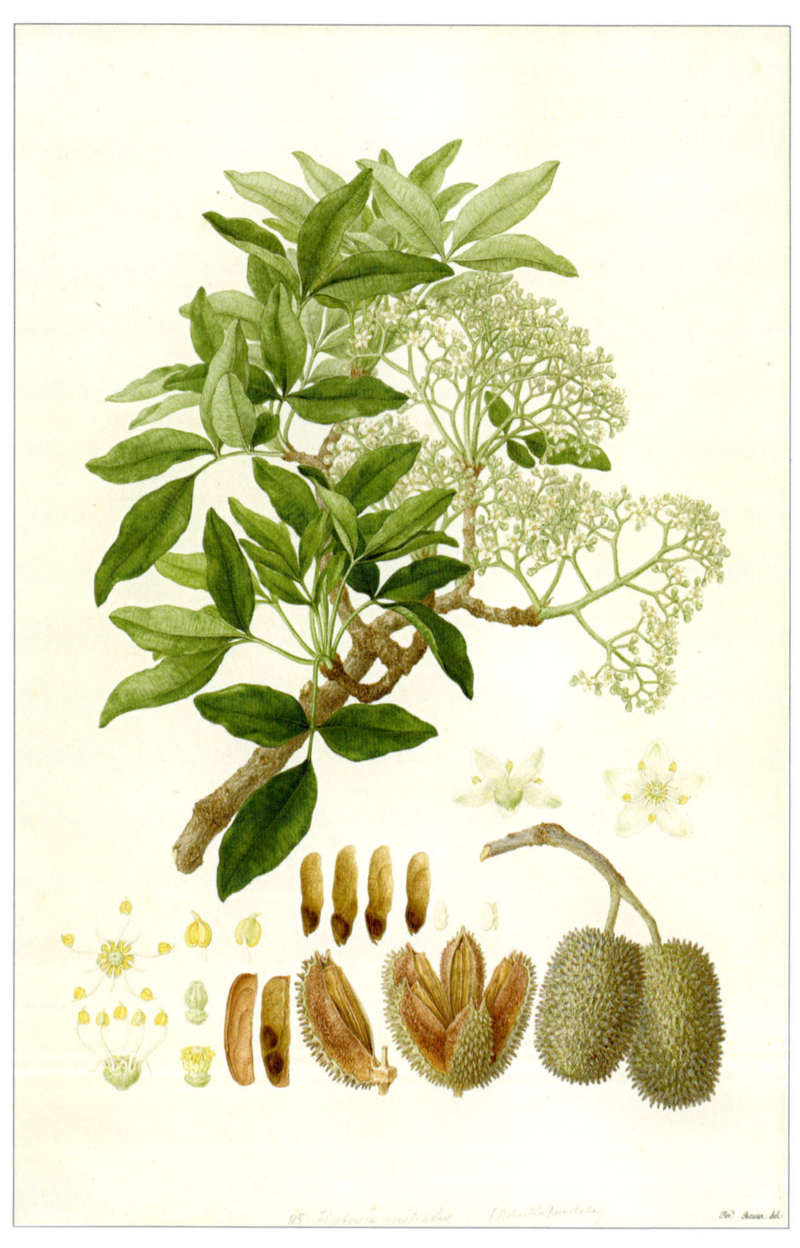

Fig. 25 Ferdinand Bauer, *Flindersia australis* (crow ash tree), 1802

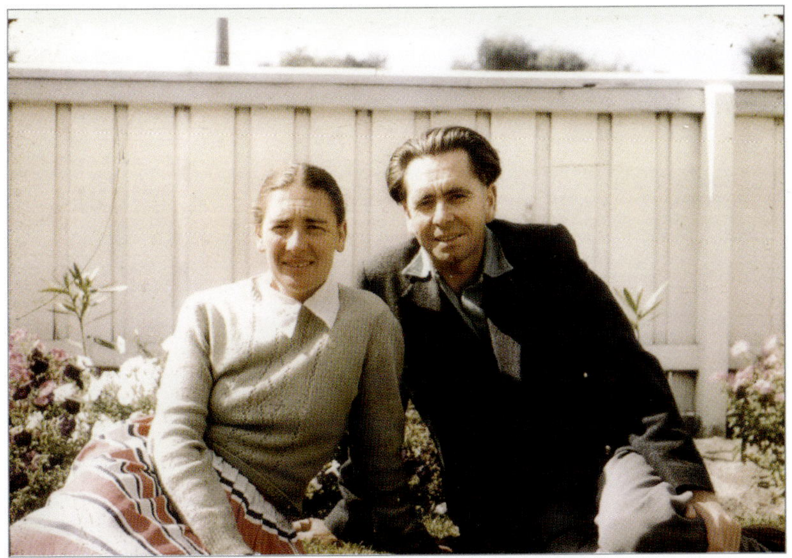

Fig. 30 Bernard and Kate Smith at Sandringham, c. 1956

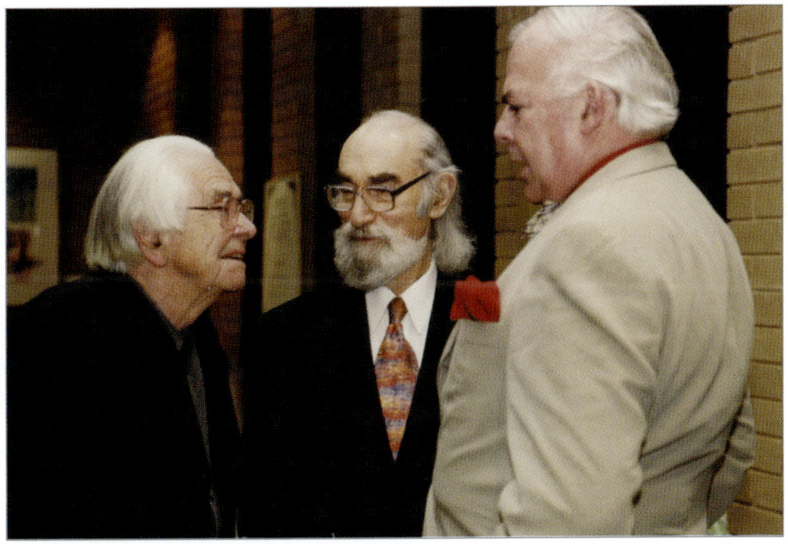

Fig. 37 Bernard Smith, Joseph Brown and Patrick
McCaughey at Brown's 90th birthday, 2008

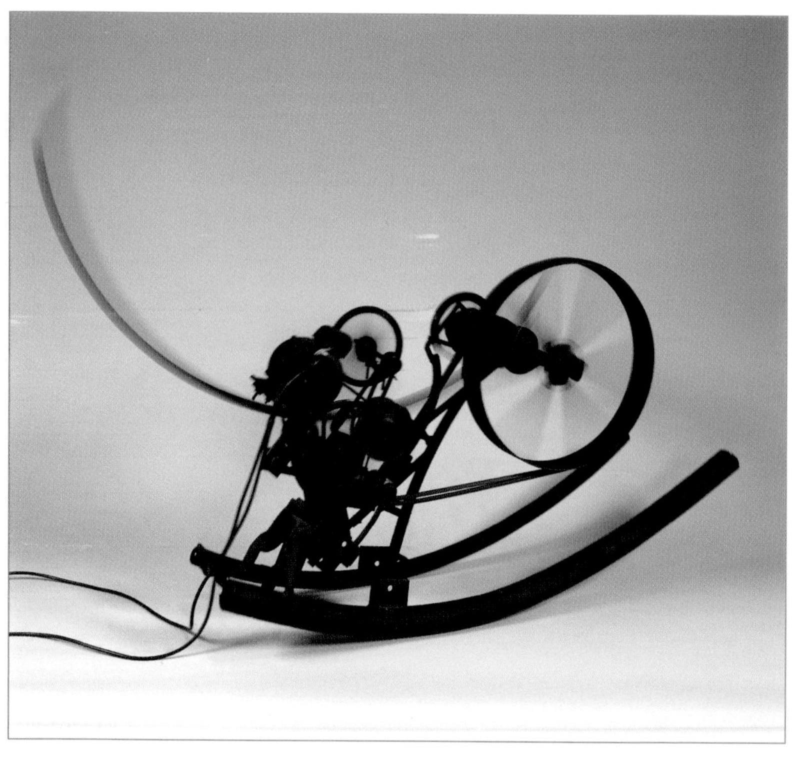

Fig. 38   Jean Tinguely, *Bascule no 1: Sisyphus* (See-saw no 1: Sisyphus), 1965

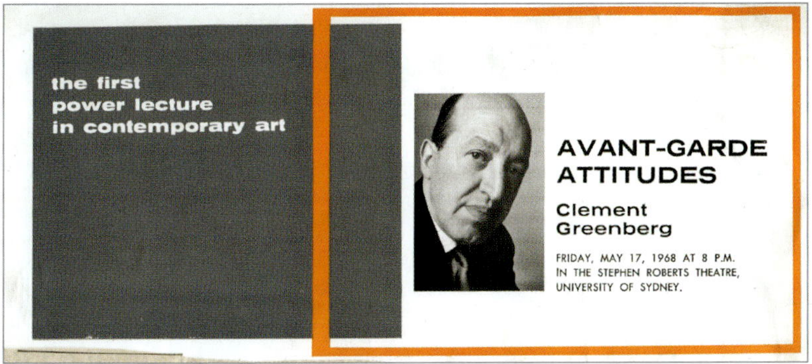

Fig. 39 Invitation to the Inaugural Power Lecture
given by Clement Greenberg, 1968

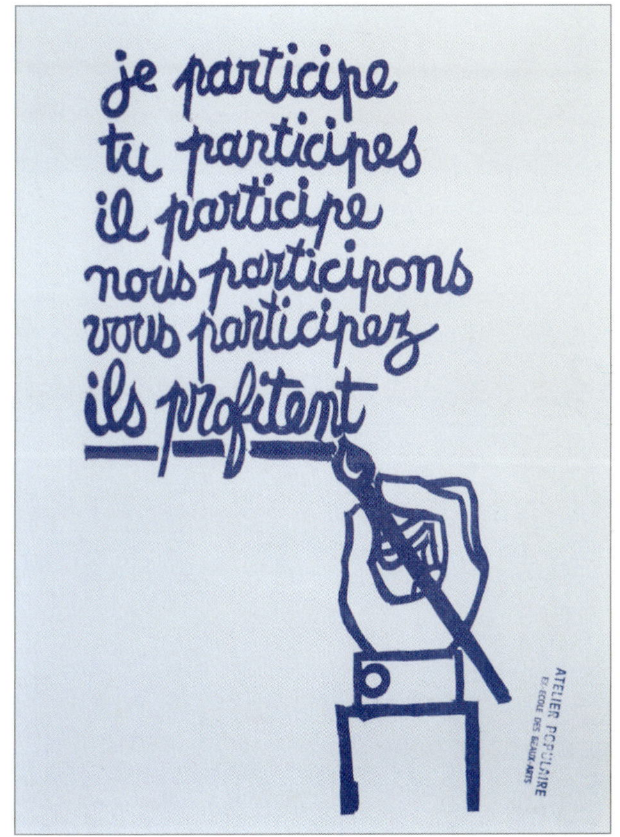

Fig. 40 *J'ai participe*, 1968

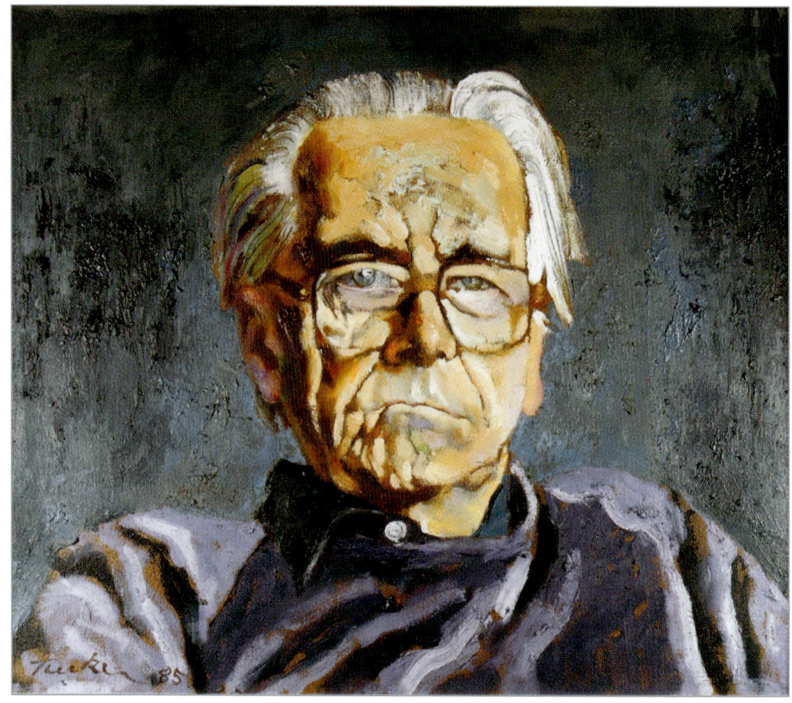

Fig. 54 Albert Tucker, *Portrait of Bernard Smith*, 1985

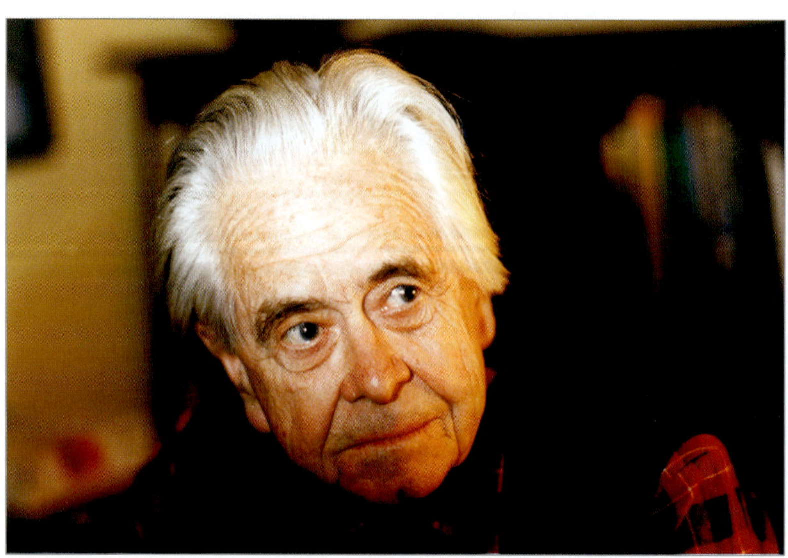

Fig. 52 Bernard Smith, Melbourne, c. 1994

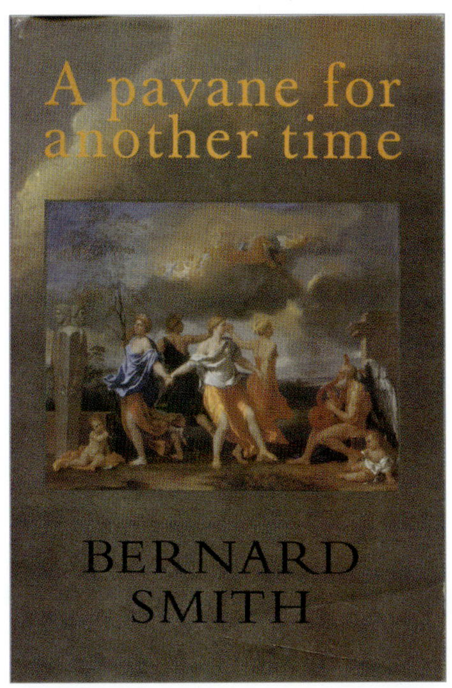

Fig. 53 Cover of Smith's second autobiography,
A Pavane for Another Time, 2002

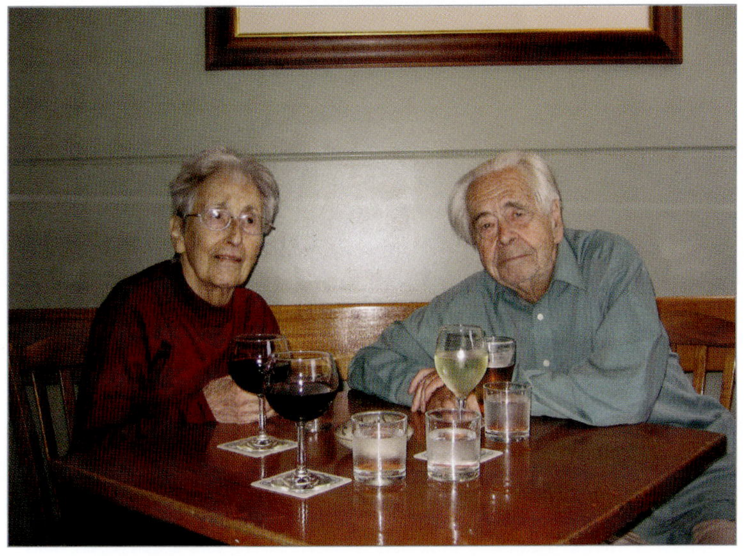

Fig. 59 Ursula Hoff and Bernard Smith at the Pump
House Hotel, Nicholson Street, Fitzroy, 2004

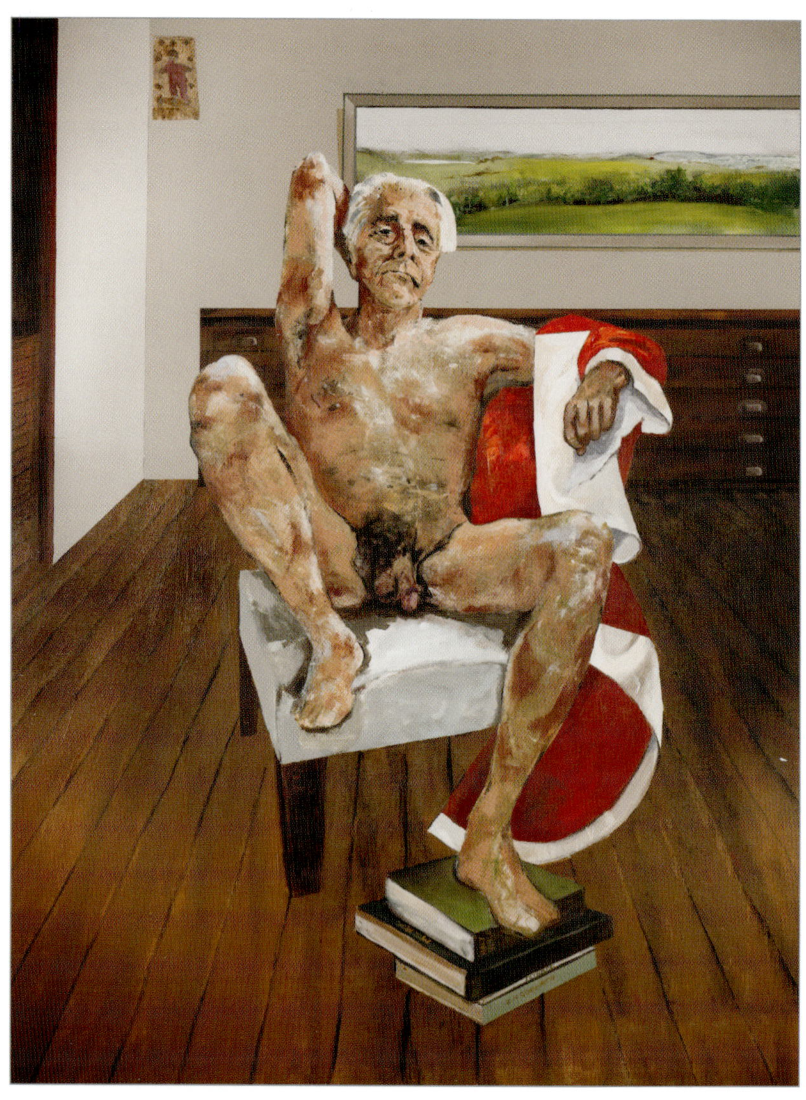

Fig. 55 Carmel O'Connor, *Portrait of Bernard Smith*, 2002

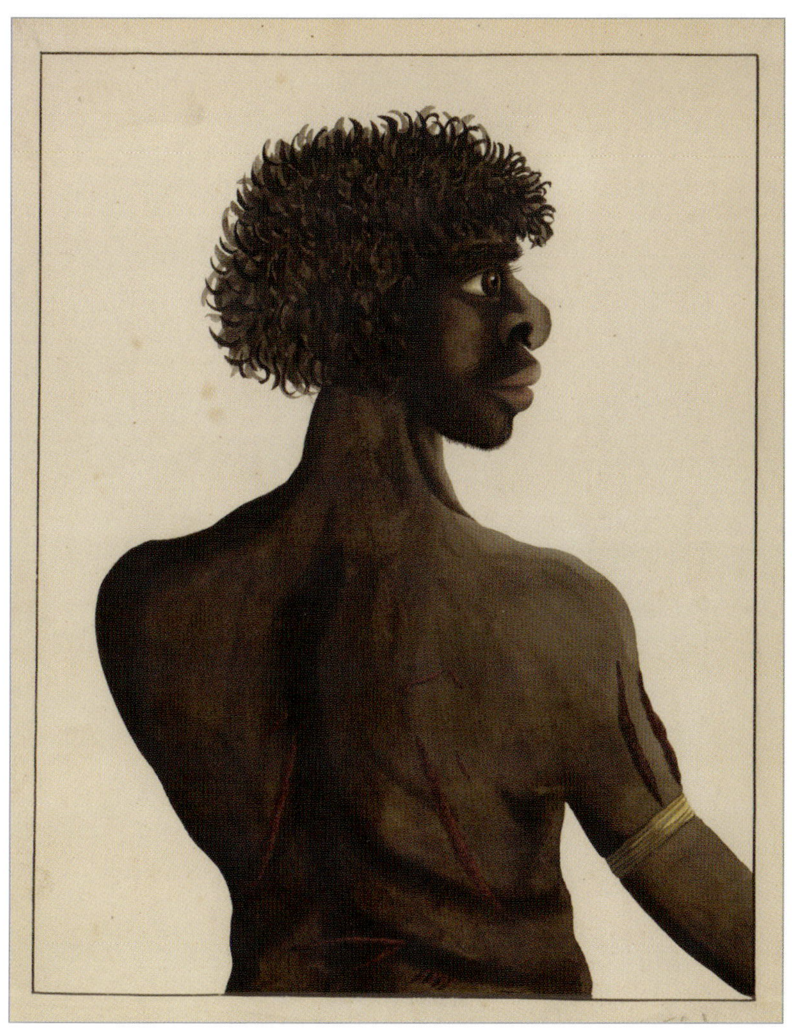

Fig. 56 Port Jackson Painter, *Half-length portrait of an Aborigine*, c. 1790

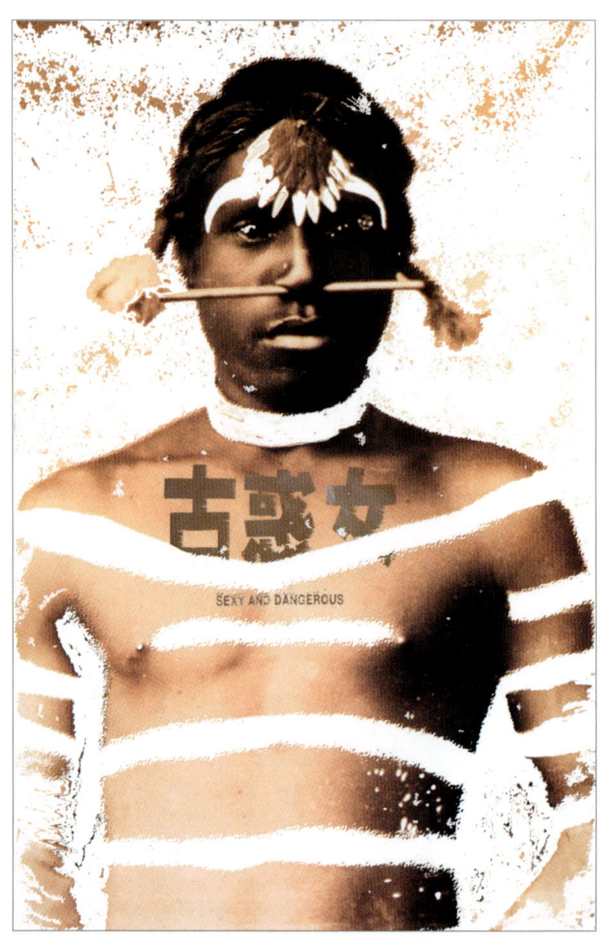

Fig. 57 Brook Andrew, *Sexy & dangerous I*, 1996

I came away with the general impression that Mr Lynn's views were much closer to those of Dr Power than the views of Dr Smith, but I felt that Dr Smith had a lead . . . in his knowledge of . . . the academy . . . [but] Mr Lynn showed that he had his finger completely on the contemporary scene, when without the slightest hesitation, after Dr Smith refused to answer the question . . . he quickly named a list of contemporary . . . artists whose work he would endeavor to acquire .[68]

Since late 1963 there had been a barrage of letters to the journal *Art and Australia* on the Read and Smith articles, including one in which Ursula Hoff judiciously articulated the unprecedented potential the Power Bequest could offer as 'a great force for progress . . . [in] provid[ing] opportunities for Australian research which lie outside the resources of present museums and university departments'.[69] In this she was agreeing with Herbert Read who still believed:

Dr Power had no intention of creating one more academic institution: I am sure he wished to question certain tendencies in traditional education and thought of a faculty of Fine Arts as a corrective of what Dr Smith might call an ecstatic worship of Apollo.[70]

Read, who had been closely connected to contemporary artistic ferment in Britain and Europe during the 1930s, may have even personally known Power, either as an exhibitor in London galleries or 'as a member of the international avant-garde'. As one of the organisers of *The First International Surrealist Exhibition* at New Burlington House in 1936, and *Surrealist Objects and Poems* at the London Gallery in 1937, Read's friendship with the French surrealists and other major artists at the 'centres of creative energy', together with his appreciation of abstraction, would certainly have given him significantly greater insight into J. W. Power than Bernard. The translation of the Power Bequest, however, still turned on the issue of it being part of the university, which many feared would transform it into a monument of the past, rather than the present.

With the demands of Bernard being an art critic and his and Kate's grown children at university or working, they decided to move closer to Melbourne University, and with the help of the architectural historian David Saunders, bought a house in Parkville. The summer of 1965 was exceedingly hot and uncomfortable. For the first time in the history of the Archibald Prize the Trustees, believing there was no worthy entry, withheld the award. Bernard considered it 'a failure of nerve', rather than confusion about the contemporary standards of portraiture, though he admitted there was some truth in the declining standards of the genre. But the controversy paled into insignificance when he received the galley proofs of Robert Hughes's *The Art of Australia* for review:

> Bob Hughes' book on Australian art will be out on the bookstalls here in a few weeks. He has put everyone in their places! . . . He praises me fulsomely at the beginning of the book, which apparently entitles him to paraphrase the first 100 pages from my three books, grabbing most of his quotations from me on the way, then of course, gives me a hearty kick in the backside a la Hughes at the end. You [David Boyd] get heavily belted . . . Arthur of course he loves. Dobell is down, Drysdale up. John Olsen gets more space than Tom Roberts. A very personal book in every way. There are sections of brilliant criticism and much bright journalistic writing—but no more real interest in the writing of history as history than a Murray River cod.[71]

Hughes may have recalibrated the history of Australian art to suit his own jaunty journalistic style and was unashamedly prepared to challenge Bernard's art-historical supremacy, but the book 'bristled with flaws'. As Hughes said, 'it was not a difficult book to write, in fact it almost wrote itself'.[72] Despite his larrikin irreverence, the book encapsulated an astute reading of Australian art and its contemporary figures, but as Andrew Riemer points out, 'his cavalier reliance on Bernard Smith's work' was bound to attract criticism. According to Penguin sources Hughes had been chronically late with the manuscript, making frequent changes because he had offended artists or gallery owners, and thus the printing process had been rushed.[73] When copies finally arrived in London for inspection the book fell to pieces with pages scattering across the floor. It was blamed on the searing hot weather melting the binding glue during the road haulage from Adelaide to the eastern seaboard. Whether because of that, or aggravated by Hughes' excessive reliance on Bernard's work, Penguin ordered the entire first printing be pulped, giving Hughes a reprieve to make further last-minute changes before the reprint.

Since 1961 and the Whitechapel exhibition Hughes had been a constant irritant for Bernard, but it was the cocky young provocateur's 'irresistible desire to offend'[74] that most annoyed him. When he read Hughes's review of *Australian Painting* (1962) for the *London Magazine* he was again reminded of how exasperating Hughes was: 'it [*Place, Taste and Tradition*] was an angry book, riddled with errors of fact and interpretation, ill researched and clogged with undergraduate Marxism. The esteem now given it is chiefly sentimental: it was after all, the first of its kind.'[75]

Bernard was often at his best when he wrote with Hughes firmly in his sight: 'The history of error has its own fascinations' or:

It would seem that Mr Nolan, Mr Pringle and Mr Hughes have all succumbed to an old medieval mode of thinking which still possesses surprising vitality today, the belief . . . in antipodal inversion, that is to say that the laws of nature operate in the southern hemisphere oppositely to those in the northern. The seasons and currents do, so why not everything else.[76]

Over the decades, however, Bernard developed a begrudging respect for Hughes. In 1981 he reviewed his *The Shock of the New* (1980), applauding his placement of modernism within a more 'human context than the rigid straight-jacket formalism into which New York critics like Clement Greenberg have sought to confine it'.[77] Describing Hughes as a 'master of the flexible and sensitive prose style' who had been 'well trained at the court of MoMA', Bernard then proceeded to take the book apart, picking out its flaws, inaccuracies and historical generalisations. Though rarely the kind of critic who set out to destroy a reputation, Bernard enjoyed stripping any crown of conceit from authors whose verbal histrionics were a cover for inadequate scholarship. By the time he reviewed *The Fatal Shore* (1987), however, he was surprised at how good it was, noting in his diary that 'Bob Hughes has redeemed himself in my eyes with this fine book.' Not only was it 'a classic of its kind' but 'a magnificent achievement . . . I did not realise that he would be capable of . . . this quality.'[78] It was a turning point, capped in 1998 when Bernard wrote to Hughes, by then the esteemed art critic for the *New York Times*, asking if he would launch his *Modernism's History* in London.

Yet Bernard also enjoyed giving with one hand and taking away with the other, especially if he had suffered grievances in the past. In an *Australian Book Review* article, he suggested that Alan Moorehead had 'filleted' his *European Vision and the South Pacific* for 'theatrical incidents' for Moorehead's *The Fatal Impact*, of which the young Robert Hughes had subsequently 're-filleted' for his *The Fatal Shore*. The 'trope', Bernard insisted, 'possessed an irresistible appeal' for these experienced journalists, and he concluded that 'Both were expatriates [who] felt the need to escape from the fatal impact of the Pacific before they were cannibalised by the savagery of their own people.'[79]

By mid-February Bernard was back on the critics' trail judging the Georges Invitation Art Prize with Alan McCulloch, Elwyn Lynn, Leonard French and John Olsen. First prize was awarded to Roger Kemp and second prize to Jean Bellette. It was not difficult to figure out who Bernard had chosen, especially as he had reviewed Bellette's work as 'lift[ing] the heart and rous[ing] the spirit of all who love good paintings. I cannot recall an exhibition in Melbourne of this quality since I began to write this column'.[80]

A highlight of 1965 was Bernard's trip to New Zealand to lecture at the University of Auckland's Elam School of Art where his old friend Paul Beadle was director and the artist Colin McCahon occasionally taught painting. Ursula Hoff owned one of McCahon's small *Waterfall* paintings and Bernard was particularly keen to acquire one from that series too. In 1964 an exhibition of William Hodges' paintings had been lent to the Auckland City Art Gallery from Admiralty House, Greenwich, and McCahon's *Waterfall* series was a direct and intimate response to Hodges' remarkable paintings, particularly the ones of Dusky Bay and other

New Zealand scenes. Bernard's admiration of Hodges predisposed him to appreciate McCahon's reunification of historical time, geographical place and aesthetic sensation, but he also saw the series as a contemporary extension of the empirical and imperial gaze of transcultural exchange.[81]

1966

In July 1966 Bernard left for six months' research in France, stopping over at the 33rd Venice Biennale where, in the magical city of Bellini, Giorgione and Tintoretto, he faced the full force of modernism. Umberto Boccioni's retrospective exhibition and the early Italian Abstraction Group impressed him, while Giorgio Morandi's small paintings reminded him 'of Mondrian and flat-patterned cubism, in the ambience of Ben Nicholson and Frank Hinder . . . an almost anonymous quality in their quietness, and . . . a sense of good taste . . . [yet] none give the impression of artists of genius or originality'. If anything he felt they were like 'craftsmen in the service of the abstract idea'.[82] He admired Alberto Burri's black on white and Lucio Fontana's dark slit and Jesús Rafael Soto's visual puzzles, but noted 'Pop is everywhere present, but rarely dominant.' He wrote his review for the *Age* in which he criticised Australia's absence at the biennale, concluding that:

> The biennale produces signs, reveals symptoms and pronounces benedictions that cannot be ignored . . . It is therefore a most formidable institution. Only the gardens are allowed to become older and more beautiful; the art is deeply committed to change.

By early July he was in Paris working on his unsung hero Gustave Courbet.

In Paris Bernard met the Grand Secretaire of the Cité Internationale des Arts to discuss Australia obtaining a permanent studio in Paris. The idea had been incubating for some time, similar issues having been discussed with H. C. Coombs, A. D. Trendall, Ralph Farrell and Hal Missingham at Australian Academy of Humanities meetings—Trendall had raised problems of establishing an Australian Institute in Rome in 1964. The Cité was a large, modern building in the Marais district on the right bank of the Seine, opposite the Île St-Louis, and was divided into studio apartments available for countries to rent or to buy. As he was interested in the Power job, the idea of the Cité studios was even more attractive given J. W. Power's French connections, and Bernard considered tilling the French soil an important prelude to securing a studio for the proposed institute. Alan McCulloch had also been shown through the complex the previous year and had steered the Australian division of AICA into making a submission to the Australian Government for the purchase of not one but three studios, arguing that they had a responsibility to rectify the 'paucity of opportunities open to Australian artists' to study overseas. The American Government had already bought 22 apartments and where the Americans led, Australia generally followed.[83]

Having arrived in Paris alone, as Kate was spending August and most of September at Ditchling with her family and friends, Bernard enrolled in an audio-visual course at the Universitaire de Besançon. He enjoyed accompanying students on excursions through the French countryside and watching film strips with grammar and vocabulary lessons. A visit to the Grotto d'Osselles, a large limestone cave in the valley of Courbet's birthplace, was an unexpected bonus. Seeing the formidable landscape in which Courbet grew up enabled a much better understanding of the artist's attachment to nature and its deeply pervasive quality in his work. Bernard would later write that 'the widening division between the country and the city, between craft and industrial production, between the alienation of urban life and the older unities of rural society' were at the core of Courbet's discontent.[84]

After completing his French course Bernard began looking at Géricault's drawings in the *Cabinet des Dessins* at the Musée Besançon, where he discovered a drawing of Titian's *Entombment* (1520). It sparked the idea for an article on the Géricault in the NGV's collection, which he published in the gallery's *Bulletin* in 1968. By September he was back in Paris at the Bibliothèque Nationale and tracking down as many Courbet paintings as he could find. When Kate arrived in Paris they caught a taxi to the Cité Internationale des Arts where Bernard had taken an apartment. Two days later a letter arrived from Ralph Farrell asking him to apply for the position of director of the Power Institute.

It was not entirely unexpected, but Kate was hesitant; she felt settled in Melbourne and wanted to stay near their children and her aged aunt. As they strolled around the Place des Vosges discussing the career move, Bernard announced he was ready to take the job. Not only would he be returning to the city where he had learnt how to survive, had politically matured and, against all odds, had achieved a university education, but it would be as the Power Professor of Contemporary Art at the University of Sydney, an offer too good to refuse. Moreover, he had already disclosed how he thought the Power Institute should be developed in his reply to Sir Herbert Read in 1964 and basing his application on this, posted it off that same evening.

Undeterred by the possible career change, he continued researching Géricault's *Entombment* and 'the apostle of realism', Courbet. At the Petit Palais in the Salle de Courbet he found 17 canvases, and another room full of Courbet's paintings at the local Besançon museum. He located Courbet's *Fileuse Endormie* (1853), *Les Baigneuses* (1853), his famous *Portrait of man with pipe* (c. 1846–49), and *le Rencontre* (1854), as well as marvellous works by Delacroix, Géricault, Girodet, David, Ingres and Tassaert at the Musée Fabre in Montpellier. On returning to Paris he learnt that Gordon Thomson had been appointed the curator of the Power Bequest, an appointment that delighted him. Thomson's credentials for the position were excellent. He had been the deputy director of the NGV, studied art gallery construction abroad on a Fulbright grant in 1955 and 1956, proven himself an astute administrator and possessed an excellent knowledge of modernist art in general and contemporary sculpture, Italian glass and furniture in particular. The news meant that the committee had arrived at their decision and it would be only a matter of time before the new director of the Power Institute was announced.

Kate continued working alongside Bernard at museums, filling notebooks with hundreds of transcribed letters and papers on and by Courbet. In London she translated copious records at the Witt Library while Bernard discussed his project with T. S. R. Boase and Ernst Gombrich, explaining that there were few books in English on the artist. Meyer Schapiro's brilliant essay 'Courbet and Popular Imagery: An Essay of Realism and Naiveté' (1941) was perhaps the only scholarly work available in English, and Bernard's biographical study and catalogue raisonné would incorporate his research on nineteenth-century stylistic change and the romantic movement.[85]

Apart from catching up with friends Arthur and Yvonne Boyd, Richard Beck, David and Hermia Boyd, and Barry and Rosalind Humphries, Bernard accompanied Mary Alice Evatt to a 'fascinating, inventive and ingenious' exhibition of Claes Oldenburg at Robert Fraser Galleries in Duke Street. The news that Moya Dyring was dying of cancer, however, came as a great shock and Bernard visited her at a private hospital in Wimbledon:

> How unkind it all is. She enjoyed life so fully and had such a gift for friendship. When I saw her last I dined with her and Michel in her studio before leaving for Besançon. Then she was full of plans for her new home in the Midi . . . had put up her studio for sale. Then her complaint was of her bad bunion and difficulty in walking.[86]

On 16 December Bernard and Kate flew out of Heathrow for Melbourne and as they crossed the vast antipodean continent and caught sight of the 'the long red ridge of the Australian interior, beautiful in the early morning light', Bernard wondered what lay ahead. Their arrival was dispiriting—'the trip from Essendon . . . even more banal than usual'—and he had still not heard from the University of Sydney about the Power position. Two days before Christmas a note arrived from the Senate of the University of Sydney offering him the position of Professor of Contemporary Art and the Director of the Power Institute. The Melbourne chapter was closing.

The first part of 1967 was spent tying up his teaching commitments, finding a replacement for his art critic job at the *Age* and organising his and Kate's departure. Bernard had been grooming Margaret Garlick, Patrick McCaughey, David Saunders and Jaynie Anderson as critics since early 1966 and the mantle was handed to the dynamic McCaughey. Forty years later McCaughey wrote to Bernard, 'I wanted to say how much I owe you . . . to giving me "my start in life" at the *Age*'.[87]

CHAPTER SEVEN: THE CONSTRUCTION OF POWER

Bernard Smith's role as director of the Power Institute of Fine Arts and the Power Professor of Contemporary Art from 1967 to 1977 presented significant challenges for him. At a personal level it took him away to a great extent from the scholarship on which his reputation had been built, involved him exercising his academic authority and operating at a senior level in university administration, and at the end of the day the strain of establishing the new institution took its toll. More broadly, at a local and international level there was a sharp turn to the left in politics and ideology, with a counterculture questioning of social democracy, public outrage about the Vietnam conflict and the increasingly manipulative powers of western capitalism. Together with the rise of feminism and sexual liberation, the period was defined as one of intense dissent. The Americanisation of art further contributed to what was perceived as a crisis in Australian cultural expression; Marshall McLuhan's 'the medium is in the message' was the rallying cry for the younger generation to challenge bureaucracy and institutionalisation, and the rules were there to be broken.[1] Within that charged atmosphere the newly appointed director of the Power Institute had to navigate his way through the turbulence of the contemporary.

The smattering of international applicants for the directorship of the Power Institute had fallen well short of the calibre sought, and even after re-advertising the position it was evident that it was not going to attract better candidates. The tyranny of distance was one crippling factor, as was the clause 'the contemporary'; few, it seemed, were courageous enough to tackle the task of establishing an institute of contemporary art in the Antipodes. Having stalled the process long enough, the University of Sydney's senate committee narrowed the field to Gil Docking, Franz Philipp, Gordon Thomson and Bernard Smith. The advice that Professor John White gave the university, whose vision complemented that of the university as 'campus bound, cloistered and rather elitist', finally recommended Gordon Thomson be offered the curatorship, while Bernard Smith was clearly 'the best man' for the Power Professorship.[2]

The appointments were always going to attract criticism, but many were pleased that at least another 'Pom' had not been appointed. Oscar Edwards, who had known Bernard since the 1940s, was more forthcoming: 'I for one would like to congratulate the university on its choice, for if it had to be an Australian, I know of no other with a more lush combination of academic qualifications, love for art, and a savoir-faire-public-relations-know-how that will be required in the launching of this difficult ship.'[3] Not everyone shared Edwards' views; there were many artists and critics incredulous that such a traditional art historian had been appointed to administer an institution defined by the contemporary. For Bernard, however, the glory of becoming a professor at the University of Sydney was the pinnacle of his academic ambitions, although in the next decade it would prove a poisoned chalice for him.

The Power Bequest had been hampered from the beginning by an overly cautious university and lampooned by the press before and well after its final legal establishment, and it was expected to be 'all things to all artists, academics, curators and critics'.[4] Robert Hughes, one of the first to tackle the problem of the function and role of the new institute, cited an anonymous writer: 'where there's a will there's often a way of getting around it, in the public interest and without doing violence to the testator's intentions.'[5] Hughes also doubted whether a person existed in Australia—apart from Eric Westbrook—capable of running an institute that had to concentrate on:

overseas contemporary art . . . and moreover who could tell the difference between Burri and Fontana, let alone between a major and a minor de Kooning or an early or late Dubuffet. The only possible solution, to import a director.[6]

Laurie Thomas, writing in the *Australian*, believed 'the fuss started' over the Power Bequest with Bernard's clash in 1963 with Sir Herbert Read. Read had suggested 'it would be fatal to give the faculty into the dead hands of historians',[7] but establishing a new department in such a loose, organic fashion as Read suggested was not Bernard's style. Almost 50 years later, the curator and art historian Ann Stephen laid the fault squarely at Bernard's feet, saying it had been disadvantaged by his imprimatur and its 'long rancorous history' a calamity of his initial mismanagement.[8] But Bernard had thought long and hard about the institute's structure, discussed it with numerous cultural cognoscenti and believed he was capable of constructing and managing the Power Institute:

> when I went up to the Power Institute, they said, 'What you've got to do, what you must teach us is contemporary art, contemporary art, contemporary art', and I said, well yes, what I'll do is what Benedetto Croce said, 'all art is contemporary art'. It may be ruins, but it was once contemporary, but there is a dual effect, you have to see it with your own contemporary eyes, and if you value it you are giving it contemporary value.[9]

That strategic resourcefulness demonstrated his shrewd use of historical slippage for the purpose of dealing with the shifting nature of the contemporary, but in the turbulent climate of the late 1960s Bernard believed any 'advocacy of the new' had to be rationally tempered while promoting criticism and arguments about the production and reception of the avant-garde.

The emphasis on the international avant-garde, using American and European standards as its measure, stamped the institute as regionalist and relegated Australia's own avant-garde as either largely invisible or second-rate, the opposite of what Bernard had been ideologically fighting for over the previous three decades. His refusal to argue for the acquisition of the best of Australia's own contemporary artists sharpened the divisions between 'us and them' and caused rifts among local artists and critics. Rudolf Arnheim, in a critical analysis of divisionism, argued that:

> Any structure is made up of directed tensions. The interplay of these vectors creates the network of relations . . . but not all vectors are constructive. Some act destructively. They disturb the structure by applying at the wrong place, at the wrong strength, or in the wrong direction . . . They . . . create tensions straining for adjustment .[10]

This encapsulates the Power Institute's history from the outset, and Bernard became both vector and target. But controversy, as Joan Kerr pointed out, came naturally to him and, while resilient by nature and necessity, from 1967 he began displaying an unprecedented level of authoritarianism. Unlike his time at the University of Melbourne, during which he managed to keep a distance between himself and the ruling elite, at Sydney he was caught firmly within the university's conservative managerial body, which he had to appease while implementing the structure of a new institute. If he were faithfully to implement John Wardell Power's will to 'make available . . . the latest ideas and theories in the plastic arts by means of lectures and teaching and the purchase of the most contemporary art of the world', and include an art library and a museum as teaching resources, it would require a firm governing hand. The emphasis on the contemporary, which for purposes of definition was deemed 'art that was not more than twenty years old at the time . . . or was the work of living, and contemporary artists',[11] was a thorny aesthetic that even the American critic Clement Greenberg confirmed as a conundrum:

> The prevalent notion is that latter-day art is in a state of confusion . . . innovations follow closer and closer on one another and because they don't make their exits as rapidly as their entrances, they pile up in a welter of eccentric styles, trends, tendencies, schools. Everything conspires, it would seem, in the interests of confusion.[12]

Inherent in the overview of the Power Bequest was the distinction between fine and applied arts, which in a contemporary context had 'became largely meaningless'; as such, it was felt that 'no rigid lines of demarcation should be established in the new department'. The breakdown of existing fields meant the history of art had to expand to include aesthetic theory, critical method, museum and art gallery curatorship, and the history of architecture. As Joseph Burke had warned, to isolate the twentieth century from the nineteenth century was 'unacademic'. Bernard, therefore, undertook to 'fashion an honest critical style that . . . approach[ed] the present without shedding the values of the past'.[13] Apart from finding staff capable of teaching art history with as much appreciation of the historical as of the contemporary, an urgent priority was to update his own knowledge of the very newest in international avant-garde art, theory and museum design.

It was also important to show the public the new international artworks that Gordon Thomson had purchased in 1967 and, with a working party of Harry Seidler, Alan Gamble, Daryl Douglas and Woodruff Hills, Bernard discussed the first Power Bequest Exhibition planned for May 1968 at Australia Square. John Kaldor, one of the founding board members of the institute enthusiastically wrote:

> What is most exciting is that the Power Institute specifies Contemporary Art, and already one collection has been bought and shown in Sydney . . . at long last, Sydney is getting a taste of up-to-date Contemporary Art, due to the excellent work of Professor Smith and the very recent establishment of this Chair.[14]

Of the 31 works acquired by Thomson, Jean Tinguely's mechanical sculpture *Bascule no. 1: Sisyphus* (1965) (fig. 38) captured what Bernard considered the leitmotiv of the collection, 'a movement away from the traditional limitations of painting and sculpture towards an exploration of the aesthetic borderlands between the two arts'.[15] The irony of Tinguely's machine art is that its 'semblance of catastrophe' sets out to destroy itself, precisely what Bernard apprehensively felt the direction of contemporary art and theory was taking.

Aesthetic borderlands and new aesthetic territories characterised the international art world and as 1968 unfolded, the tumultuous political events in Europe formed a backdrop of revolutionary dissension. Violent student riots in Paris and elsewhere, large peace and 'ban the bomb' marches, anti–Vietnam War demonstrations and military intervention to end the Prague Spring were stark reminders of the ongoing Cold War. Australia's own counterculture may have looked placid by comparison, but it was not immune to the fallout. In 1966 and 1967 it was revealed that the CIA had financially backed 'magazines, books, concerts, art and congresses', including Australia's *Quadrant* magazine, as part of their 'manifest destiny' program. Bernard knew all this. *Quadrant*'s editors were Peter Coleman and James McAuley, with Elwyn Lynn an associate editor and Joseph Burke, who had previously been on its editorial board, a member of the Congress of Cultural Freedom, now known as having operated as a front for the CIA.[16]

Bernard had been monitoring the USA's cultural ascendency for almost two decades and there was no holding back the tide of its avant-garde thrust. In June 1967 when MoMA's *Two Decades of American Painting* arrived in Melbourne before travelling on to Sydney, the reception for abstract expressionism had been electric. Patrick McCaughey declared 'these are the greatest paintings we've seen since the war' and 'the myth that all American painting was over-scaled, over-rated and over-promoted dies on the spot. The illusion that Australian painting was just as good but somehow went "unrecognised" was exploded.'[17] The following year the NGV opened its new St Kilda Road building with *The Field* exhibition, devoted entirely to a new generation of post-painterly abstractionists.

In May 1968 Bernard, working with Alan McCulloch and no doubt encouraged by Elwyn Lynn, brought the famous American art critic Clement Greenberg to Sydney as the guest of the Power Institute, the Commonwealth Fund and the Carnegie Corporation.[18] Greenberg was a logical choice to deliver the Inaugural John Power Lecture, titled 'Avant-Garde Attitudes', and to give the key lecture at the UNESCO Seminar on 'Criticism in the Arts', also held at the University of Sydney (fig. 39). His championing of the physicality of the medium as embodied by America's post-painterly abstraction, action painters and hard-edged practitioners, gave him a commanding influence, but the power of the man who had helped package American abstract expressionism as a politicised 'aesthetic national mythology' during the 1940s and the early phase of the Cold War was, in Bernard's view, already on the wane. If he had been impressed with the American critic's essays and criticism in 1962, by 1968 he had changed his mind and his invitation to Greenberg was undoubtedly another veiled attempt at hitting out at the USA's cultural imperialism.

Greenberg's visit helped localise Australia's own perceptions of its avant-garde position, though not everyone shared McCaughey's belief that he had raised 'the level of expectation in critically assessing new painting in Australia'.[19] According to John Stringer '[he] did more to disillusion artists with his teachings than to recruit new converts' and Terry Smith believed that his 'racing form-guide to the history of art', though 'compelling in its simplicity', damaged the critical foundations of art history.[20] But art and its history was not an easy game and, as Greenberg claimed, it never proceeded neatly; what mattered was quality and ultimately that came down to a matter of self-critical experience—in other words 'the avant-garde is left alone with itself'.[21] The difficulty of aesthetic judgement, or determining good art from bad, was either 'intuited' or evaluated by the yardstick of experience. This sounded very like Herbert Read in 1933—'Positive criticism begins as an impulse to defend one's instinctive preferences.'[22] A Melbourne artist and critic at one of the informal gatherings arranged for Clement Greenberg captured his 'anti-doctrinaire attitude':

Greenberg, very much the visiting guru, was chewing his cigar and had all these slides of the Americans; as we looked at the slides . . . then looked to Greenberg . . . he'd say, 'No, no it's no good', and he'd go to the next one and say 'that's terrific', or that's 'OK'. After about twenty slides one young critic asked Greenberg why the brevity of explanation, and taking the large Havana out of his mouth, Greenberg replied 'just a matter of experience, son'.[23]

Bernard found this subjective form of evaluation unacceptable, even in the fluid climate of 1968. For him art criticism demanded rigour and accountability:

> The function of the critic is not to lull the public into agreeing with his own particular prejudices, but to arrive at certain evaluations, certain conclusions after he has arrived at a standard of values which are more or less objective. It is his business to examine the past in the light of the present, to take up from the history of the past those aspects of art which have manifested themselves . . . and which will prove useful in weighing the position, standard, direction and impetus of our contemporary culture.[24]

Elwyn Lynn, though friendly with Greenberg, parodied him as a figure who 'came amongst us as the great healer', rather than 'an iconoclastic divider', but conceded that his refusal to 'deepen' discussions was inadequate.[25] Lynn's attitude to art and public criticism was to advance a more professional structure, one in which:

> the role of the art critic is unique, because he is the only free agent operating in the (art-world) context. As such he is in a position to act as a check on the activities of dealers, collectors, journalists, and museums, which at the present time seems to grow more outlandish and reprehensible every day.[26]

With Clement Greenberg spot-lit in the contemporary arena, Bernard stood at its edge watching the myth exploding. At the Inaugural John Power Lecture Greenberg asked the audience for questions, to which one young wit announced, 'Why are we talking about flatness and opticality when Andy [Warhol] might be dying?'[27] Bernard, however, must have taken some satisfaction when Greenberg 'admitted that [while] the Antipodeans had faults, they impressed him more than other artists', ostensibly because of their fertile artistic quality, but he also cautioned that 'to take sides in the Antipodean-abstract skirmish' was to deny art its innovative rights.[28]

At Greenberg's final farewell chat to the Power students David Saunders captured something of the critic's uncritical arrogance. Describing it as taking 'the form of comments on Australia. There were only four comments he [Greenberg] had to make but his pondering drawl spun out for three quarters of an hour and he made it quite enjoyable.'[29] Before Greenberg left Australia Bernard was already on an aeroplane heading for Europe. The issue of the collection, the curator and the proposed gallery or museum of contemporary art remained a top priority, particularly as the J. W. Power Collection was a crucial teaching resource. Gordon Thomson had resigned partly for family reasons, but mainly because of problems with the release of funds for acquisitions—misunderstandings with Bernard, whose 'impenetrable ego' and skill of turning everything to his favour made Thomson's job unworkable.[30] It was decided that Bernard would test his hand at buying for the Power Collection. He informed the vice-chancellor that the Venice Biennale 'provides the best single conspectus of international art . . . available anywhere and is, therefore, one which I can barely afford to miss'.[31]

Another objective was to look at modern gallery design and on his way to Venice Bernard stopped at Tel Aviv and Jerusalem, where he visited the Israel Museum. Its brilliant lighting, materials and colour, floors and walls, lifts and doors, entrances and exits, exhibition and art storage, administration and public spaces made it, in Bernard's opinion, 'one of the great modern museums of the world'.[32] This was just the first stop and in the next few months he saw many modern galleries in Italy, France, Britain, Germany and the USA. His wider objective was to look at the world's best artists, make purchases for the collection and find out whether the Italian Government would assist with donations of books and photographs for a new research library in Australia. After three days at the Venice Biennale he made a list of who he considered the most outstanding artists. These included Alberto Burri, Anthony Caro, Eduardo Chillida, Sonia Delaunay, Jim Dine, Jean Dubuffet, Alberto Giacometti, Lucio Fontana, Hans Hartung, Louise Nevelson, Victor Vasarely, Eduardo Paolozzi and Mark Tobey. With limited funds of $28,000 he purchased 58 works, one-third of which were bought from the major contemporary art fair *Documenta IV* in Kassel, Germany. The most significant of those were the Fontana, an Enrico Baj collage, a black-and-white porcelain relief by Vasarely and a Hartung painting. With inimitable meticulousness he also made lists of major galleries in Milan, Rome, Paris, London, Stuttgart and the main cities of the USA, noting the universities that were active in teaching and collecting twentieth-century art.[33]

In Paris Bernard inspected the University of Sydney's newly purchased residential studio at the Cité Internationale des Arts, dedicated to the memory of Moya Dyring. With an introduction from Oscar Edwards he met the art dealer Daniel-Henry Kahnweiler. As he intended to provide a profile of J. W. Power in his inaugural Power Lecture, he was keen to find out as much as possible about that forgotten expatriate who had left his wealth to his alma mater. Kahnweiler, who had handled Power's paintings at his Galerie Louise Leiris, told Bernard 'we all knew Power, but . . . as an artist . . . [not] as a rich man and a surgeon'.[34]

Bernard also found himself at the centre of student unrest, with the aftermath of the May riots resonating through the Parisian streets and buildings. Revolutionary posters were plastered everywhere and he acquired several for himself. They represented the visual and verbal working mutually, the medium of the message brilliantly capturing 'the dichotomy that exists between the workers and the managerial level in a capitalist society'.[35] They also testified to the importance of public art as a handmaiden to social reform, so potent in France's history and seminal to Bernard's ideology of art and society (fig. 40).

From Paris Bernard and Kate, who accompanied him to all his meetings and acted as his secretary and interpreter, travelled to England where he discussed problems establishing an institute of fine arts with numerous directors. He bought books on European art and architecture in the period 1750 to 1880 for his undergraduate courses; MoMA's Bernard Karpel was asked to draw up a list of more contemporary books. Arriving in the USA, Bernard's priority was to discuss methods and course structures on the contemporary and he called on Waldo Rasmussen at MoMA, numerous museums, and Yale University and School of Art. He also caught up for a postmortem discussion with Clement Greenberg about the critic's visit to the Antipodes. When Greenberg told him 'you Australians . . . are all so honest, so naïve' Bernard could not help but feel, and not without some contempt, that he was just like most critics from the Northern Hemisphere who believed a young nation so geographically and culturally removed from the great metropolitan centres could not be of any real importance.[36]

Cultural eclecticism

On 11 June 1969 Bernard gave his inaugural lecture as the Power Professor of Contemporary Art in which he depicted J. W. Power as an alienated man.[37] This view has recently been rejected and it raises the question as to whether Bernard had recalibrated Power through his own outsider lens. In establishing something of Power's personality he outlined the expatriate's beneficent intentions and why the institute was uniquely positioned to question the relationship of art to contemporary society.

After Power left Australia and gave up his medical career he had acquired a 'curious, eager, omnivorous' appetite for the avant-garde that enabled him to penetrate some of the more important artistic circles in London, Paris and Brussels.[38] Yet the 'alienated cosmopolitan' chose to endow an Australian university as a beneficiary of his wealth, rather than a British or French institute—the European crisis and World War II had clearly been a major factor in Power's decision. Bernard believed that by mediating the geographical distance which plagued Australia, and by 'sharpen[ing] the dialogue between theory and practice', Australian artists could compete with their international counterparts and could develop a better sense of their intellectual and creative originality. At the same time it was important 'not [to] neglect the grass-roots of our own culture' and he signalled the study of Australian art and architecture as well as Asian and Oceanic art. But for art history and international theory to become a vital discipline in an Australian university, inter-institutional cooperation, travel to major collections other than in Sydney, as well as abroad, was necessary. While establishing a global relational position he wondered whether, in the age of readymades and mechanical reproduction, this was necessary.

Bernard's intense interest in the 'second machine age' had been consistent since the 1930s; 'if we are living through the last days of painting as men of the sixteenth century lived through the last days of the illuminated manuscript' the question, he said, had to be asked whether artists or 'art could survive in the modern world'.[39] Adopting a manifesto-like tone, he hypothesised about the artist in the modern industrial world:

The happy producer asserts that art will survive if it is prepared to adopt the methods of modern industrial production without question. The artist will become a designer . . . at the . . . end of the industrial process . . . and produce his work for a large market. His name will become a brand name . . . General Motors will be replaced by General Multiples.

His prophetic parody continued:

The mass media will disseminate the artist's reputation . . . the independent art critic . . . will become as much of an anachronism as the independent artist expressing his feelings in prestigious, handcrafted objects. He will write blurbs for the super dealers . . . Art will be cheap . . . and available to all in the suburban super-market . . . [and] to twist Lord Acton's phrase: 'Mass production corrupts artistic value, and absolute mass-production corrupts artistic values utterly.'[40]

A correlation existed between this lecture and Bernard's 1938 Teachers Federation Art Club critique of Australian art and education in which he had quoted Alexis Carrel's *Man, the Unknown* (1935):

Aesthetic activity remains potential in most individuals . . . [but] we have been transformed into machines . . . He manufactures only single parts . . . never makes the complete objects . . . In sacrificing mind to matter, modern civilization has perpetuated a momentous error . . . industry has deprived the worker of originality and beauty.[41]

Bernard concluded his lecture with a plea for a continuity of past traditions within the bounds of contemporaneity:

if the liberal tradition is to be sustained in the powerful new areas of mass-communication, critical modes of procedure will have to be developed . . . We need an etymology and semantics of the visual image as rigorous as that of the word . . . a deepening concern with the uses to which visual imagery has been put from the Egyptian tombs to its latest uses in colour television and holography.[42]

Yet Bernard was still optimistic about the future of the Power Institute and, as Richard Larter observed, he appeared like a man moving sure-footed across the modern landscape.[43] The inaugural John Power Lecture had been presented by Greenberg and the recently appointed lecturer Donald Brook had just delivered a brilliant and 'closely argued denunciation' of Greenberg's ideas in the second Power lecture. Elwyn Lynn's first bounty of international art had been bought and John Kaldor's Art Project, Christo and Jeanne Claude's *Wrapped Coast, Little Bay, Sydney,* had used a team of university students under the artists' direction to cover the cliffs with 1 million square feet (929,000 square m) of polypropylene 'to brilliant effect and great publicity'. Bernard and Kate helped with the wrapping. Though dismissive of the massive art installation as 'derivations of dada' or 'a kind of blown up Duchamp', Bernard conceded it was very good, even if 'it [wa]s not the business of a University to promote publicity or controversy . . . but it is certainly a university's business surely to see that public matters and controversial matters are discussed.'[44]

Postmodernism's maelstrom

Art is not the name of a distinctive kind.
It is a shifting bundle of cultural kinds.
Donald Brook[45]

During the late 1960s and early 1970s 'the status of the work of art as a privileged object, as a special thing in itself' was questioned. Concepts of 'high-art' were deconstructed, 'Pop Art was in its prime, Minimalism was multiplying and Conceptual artists had begun their tactical offensive.'[46]

Debates about the new pluralism and collective socialisation were captured by the slogan 'anything goes', and with 'painting under siege' a burgeoning, diverse consumerist art market growing, Bernard, who usually rode the cultural demands of the times, must surely have occasionally felt that he was walking on shifting sand. Establishing the teaching of art history within such currents may explain his dogmatic insistence on the institute being constructed along traditional academic lines of teaching.

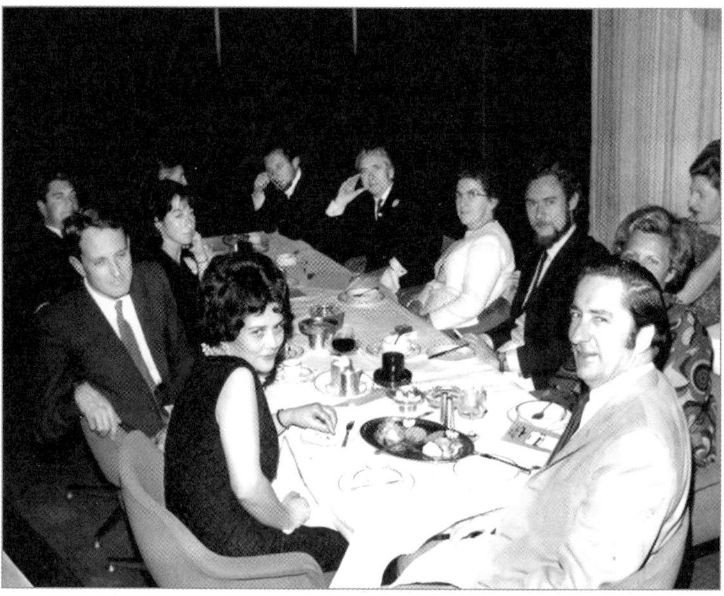

Fig. 41 Power Institute staff dinner at the Summit Restaurant, 2 August 1969

His first staff appointments included the Melbourne architectural historian David Saunders, the young art history graduate and Marxist Terry Smith, and Jocelyn Grey, also from Melbourne, as tutors, and the British artist, theorist and critic Donald Brook, a graduate of Durham University, England, and more recently of the ANU (fig. 41). By mid-1968 Anthony Bradley had been appointed librarian and Bernard, who was keen to appoint Daniel Thomas, encouraged him to apply for the curator's position and establish a museology course. Though interviewed, Thomas decided 'to hang on' at the AGNSW—it was then in the process of being upgraded, whereas the Power Gallery at the time 'was not even a real prospect'.[47] Consequently Bernard invited Ursula Hoff to join the institute and to establish a third-year course on seventeenth-century art, introduce museology as a course and become editor of the Power journal. Though tempted, she declined when the NGV recognised her scholarly contributions and promoted her to a position in which she could devote herself more to full-time research and publications. By February 1969, Elwyn Lynn had taken over as the Power curator and Anton Wilhelm, a graduate of Vienna and Innsbruck and a specialist in seventeenth-century art and architecture, had been appointed. The staff also included Bert Flugelman and Guy Warren as lecturers in practical classes, otherwise known as the Creative Art Workshop or the Tin Sheds. Other staff included Eneide Mignacca, Jennifer Sherwood and Joan Kerr, while Marr Grounds and the artist Lloyd Rees, both from the School of Architecture, also lectured. Undergraduate teaching began in 1968, the honours year in 1971, with a course on Asian art introduced in 1974.

'Modernism', Peter Beilharz writes, 'is always looking backwards. Part of its identity precedes it, existing as . . . a reference.'[48] Bernard epitomised modernism's traditions and relished looking backwards, which was why many considered him unsuitable for the Power professorship. Yet within that traditional frame he had helped professionalise art history in Australia by marshalling a global historiography. At the opposite end of the spectrum was postmodernism's precursor, Donald Brook, an intellectually creative and theoretically advanced internationalist whose open platform polemics mirrored the deconstructive, reformative times. After completing postgraduate studies under the philosopher John Passmore at the ANU in 1965, Brook was appointed teacher-in-charge of the School of Art in Canberra, but it was his radical style of thinking and writing, particularly his art criticism for the *Canberra Times*, that generated excitement (fig. 42). As an outsider from England, Brook saw Australia's modern art world divided into two camps: international American modernism and those concerned with cultural identity as conceived by Bernard's antipodean paradigm of figural mythography. Brook was prepared to confront both and 'shift the bundles' to a new polemical level. To all appearances he was the perfect appointment for the Power Institute, where he lectured on aesthetics and sculpture.

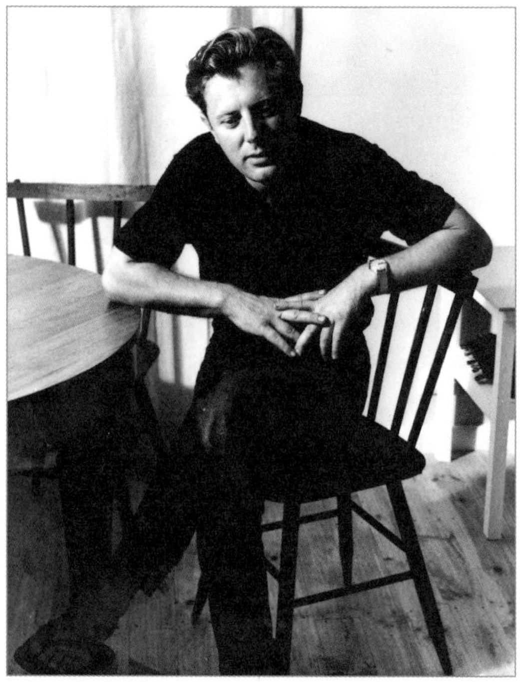

Fig. 42 Donald Brook, 1967

Brook's well-received Power Lecture, 'Flight from the Object', proposed a new way of perceiving art through a critical analysis of its 'object-hood', and argued that the traditional idea of art as a special object, elevated by its 'pedestal' distinctiveness, had isolated it as a thing in itself. By dismantling art's privileged position within a minority market, the cultural value of production, distribution and reception would be dramatically reorientated. It was theory and cultural history at its innovative best and the majority of students found Brook an inspiring beacon within the Australian contemporary art world.

Initially the department's collegial atmosphere was constructive and friendly. Students found it particularly well balanced, solid and dynamic, with Bernard perceived as an approachable old 'lefty' with conservative traits and whose linear tree of art history with its connective, stylistic changes reached back to the Syrians, a coherent and logical foundation.[49] Robyn Ravlich, a student at the Power Institute in 1969, described him thus:

[His] lectures were more sedate and highly composed: he'd enter the lecture theatre, an elegant trim figure with hair slicked back . . . and as the slides began to flicker on the projection screen with images of European art from the nineteenth century, he'd bring them to life. Not only aesthetically, but illuminating all the social, political and economic circumstances and thought that went into paintings such as David's *The Death of Marat*, and Gericault's *The Raft of the Medusa* . . . [He] lectured on Courbet, Corot, Cézanne and Van Gogh with tenderness and passion, showing us . . . the alienation of rural workers and the emptying of the countryside as industrialisation gained strength and fed the cities . . . This was his backdrop to twentieth century modernism, with a Marxist flavour.[50]

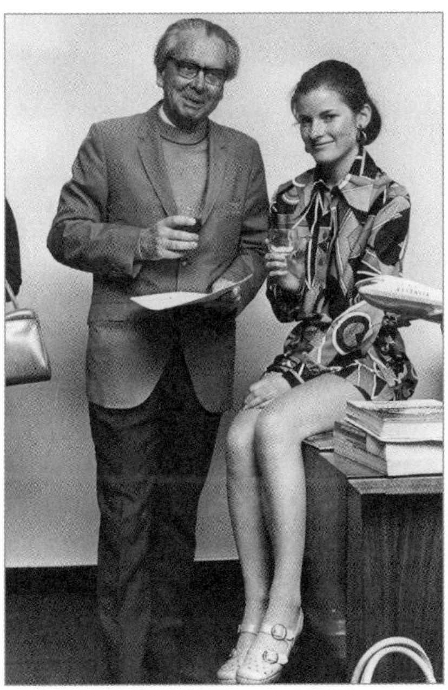

Fig. 43 Bernard Smith with Power Institute
student Catherine De Lorenzo, c. 1970

By early 1969 Donald Brook had initiated an interdisciplinary colloquium between science, technology and the fine arts, aimed at addressing art scholarship, environmental design, creativity and 'adjacent interdisciplinary regions'. The idea was to produce artworks within a multidimensional parameter, using new technical tools and materials and applying innovative psychological and perceptive ways of appraising art.[51] It was the platform for the non-institutional Tin Sheds, an experimental paradise for the making of art. As Brook said:

> The Sheds were and weren't a part of the University . . . [they] collected the malcontents of the 'system' [and also represented] an intellectual shift within art education . . . like the Yellow House and Inhibodress, [they] became home to radical art practices that were not tolerated in established art schools . . . The Sheds was one of the first places in Australia to recognise the need for a 'laboratory' for experimentation around art and the built environment.[52]

Such experimentation within the university was at first opposed by Bernard, as Marr Grounds discovered when he lobbied for Fine Arts students to have contact with the art workshop; 'He told me . . . that the teaching of art and the studying of art are two different things . . . art teaching belongs at the trade school [and] has no place in the University . . . [which] is a place for intellectuals . . . he felt very strongly that way . . . in the beginning.'[53] Perhaps Bernard still had Herbert Read's 'laboratory style art school' in mind, but eventually he relaxed his attitude and became supportive of 'the democratising effect . . . the Sheds had to offer'.[54]

By the early 1970s the unified mood of the department had turned. Taking his 'god professorship' seriously and insisting the institute be established along traditional lines similar to the Courtauld Institute—a requisite if students wished to move on to postgraduate degrees at international universities—Bernard's unilateralism began to alienate staff and students, his manner and methods out of kilter with the times. In his 1967 article 'Wither Painting?' Bernard foreshadowed the postmodern as 'the peculiar delusion of twentieth century arts or will it be seen as the birth of a new language of vision. I don't think we can know the answer to that', but by 1970 he did.[55] While the Power Institute could boast it had an exciting theorist trained in the British analytical philosophy manner, Brook's aesthetic criticism and liberationist theories struck at almost everything on which Bernard had based his intellectual and historical praxis. Bernard saw Brook's neo-Kantian, phantom aesthetics and 'linguistic modelling' as reducing art and its history to a situation in which the subject–object relation existed only as a relation, not as a reality.[56] As Brook later put it, 'Meaning and truth are simply spoils to the victors in discursive conflict on the cultural worksite.'[57] Brook, however, saw Bernard as the executive of the traditional trope and anchored so deeply in the past that his concept of the contemporary was incompatible with what the present needed. Bernard was interested in the detail of cultural change, whereas Brook was interested in the shifting; and each came to represent each other's nemesis.

As tensions increased, arguments became ferocious and walls were erected, psychologically and physically by the shutting of doors; Elwyn Lynn refused to communicate and became reclusive, his bunker mentality a response as much to Bernard as it was to Brook, the latter determined to diminish or to eradicate Lynn's curatorial independence by insisting that buying artworks for the Power Collection be rotated among the staff. Lynn's relationship with Bernard had already soured in 1967 when Bernard reviewed his book *Sidney Nolan: Myth and Imagery*, claiming that 'it leaves much to be desired'.[58] Having worked so extensively with Nolan for the Georgian House monograph in 1962 Bernard's vindictive review set out to show his superior knowledge of Nolan, but it was a mean pettiness that many saw as a form of intellectual bullying. With both men possessing volatile tempers, the Power Institute became a site of truculent insults, often resulting in Kate Smith ringing Lynn's wife Lily to warn her 'that Bernard was on the war-path and that Jack [Elwyn] should keep out of his way'.[59]

As collegial relations deteriorated, even the congenial David Saunders, who had been a mediating presence in the department, joined the ranks of the disenchanted. Bernard's refusal to promote him until he gained a PhD from the Faculty of Architecture was seen as grossly unfair and another of Bernard's power tactics. Saunders eventually took a professorial post at the University of Adelaide in 1977. By late 1972 dissension was rampant with students publishing the article 'Who has Power in the Department of Fine Arts?' in *Honi Soit* and circulating it as a pamphlet. Aimed squarely at Bernard's refusal 'to discuss the general rigidity of the Department' or consider student representation at staff meetings, he was accused of 'old ideas of the master–student relationship' and the 'all-powerful Professor syndrome'. The issue of authority versus the democratising of the institute's management, spearheaded by Donald Brook's vociferous and often seductive rhetorical art politics, was not contained within the university. When the exhibition of the Power artworks opened at the NGV in January 1972, the Power Institute's internal squabbles and the University of Sydney's mismanagement of the Power Bequest funds were exposed by Patrick McCaughey's 'Signs of a Power Struggle for the Fine Arts in Australia' in the *Age*.[60] The fuse had been lit for a bonfire of the vanities.

When Bernard began supervising the feminist Joan Kerr's masters thesis in 1973 he was challenged in different ways. With Kerr's indomitable personality, strong political views, irreverence for authority and determination to do history her way there was an immediate clash. Yet, while their relationship was confrontational, he was supportive of her research on colonial church architecture and appreciated her revisionist historiography. Kerr's rehabilitation of minor and marginalised artists was not dissimilar to Bernard's own approach and, with her immense appetite for facts, she was a natural collaborator in the dictionary project that Bernard had begun with Eve Buscombe and which Kerr took to completion in 1992. When he reviewed her *Heritage: The National Women's Art Book* (1995) his wit had the final word: 'at the end of her voluminous acknowledgements, Joan tells that once again her "survival was entirely due" to her husband. If that is so and she is not just being "nice", which is not quite like her anyway, then the Australian Women's movement owes a great deal indeed to James Semple Kerr.'[61]

As the divisiveness of the department escalated staff either opposed Bernard or refused to meet him or even each other. Bernard recalled that the situation was one of complete disunity. Many could see that his authoritarianism would be his downfall and yet years after his retirement he maintained that he was neither 'by temperament or conviction [authoritarian]. Indeed positions of authority have always made me feel a trifle uncomfortable: I may have exerted influence at times but not power.'[62] Minerva's owl, that symbol of objective wisdom, was nowhere in sight and Bernard was unable to see his shortcomings.

George Steiner captures the type of vitriol that develops among academics when there is bloodletting in the corridors:

A strange violence can inhabit abstract thought and scholarship. It expresses itself in the *odium* of academic disputes, in the unforgiving acidity of mandarin debates . . . The motives may lie in the isolation of pure erudition from the roughage and compromise of ordinary existence. It may point to the envy felt by the cloistered intellectual . . . for those who must put their skills and beliefs to the test of the pragmatic.[63]

The unforgiving vitriol reached crisis point when Donald Brook, while still a member of staff, wrote a series of scathing articles on the Power Institute, claiming it had 'started badly and that there is no reason to think it will improve without a radical change in policy'. In his view, Bernard could have changed the nature of art education in Australia, but missed the opportunity.[64] His attacks on the curator and the director, as well as his provocative reviews in the *Sydney Morning Herald* on local Sydney artists and dealers, created an antagonistic groundswell. Bernard could hold out no longer and told A. D. Trendall about the appalling situation. A plan was hatched to remove Brook from the Power Institute by encouraging him to apply for the new Chair of Fine Arts at Flinders University in Adelaide. In a letter to Joseph Burke, Brook wrote, 'I am told that nothing or nothing important happens in Fine Arts in Australia unless your opinion has been sought'.[65] Trendall also asked Burke to write Brook a glowing reference, in which Burke frankly stated:

he will from time to time parade esoteric learning in a way which reminds me of the flourishes with which some of the eighteenth century composers embellished their sonatas. At the same time his performance is both distinguished and well considered . . . [but] I have heard him criticised for being divisive.[66]

Despite his faults, captured effectively by John Passmore as 'a man of strong views . . . [who] sometimes offends people . . . I should not regard diplomacy as his strongest point, a judgement in which I am sure he would concur', Brook's application for the chair was successful.[67] Many considered him a brilliant man who had fought to save Australia from sinking into its antipodean desert and saw him as being integral to the development of a postcolonial, cosmopolitan theory of new art. At a time when contemporary national identity and regionalism had increasingly become irrelevant he was 'a prescient but ultimately lonely participant', arguing against a parochialism that regularly beset the Australian art world.[68]

Bernard's difficulty in handling the new type of art historian was not just about defending his position or being displaced; the more he saw art becoming ambiguous the more he asserted a historically structured form of teaching. Being superseded by a new generation of art historians and critics was inescapable, but the new internationalism and provincialism argument was not new either; it was another version of his antipodeanism argument that he had consistently defended and written about since the 1940s. With history permeating the present, those who came after Bernard were progressive to a point, but even in shifting their discourse to new levels, tradition retained its status as an alternative vision.

In 1973 Bernard gave a paper titled 'Making of the Future' at a Visual Arts Weekend at Spode in England. The modern movement, he pronounced, had begun to lose its impetus by 1968 when the 'capacity of *new avant-garde* movements to shock [was] declining rapidly'; indeed, he said, 'the device of shock itself is becoming . . . an act of ironic impotence'.[69] In the 1970s, however, Australian avant-gardism was intent on deconstructing the spectacle and subverting the real. The message was a mixture of anti-authoritarianism, ambiguous signs and 'blurred divisions'; and performance art, particularly in Melbourne, 'rejected the most cherished ideas of modernity and social normality'. Stelarc's *Body as object*, Domenico De Clario's *Interruption* installations, Ivan Durrant's dramatic *Slaughtered cow* at the NGV, Kevin Mortensen's *The seagull salesman*, and Peter Tyndall's camera head and autobiographical gaze, were some of the best of these performance works.[70] In Sydney, at the short-lived Inhibodress art space, Peter Kennedy, Ian Burn and Mike Parr introduced anti-commercial, avant-garde conceptual performances, and at The Yellow House in Potts Point, weirdly wonderful exhibitions and manic, wild performances enticed the counterculture and its 'disaffected artists, musicians [and] poets'.[71] Bernard often dropped by as an observant witness, but resisted enticement.

As a new generation of art historians emerged to challenge the old moderns Bernard found his polemics on the contemporary increasingly attacked or used by younger neo-Marxist art historians to assert their divergence. The provincialism problem, first promulgated by Ian Burn and then more extensively by Terry Smith in 1974, took Bernard's work as a foundational matrix to develop a contemporary critique of cultural hegemony, metropolitan centres and their provincial dependants. In that Bernard was simultaneously displaced and centralised. His concept of antipodean inversion was adopted, interrogated and reconstructed, but essentially it remained at the core of a new plateau of revisionism. For the new art historians and many anthropologists, ethnologists, visual cultural theorists and mainstream intellectuals, Bernard Smith was an inescapable presence whose footsteps were always ahead of them.

Glebe

Caring is not all that fashionable these days.
Bernard Smith[72]

By August 1967 Kate and Bernard had bought a large, roomy house at 23 Avenue Road, Glebe, within walking distance of the university. 'It is all very exciting and challenging', he wrote to his mother, but admitted, 'he also wished he was back in Parkville'. Not only was the job daunting, but Kate was unhappy at being uprooted from her family and found Sydney's cultural life shallow compared to Melbourne. A few lines copied in her diary from Randolph Stow's *The Merry-Go-Round in the Sea* (1965) captures something of her discontent:

I can't stand this arrogant mediocrity. The shoddiness and the wowserism and the smug wild boys in the bars . . . And the unspeakable boredom of belonging to a country that keeps up a

sort of chorus: Relax mate, relax, don't make the place 'too hot'.
Relax you bastard before you get clobbered.

Though as Kate and Bernard got to know their neighbourhood Kate's passion for its architecture and preservation of the buildings developed into a serious research project and conservation program. From middle-class Glebe Point to the less privileged areas of Bishopthorpe (also in Glebe) and areas closer to the city, many houses were in appalling condition, but far from being 'a slum' suburb, as the Town Planning Department suggested, they found its working-class ambience appealing. 'It[s] earthy friendliness, and lack of pretence', as Max Solling has described, was exactly their sort of place.[73] Theft, however, was prevalent, and after their magnificent ceramic *Angel learning to walk* by John Perceval was stolen, bought from Perceval's 1958 exhibition for 80 guineas, Kate and Bernard kept an old broken sofa and refrigerator on their verandah to deter further burglaries.

The Glebe community had always been a mixture of students, professionals and tradespeople, but when the Askin Government began tearing down houses to make way for a massive freeway the people galvanised. Under Kate and Bernard's leadership they established the Glebe Society, and while Bernard was an effective leader and spokesman who relished the opportunity to resist bureaucrats and take to the streets with public protests, Kate was the driving force (fig. 44). The society played a crucial role in the Whitlam Government's decision to purchase 42 acres (17 ha) of Bishopthorpe, which, according to Bernard, was the first piece of urban conservation undertaken in Australia. As Bernard's son John said, 'A bulldozer was no match for Bernard, as many of us have found when we tried to stop him from doing something he had set his mind to.'[74]

Bernard also protested against the war in Vietnam, at both a street and aesthetic level. On 3 October 1968 he opened an exhibition at Ann Lewis' Gallery A, claiming it was 'a gesture of dissent' in line with what he had seen during his recent overseas trip:

from Jerusalem to San Franscisco a new . . . social involvement [was obvious]. It differs . . . from the involvement of the old left

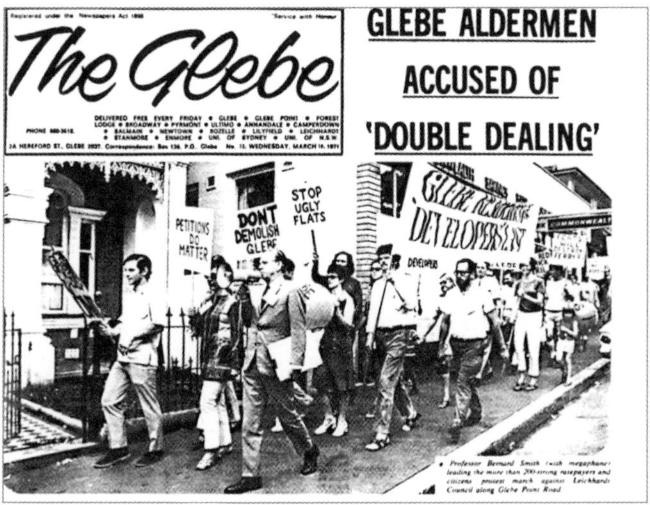

Fig. 44   Bernard Smith leading protesters at Glebe, March 1971

of the 1930s. Then involvement meant the politicisation of art . . . The new dissent is not tied to party . . . [it] cuts across stylistic divisions, and sees the creative artist as actively and even provocatively involved in social change.[75]

In many ways Bernard found this new dissent invigorating and, though he tried to remain critically balanced, his speech was weighted with fighting words. He referred to the peace conferences of the late 1940s and 1950s and called for action from the Commonwealth Government; 'It is certainly time we stopped conscripting young men . . . The old are given the power of forcing the young to kill and they wonder why the young are in revolt.'[76] Bernard's activism remained as vigorous as it had been in the early 1940s when he was a committed communist and the opportunity of going to the barricades or joining the protesters was enthusiastically embraced.

By 1972 the conservation movement and the community had become a force that cut across traditional political lines, attacked bureaucratic ineptitude and mounted increasingly coherent and successful campaigns. As a 'cultural activist' Bernard also became involved and committed to the Glebe Estate Workshop, which provided the community with opportunities to produce their own arts and crafts, an ethos befitting his socialist and guild beliefs. Given the departmental turmoil at the Power Institute, the success of the 'Save Glebe' campaigns may well, at times, have saved Bernard's sanity.

In 1973 Bernard and Kate published *The Architectural Character of Glebe Sydney*, with Bernard coining the term 'Federation Style' to cover red-tiled houses built around 1900. The Melbourne architect Neil Clerehan, on learning of this, wrote informing him that he had previously used the term in an article written in 1959 or 1960 for the *Age* or the Council of Adult Education. Bernard replied, 'Naturally I am intrigued by your use of the term . . . and should like therefore to have the precise context.'[77] Clerehan, however, was unable to locate the article and Bernard refused to accept without proof that Clerehan had pioneered the term. In 2003 he wrote:

In 1969 I suggested that all those red-roofed houses that became so popular here at the turn of the century might be better called the Federation style rather than Edwardian or Queen Anne style. Some architectural historians are still unhappy about accepting Federation as a generic, visual style, but estate agents now seem to have no trouble with it . . . Hegel's owl has at least perched itself on an Antipodean red-tiled rooftop for me.[78]

By the end of 1972 Gough Whitlam had displaced William McMahon as prime minister and his social reforms heralded a new humanism that pulled Australia forward into the modern era. Without delay Whitlam injected optimism into the arts and, in an article 'The New Commonwealth Patronage and the Arts', Bernard exclaimed 'Mr. Whitlam, on coming to power, placed the arts in his Department and doubled their budget from seven to fourteen million dollars. It is too early to assess the long-term effects of the new patronage; but already cynicism had been replaced by hope.'[79] Whitlam's creation of the Australia Council for the Arts also included an Aboriginal Arts Board, which received an outstanding 147 grants totalling $531,000. Bernard and Kate applauded this important step in acknowledging, supporting and preserving Indigenous culture through theatre, painting, filmmaking and writing, and eventually it would have significant implications for Bernard's concept of the Ruth Adeney Koori Award.[80]

Though wary of the dangers of bureaucratic power and the inherent elitism that usually accompanies institutional or governing bodies, 'Elitism', Bernard said, 'is the most difficult of all charges to refute. All the arts are deeply entrenched in elitist situations that are neither natural nor desirable', adding 'how can the [Australia] Council help modify the view held by most Australians that the arts are fringe benefits for the privileged? Only . . . by a realistic awareness that our cultural values are moulded by social institutions far stronger than the Australian Council for the Arts.'[81] If Bernard's anti-elitism was mirrored in his solid relationship with Glebe and its residents, he also applied it to all aspects of his personal and home life. When Kate decorated their sitting room with a large, orange Indian cover for the day bed, Bernard insisted that the walls be painted red; as she noted, 'No danger of looking like a Toorak drawing room now.'[82]

In 1975, with politics entering an unprecedented explosive level, Bernard, acting as the Master of Ceremonies for a Whitlam rally fundraiser at the Paddington Town Hall, threw everything into mustering the crowd's enthusiasm. When the Liberals gained an overwhelming victory on 13 December, Kate dejectedly wrote in her diary, 'Fraser Victory, "a good honest government" but a cruel face.' Labor's defeat was a blow to both Kate and Bernard, but she also often suffered the consequences of her husband's heavy workload and university commitments, and on their 33rd wedding anniversary she noted in her diary: 'Peach', as she had always affectionately called Bernard, 'no doubt has an inbuilt reason for not knowing the day or year even after help . . . We seem to have learnt to give the other freedom to live independently. I would have preferred something less detached'.[83]

Tahiti to Leningrad

Bernard's research on Cook's voyages had progressed little during his directorship of the Power Institute and he returned to it only sporadically during the university's long summer breaks or when he took study leave.

Tahiti had long intrigued and beckoned him and he was curious to see if it retained any of the languid sensuousness that had fired sea voyagers and missionaries during the eighteenth and nineteenth centuries, or the 'free-love' arcadia of Gauguin. He and Kate visited it briefly in 1973 before heading to England to continue his research on the British Enlightenment and its romantic and neoclassical periods.

Economic transformations, Bernard believed, were the key to human progress and his new project on art and industry attempted to delineate art as a social utility and establish a new model of historical inquiry. Terry Smith was in England at the time and wrote to Joseph Burke that 'Bernard seemed in his element working away at a book on Art and Industrialisation.'[84] The image of the older Smith contentedly writing his Marxist paper and his young protégé delivering a lecture at the Royal College of Art on 'Art and Language' captured the inevitable changing of the guard. In September Bernard gave his paper 'Art and Industry: A Systematic Approach' at Spode House in Rugeley. It was a trial run for the seminar paper he would give later at the Warburg Institute. In the meantime he and Kate visited Russia, the seat of communism and what had once been for Bernard a mecca of his early political and socialist ideologies.

As the couple waited to board an Aeroflot plane in Copenhagen, a woman approached inquiring if it were going to Leningrad; it was Nina Christesen. On arriving at their hotel they were given keys to their rooms, 'nine inches [22 cm] long and weighing what felt like two pounds [0.9 kg]'; they passed a female attendant whose job was to guard the stairs all night and, on finding their rooms, discovered comfort was very basic. The taps screamed and ran lukewarm, reddish water and there were no plugs, nor could their doors be locked or closed; it was the Russia of Dostoyevsky. The next day they visited the old university where Lenin graduated as a lawyer, 'having never attended a lecture', and they visited The Hermitage, formerly the Winter Palace. They strolled through the Arts Square with its statue of Pushkin, saw the little Opera House, the Russian Museum and Smolny Monastery on the River Neva.[85] From Leningrad, still accompanied by Nina Christesen, they flew to Moscow where 'the Kremlin glittered like golden onions' and they found the Cathedral of Saint Basil, built in the reign of Ivan the Terrible, amusing with its collection of brightly coloured domes. At the Pushkin Museum Bernard saw masterpieces by Cézanne, Van Gogh, Gauguin's *Self-portrait* (c. 1890), Monet's *Dejeuner sur l'herbe* (1863), and some early Picassos confiscated during the revolution. Kate was reading Solzhenitsyn's *The Cancer Ward* (1966) and copied a few lines in her diary:

> One should never direct people towards happiness because happiness too is an idol of the marketplace. One should direct them towards mutual affection . . . [as] only human beings can feel affection for each other, and that is the highest achievement they can aspire to.

It captured a quality of her relationship with Bernard, one based on mutual affection in its highest form. They were so attuned to one another in companionship, cultural matters and journeying, and there was never an idle or empty moment. Yes, there had been hurt and pain with Bernard's womanising and his incessant, heavy workloads had created at times an emotional detachment, but that was balanced by a sense of productive independence in their lives. Over the years they had always maintained a warm affection that, for Kate, was far easier and more comfortable than fire in the belly.

Returning to England, Bernard gave his paper 'Art and Industry' in one of Ernst Gombrich's work in progress seminars at the Warburg Institute. Discontented with inadequate conceptual framing of stylistic shifts and 'movement sequence', he offered a study of the two-tier system, the academic and industrial systems for education and production of works of art. It was an extenuated lesson in mechanical invention, object status, value systems and artistic evolution from about 1750 to the present, with an emphasis on the binary relationship of art and industry. The root of cultural evolution as he saw it, was 'not the novelty but the intensity with which the passion for the mechanical invention swept Britain in the eighteenth and nineteenth centuries . . . the industrial system has not, however, replaced the fine-art system. They have developed . . . parallel to one another in a two-system situation.'[86] Apart from labouring his conspicuous attachment to the sociological relationship of the crafts to the fine arts, he argued:

> industry has not only been imaged by art, it has influenced art and influenced ideas of art, and produced its own arts, such as film .[87]

Whether Bernard knew of the social theorist and poststructuralist Jean Baudrillard's *System and Objects* (1968) and *Consumer Society* (1970) is not known, but he did know of George Kubler's *The Shape of Time* (1962), in which the 'division of the arts' is discussed. It complemented his archaeology of historical materialism, which had been a consistent part of his analysis of art and society since the 1940s and would continue to be. In 1987 his article 'Marx and Aesthetic Value', published in *Art Monthly*, continued that discourse—as he proudly declared, 'I'm a Marxist to the extent that I'm an historical materialist . . . I believe technology to be the prime mover of historical change.'[88]

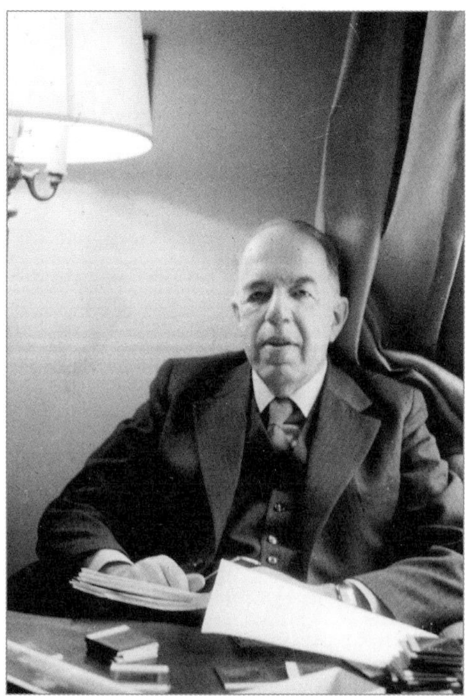

Fig. 45 Ernst Gombrich, March 1974

Bernard's rapport with Ernst Gombrich, whom he considered the foremost art historical genius of the time, was a curious one (fig. 45). They shared an intellectual alignment in their conceptual approach to roots of style and the use of perceptive and empirical methods as tools of cultural inquiry. Both possessed a clear logic that enabled them to see complex connections and each investigated art as a formal process of inheritance. Bernard's pattern of gravitating towards displaced Europeans, whether a subconscious attraction or one based on the status of outsider-ness, was understandable and perhaps he hoped that Gombrich would be a portal for his re-entry into the international world of scholarship. The reception of his paper at the Warburg Institute, however, must have come as a shock when the normally polite and self-contained Gombrich ferociously criticised his material. This trial by fire was part of the great art historian's tactics, as Christine Harris, a postgraduate student at the Warburg Institute and previously a student at the Power Institute, recalled:

Invariably the heavies—Gombrich and Otto Kurz particularly— would tear the paper to shreds, so Bernard wasn't alone in this respect [All postgraduate students were expected to give seminar papers]. But I felt that someone who was rather older than the usual post-doctoral students . . . could have been treated more sensitively. Michael Baxandall and the librarian Joe Trapp were much nicer people. Fierce criticism would have been ok, I suppose, [but] what shocked me was that when everybody went to the tea-room afterwards, I hung back waiting for one of the professors to go and sit with Bernard, and they totally ignored him.[89]

Such brutal criticism and dismissal from elite scholars like Gombrich and Kurz would have demoralised most, but for Bernard it simply reinforced his resilience. Humphrey McQueen believes that 'With Bernard criticism was considered, accepted then constructively used'. Despite the Warburg assault he gave the paper again at the University of Cambridge in the Department of Art History and at the Courtauld Institute, where it was constructively discussed.[90] He also submitted it to *Studio International*, in which it was published in 1974. That reinforced his belief in its intellectual substance, and served as a gesture to Gombrich that he was not easily dissuaded. He later included it in his book of essays *The Death of the Artist as Hero* (1988).

Cultural liberalism

I like not only diversity, but committed diversity.
Bernard Smith[91]

Donald Horne believed that Australia in the early 1970s was culturally and economically hampered by 'the British connection, provincial and enervated elites, plus unadaptive and unenterprising businessmen'.[92] This dramatically changed when Gough Whitlam opened up government resources in favour of the fine arts and in particular the establishment of the new Australian National Gallery (ANG). The acquisition of Jackson Pollock's *Blue poles* (1952) and Willem de Kooning's *Woman V* (1952–53) raised energetic discussions about the status and value of art objects, with many people considering this 'the most flamboyant example . . . of conspicuous waste . . . by Canberra's centralised bureaucracy'.[93] Bernard's interest in aesthetic value versus the market value of the artwork in a competitive capitalist system was suddenly topical and highly relevant.

In April 1974 *Blue poles* was displayed at the AGNSW with the travelling exhibition *Recent American Art*. Long queues of people waited to see Australia's most expensive painting and the spectacle of aesthetic consumption was perhaps the most conspicuous it had been since the great international exhibitions of the 1880s. For Bernard the Pollock represented 'the impingement on these shores of the dominance of American art', and he saw it as just as much of a challenge as it had been at the height of the Cold War and the USA's cultural imperialism of the 1950s. Its abstraction, or to use Derrida's description of painterly language, its 'irreducible specificity' and 'presumed mutism of "the-thing-itself"',[94] was a fashionable form of worship to which Bernard did not subscribe. While the government was signalling its intentions of buying expensive paintings, Bernard believed it was stepping ahead of itself and foolishly alerting 'the international art market that [it was] seriously interested in collecting' the top shelf at no matter what price.[95] Though Whitlam presented himself as a progressive modernist, Bernard felt that caution would have been far preferable, especially when it came to abstract art. He later qualified his reaction to *Blue poles* in Greenbergian terms:

> If I had to decide which was the better painting between Jackson Pollock's *Blue Poles* or Rembrandt's *Night Watch*, I just seem to know, instinctively almost, which is . . . better . . . Because for me painting is at its best when it does not obliterate meaningful references to things beyond its structure, whereas architecture and music may do this and be better for it . . . it is not necessary to reject the human form.[96]

Kate, on the other hand, thought *Blue poles* was a fine and dramatic work and, as a musician, understood the connective qualities of artistic abstraction and emotional impulses.[97]

Bernard insisted there was nothing new about abstract art. Its origins were in Neolithic crafts, such as basketry and ceramic design, but in its contemporary mode, the diminution of its purity of expression or mark making relegated it to 'a second-order visual art'[98]—it was an argument he applied to the Central Street Gallery artists and what he saw as 'their narrow commitment to minimalism'. He told Paul McGillick that the group, with its strong commitment to the new international abstraction, 'was taking paintings to a kind of cul-de-sac', adding 'I like not only diversity, but committed diversity.'[99]

In March 1974 Bernard heard the news that Bertha Chivers, 'Mum' Keen's daughter, had died. With her passing, Kate said it was 'the end of his childhood'.[100] He attended her funeral and met old friends he had not seen for many years; yet, contrary to what Kate thought, it reopened memories that had been neatly tucked away. Unexpectedly Bernard found himself wanting to delve into his past and relive the part of his life that had been so crucial in forming his identity and which, it seemed, was no longer suited to the contemporary art world of Sydney. T. S. Eliot's words capture this realisation: 'What might have been and what has been, point to one end, which is always present . . . Round the corner. Through the first gate. Into our first world'.[101]

The last days of Power

Bernard could not have foreseen how fraught the construction of the Power Institute would be and by 1974 it was taking its toll. He applied for the directorship of the recently established Humanities Research Centre in Canberra and wrote to Ernst Gombrich for a reference, conceding 'I have no doubt that the Power Institute has reached a stage where it might well benefit from the ideas of a younger man.'[102] According to Ian Donaldson he would have been a brilliant appointment, except that he wanted to spend three days a week in Canberra and four days in Melbourne, an unacceptable arrangement.[103] Bernard knew that his days at the Power Institute were numbered; not only had he moved beyond it, or was being moved out of modernity's frame, but the fact was that in both spirit and mind he had grown 'grey in grey' as Hegel said, a seasoned maturity parenthesised by traditional values that no longer suited the contemporary.

There was, however, still much work to be done. By 1975 the gallery was yet to be built and the collection, consisting of 450 works of art, 140 acquired as gifts, plus 140 paintings, 200 studies and 700 drawings of J. W. Power's personal artworks, all lay hidden on the top floor of the university's Fisher Library. Problems about who would design the gallery were the stumbling block, with Bernard firmly in favour of Harry Seidler. The university wanted its architect Keith Cottier, but Bernard advised the vice-chancellor that 'We require a building which is itself a work of art' and insisted on someone outside the university's internal system. Bernard was only too mindful of the nepotism that had occurred with Roy Grounds and the Arts Centre complex in Melbourne:

As I have taken a stand on the appointment of an architect for the Power Institute Building, I ask your patience in permitting me to put my case in more detail . . . The view has been expressed that 'the Seymour Centre can form, with the Power and Music

Buildings, a complex that will foster an interaction of thought and activity between various disciplines involved'. It is true that propinquity and neighbourliness can, and often do, foster such interactions. But they cannot be forced.

He argued against the notion that:

the arts [of] theatre, music and the visual arts are more likely to relate to one another than to other departments within the university . . . In our own case a more creative interchange . . . has taken place. . . between the Department of Electrical Engineering.

And he continued:

one architect's style would be undesirable . . . [and create] . . . a sort of artistic ghetto . . . Some visual expression of difference, within the larger unity, is desirable.

A different emphasis is required for the Power Building. Dr Power was interested in bringing contemporary art of high quality from other countries to the people of Australia. The emphasis here is upon standards and internationalism . . . his intentions would be best served . . . in the international style . . . I want to stress again that Seidler and Associates are the best and most logical choice for the Power Building. Dr Power's taste was formed by the International Style . . . Seidler, through his training with Gropius, Albers, Breuer, and Niemeyer, was more thoroughly trained in this tradition than any other Australian artist . . . and expresses it in its purist form .[104]

As convincing as he was the issue could not be resolved. The university's parochialism inhibited innovation and Bernard might well have thought of Sir Kenneth Clark's definition of provincialism: 'simply a matter of distance from the centre, where standards of skill are higher and patrons more exacting'; Clark had also warned that the worst feature of provincialism was complacency, a self-protective measure that preferred insularity to innovation, the commonplace to international standards.[105]

With retirement in sight, Bernard turned his mind to his much-neglected writing and put together a critical anthology of essays, *Documents on Art and Taste in Australia 1770–1914* (1975). Written on or by artists who were active between Cook's landing on the eastern seaboard of Australia and World War I, they illustrated developing attitudes towards a colonial culture. A second group of essays under the title of *The Antipodean Manifesto: Essays in Art and History* won the 1976 Wilkie Literary Prize for nonfiction—they represented what Bernard considered to be his best research and writing, in particular his piece on Coleridge, which had not been accorded the reception he felt it deserved. As he explained to Frank Eyre of Oxford University Press in Melbourne, 'I have chosen them in order to make somewhat more explicit the development of my point of view from a Marxist position (. . . which I have never entirely abandoned) in seeking to face up to the questions related to art criticism, art theory, history, nationalism etc.'[106] If he were no longer 'contemporary' then at least he could cast judgement on what had once been contemporary.

Having attended Donald Friend's 60th birthday at the Holdsworth Gallery, Woollahra, Bernard noted in his diary on 16 March that the artist was looking 'fat and decadent', so dreadfully different from the man he had known at the artists' enclave Merrioola in the 1940s. Friend's early paintings, however, were beautiful and showed, among other stylistic influences, that of Goya, and Bernard bought two. In June Lucy Lippard flew in to Sydney to give the Power Lecture, but both Bernard and Kate thought she was lightweight and her brand of feminism illuminated the ever-widening generational gap.

It was a relief for Bernard to leave Sydney in mid-1976 when he was invited to give lectures at several British universities. The British art historian Peter Quartermaine had discovered *European Vision and the South Pacific* in the late 1960s and he used it to shape his course in Australian studies at the University of Exeter. In the following decade Bernard's work played an important role in reinvigorating British colonial studies. Similarly, Michael Rosenthal claimed that Bernard was a 'hugely influential figure' in imperialist and colonial revisionism and that 'the starting point had to be [his] *European Vision and the South Pacific*'.[107] Ironically, Bernard felt professionally more appreciated in Britain than he did in Sydney where, in his last months of institutional power, he retreated to his office and tried to achieve some form of control. Yet to many of the younger students he remained the esteemed scholar, someone with real gravitas and held in high regard.

Generally, however, it was felt that Bernard had entered the twilight of his academic life and even he began setting in place a number of projects to occupy himself in retirement. In spite of his misapprehensions, he had achieved a great deal, initiating the John Power Lectures, the Power Research Library, the Museum Studies course, the artists' studio in the Cité Internationale des Arts, overseas student study tours, the dictionary project and the Power Foundation for Fine Arts. He had also trained and had influenced many students who developed successful careers in the discipline of art history and the arts. Shaping a new institution from the ground up had been extremely demanding and, when he retired in late 1976 at the age of 60, he was unapologetic about having 'no great affection' for the intellectual tone of the university.

Bernard had always measured himself against overseas institutions and scholars, but as Terry Smith said of those early Power days, 'you had to work with what you had', and Sydney was a far cry from London or New York.[108] It was not until Bernard was in his 90s and had the Hegelian distance to digest the criticism of his management during his Power decade that he considered he had failed to implement a 'first rate structure', one abreast of some of the most contemporary academic international programs, but at least he had tried.

CHAPTER EIGHT: THE CONSTANT REVISIONIST

History . . . is a kind of criticism. It seeks to correct prevailing views about what has occurred.

Bernard Smith[1]

As 1976 drew to a close Bernard wrote in his diary, as he usually did at the end of each year, what he hoped to achieve in the following one: '[I] have in mind to begin work on three books, an autobiography to 1939; work on the art and industry material, and a book on the theme of Neighbourhood Workshops.' There would be no soft armchair or a slowing of the days for this scholar after his retirement from the Power Institute; it was full flight as usual, a spectacular combination of Minerva's contemplative owl, the telescopic sight of the eagle and the ceaseless drive of a man with still much to say. Over the next three decades he would write two volumes of autobiography; a biography of his old comrade Noel Counihan; edit a festschrift for Jack Lindsay; and revisit in extenso the voyages of Captain Cook and the artists of the First Fleet. In addition to that impressive output he wrote a plethora of articles, but it was only after he got 'the old man of the sea off his back' in 1989 that he felt the time had come for him to be part of the postmodern present by parenthesising modernism.

On their return to Melbourne Bernard and Kate bought a house in Fitzroy, a suburb with a working-class ambience and a delightful mix of nineteenth and early twentieth-century cottages and buildings, similar to their beloved Glebe. Their double-storey terrace Jeansville, at 167 Nicholson Street, was within walking distance of the university and the State Library of Victoria. The Carlton Gardens and the Royal Exhibition Building were directly within sight, and it was a short stroll to Brunswick Street, which had begun its bohemian transformation with small print galleries, cafés and artists' studios. The couple resumed an active social life with family, friends, colleagues and students, and Kate was pleased to be back with their grandchildren.

Throughout their time in Sydney Bernard had continued to engage in extra marital affairs, but with this new 'retirement' phase, Kate demanded that he stop his womanising or she would leave him. Knowing that he could never do without her, he reluctantly fell into line. Some 30 years later he admitted that he had given her a very hard time with his affairs but in 1977, with a renewed commitment and more time together, a mellowness and relaxed enjoyment of each other's company developed. Bernard began accompanying Kate frequently to concerts and the theatre, and read to her in the evenings, usually Proust—her eyesight had been deteriorating for some years. He often played with his grandchildren; in short, he became a family man. The reinstatement of his routine of rising early and working in his study until 4 pm remained a priority, and only after that time would he take visitors. Kate was a marvellous regulator of social intercourse and was always on hand; if Bernard showed signs of impatience with guests, she would 'nicely' sabotage his rudeness, jokingly put him in his place and rescue them.[2] Patrick McCaughey, then head of Fine Arts at Monash University, frequently called, as did Humphrey McQueen and Jim Davidson. Ursula Hoff, whose career had been resurrected as the adviser for the Felton Bequest, visited when on leave from her job in London, and Anne Purves of the Australian Galleries, Melbourne, always enjoyed discussing art with Bernard. Joseph Burke occasionally invited him to University House for lunch but only once to the Melbourne Club.

Both Bernard and Kate 'believed that it was the responsibility of individuals to actively support the arts through purchasing works', and throughout their marriage they had amassed a large, eclectic collection.[3] In June 1977 it comprised 287 works, including paintings, works on paper, sculptures,

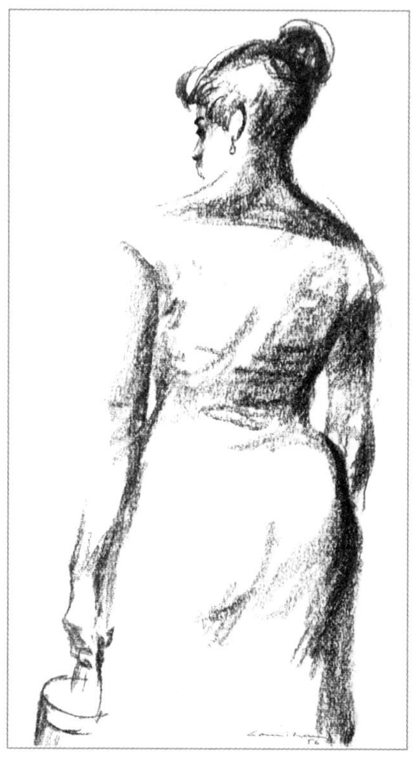

Fig. 46 Noel Counihan, *Venetian prostitute*, 1956.

ceramics, carvings and textiles.[4] Many works were by friends, though not all had been in need of support, and they were usually bought directly from the artists' studios. There were works by Moya Dyring, Hermia Boyd, Thea Proctor and several by Noel Counihan, including a drawing of a Venetian prostitute, a reminder of Bernard's sensual northern summer of 1949 (fig. 46). Their walls featured a Margaret Preston monotype of Mosman Bay, several Francis Lymburner drawings, Sali Herman's 1948 oil portrait of Bernard, and Grace Cossington Smith's *The school cape* (1916). In his study hung Jean Bellette's *Above Fornalutz* (1963) and Vic O'Connor's *Refugees* (1942), as well as John Perceval's *Romulus and Remus*. An Eric Gill wood engraving reminded him of Kate's beloved village of Ditchling and Gerard Dillon's painting of two boys fishing for crabs in Connemara, bought in 1950, of his Irish origins. More contemporary works included an Enrico Baj, a Mike Brown, a Tony Tuckson and one of Richard Larter's nudes.

Bernard was particularly proud of the Eugene von Guérard, *Forest scene near Kiama* (1863), for which he had paid only 35 guineas, but ultimately it was a collection that reflected his journey among artists and his own aesthetic history.

Ever attendant to the march of the people, Bernard kept an eye on local politics and community affairs. The local councils had adopted a policy of confrontation about the new F19 Freeway, narrowing Alexandra Parade to obstruct its exit; 'It's War' a *Herald* banner headline declared. One evening he walked down to Alexandra Parade where a group of protesters had bunkered down for the night. It was 25 November 1977 and he spoke to some of them about the heavy police move the previous night in which two arrests were made. Having waged and won a battle with the authorities about the proposed freeway in Glebe, he was extremely sympathetic to their cause.

In the footsteps of Cook

As the troubled waters of the past decade receded Bernard resumed working on the Hakluyt Society project, the *Art of Cook's Voyages*; pressure was also mounting as the bicentenary of Cook's death approached. He had re-sailed the seas, figuratively speaking, many times with the navigator and artists attached to the First Fleet, and Cook's bounty had certainly been Bernard's scholarly blessing, for through those voyages he had learnt how others used geographic distance, empirical observation and perception as investigative tools:

> You are . . . carefully to observe the nature of the soil and the produce thereof; the Animals and Fowls that inhabit or frequent it; the Fishes that are found in the rivers or upon the coast, and in what plenty; and, in case there are, peculiar to such places, to describe them as minutely, and to make accurate drawings of them, as you can.[5]

The written word may have established Bernard's reputation, but the image remained central to it: 'Words are often forgotten but images remain', he said. In 1975 Bernard and the German curator Rüdiger Joppien, at the time a visiting Fellow at the Humanities Research Centre in Canberra, decided to collaborate on the catalogue raisonné of the art of Cook's voyages. By 1978 Bernard had activated a comprehensive research program in which he planned to visit major international galleries and collections that contained artworks, ornaments and objects collected during Cook's three voyages. In Hawaii he gave a paper 'Art as Information' at the Honolulu Academy of Arts and the lecture 'Cook's Posthumous Reputation' at the University of Hawaii. Occasionally he reversed his praxis of 'seeing is conditioned by knowing' to 'knowing is conditioned by seeing' and engaged a local Hawaiian fisherman to take him to the spot where the artist John Webber had drawn the promontory of Kealakekua Bay. On another occasion he and Kate stayed at the Volcano Hotel situated on the edge of the Kilauea crater, one of the world's most active volcanoes. With a photographic print in hand of a 1772 painting, purportedly by William Hodges, they were driven around the volcanic rim and walked through a lava tube in an attempt to recognise features captured by the artist.[6] Twenty years later, aged 83, in the company of art historians, Bernard's second wife Maggi and his son John, he travelled by boat from Doubtful Bay to Dusky Sound on New Zealand's wild west coast of the South Island. Following in the footsteps of Cook and William Hodges he clambered and was hauled up to the site of the waterfall where the artist had painted in 1773. Cook had recorded:

> Being a fine afternoon I took Mr Hodges to a large Cascade which falls down a high mountain . . . He took a drawing of it on Paper and afterwards painted it in oyle Colours which exhibits at one view a better description than I can give.[7]

With a photocopy of the original painting, Bernard compared Hodges' scene with that in front of him; it was essentially unchanged (fig. 23).

In a conference paper at the Simon Fraser University in Canada in April 1978, Bernard called for a revitalisation of Pacific Studies, suggesting that J. C. Beaglehole's narrow focus on Cook's iconic reputation had cast a huge shadow on the study of the Pacific (fig. 47).[8] That, he said,

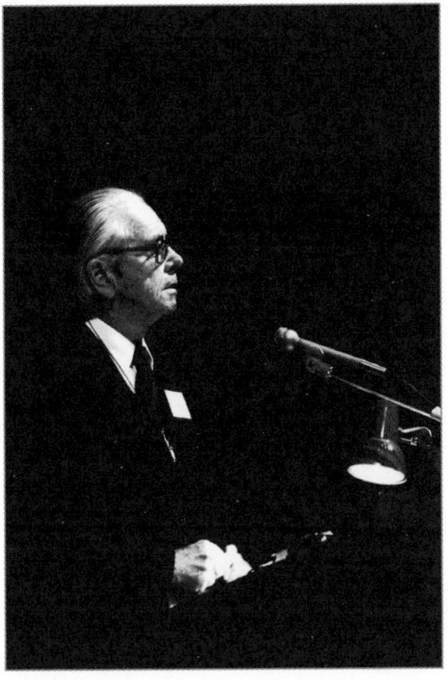

Fig. 47 Bernard Smith at Simon Fraser University, Vancouver, 1978

had to be questioned and the entire program of historical investigation expanded: 'It has not been part of my intention to discredit the achievements of Cook. My intention has been to suggest that it is timely that they be placed in a new perspective.'[9] The hero was an important part of British eighteenth-century imperialism and Cook had been portrayed as the pacifist purveyor, rather than the perpetrator of violence and disease. Even in death all accounts of Cook's voyages had celebrated him. Truth, however, was highly selective and Bernard, who believed in 'history as critical enquiry', considered it was his job to prove that even as a kind humanist James Cook eventually recognised his error of destroying arcadia. He quoted the young French lawyer and eulogist Pierre-Édouard Lémontey, who wrote in 1787:

Aren't the benefits of Cook rather mixed . . . Praise, praise civilised peoples, wise nations exalt those discoveries that flatter your pride, increase your wealth, perfect your knowledge. It is not you who will pay for your happiness but what you have made of all those small tribes of which your barbarous curiosity has violated . . . by the fatal presence of your vices and your needs . . . The eulogy of Cook is only a calculus of egoism, and its laurels will perish on the theatre of its glory.[10]

At Hawaii and Vancouver Bernard met many young scholars and his reputation as a major specialist of Cook's voyages was cemented (fig. 48). He also realised the need to throw open the door and invite other historians more adept and qualified than he was to enter the debate; 'Historical causation is notoriously multiple rather than singular', he wrote.[11]

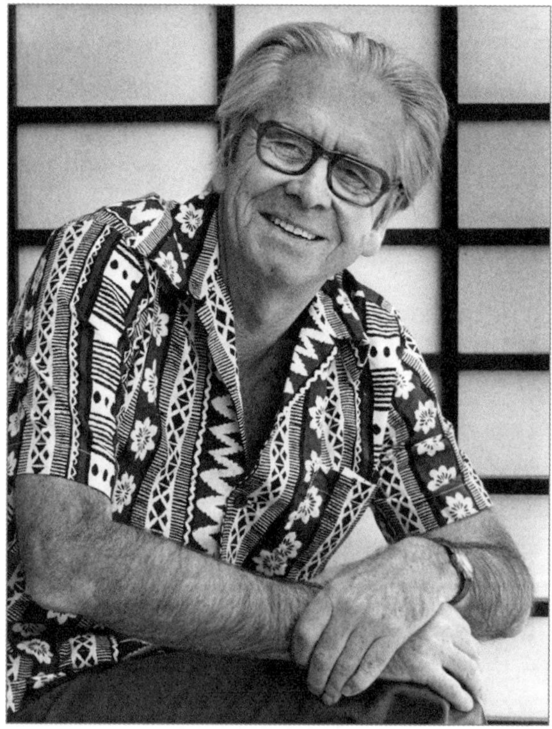

Fig. 48 Bernard Smith, Hawaii, 1978

In London Bernard looked at paintings, artefacts and papers in the major museums and galleries, including the Linnean Society, and visited the Fitzwilliam Museum in Cambridge to reassess *Scene in Otaheite*, a painting attributed to John Webber. At Anglesey Abbey he compared

William Hodges' first version of *A view taken in the bay of Otaheite Peha* (1776) with another version, *Tahiti Revisited* (1776), at Admiralty House in Greenwich, London. There were clear differences. One had been painted for public viewing at the Royal Academy, the other for the Royal Naval collection. The first version showed two naked Tahitian women, while another female had been added for the Admiralty House painting. The elevated platform with a shrouded corpse, 'motifs of death and transience', and the large figure of the pagan god Tii may have been an essay on the popular theme of '*et in Arcadia Ego*', but Hodges, as Bernard suggested, also 'aspired to the production of an alternative dream', one of 'a tropical paradise of sunshine, sensuous . . . women more beautiful and more tempting than Italy'.[12] This was aimed as much at the tourism trade and promoting the potential of a grand tour of the South Pacific as it was representative of the sensuous noble savage of the New World.

The scale of the Cook project was so immense that on returning to Melbourne Bernard applied successfully for an Australian research grant towards the cost of photographs, and he also selected a team of eight scholars to help with the project. The team included Dr Andrew David from the Admiralty Sailing Directions and Hydrographic Office in England; Dr Peter Gathercole, Keeper of the Museum of Archaeology and Ethnology in Cambridge; Dr Rüdiger Joppien, Curator at the Museum of Decorative Arts in Cologne; Dr Adrienne Kaeppler, Research Anthropologist at the Bernice P. Bishop Museum in Honolulu; Dr Helen Wallis, Superintendent of the Map Room at the British Museum; Dr Peter Whitehead, Department of Zoology at the British Natural History Museum; and, he hoped, a botanist and an ornithologist from Australia. The outcome was to be the publication of a complete illustrated catalogue of all the known material from Cook's three voyages, accompanied by the highest scholarship. The proposed seven volumes would be a major contribution to the study of the Pacific region and a clear account of late eighteenth-century European ideas and science, but it never fully materialised. In conceptualising the enormous project, which involved more than 3000 items—only 30 to 40 per cent of which had ever been published or fully described, illustrated or seen—Bernard's meticulous research criteria came to the fore:

The art of authenticity, the onus of correct and full attribution . . . details of recto and verso . . . what is now required is an exhaustive and systematic [visual] presentation of the material as basic source material, comparable to the establishment of a text. Both Banks and Cook, on several occasions, insisted that the drawings made on the voyages would provide a better idea of the matter under discussion than their own words.

He confirmed this with an example:

The drawings sometimes contain conclusive evidence on matters about which the written record is silent. A well-known example is the use of the gourd helmet in Hawaii for which John Webber's drawings provides the sole evidence.[13]

While he was successful with the grant and the scholars started their work, things did not go to plan. Yale University Press pulled out of the project despite its initial enthusiasm and there was conflict with the Natural History Museum's publishing program due to an overlap on the natural science drawings. It left Bernard 'to salvage what remain[ed] of the project', but 'on a less ambitious scale',[14] and it became a protracted and exhausting affair. Instead, a number of other important publications resulted, including *Baudin in Australian Waters: The Art Work of the French Voyages of Discovery to the Southern Lands, 1800–1804* (1988), edited with Jacqueline Bonnemains and Elliott Forsythe; *The Art of the First Fleet and Other Early Australian Drawings* (1988), edited with Alwyne Wheeler; and, in 1985 with Rüdiger Joppien, finally two volumes of *The Art of Captain Cook's Voyages*; the third volume, *The Art of Captain Cook's Voyages: The Voyage of the Resolution 1776–1780*, was completed in 1988.

Since returning to Melbourne in 1977 Bernard had acted as a de facto adviser to the Department of Fine Arts at the University of Melbourne. When Joseph Burke retired from the *Herald* Chair of Fine Arts, Bernard, who was on the advisory committee, encouraged Martin Kemp, the British Leonardo da Vinci specialist, to apply for the chair. It was thought

that Kemp could make a considerable contribution to Renaissance studies, particularly as that field had not been adequately filled since Franz
Philipp's death in 1970. Kemp was interviewed and offered the position,
but declined due to his scholarly interests, the tyranny of distance and the
challenge of working in Melbourne; the position was taken up by Sister
Margaret Manion. In April 1979 Bernard was made a senior associate
in the department and began supervising postgraduate students, a role
he enjoyed and in which he offered constructive advice borne of sound
judgement and immense scholarly experience. As a cultural elder, whose
past was now of historical interest to younger historians, he gave generously of his time and provided access to his private papers. His sense
of 'positioning everyone historically' was invaluable to students and to
researchers such as Janine Burke,[15] Humphrey McQueen, Ann Galbally
and Richard Haese, with Bernard often reminding those who sought his
opinions, 'I knew them all. I lived through it. I saw it happening.'[16]

Being made an Honorary Doctor of Letters from the University of
Melbourne in 1976 was validation of his stature in retirement—Bernard
would later receive the award of *Chevalier de L'ordre des Arts et des Lettres*
by the sectrétaire D'État à la Culture Nomme in 1981 in recognition
of his role in the Cité Internationale des Arts and his scholarship on
European maritime voyages, particularly those of the French in the
Pacific; a Degree of Doctor of Letters (Honoris Causa) conferred from the
University of Sydney in 1997; and lastly, the Australia Council's Visual
Arts and Crafts Emeritus Medal for his contribution to the visual art of
Australia in 2004. Yet he always maintained that he never was, or felt part
of, the establishment. Admiration was affirming, but he always carried
such recognition with humility. Nevertheless when Anthony Bradley and
Terry Smith published a festschrift, *Australian Art and Architecture: Essays
presented to Bernard Smith* (1980), honouring his contribution to art
historiography, he proudly accepted the title of 'father of Australian art
history' and moreover fully agreed with them that he had brought 'order
to a field which lacked guiding principles of organization'.[17] The new
director of the Power Institute, Virginia Spate, also wrote, 'Things are
going pretty well here—it's a very nice department—and I must say it's
perhaps only by occupying the bed of nails that I have become conscious

of how much you have achieved in the ten years here.'[18] After the agonies of administering such a bureaucratically sensitive organisation, finally his efforts were being recognised.

One evening after a book launch at the University of Melbourne, Bernard and Joseph Burke had dinner at the Lemon Tree, on the corner of Grattan and Rathdowne streets in Carlton, where they discussed, among other things, the demands of the public life of a scholar. Burke was tired and needed a rest from public commitments; as he said, 'We art historians don't have much opportunity to see nature, we are always in the galleries and museums.'[19] Bernard felt sorry for him; he had always strived for a balance in his academic life, except perhaps during the difficult Power Institute period, but even then he regularly travelled and made sure that his research activities involved much more than galleries and museums. Ever mindful of academia's shackles Bernard never lost sight of the real world or the common people, and if his professional life threatened to consume him, he would either retreat to his study to centre his thoughts and balance his world, or walk. Some of that had to do with Kate's great love of botany, but he had always been a great walker, even before Murraguldrie, where long rambling treks had enabled him to replenish his soul through a type of Darwinian reverence for nature. The mechanisms of survival had been learnt from an early age and Bernard's ability for self-preservation was always a priority.

Return to the margins

Shortly after retirement Bernard began writing his autobiography; it would take six years to recount his life from a state ward to a young critic of art and society. Janet Malcolm suggests autobiography and the presentation of the self is 'an exercise in self-forgiveness. The observing "I" of autobiography tells the story of the observed "I" . . . as a mother might. The older narrator looks back at his younger self with tenderness and pity, empathising with its sorrows and allowing for its sins.'[20] As Bernard re-read his diaries and contacted old friends such as Jack Carns, one of Tottie Keen's wards, he found tracing his roots cathartic. At Rose Anne's 90th birthday in Brisbane, Bernard asked his mother to write down her early memories and for any photographs and letters she had kept. In a letter to Jack Lindsay Bernard explained:

> My mother was of Irish Catholic peasant stock and . . . born on the feast of Augustine. . . I was baptised in the Church of St Augustine of Hippo, Balmain, Sydney, but I was born illegitimate . . . my [foster] mother was an excellent Congregationalist . . . [and] for many years I went to a Salvation Army School. So I had mixed beginnings. But it all gives me a metaphysical interest in Augustine's boy Adeodatus.[21]

Lindsay replied, 'What a theological mix-up.'[22] When Vincent Buckley read Bernard's memoir he understood completely the type of background that he had experienced; 'I feel a peculiar rapport with this book . . . because my mother, too, for many years acted as a foster mother, and I am familiar with the disturbances of "boarding" children and with the . . . drift and drudgery of their natural mothers . . . so I know how they may be gathered in, and nurtured, and let go again'.[23] But the root of Bernard's early life was not so much about his absent mother, but his relationship to society and his 'acute sensitivity to the politics of the unequal exchange'.[24] Throughout his childhood he had often turned to the Book of Daniel in the Bible, in which the child who spurns the nourishment of the elite for the simple food of peasants survives the lions' den:

> Children in whom was no blemish, but well favoured, and skilful in all wisdom, and cunning in knowledge, and understanding in science, and such as had the ability in them to stand in the king's palace (Daniel 1:4).

He kept this ulterior template close throughout his adult life. It explains his use of St Augustine's illegitimate boy, Adeodatus, in his autobiography. As he said to Brian Johns of Penguin, 'I suppose it could be called an analogical or even an anagogical autobiography.'[25] Impoverishment had propelled Bernard to excel or to redeem himself and his account of his rite of passage from boyhood to young manhood was a touching analysis of his place within society as well as a brilliant study of interwar Sydney.

On Friday 22 February 1984 Bernard received a telephone call from Brian Johns informing him that *The Boy Adeodatus: The Portrait of a Lucky Young Bastard* had won the National Book Council Award for Australian Literature, the Victorian Premier's Literary Award, the Nettie Palmer Prize for nonfiction and the Talking Book of the Year Award. 'Great mutual enjoyment!' was how he described his achievement to Kate. With extremely favourable reviews and an invitation to participate in the Adelaide Writers' Week, Bernard proved he had another feather to add to his professional hat: that of the successful, independent author. In keeping with his disdain for accumulating wealth, he used some of his prize money to help establish the Nuclear Disarmament Party.

In the heat of late February 1987 Bernard met poets and writers on the banks of the Torrens River in Adelaide, including Amanda Lohrey; the New Zealand-born English poet, Fleur Adcock; the Indigenous Aboriginal civil rights activist Faith Bandler; and authors Tim Winton, Ian McEwan and Graham Swift. It was a sweltering 41 degrees when it came to his day in the tent. Helen Garner began with a polished reading from her *Postcards from Surfers* (1986), followed by Bernard who read from *The Boy Adeodatus*, and three of his unpublished poems from the 1940s: 'Easter Rising', 'The Ballad of St. Phar Lap', and 'Woolloomooloo'. He explained to the audience that the book was about the getting of wisdom, which involved three steps: 'the first step was to recognise oneself . . . the second . . . was the recognition of death . . . [and] the third step was the recognition of the other . . . recognition not in an intellectual sense, but to be able to see oneself and see one's humanity in the other'.[26]

On reading *The Boy Adeodatus* in 1997 Ihab Hassan wrote to Bernard: 'I feel our friendship has suddenly lengthened by some eighty years and my knowledge of Australia deepened by several cultural layers.' Hassan recognised the cultural and intellectual forces that had shaped Bernard's 'uncommon childhood', writing that 'it seems that we read the same boys books, you in Australia, I in Egypt, which may attest to "cultural imperialism" in one of its more benign modes.'[27]

Not long after completing his first autobiography, Bernard began research for a second volume, provisionally called 'Memoirs of a Political

Decade', to deal with developments in the 1940s, but he did not find it easy 'interweaving the personal and the political'.[28] It would be another 15 years before this memoir was published.

Shortly after his literary success his mother's health began deteriorating. Rose Anne had moved to a nursing home in Melbourne to be near her daughter Isabel and Bernard, and on one of his last visits he found her heavily sedated, pitifully feeble and her feet swollen with the beginnings of gangrene. By mid-November 1986 a priest was called to give the last rites and she died the following day, aged 96. It had been a long, hard life in which she had loved Bernard from a distance, and now the sad harp of his origin was gone. His mother was not the only one who had declined; Kate had developed a swollen liver and spleen and she required medical treatment. By the end of November her haematologist had broken the news that she was suffering from chronic myeloid leukaemia. She took the news with a stoicism to be expected from a woman of such enormous self-control, but for Bernard the reality that his faithful partner's life was to end was indescribably sad. The prognosis gave her anywhere from a few months to 15 years, depending on how well she responded to treatment; Bernard noted in his diary: 'I shall have to give her [all] my attention. But she accepts that she has had a full life.' With his days dictated by Kate's health he reorganised his priorities, but continued with his work methodically cataloguing his papers and books and embarking on new articles and lectures, but never neglecting the woman he so much loved and who was now the centre of his attention.

The spectre of Truganini

We need courage to face our colonial hang-ups.
Bernard Smith[29]

Bernard knew what it was like to 'dwell invisibly in the unnameable centre of time'; as a state ward he had resided at the edge of society and had slept the dislocated dream of illegitimacy.[30] Midway through writing his first autobiography he was invited to give the 1980 Boyer Lectures, and had initially thought of talking about the legacy of illegitimacy. A colleague, however, suggested he might transfer the tragedy of his personal separation to that of the loss of human dignity and dispossession encountered by Australia's Indigenous inhabitants. Bernard had always skirted around issues of Aboriginality, primarily because his scholarship had been based upon the longue durée of western civilisation and not the 'mythological underpinnings' of Australia's Indigenous lore. Moreover, he knew his own limitations when addressing Indigenous Australian art and culture. He was not an anthropologist, nor was Indigenous art very visible in the middle decades of the twentieth century, except as Daniel Thomas has pointed out, 'in small doses, and in artistically marginalised spaces'.[31]

Yet Australia's modern identity had developed under conditions of cultural displacement and geographical distance, as well as the repressive guilt associated with 'the locked cupboard of our history'.[32] In 1980 Bernard was ready to deal with 'the great Australian silence' and his Boyer Lectures, 'The Spectre of Truganini', were powerful essays on the ethics of conquest and the decimation of Australia's Indigenous peoples. Invoking 'the colonial crime' as tragedy and the present as having potential for redemptive atonement and liberation, he took the moral high ground and brought the past into the present, quoting the American Declaration of Independence: 'all men are created equal, that they are endowed with certain unalienable rights, that among these are life, liberty and the pursuit of happiness'.

There was, however, a muted connection to his roots. 'Australian morality is a history of damaged goods', he said, and who better to talk about the unequal exchange than the bastard boy from Balmain.[33] The price of survival had always interested him, whether the convict, destitute, state ward, Australian Aboriginal, or the marginalised, it resonated deeply with his own sense of the alienated self. Now he was asking a different type of question, one he later articulated as '[history] is often a criticism of silence, of that story which has not been told and must be told.'[34]

Bernard's academic cabinet brimmed with stories of Europe's imperial impact on the South Pacific and of empire on imagination and art. It was a Eurocentric gaze that had occupied him; as Heinrich Wölfflin said, 'vision itself has a history'.[35] The early exploration and settlement artists had primarily recorded the outcast Indigenous as a 'curiosity' in an alien land, their art regarded as ethnographic information. Plaster casts of the Tasmanian Aboriginals by Benjamin Law, including those of Truganini and Wourredy, had been kept in anthropological museums throughout Australia and Europe since 1837 and rarely shown; the memorialisation of a race and the moment of contact between the European and native was seen as a transaction, most often of a fatal kind. Truganini, 'the tragic old muse' and allegedly the last full-blooded Tasmanian Aboriginal, 'the ultimate victim of the European invasion', haunted the landscape, but it had been a silent spectre (fig. 49).[36]

During the early twentieth century, as western artists borrowed tribal forms to create new hybrid aesthetics, primitivism encircled much of their art. Bernard, however, had preferred to look at the politics of identity and sociological transitions within the industrialised world. When he first saw Margaret Preston's art in the 1930s and 1940s he considered her appropriation of Aboriginal symbols as a form of cultural nationalism, rather than innovative linear formalism. In 1950 James Cant exhibited his paintings of Arnhem Land cave drawings in London, based on photographs from C. P. Mountford's expedition of 1948, but they were seen not as the artist intended, to 'recapture . . . the spirit of those primitive aborigines in a form that will allow the artists of a modern civilisation to appreciate their beauty', but as mere copies of Stone Age art.[37] Bernard's tendency to exclude Indigenous art in his historiography was understandable, but it also placed him as a victim of Eurocentric politics. It had taken Yosl Bergner, Vic O'Connor and Noel Counihan to first reveal the haunting plight of contemporary urban Australian Aboriginals and their persona non grata status; as Bernard wrote, 'Tragedy nor any dark passion of the spirit', did not enter Australian art until the 'eve of the Second World War', but even then it was the white fella's gaze.[38] In an article by Ronald and Catherine Berndt in *Meanjin*, 1950, which Bernard would have read, Australian Aboriginal art, they claimed, possessed the same artistic criteria as that of all civilisations:

[it] is more than just beautiful drawings, carvings or workman-
ship, possessed of graceful lines and aesthetic values—the external
expression of the 'soul' of the people. It fulfils a vital need in the
culture, and is dictated by tradition, religion and mythology.[39]

By the late 1950s there was a shift in Bernard's response to the plight
of Indigenous Australians. Arthur Boyd had begun a series of paintings
titled *Love, marriage and death of a half caste*—works that captured the
harrowing interracial relations subverted by the 'fear of white society'—
but these were mostly coolly received. David Boyd's dramatic series *The
explorer* and *The Tasmanians* belonged, as Bernard wrote, 'to the world of
Notting Hill riots, Sharpeville and the trial of Albert Namatjira', but the
critics so abused the artist's work and his theme of brutal extermination
that 'Boyd had to leave the country to find a more liberal audience'.[40]
When Tony Tuckson's acclaimed exhibition *Australian Aboriginal Art*
toured all Australian state capitals in 1960 and 1961, Bernard's awareness
of Indigenous aesthetics was further awakened, yet he was still treading
'the boundaries of Aboriginality' cautiously and was reluctant to take the
step from ethno-aesthetics to art history.[41]

By the time W. E. H. Stanner gave his Boyer Lectures in 1968, the
dialogue on racial relations had moved to a new, confrontational level
in which the hidden skeletons of the past were brought out and into the
European Australian conscience. But it was not until the Aboriginal and
cultural rights protests in Redfern, Sydney, during the early 1970s and
Gough Whitlam's establishment of a Department of Aboriginal Affairs
and his landmark gesture of pouring sand into the hand of Gurindji
elder Vincent Lingiari, that Bernard saw the urgent need for Indigenous
cultural recognition. It had taken him a long time to arrive confidently
at the Indigenous frontier and its moral and aesthetic territory, and he
expressed this by gathering up the human condition with its culture of
forgetfulness and putting universal justice on trial.

In Ian McLean's *How Aborigines Invented the Idea of Contemporary Art*
(2011) Bernard is categorised as an apostle, a messenger, a missionary and
a leader of reform; Bernard's Boyer Lectures reinforce this:

> Between our history and our pre-history, between our Eden and
> the expulsion of 1788, lies a lawless terrain in which our courts
> stumble . . . We have been caught out as it were red-handed play-
> ing the genocide game, corrupting Darwinism for our purposes as
> the Nazis corrupted Nietzsche, and Stalin corrupted Marx.

His words transmitted accusation and verdict with heavy pronounce-
ment, the crime and blame to be collectively shared, and its effect on
listeners was moving. He brought to court Darwin and Marx: 'Darwin's
theory of natural selection reduced the status of the Aborigine from that
of the perpetual servant to that of the entrapped animal about to die.'
Marx, he said, 'reinforced that vision of history as a moral drama'.[42] The
missions and reservations into which Indigenous people had been 'herded
. . . helped to throw a white blanket of forgetfulness across the central
tragedy of Australian settlement'—out of sight and out of mind. The
Stolen Generations had not yet emerged into the light, but the tragedy
of alienation and separation was alive, just hidden in dusty pastures and
deplorable settlements. As a state ward Bernard knew the 'thin line' that
had demarcated him within society, so thin you sometimes hardly saw it,
but the pain of anonymity had been his too, even though he was one of
the lucky ones. It is why his lectures were so powerful and so disturbing.
He had transferred his own marginality across the great divide of guilt
and it cut deep into the 'white fella's' psyche.

In 1980, though he had 'not yet got' Captain Cook, 'the old man of
the sea', off his back, Bernard confessed it was time that he and others
'should talk less about the "shoes and ships and sealing wax" and turn to
the arithmetic of our shame',[43] for it was only in confronting the debase-
ment and atrocities that had occurred and were still occurring to Australia's
Indigenous people that any honorable reparation could begin. In response
to Bernard's Boyer Lectures, Jack Lindsay wrote that it was 'Good that the
question of aboriginal culture is now being so effectively defined. Of course
in my day one couldn't see it clearly like this'.[44] Once again Bernard was
ahead of the pack; as Fay Brauer observed, it was a decade before Eddie
Mabo's fight for reconciliation, but Bernard's Boyer Lectures articulated
what would move the arguments forward—'progress and the storm'.

Homage to Jack

Bernard's next literary exercise was Jack Lindsay's *Festschrift*. It began to take form as he was writing his entry on the Lindsay family—Norman, Lionel, Percy, Daryl and Ruby—for the *Australian Dictionary of Biography*. He was also finalising the proofs of his autobiography and the first two volumes of *The Art of Cook's Voyages*, as well as working on the second edition of *European Vision and the South Pacific* for Yale University Press. He had a knack of working on several projects at the same time: 'double-tasking keeps things fresh', he told Rüdiger Joppien.

Jack, the son of Norman Lindsay, was one of Australia's best 'outsider' intellectuals, a 'phenomenon as a poet, novelist, historian and playwright, both in the scope and quantity of his writing'.[45] He was also a communist whose *A Short History of Culture* (1939) had profoundly influenced Bernard, and for that and much more Bernard wanted to rehabilitate Jack's reputation. For the *Festschrift* he brought together 15 writers from Australia, Britain, the USA and the Soviet Union to pay tribute to this expatriate intellectual whose prolific output in 60 years consisted of more than 150 books, translations and edited volumes. There were many reasons why Australia should recognise Lindsay, not least because he had corresponded with Freud, Sartre, Brecht and Yeats, and had counted Tristan Tzara, Kenneth Slessor, Paul Éluard, Edith Sitwell and Dylan Thomas among his friends. As Jack put it:

> One of the reasons for my work not being taken seriously by critics is that they don't know what the devil I am. I've worked in almost every field. Often heretically. The establishment ignores me as the one creative writer who refused to succumb to the Cold War . . . All good writers did, ergo I'm a bad one, or rather I'm just not there at all . . . I think one can say that from the outset when I invaded England as the deadly serious emissary of the (NL) Australian Renascence, I have been odd-man-out.[46]

Like Noel Counihan and Gustave Courbet, Lindsay was a victim of politicised discrimination and, like Bernard, had been an active voice of protest during the Cold War. John Arnold points out that Bernard and

Lindsay's 'respective Marxisms had many common threads. Theirs was the Marxism of the early Paris manuscripts, a "humanist", rather than a "determinist", one'.[47] Moreover, Lindsay's biographies of artists 'provided a comprehensive view of the bourgeois world' and the dramatic social and cultural changes of the eighteenth and nineteenth centuries, the very territory in which Bernard's intellectual strengths resided. The *Festschrift* met both a personal and political obligation and it typified Bernard's attraction to the marginalised or alienated intellectual. As Lindsay wrote:

Hegel saw alienation as simply a necessary phase of the spirit's process of objectifying and realising itself: the moment of separation and division when the spirit confronts the objective world as otherness, before it proceeds to overcome the antagonism by grasping the essential unity of the opposites and thus discovers the alien thing as an aspect of itself.[48]

This captured Bernard's ontological relationship with the world and with himself. To his few closest friends and family he could be 'playful, loving, reliable, tenacious, empathic', but most knew Bernard as 'argumentative, tough, uncompromising, opinionated, provocative, challenging and single-minded, with impossibly high standards'.[49] As Patrick McCaughey put it, 'A strange pattern of encouragement and admonishment, of personal friendliness and public excoriation . . . characterise[d] my later relations with Bernard Smith.'[50] Though a 'fiercely competitive man', Bernard brought a rigorous intelligence and concrete reality to his understanding of cultural phenomena, one where 'humanity was his objective'.[51]

In his 1964 journal Bernard quoted Blaise Pascal: 'If all men knew what each said of the other, there would not be four friends in the world.' He may have been thinking about the Department of Fine Arts of the University of Melbourne or the Sydney and Melbourne circle of art critics, but Bernard did not actively seek close relationships; autonomy was too precious. His friendship with Lindsay Gordon in the 1930s had been richly rewarding, but career and marriage changed those dynamics. As his academic life progressed the *vita solitaria* was essential to his productivity. His study was where his arguments originated and his battles took place on the page, substantiating his discourse and himself (fig. 50). Among fellow scholars at the Australian Academy of Humanities he was considered congenial, reliable, pragmatic, his commonsense arguments cutting to the heart of matters, but he had a tendency to exclude himself socially. Distance was preferable, not only because it was deeply embedded in his psyche but also because it provided a relational objectivity to observe contemporary intellectual and cultural patterns. As Tim Bonyhady has noted, it was Bernard's wide-ranging and 'powerful set of cultural arguments' that clarified and gave shape to antipodean discourse, and which made him one of Australia's most enduring intellectuals.[52]

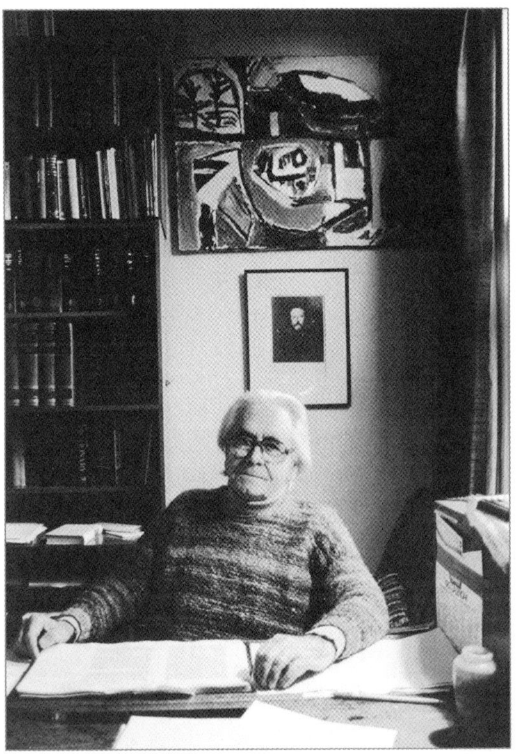

Fig. 50 Bernard Smith in his study, Fitzroy, 1987

As a utopian, Bernard believed in the future and in the younger generation. He found generational change exciting and it helped him absorb the Zeitgeist of the day. When Paul Taylor, a highly productive 'flamboyant wunderkind', swept onto the Melbourne art scene with the journal *Art & Text* Bernard applauded his ambition to revitalise the institutionalised impotency of art discourse. Bernard had already noted Taylor's rapier wit and intellectual stretch in an interview that Taylor had conducted with Clement Greenberg, published in *Art and Australia* in late 1979. Anyone as capable as Taylor at dismantling false gods was certain to gain Bernard's approval.[53] Moreover, Taylor and his colleague Paul Foss 'channelled' Bernard's early theories of cultural imperialism and the importance, or unimportance, of locality and provincialism, depending on where one stood. That had been one of Bernard's main intellectual thrusts in 1959 with the Antipodeans and under Taylor's new avant-gardism of appropriation a new image of Australian art was being reconstructed within the global landscape.[54]

Bernard also found several post-conceptual artists such as Imants Tillers and Juan Davila appealing for much the same reason. He admired their reworking of Australia's mythic alienation and geographical nihilism and he liked how they had identified the political and cultural dystopia beleaguering Australia in the postmodern era. He believed this notion of an antipodal shift was a way of 'seeing provincialism as an advantage rather than a curse' or, as Charles Green put it, 'the metropolitan centre's authority had become problematic; the personal self had been shown to be a construction woven from language and discourse; and the difference between private and public life had evaporated.'[55] Taylor was moving the argument forward and in 1982 he asked Bernard to contribute an essay to *Art & Text*'s surrealism issue. That invitation rehabilitated the ageing art historian within contemporary discourse while recasting him historically—a perfect solution.

Vox populism

The *Popism* exhibition at the NGV curated by Paul Taylor in 1982, and the *Vox Pop* exhibition, also held at the NGV, in January 1983, were the impetus for Bernard picking up his paintbrushes. It was 45 years since he had painted, but on seeing the works of Peter Booth, Paul Boston and Lutz Presser he was surprised by the urge. Moreover, it coincided with him writing about his artistic aspirations in the late 1930s in his autobiography and perhaps he had a sense of 'unfinished business'. Inquiring at Roar Studios in Brunswick Street as to whether there were studio spaces available for rent, he ordered canvases, brushes and paint to be delivered to Jeansville, and thought about his subject matter.

In his *Popism* essay, Paul Taylor argued 'the snap-shot is the real version of the real' and 'photography in its general usage is the amateur visual medium at its most perfect'.[56] Taking his cue from that, Bernard took his camera to the streets and photographed protests, public gatherings and celebratory events, including Circus Oz, Chinese New Year and the Moomba Festival. These 'snap-shots' became the composition material for his paintings. In a letter to Jack Lindsay he related how much he was enjoying 'painting people . . . [at] carnivals, anti-nuclear processions, our May Day and Anzac marches, plenty of colour, perhaps a bit naive in places (one has to relearn half learnt techniques of years back) and, I hope eventually, some pertinent social comment'.[57] Both the subject and the mechanical method of reproducing the image suited his Marxist belief in a broad, democratic base of the community, but artistic production required reception, and Bernard decided to hold his first one-man show.

Geoff Hogg, an artist whom Bernard had befriended, offered him the use of one of the front towers of the Victorian Trades Hall in Lygon Street, Carlton, as a studio. It was a time of burgeoning public arts programs, with Arts Victoria and the Australia Council funding collaborative projects, including the Art and Working Life Programme of which Hogg was in charge. At the Victorian Trades Hall, where people worked in a large communal workshop, Bernard insisted he would rather be with the workers than isolated in the tower and so duly set up his easel among the activity. Most likely it reminded him of the EAM or SORA, where people, ideas and practice all met under one roof.[58]

In mid-January 1985 Frances Lindsay, who ran the University Gallery at the University of Melbourne, came to the Victorian Trades Hall, looked at Bernard's paintings and offered him an exhibition. He was thrilled, but insisted he would exhibit under his pseudonym Joseph Tierney, just as he had done in 1940. In the catalogue introduction Lindsay wrote,

'The message in Tierney's early paintings [*Lot* and *Pompeii* were included in the exhibition] is as pertinent today as it was in 1940. In the 1980s the threat of nuclear holocaust is an awesome reality, as was the fascist destruction of Western Europe.' Politics was never far away in Bernard's life and while his paintings celebrated ordinary folk, public participation and the community spirit, they were very much about his Marxist utopianism—'the hope is in the waiting'. The exhibition was well attended by many old friends, but the experience of a one-man show was not the thunderbolt he had hoped, simply an 'unnerving experience'. He sold three paintings; Frances Lindsay expressed an interest in acquiring one for the university collection and Joseph Brown offered to act as his agent. Bernard, however, realised that the best contribution he could make was in writing about art and he duly returned to his desk.

In April 1985 copies of the second edition of *European Vision and the South Pacific* in its new, enlarged format with colour images arrived. It came soon after the publication of his and Rüdiger Joppien's much-awaited first two scholarly volumes of *The Art of Captain Cook's Voyages* (1985), made possible through a grant from the Australian Academy of Humanities and the Utah Foundation, and published by Oxford University Press. Many museums, recognising Bernard's importance, had waived their reproduction fees for the reprint of *European Vision and the South Pacific*, and finally the book began to receive the attention it deserved. Joppien has said of Bernard's magnum opus that 'it remains a lighthouse', and Humphrey McQueen has pointed out that Americanists honour it as 'essential for their comprehension of Herman Melville, and not only *Moby Dick*'; it was equally a seminal text for anthropologists, cultural historians and artists as much as for scholars of Pacific history.[59] Oskar Spate celebrated the handsome edition, but begged to disagree with Bernard's premise that 'the opening of the Pacific was the prime external factor contributing to the emergence of a scientifically acceptable theory of evolution'. Spate, perhaps provocatively, thought there was sufficient evidence 'to suggest that evolution was bound to evolve',[60] but he iterated what he had written 25 years earlier when he first reviewed the book: that *European Vision and the South Pacific* 'was a great achievement and had been the flagship in the intellectual exploration of the Pacific'.

Spate and Bernard were fond of each other and Bernard credited him with having been more conceptually challenging than his supervisor J. W. Davidson during his postgraduate studies. Spate understood Bernard's broad interdisciplinary vision and his literary and poetical sensibilities as key factors in analysing the cultural tenor of a period and the romanticised notion of the noble savage. In 2012 the Australian Indigenous Studies scholar Philip Morrissey similarly noted that Bernard's historical interrogation of European possession was heavily inflected by the romantic notion of literary and Enlightenment philosophy, but added that 'his Marxism counteracted this', thus giving it a more critical and empathetic edge.[61] Another reviewer questioned whether Bernard should have updated his material on cultural relativism, to which he replied that to do so would have required another book and he 'saw no reason for a "face lift". If my point of view now seems a trifle old fashioned I hope at least it has acquired the dignity of age'—a view he took with any re-editing of his books.[62]

In an interview in 1987 Bernard spoke of how his initial research in England had made him 'look back at his own intellectual origins' and cultural inheritance. The historian Greg Dening believed 'Culture' was an 'analytic concept . . . of all human behaviour considered as expression and communication. Culture is an observer's construct.'[63] As one of Australia's most astute observers and critics of modern Australian society, Bernard's analysis of its cultural origins remains an authoritative benchmark.

At a meeting of the International Cultural Corporation of Australia in Sydney on 25 July 1985 it was agreed that an exhibition *Terra Australis: The Furthest Shore*, planned for the bicentenary, be based around Bernard's *European Vision and the South Pacific*. The committee members included Daniel Thomas, Edmund Capon, Virginia Spate, Barry Pearce, William Eisler and Bernard. Once again he had to turn his mind to European imperialism and colonisation, but the result was an exceptional exhibition that brought together hundreds of objects and pictures and which paid a magisterial tribute to Bernard's groundbreaking scholarship.

Counihan and the class struggle

England . . . has its Hogarth, France its Daumier and Germany its Kollwitz and Australia its Counihan. Such artists are rare birds in danger of becoming extinct . . . today it does not surprise me that Counihan was singled out . . . [as] the whipping boy, the scapegoat of the show. And not because he was a communist, but because he died one. Such people are not readily forgiven. Remember Courbet.
Bernard Smith[64]

When Pat Counihan rang in July 1986 to say that Noel had suffered a massive heart attack and died, Bernard wrote in his diary, 'The end of a noble life'; he also made the decision to write the biography of Australia's own 'stormy petrel of art'. With the first volume of his autobiography completed, he was in a position to take on another literary project, and as Noel had already drafted some 20,000 words on his early life, superbly written in a clear and fresh style, Bernard was able to use this much in its original state. He also felt obligated to write about Noel's life, not only because he had been such an important critic of his own society, 'address[ing] his work to the suffering, to Modernity's victims,'[65] but because his ethics and politics and 'interest in the working class and a respect for its labour', correlated so closely to Bernard's.[66] In writing Counihan's biography, however, Bernard wanted to 'redress a situation' for which he felt partly responsible; he was referring to his role in cementing Noel's reputation as a Social Realist. But Counihan had been more than capable of managing his own artistic reputation and political career, and that admission was plainly an excuse for Bernard to address his own political history, admitting 'there's no history until it's written. That's why the memoirs of Noel [are] important'.[67]

The biography would enable Bernard to be an authorial participant and place on record his recollections and views about his contemporaries; after all, he knew them too—Dobell, Bergner, O'Connor, the Lindsays, the Evatts, the Boyds, Tucker, Gleeson, Nolan, Perceval, Westbrook and so on. Richard Haese has pointed out: 'The reader who comes to this book with some sense of Smith's own ideological history will find considerable interest in the interweaving of the lives of both biographer and subject.[68] For Bernard it was as much a historical document as another mask that allowed him to wield 'the whip with the velvet thorn' and cast judgement on his friends and foes while writing himself into history.

Both Bernard and Counihan believed that artists had to be accountable for what they produced, just as the worker was responsible for the utilitarian object; each was validated by the existence and the reception of their products. Art, even in its most special and elite sense, should address not only the refuge of dreams, myths and misconceptions, but mirror the social and political conditions of the common people in a world struggling with post-industrialisation. As Counihan put it, 'it was a function of realism to disclose what good taste preferred to conceal', which is why he painted the underdogs of society, the workers, the poor, the urban Indigenous, the destitute and the sick. In 1944 he had gone to the Wonthaggi State Coal Mine to paint the miners, primarily because they had not received recognition for their part in the war effort. Accompanying them underground, Counihan sketched by the light of his helmet lamp in the dark, cramped, muddy pits. His 1947 linocut *Cough—stone dust*, with its economy of line and the bent posture of the miner as he coughs out his 'dusted' silicosis lungs, captured the victim of his working environment; an image as haunting as Courbet's *The stone-breakers* (1849–50) or van Gogh's peasants.

Counihan once told Bernard and Kate that he had never visited John and Sunday Reed's home, Heide, simply because he had never been invited and it was unlikely that he ever would be. When Yosl Bergner was invited to Heide, Reed had accused him of taking a £5 note from the mantelpiece. After Bergner told Counihan what had happened and assured him he had not stolen the money, Counihan took him to John Reed's city office and announced 'that a rich man had no business leaving notes lying about and then accusing impoverished guests of having stolen them'.[69] Aware that the art world was a battlefield riddled with divisive temperaments, intrigues and individuals capable of ruining careers and reputations, Counihan had the courage and the conviction to expose the 'unequal exchange'; it was why Bernard admired him, even at his most politically doctrinaire and argumentative, though he later told Manning Clark:

I know it's not possible to tell the truth about others: but there are so many who should be remembered despite that, and I feel sad about others who will be forgotten, even the scoundrels. Death should not be so final but it is . . . Trying to cope with Noel Counihan's biog[raphy] is daunting enough. What arrogance and pride, but a man of faith and honour.[70]

Marxism, Bernard said, was a complex business and Counihan, who had been both a comrade and a conduit for his own political convictions, offered one of the closest examinations of humanity and the unifying struggles of art and politics.

Farewell journey

While Bernard ploughed through Counihan's life he watched his wife struggling with hers. On 29 April 1988 Bernard and Kate left for London on what was to be her 'farewell journey' to say goodbye to her family and dearest friends. Despite Kate's illness it was business as usual for Bernard, conferring with Cook scholars, checking sources at various British museums and galleries, and meeting his publisher, John Nicoll of Yale University Press. He attended the Hayward Gallery at the South Bank Centre to preview the *Angry Penguins* exhibition, where he met the British curator Sandy Nairne; Australia's Zelman Cowen, who was, at that time, Provost of Oriel College, Oxford; Sidney and Mary Nolan; Janet Spens (McKenzie); and, from the National Gallery of Australia, Sara Kelly who had helped organise the exhibition. Margaret and Gough Whitlam strolled around the exhibition, discussing the art and teasing one another.[71]

The exhibition of 176 works was the brainchild of Sandy Nairne and Richard Francis, former curators of modern art at the Tate Gallery. They had discovered Australian expressionism on a visit to Australia and considered the artists associated with John and Sunday Reed's coterie at Heide, namely Nolan, Tucker, Perceval, Arthur Boyd, Charles Blackman and Joy Hester, and the Social Realists Noel Counihan, Vic O'Connor and Yosl Bergner, 'enunciated . . . a critique of modernism' that was considerably more energetic than what existed elsewhere during the war years.[72] Their ignorance of that Australian artistic coruscation had been partly due to the generational veil—Bryan Robertson's 1961 Whitechapel exhibition *Recent Australian Painting* long forgotten—and that restaging of Heide's *Angry Penguins* and the poetics and politics of Melbourne's artistic fermentation not only highlighted the dogfights, artistic self-determinism and intellectualism, but also illuminated a unique aesthetic urbanism.

Bernard had contributed an essay to the catalogue that sought to reconstruct the colourful tensions of the times. As he pointed out those tensions were a complex conflation of wartime political issues, philistinism, xenophobic nationalism and a 'petrified culture' against which young artists and intellectuals of the left raged.[73] Melbourne was 'a storm centre' and it was only to be expected that the clash would be more dramatic and brutal there and that a distinctive antipodean school of painters would emerge from it. In his review of Richard Haese's *Rebels and Precursors* (1981) Bernard had agreed about the revolutionary mood of the period, but disagreed with Haese's interpretation of the political situation. Haese, according to Bernard, had misjudged the extent of communism's ideological capacity to inject a greater humanism into the artistic equation, which played out vividly between the Heide camp and the Social Realists. But Bernard's corrective criticism erred on the reflexive side, even if his perspective was ultimately about historical truths:

Hope is central to Marxist thought . . . it is an extremely powerful social myth . . . Melbourne social realism was not based upon hope, nor was it about the optimistic aspirations of the working class . . . Melbourne social realism was a sombre art, not defeatist, but almost elegiac . . . it is an art possessed of great human dignity.

In contrast he wrote:

The war-time art of Nolan, Perceval and Arthur Boyd . . . remained immature and unfocused; they were all still very young men, obsessed by personal problems and predicaments . . . and their art lacked the distancing and objectifying structures that they achieved later.[74]

Being an eyewitness or participant mattered, as Bernard so often reminded people. He experienced a similar occasion in 1984 when he launched a formidable rebuttal to the curators Christine Dixon and Terry Smith and the academics responsible for the exhibition *Aspects of Australian Figurative Painting 1942–1962: Dreams, Fears and Desires* at the S. H. Ervin Gallery in Sydney (fig. 51). Their interpretation of the period, he claimed, was not an accurate reading and 'those . . . who are now ambitious to rewrite Australian art history' stood to be corrected. He disagreed with Virginia Spate about 'enforced isolation' during the war years in Australia, which he had addressed in his Macrossen lectures; nor did artists paint in a state of fear, 'those who fear sit petrified or run for it', and 'the concept of alienation is . . . an extraordinarily blunt weapon to use on these paintings', and so forth. Terry Smith 'got it wrong', the Antipodean intervention was not a 'liberal middle ground' response to the Cold War; it was certainly a product of it, although it was not intended 'as a Melbourne–Sydney dog-fight . . . but it was quite enough to start them all barking'.[75] As arguments raged and insults were hurled, the father of Australian art history was having a field day imparting his lesson about recovered criticism, of which he felt strongly— 'Although the recovery of criticism is an important part of art historical writing, as is the delineation of avant-garde movements, the acceptance of their value at face value, results in superficial history.'[76]

Bernard was similarly provoked to write an aggressive riposte to several British critics' condescending reviews of the Hayward exhibition, which had excavated the same old argument about isolation and myth-making. It was published in the British art journal *Modern Painters*, and Bernard lambasted the 'imperious (imperial?) superciliousness' and 'insufferable' and 'overweening arrogance' of the critics. It was not just 'a case . . . of tunnel vision but of tunnel rhetoric . . . which has flourished in Britain whenever [they] . . . are faced with art from its former colonies'. The British psyche, he insisted, needed to demote Australians in order to invoke their superior cultural hegemony; it had been evident in their

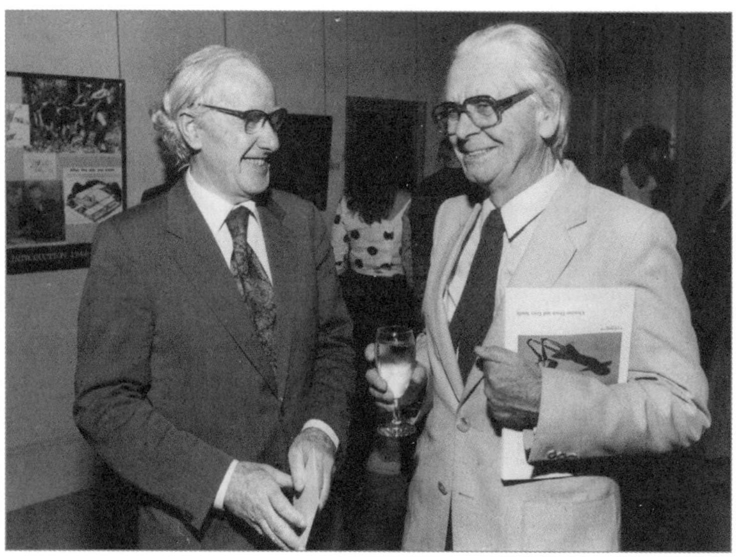

Fig. 51 Sidney Nolan and Bernard Smith at the exhibition *Aspects of
Australian Figurative Painting 1942–1962* at the S. H. Ervin Gallery, 1984

reaction to all the large exhibitions of Australian art shown in London
since 1898. Moreover, he accused them of depicting 'contemporary
Australian artists . . . [as] the new white noble savages, stand-ins for those
darker ones that Anglo-Celtic settlers had displaced . . . in the 19th century.' The patronising critics had simply repeated the same old atavistic
'apothogems . . . writ[ten] within a sub-cultural discourse designed to
invoke contempt'. One critic had mentioned second-hand conventions
and the so-called dependency of Australian artists on reproductions of
European masterpieces, to which Bernard sarcastically hypothesised,
'how many European masters does a practising artist have to study in
order to become a master himself?' In arguing about provincial originality versus metropolitan exclusivity as a qualifying value-status system,
he also prepared his own rhetorical rebirth, claiming that 'the history
of modernism is still written very largely in terms of those Eurocentric
models from which modernism itself as an art practice had broken away'.
The model, he said, had to be challenged.[77]

At the Menzies Centre for Australian Studies in Russell Square,
London, the director, Carl Bridge, gave Bernard a visitor's room where he
pondered the stylistic parameters and the generic character of modernism,

concluding that as 'late modernism and post-modernism have become institutionalised' the case was ripe for analysis; and who was better to write a revision of modernism and rake through the already cooling ashes of postmodernism than the participant critic and cultural historian himself.

At the Tate Gallery Bernard saw a brilliant David Bomberg exhibition, noting 'the English are beginning to discover at last their important 20th century artists'.[78] Bomberg had been a student of the Slade School of Art in London before World War I and had produced exciting figurative works in a Vorticist, Cézannesque style, based on industry and the worker; he was also a communist who had visited Russia in 1933. That immediately elevated him in Bernard's eyes. At the Whitechapel Gallery he saw an impressive Clifford Possum Tjapaltjarri exhibition of large Central Desert canvases. Their spectacular visual language, Bernard imagined, would undoubtedly unsettle the British critics as another 'subcultural' art from the isolated periphery. A retrospective of Michael Sandle's sculptures and drawings, also at the Whitechapel, reminded him that he had tried to buy one of Sandle's works for the Power Collection in 1968, but the size and cost had been inhibiting.

Once back in Australia, Kate's health deteriorated; dizziness, the appearance of red blotches on her skin and frequent nosebleeds indicated her condition had shifted from chronic to acute, and she was hospitalised. After four blood transfusions Bernard recorded in his diary that it was one of the saddest days of his life because he knew that this was the beginning of the end of Kate's life. With her health so delicate he needed to be close to her most of the time and, though he managed to keep to his strict work routine, other activities dropped off as he nursed her. The Counihan biography occupied most of his time, with Pat regularly dropping in bundles of the artist's papers, but he also began working on a book of essays, *The Critic as Advocate*, and his lecture for a special series of 1988 Boyer Lectures that was to include seven other prominent intellectuals discussing issues relevant to Australia's political, humanist and cultural condition.[79]

Since Bernard's Power Institute days there had been a shift in his engagement with society; at one point he claimed 'the past is not a place to live in'. In his 1988 contribution to the Boyer series he tracked the geopolitical movements about Australia's multinationalism and its crucial relationship with South-East Asia. With his political mask removed, he addressed the issue of independent sovereignty, a pro-republicanism that might better protect our cultural values and identity, and eloquently castigated those who clung to a 'paralysing nostalgia' of colonial and imperial dependence. With clarifying logic he proposed armed neutrality, bipartisan multiculturalism and a national autonomy that would ensure Australia's global future.[80]

In Jeansville, however, a subdued gravity settled over their lives, further saddened by the death of Bernard's long-time friend Lindsay Gordon on 13 October 1988. Two weeks earlier he had dedicated his book of essays to Gordon, but a premonition changed it from 'To Lindsay Gordon who steered me down the track' to 'To the memory of Lindsay Gordon'. On 12 November Vincent Buckley died at the age of 63, bringing mortality even closer to the couple's doorstep. Bernard attended the requiem service at Newman College where the poets Peter Steele and Chris Wallace-Crabbe gave magnificent homilies to one of Australia's most admired literary essayists, poets and public intellectuals.

While Bernard watched over Kate and attended to her medical needs, a constant stream of colleagues and students visited. On good days he and Kate attended exhibitions and on one occasion Grahame King took Bernard to the Victorian Print Workshop in Gertrude Street to see a small portfolio of Noel Counihan's prints that had been posthumously printed, but largely he was housebound.

The final obstacle to Bernard's understanding of Indigenous art was removed when he was asked to review *Dreamings: The Art of Aboriginal Australia* (1988), edited by Peter Sutton and published to coincide with a large exhibition touring the USA before returning to the Museum of Victoria in September that year. Issues such as the politics of representation and how to apply the term 'art' to things made by the Indigenous peoples of Australia were addressed in a clear, didactic manner; particularly how western critics tended to interpret this distinctive culture 'as an act of cultural colonisation'.[81] Bernard considered it a thorough and excellent piece of research in a genuinely new spirit of inquiry; it was sensitive to the richly complex Dreaming of Indigenous Australians' ancestral past and its organic present, and he found the essays and art so exciting that it confirmed his decision to endow a memorial prize in honour of Kate. Pondering his own mortality, he decided it would be called the Tierney-Challis Prize for Aboriginal Art.

The gatekeeper

As Kate's condition deteriorated, she was hospitalised for more blood transfusions, but expected to return home. On 7 January Bernard received a telephone call to inform him that she had died. That night he wrote in his diary 'My dear wife Kate, fond and beloved wife of forty-eight years died at 4.30 pm this evening. I was desolated'.[82] As his grief subsided it was replaced by an unendurable silence:

> The object now is to retain the realities of living that we developed over the years, in that way perhaps I can gain some strength in my loneliness from the strong shadow of her memory, of her cheerfulness, love and companionship, her selflessness and great love of her family and wide circle of friends. Her loss to me means that I shall end my days in a different world.[83]

Kate Challis, who had been Ruth Adeney and became Kate Smith, believed in the decency of people and her warm, considerate manner had endeared her to everyone she met. She had been Bernard's great fortune and he had always held the greatest admiration and respect for her magnanimity and grace. There had been real affection, love and humour between them and she had been immensely proud of his development and achievements, but she had also worked hard, striding through his vast intellectual landscape. Along the way she had smoothed many difficult patches, pacified antagonists and diffused unpleasant encounters, and had been prepared to shepherd him back, even when his infidelity tore at her affection. She was a pragmatist who had nurtured Bernard as a work in progress, but it had not been easy; a few lines by Mary Gilmore, copied into her diary reveal this:

Never admit pain/Bury it deep
Only the weak complain/Complaint is cheap
Cover the wound, fold down
Its curtained place
Silence is still a crown/Courage a grace[84]

While she had made time for herself, her music, her weaving and their grandchildren, ultimately she had given most of her attention to the man she had helped shape. Only after her death does a decline begin in Bernard's work, and had Kate lived, perhaps he would not have strayed over the boundary lines that she had carefully marked, nor dived so deep into the waters of postmodernism and risked the dangers of intellectual diffusion, or the damage of foolish egocentrism.

During the following months Bernard replied to hundreds of letters of condolence. Manning Clark, typically theatrical, but equally warm, assured Bernard, 'I think of her as a KINDRED SPIRIT, to the impression in her face always holding out the promise that it would be possible . . . of being an ENLARGER of life and not one of the STRAIGHTNERS and LIFE-DENIERS'.[85] Humphrey McQueen captured a quintessential quality: 'there was her no-nonsense attitude towards the world and its vanities. She was earthed in a way that sorted out what was important.'

As Bernard dwelt on Kate's absence he admitted that 'much of the savour of life has gone'. Grief turned to depressed loneliness, and even 'the relish of work was no longer there when K's presence is no longer about the house'.[86] With Kate's death, however, Bernard's gatekeeper had left the door open and he was free to roam. He had always needed a woman—or several women—in his life, a legacy perhaps of 'Mum' Keen, her daughter Bertha and his absentee mother. At the age of 73, his single status reinstated, and virile in mind and body, he went in search of a new partner. He propositioned old and young women, colleagues, postgraduate students, as well as 'his sweet little cleaner Mary', yet Kate's spirit haunted him and not a day passed without him thinking and referring to 'My Kate'. Faced with her corporeal absence an almost elegiac memory pervaded his life for more than a decade, diminishing only in the last years of his life as he edged towards his own death.

RAKA

Bernard had been gathering ideas for a memorial to Kate and they all pointed towards the one area he had neglected, Indigenous Australian art. There was Kate's small manuscript *Tales from Sydney Cove*, written in 1951, about the first days of settlement and the contact made with Australia's Indigenous people:

> The chapters on Arabanoo, Bennelong and Balooderry tell of the early attempts of the white men and the natives to live together, and of the troubles that arose. It was more than difficult for men of such different cultures to understand one another. Yet the attempt *was* made, and at times even affection seemed to grow up between them.[87]

Intended for school children, all attempts at publishing it had failed. Sam Ure Smith felt it had limited appeal and Clem Christesen warned that the publishing business was 'beggared'. Bernard approached Angus and Robertson, but also received a negative response, and eventually in 2000, well after Kate's death, Bernard had it published with Helicon Press 'when reconciliation with Australia's first peoples [was] a burning issue on the political agenda'.[88]

Jim Davidson's editorial for *Meanjin*'s Australian Aboriginal issue in 1977 also provided an excellent template for a memorial prize:

> Apart from raiding it for a name, *Meanjin* has not hitherto paid much attention to Aboriginal culture: for many years it seemed separate, a forbidding terrain of secret, ancient rites patrolled almost exclusively by anthropologists—for obvious reasons—no black creative writer arose to interpret this world for us. This situation has now, partly as a result of increasing Aboriginal urbanisation, changed dramatically. The worlds have come closer together. In the last dozen years or so, and with increasing acceleration, Aboriginals have produced first poetry, then a novel, a theatre group performing original plays, and soon . . . film. What we are witnessing . . . are the first attempts to use the white man's art forms to articulate an Aboriginal identity.[89]

On the first day of February 1989 Chris Wallace-Crabbe and Dinny O'Hearn arrived at Jeansville to discuss Bernard's plans. He had contacted the anthropologists Ronald and Catherine Berndt about an appropriate Indigenous word to name the prize, but the suggestion of RAKA, meaning five fingers, came from the linguist Tamsin Donaldson. This could represent the five artistic disciplines of the cyclic prize, with painting, film, nonfiction, poetry and theatre awarded on a rotational basis. It was also a neat acronym for Ruth Adeney Koori Award.[90]

The prize of $10,000 was not only the first major Indigenous award in Australia, but it would be awarded to a person of 'Aboriginal descent, whether of full-blood or of any other blood', and the newly established Australian Centre at the University of Melbourne would oversee its management. The only way that it could be financed was for Bernard to sell a substantial part of his art collection, but for a Marxist who believed 'speculative consumption' was potentially corrupting, disposing of his collection was not a difficult decision.[91] Robert Blakeney from Sotheby's Auction House was called to assess the more important works, with Grace Cossington Smith's *The school cape* valued at between $80,000 and $100,000—it fetched $93,000—and with further sales, including Donald Friend's *Monkeys*, a Richard Larter and a Tony Tuckson, Bernard was able to announce proudly that 'the first step to the Kate Challis Prize had been made'.

On 18 June 1989 Bernard walked to the Trades Hall in Carlton to attend the memorial service for the former secretary of the Communist Party of Australia, Ralph Gibson. Deidre Moore, the woman he had an affair with 45 years earlier and had not seen for many years, was there, and together they listened to eulogies by John Halfpenny, Lloyd Edmonds and Manning Clark. The following day Bernard flew to Sydney to attend Valerie Walsh's funeral at the Salvation Army Citadel in Marrickville. He had grown up with Val, another of 'Mum' Keen's state wards, but had not realised she had remained a strong Salvationist. He was asked to say a few words about their childhood friendship in Burwood, and on his flight back to Melbourne he reflected on how he had sung Salvation Army hymns in memory of Val that day and the 'International' to honour Ralph Gibson the day before.

As Bernard adapted to living alone his daily routine became more important than ever. He was working on essays for *Imagining the Pacific*, as well as the Counihan biography, but Kate's absence festered like a wound. This time the act of mourning was his duty and his right. Others commented on his solemnity and even his Saturday evening gatherings or 'symposias' at Jeansville were strained, sober events.[92] In August he flew to England with his daughter, Elizabeth, to scatter Kate's ashes on the South Downs.

That period of sadness was further compounded when Peter Townsend, the editor of *Australian and International Art Monthly*, rang Bernard and broke the news that the English art critic Peter Fuller had been killed in a car accident. Fuller had planned to visit Melbourne later that year and stay with Bernard, who was visibly shaken: 'A tragic loss [to] English art and criticism. And just at the early peak of his career; what a waste.' Bernard believed Fuller 'was the first British critic to develop a serious interest in Australian art and its relationship to British art', unlike Sir Kenneth Clark or Herbert Read, and what was more, he wore his intellectual honesty on his sleeve. He admired Fuller, 'I like hard cases', and identified strongly with Fuller's attempt to reanimate visual culture, reverse the trends of reductivist aesthetics, and in particular his feeling for tradition, regionalism, his re-examination of roots and his attack on postmodernism. Fuller thought postmodernism 'treat[ed] tradition as a load of old junk to be dismissed and ruthlessly exploited'; but Bernard also applauded his antipathy towards the American hegemony of abstract painting.[93] While he read Fuller through a rose-coloured lens, admitting he often felt as if he were 'traversing his own past'—especially in Fuller's study of Marx, Ruskin and Morris—Bernard was nevertheless critical of the British art historian's theoretical prevarication, yet in many ways he had regarded Peter Fuller as the art critic most likely to inherit his baton; but death had snatched his heir.

The Celtic temperament

Within a year of Kate's death Bernard met Margaret Forster, a spritely, charismatic and intelligent woman of Irish parentage, whose appetite for life, laughter and fun was a great diversion from his grief. She was also well acquainted with the art world, having known Arthur and Yvonne Boyd, Jean Langley and many of Melbourne's cultural figures for more than 50 years, and Bernard found her excellent company. 'Maggi', as she was known, was sensitive to Bernard's territory, but she also wanted to be part of his topography and at first he happily accepted her into this part of his life as their courtship unfolded. As he put it, 'We relate so well together both in our talk and in our more sensuous relationship', but he warned, he was not a monogamous creature.[94] He also proposed that his granddaughter, Kate, who was studying Fine Arts at the University of Melbourne, move into Jeansville, and consequently he experienced a new lease of life and a revival of pleasure.

Young Kate stayed for almost 10 years, during which time she grew to admire the man who had been such a remote figure in her childhood. Her grandmother, after whom she was named, had been a wonderful role model, but she found her grandfather's intellectual tenacity inspiring. They talked 'philosophy, art, literature, politics . . . and the way in which information, culture and values are propagated'. But it was his extraordinary wit, linguistic play and irony—though his sense of humour was usually very specific—which she equally enjoyed. She also saw a man who never complained, was optimistic about the future, loved life and viewed 'the past, including his own . . . with a curiosity and respect'.[95]

At first Maggi was good for Bernard and on 30 July 1995 they were married, but it was a partnership destined to flounder. With the demands of his work and his predatory need for women, old patterns were resumed, fissures developed and their lives together unravelled; as Bernard admitted to a friend, 'My marriage has its ups and downs. The Celtic temperament is so different from the Anglo-Saxon.'[96]

Ian McLean, one of Bernard's last postgraduate students, believed Bernard belonged with some of the major western Marxist scholars and cultural historians interested in the discourse of cultural studies. As one of the surviving traditional 'patriarchs of the old art history', along with Erwin Panofsky and Ernst Gombrich, Bernard's 'cross-disciplinary modes', as exemplified in *European Vision and the South Pacific*, were 'a typical and brilliant piece' of Warburgian inheritance, and a prime example of 'proto-cultural studies'.[97] Bernard, however, had displayed that type of intellectual inquiry from the outset, as early as his 1940 education department thesis on the romantic movement; he had always taken a long view, searching for missing links in the historical chain of events and ideas. McLean also noted 'the most distinguishing feature of the new art history is its claim to suspend aesthetic judgments in favour of ideological analysis,' a position Bernard usually resisted, believing history was not a closed discipline, but rather that contingency produced causality, and central to this was the capacity of art to illuminate that which was known, as well as what was unknown or unwritten. As the art historian Rex Butler suggests, for Bernard 'there is a truth to vision outside of discourse'.[98] The role of the art historian was to decipher that relationship 'between appearance and cognition'.

Ever since the *Antipodeans* exhibition in 1959 Bernard had no shortage of hostile criticism, and by the late 1980s a younger generation of Marxist art historians began to question his orthodoxy and dominant position. Ian Burn, Nigel Lendon, Charles Merewether and Ann Stephen felt it was time to rewrite Australia's cultural history and challenge the colossus of art history. Their book *The Necessity of Australian Art* (1989) rehabilitated William Moore's *The Story of Australian Art* (1934), which had been superseded by Bernard's *Place, Taste and Tradition* in 1945 and his updated editions of *Australian Painting* in 1971. They also accused Bernard of inhibiting interpretation and not identifying a distinctive Australian identity outside 'the circularity of between Europe and Australia'.[99] Yet it was precisely the Eurocentric cultural inheritance that incited Australians to 'refer back' and to 'mediate influences' or 'wilfully disrupt' received styles so as to reposition themselves within their own locality and unique present.[100] As Bernard said, 'Even if the past is another country the historian has to find a way to get there.'[101] Simply, Bernard's aesthetic gaze was considerably more dependent upon overseas models and inclined towards a universal modernism than the 'Nolanesque' or 'Streetonesque' paradigm. While John Brack thought Bernard might have written Australian art history better, in the middle decades of the twentieth century 'he [wa]s probably the only one who could'.[102]

Leon Paroissien believed *The Necessity of Australian Art* was an important and inevitable process of contemporising the historiographical nature of the discipline.[103] The authors' attack, however, took Bernard by surprise, and whenever he found himself backed into a corner, he usually responded with combative determination and flaring brilliance. With a blow-by-blow critique he cogently argued against the neo-Marxist art historians' reading of his work, writing, 'contingency is the guard dog of history that protects it from invasion by theoretical fictions.'[104] Though Burn, Lendon, Merewether and Stephen's theoretical dismantling of Bernard's scholarship was an obvious 'oedipal revolt' against his reification, it prompted others to follow and to evaluate his position. Richard Haese took aim at 'Bernard's rather jaundiced view of Australian attitudes towards its artists and their art' in his review of the third and enlarged edition of *Australian Painting 1788–1990*,[105] while David McNeill wrote 'If [William] Moore is the Vasari of Australian art, then Bernard Smith is our Vico. In *Place, Taste and Tradition* Smith relegates anecdote and chooses instead to chart the complex intersections of inheritance, locale, patronage and politics.'[106] Despite the generational change, Bernard was not about to bow to the new cultural theorists and he continued to plough the historical field of modernism with the same investigative analysis that he had always used. The battle was not yet over.

In 1992 David Bindman, then head of Art History at University College, London, offered Bernard a visiting professorship. As he arrived in London he was overcome with nostalgia; 'A kind of gentle sadness hangs over [the city] . . . because wherever I go I am reminded of places that I first visited with Kate. For me her presence is all over London . . . it is not depression of course, just the overarching sadness of life.'[107] He stayed at Arthur and Yvonne Boyd's house in Grove Terrace, Hampstead, where the Australian artist Gary Willis oversaw the ebb and flow of family and guests. Bernard chose a small attic room on the third floor 'where the maids must have slept'—workers' quarters always appealed to him—and in the evenings he would walk on Hampstead Heath. As he worked on his 'Modernism and Post-modernism' paper he would often discuss issues with Willis, who felt that the great art historian 'was simply off track'. He changed his mind when he heard Bernard give his paper at the Menzies Centre; his rearguard approach, which 'had been defined by modernism's end', made sense after all.[108] In the following months Bernard delivered his paper at the University of St Andrews, where Martin Kemp was Professor of Art History; at the University of Coventry in Michael Rosenthal's Department of Art History; and at Peter Quartermaine's department at the University of Exeter—every time reformulating his argument.

In April Bernard announced to Yvonne Boyd that he was 'about to go up to Leeds to an art historians conference and enter the deep waters of postmodernism'.[109] Most of the papers were 'first rate' and prepared him for what lay ahead. As Ken Wach recalled:

Bernard . . . told me that he was 'scouting around' checking up on Post Modernism and its positions. He said he was planning out and researching a new book (to be his 'magnum opus' . . . and was keen to hear at first hand as many of the experts as he could manage . . . He went to many of the conference sessions (totally flat out, working hard and taking it all in).[110]

His presence at the conference and engagement with mainstream international art historians announced him as a contender on the discourse of the collapse of modernism. Bernard relished conversation and criticism because it helped him to define his arguments, in turn helping him redefine his identity among the younger art historians. In July 1992 he flew to Hamburg and caught up with Rüdiger Joppien before travelling to Berlin for the XXVIII International Congress of the History of Art where he mingled with 'luminaries' of the international art world, such as 'Werner Hofmann, Stephen Bann, Peg Weiss . . . the "new art historians" Keith Moxey, Whitney David, John Clark (the only Australian speaker) [and] the *October* contingent of Benjamin Buchloh, Rosalind Krauss, with Serge Guilbaut and T. J. Clark and Yves-Alain Bois [*sic*] in tow'.[111] The forum, according to Fay Brauer, was an exciting exchange of art historical knowledge and theoretical discourse centred on American cultural imperialism, the Cold War and its aftermath[112]—the very territories that Bernard had been traversing for decades. He had not experienced such an intellectually challenging feast for some time and it gave him ample material to consider and structure his revision of modernism.

It was 43 years since Bernard had been in Germany; so much of it had then been rubble, but now he saw rebuilt cities. He found Weimar 'an ideal Enlightenment city— the urban spaces so beautifully related, such a wonderful place to walk about in with dignity . . . I am so pleased that I saw it before it is transmogrified by McDonald's and Coca Cola's visual pollution', he told Joppien.[113] Back in London, Martin Kemp launched *Imagining the Pacific* at the Menzies Centre, a book containing Bernard's best essays on eighteenth-century imperialism of the Pacific; it was dedicated to Charles Mitchell and A. D. Trendall, the former having taught Bernard how to ask questions and navigate the oceans of empiricism, the latter helping him build a secure, intellectual framework within a global landscape.[114]

On his return to Melbourne, the Marxist sociologist Peter Beilharz, a lecturer at La Trobe University, approached Bernard with a proposal to write about him. Beilharz had discovered *European Vision and the South Pacific* and *Place, Taste and Tradition* and was excited by the art historian's 'strikingly contemporary way of seeing', his 'architectural thinking', political insights and 'antipodean optic'.[115] After four years of working his way through Bernard's immense archive and discussing the sociology of colonisation, the annals of art and the boundaries of politics with the ageing Marxist scholar, Beilharz produced the first major appraisal of the cultural historian's work. *Imagining the Antipodes: Culture, Theory and the Visual in the Work of Bernard Smith* (1997) recognised Bernard's central operative of 'the antipodes as a relation, not a place', one defined by the continual movement and interchange of 'cultural traffic' in which 'each is defined by the other, Europe by the Pacific, Australia by Europe'.[116]

Further scholarly evaluations of Bernard's most influential work, as well as recognition of his intellectual integrity, were also beginning to emerge—the Egyptian-born American literary theorist Ihab Hassan was but one of a growing line of international admirers who recognised Bernard's yearning for, and translation of, historical truths, and his impressive record for tackling huge, fertile projects. In 1996 the ethnographic historians Nicholas Thomas and Diane Losche convened a large conference on colonial and postcolonial theories at the ANU in Bernard's honour. The conference, 'Reimagining the Pacific', was a tribute to

European Vision and the South Pacific, and revealed his penetrating influence on postcolonial discourse and cross-cultural studies. Acknowledged as the starting point in opening up the field and as an authority of world history, Bernard was, as Dinah Dysart and many others discovered, 'still an innovative and subversive mind',[117] whose 'intellect was driven by itself'.[118] Bernard, however, confessed to Ursula Hoff that he found the excess of adulation embarrassing and that he was much 'more accustomed to contention'.

In 1996 the position of the *Herald* Chair of Fine Arts became vacant again and Bernard threw his support behind one of his old students, Jaynie Anderson. He had known her since 1962 as a student in the Department of Fine Arts, advised her on her master of arts thesis and was instrumental in her postdoctoral acceptance at Bryn Mawr College, Pennsylvania. While Anderson, a Giorgione specialist, faced considerable competition, Bernard argued vehemently that she should be appointed; as he said, 'I do not know of any Australian-born art historian who has been better trained professionally and has been more productive in the traditional fields of European art history'.[119] Anderson duly became the third *Herald* Professor of Fine Arts.

Peter Townsend's suggestion that Bernard should be asked to deliver a lecture on his current project *Modernism's History* at the Tate Gallery was taken up and on 23 August 1997 Martin Kemp introduced him as 'One of the founding fathers of art history—both inside and outside Australia'. He also said that Bernard was 'more than somebody who writes about art . . . [he] was at the heart of it . . . like Clement Greenberg, like Herbert Read . . . and his radicalism had not diminished but may have become greater'.[120] Bernard may have winced at being classified with Greenberg and Read, but he would have appreciated being called 'radical'. His lecture was clever, witty and a dialogically clear post-mortem of modernism, and he told his audience that 'a complete biography . . . cannot be written until its subject is dead. Equally, the history of a period style cannot be written until it has ceased to dominate the period that gave birth to it.'[121] Officiating over modernism's burial was understandable for an art historian of Bernard's age and calibre, but hovering on the margins as a midwife to postmodernism's delivery was a risk. Postmodernism's hybrid character collapsed time, destroyed distance, played with displacement and employed paradigms that dishonoured traditions and deconstructed history; it was not Bernard's territory.

The postmodern turn

It seems to me that it's time we began to consider the historical sources of modernism and postmodernism from a global rather than a European viewpoint.
Bernard Smith[122]

Lévi-Strauss wrote 'There is no history without dates . . . for history's entire originality and distinctive nature lies in apprehending the relation between *before* and *after*.'[123] History excavated and criticised, but art history distinguished stylistic differences. Such pressure points in historical change were important for understanding cultural ancestry and by 1990 Bernard was turning his mind to the relationship between modernism and postmodernism. Oppositional ideas, modes or styles produced waves of nostalgia, as well as introducing new concepts of vision, so when it came to understanding postmodernism his position was that: 'the only way to justify the use of such an awkward term as postmodernism was to take it to be a description of a dialogue with modernism'.[124]

Defining modernism, especially antipodean modernism, had concerned him since the 1940s:

The importance of the radicalism of 1940 is that it was a radicalism of modernists who developed a radical critique of modernism itself. The critique of modernism did not begin in the 1970s when terms like post-modernism became fashionable, it began when modernism began.[125]

Not only should modernism be defined so as to clear the ground for the postmodern condition to be more readable, it also involved identifying modernism's beginning and its end or, as T. J. Clark suggested, when it had reached its last flowering. Conceiving the modern movement of the twentieth century, also known as formalism, as substantially a cultural product of the late nineteenth century—its roots lay in British art criticism, Russian literary concepts and, as Bernard saw it, where 'form and technique are the means to and the goal of artistic creation'—he believed Malevich was a primary exponent.[126] While the foundation of modernism may have begun with humanity's double routes—the conflict and contingency of Christianity and paganism, when secularism and spiritualism changed people's vision of themselves—Bernard identified its more significant actualisation with the imperialist colonisation of the exotic, and the political, aesthetic and philosophic revolutions derived from the Enlightenment, particularly those of Descartes, Rousseau, Winkelmann, Hegel, Hume, Locke, Darwin and Marx, to name some. These great thinkers permeated or saturated what came after, and as each generation created a new style, whether in art or ideas, a counter-displacement created a fast-moving slurry of avant-gardisms.

Roger Kimball suggests that the Enlightenment 'looks to culture as a repository of values that transcend the self, postmodernism looks to the fleeting desires of the isolated self as the only legitimate source of value. For the postmodernist, then, "culture is no longer seen as a means of emancipation, but as one of élitist obstacles to this".'[127] Ihab Hassan also believed 'modernism and postmodernism are not separated by an Iron Curtain or a Chinese Wall; for history is a palimpsest, and culture is permeable to time past, time present and time future. We are all . . . a little Victorian, Modern and Postmodern, at once.'[128] While he preceded Bernard in the postmodern debate, there were intellectual affinities between these two men that made them co-voyagers, but Hassan had asked whether postmodernism needed to be distinguished, let alone named, for 'history moves in measures both continuous and discontinuous'.[129] It was an argument that did not entirely suit Bernard's sense of identification and boundary, and in committing to write modernism's history, he had to both 'trace its limit' and name postmodernism.

The 'anarchic hope' and 'emancipatory effect' of modernism, as the American art critic and historian Hal Foster has argued, was 'a time of pure presence, a space beyond representation'.[130] That corresponded to

Bernard's view of modernism as a critique of modernity and modernity as a 'slab of history . . . [with] no meaningful end', thus endowing it with a conceptual eternity that overrode postmodernism's arrival.[131] Yet this slippery paradigm, Bernard thought, had to be brought under a more taut, periodising umbrella that he called 'the Formalesque', and to which he applied a pragmatic Hegelianism and theories of cultural determinism.

Traditions, however, hold their own timeworn residences and the anachronistic offence of the past sat uncomfortably with postmodernism's 'schizophrenic pastiche'. During the 1970s Bernard had watched the discipline of art history being 'written out' as it crumbled into an indistinct ravine of post-structuralism and cultural studies, or 'Baudrillardian nightmares', as he called it. As the Power Professor of Contemporary Art he had fought hard to preserve the discipline from diffusing at its core, despite the new art historians regarding him as a 'vanishing mediator' and 'a monument to another time'.[132] While Bernard tried to work his way around the new art historians, he still saw cultural studies as a hybrid discipline circling over art history's Promethean liver, hacking at it only to let it recover slightly before hacking at it again. Throwing his hat into the contemporary debate on modernism's end and the birth of the new 'post-mod' was an heroic step, one in which the gallows were within sight, particularly as younger, dynamic cultural theorists and art critics had been writing extensively about the subject for more than a decade. Bernard, however, was optimistic that he could survive the international lions' den: 'If it is to survive as a distinct discipline, art history will have to retain confidence in its capacity to create generic styles which have served it so well in the past.'[133]

But Bernard was also becoming tired and his intellectual prime had passed. After turning 80 there was a notable lack of vigour in his quest for knowledge and his thesis on modernism tended to rely on what was known and not what was new (fig. 52). Based on the Aristotelian notion 'that all art is mimetic, a position', he told John Nicoll at Yale University Press, 'that most "postmodernists" would now appear to support', his new work, originally titled 'Reframing Mimesis',[134] was an analytical and pedagogical revision of modernism. Perhaps Nietzsche was not far off when he wrote:

There is no set of maxims more important for an historian than this . . . that everything exists, no matter what its origin, is periodically reinterpreted by those in power in terms of fresh intentions; that all processes in the organic world are processes of outstripping and overcoming, and that, in turn, all outstripping and overcoming means reinterpretation, rearrangement . . . The evolution of a thing, a custom, an organ is not progress towards a goal . . . Rather, it is a sequence of more or less profound, more or less independent processes of appropriation.[135]

Bernard had always centred his scholarship around the dynamic tensions of European hegemony and imperialism. He took 1890 as his starting point, when 'the old avant-garde' and its magnetic characters gave value to identifiable genres and when disciplines were intact and cultural imperialism was highly interactive and time more measured. Modernism, he wrote,

possesses a powerful normative usage that 'modern' has kept recurring as a description of present-day social phenomena, to which of course is attached a stretch of recent past . . . So what about 'modern' and 'contemporary'? Let me put it in a metaphor. They are both kites well adapted to the wind of time. But modern has a longer tail. So it maintains a steadier course whereas 'contemporary' is more buffeted about in the squalls of fashion . . . 'Postmodern' attempts to bring down the flight of the modern and transform it into a period style.[136]

By the late twentieth century, Bernard believed that simplicity had been consumed by a surfeit of post-structuralist theories and that 'to decipher the aphoristic and gnomic profundities was tiresome'. The individual, artist and intellectual were being displaced by a morphologically deconstructed world in which distance was being destroyed and time collapsed. It was the business of historians to grapple with disunity and diffusion and provide some form of identifying parameters; as he said, 'Metanarratives will be written long after Lyotard is dead, long after my generation have ceased to indulge in their *fin-de-millénnium* anxieties.'[137]

As a global phenomenon, postmodernism—a term that Perry Anderson has pointed out originated in the Hispanic world of the 1930s to 'describe a conservative reflux within modernism itself'[138]—was neither regionalist, nor avant-garde, but a result of universalising contingencies that had 'eroded the elitism, the exclusivist, anti-democratic forms of validation'.[139] With formalism having collapsed under such forces as the Vietnam War, the women's movement and global hegemony, Bernard mimicked Hassan and wondered whether 'a "period style" exegesis [w]as still relevant for an art historical study of the recent past', but added 'My own feeling is that if the concept of "period style" is no longer available to art historians . . . then one powerful tool in the discourse is no longer available.'[140] Perhaps he was mourning a lost past or, as Juliette Peers has suggested, 'search[ing] for the holy grail of modernism',[141] but Bernard was adamant that his book was 'a history' and not a theoretical quarrel or an 'address [to] all the problems we are at present confronted with'.[142]

Yet *Modernism's History* (1998), a culmination of eight years' work and his grand historiographical narrative on global institutionalisation, was, as Bernard said, a 'critical synopsis' and an 'original rethinking of Modernism'. Furthermore, his insistence on introducing a new overarching generic term, 'the Formalesque', to describe modernism as a period style, 'avant garde until 1914, dominant until 1960', alarmed almost everyone, except himself. Hassan, however, thought it the best solution that he had come upon for distinguishing the so-called modern from the postmodern; after all 'Modernism was done'. Ernst Gombrich, art history's exemplary old statesman, also incorporated it in his *Preference for the Primitive* (published posthumously in 2002), and while the *Oxford English Dictionary* accepted the term, Bernard told his granddaughter, 'Modernism, postmodernism, and the formalesque. Yes another of my new coinages. It will probably die on the vine, but it's fun finding sensible words to replace ones that have been over-handled and used up.'[143] Terry Smith advised him that by dropping the universally used term 'modernism' and substituting a term that 'privileges matters of form . . . and which, with "esque" on the end implies a conditional "in the manner of" something which is yet to be established would be to surrender all modernist art to Greenbergian formalism'.[144] Another critic felt it conjured up 'revivalist eighteenth century topiary or jardinières, rather than Wyndham Lewis's Vorticist works from the first Machine Age'.[145] But Bernard said he was being 'historical not hysterical' and moreover, that the term 'Formalesque', he believed, would hold, an assumption that further alienated the reader.[146]

Despite his 'pretentious neologisms' and 'totalising histories', in which Fay Brauer pointed out that he had made the unforgivable error of omitting significant individuals, and especially women, *Modernism's History* was a learned, though pedagogically strained, revisionist history. Its reception, rather like that of his two paintings in 1940, received a 'silence of contempt', which Bernard excused on the pretext that his reputation was based on his early masterpiece *European Vision and the South Pacific*. Critics, he said, could not accept that he could also be an expert on contemporary history:

> If you go from one area to another, people decide that since you are specialist in Eighteenth century European and Pacific history, why should you know anything about twentieth-century art in Europe and North America? But I am linking it in my book with my notions of cultural imperialism . . . [and] taking a world view. People could say it is Euro-centric but this is where Modernism began before it was taken up brilliantly in the United States. The only advantage I've got, which I made clear in the book, is the advantage of distance.[147]

If, as Ephraim Lessing wrote, 'disputes alone nourish the spirit of inquiry, prevent prejudice and prestige from ossifying, and painted untruth from masquerading as truth',[148] Bernard's canalisation of modernism and his argument with postmodernism had failed. He once told Terry Smith, 'I wonder how long it will take for Oz critics to give my texts the same considered attention that they give Foucault, who though a cogent thinker, just reeks of bad faith in his failed attempt to unify power and knowledge. Power corrupts knowledge.'[149]

While critics from the Northern Hemisphere were generally dismissive of Bernard's book, those closer to home were even more negative. Fay Brauer considered his 'teleological vision' had suffered and criticised his 'circuitous' and, at times, 'incohesive digressions'. She also noted: 'By comparison to those intent upon resurrecting the legacy of Formalist Modernism, Smith may be located as saying the last rites over the twitching corpse in the hope that it will be consigned to eternal rest.'[150] Ian McLean similarly felt that in 're-naming' the unsettled period of modernism Bernard was prematurely foreclosing the debate on a discourse still very much polemically and vigorously alive.[151]

When Patrick McCaughey accused his old teacher of congesting art history with 'old fashioned' distinctions and suggested that 'the penalties of the long-distance view' had taken their toll, not to mention that his reading of the twentieth-century moderns was 'a poor wretched, diminished thing', he also made the fateful mistake of relegating Bernard to the past.[152] Generational conflict was inevitable, but to be considered obsolete was unbearable and in defending his intellectual integrity Bernard vigorously replied to McCaughey's 'demolition job'. The verbal warfare and barbed wit between the great elder of art history and McCaughey, then director of Yale Centre for British Art, played out in successive issues of the *Australian Review of Books*. It gave Bernard a public forum for 'wielding the whip' and admonishing his former pupil, while also providing the incentive for him to defend his discourse on modernism, its periodisation as 'the Formalesque' and his defence of art history as a discipline.[153]

CHAPTER NINE:
PERMISSIBLE LIMITS

In the circumstances, it is futile to apologise for egoism.
Oskar Spate[1]

Bernard's need to be part of the art world remained as strong as it had always been and in 2000, while still on the scholarly circuit promoting *Modernism's History*, he was invited to sit on a panel discussion on 'Periodisation' at a Comité International d'Histoire de L'Art (CIHA) conference at the National Portrait Gallery in London. It was not an edifying experience. Ross Woodrow, who was present, said that Bernard was a 'representative scapegoat for all those "old art history" ideas about historical periodisation,' as demonstrated in Bernard's recently released *Modernism's History* (1998).[2] Nevertheless Bernard 'mounted a spirited argument . . . for the traditional framing of history' as opposed to postmodernism's vague pluralisms, but his discourse began to unravel as he reminisced about his years at the Warburg and Courtauld institutes and how he had stood 'on the shoulders of giants'.[3] Using antiquated metaphors and his generic coinage 'the Formalesque', and insisting that if art history were to survive as a discipline it had to remain defined, Bernard's argument had lost its contemporary relevance. A 'bemused' sense of redundancy was registered by the audience and it was a sad moment for the old art historian.[4] The thought of retiring, though, never occurred to Bernard, as his resistance to dislodgement was too deeply embedded in his psychological armour for him to disappear into art history's archive.

Personal vanity and belief in his intellectual potency meant only one thing: the battle would continue.

Ernst Gombrich wrote that 'the best tribute . . . one can pay a scholar is to take him seriously and constantly reappraise his lines of argument', and while Gombrich was referring to G. W. F. Hegel, this could have been applied to Bernard.[5] In 1998 Gombrich wrote to him about Anthony Blunt, 'Of course he was intelligent, but I am not so sure that he was a great scholar. He could never have written such a book as yours, since, I think he was afraid of ideas after he became disappointed with Marxism.'[6] Bernard claimed that Gombrich had always taken him seriously, the latter having once written, 'I consider it [*European Vision and the South Pacific*] a standard book on this novel and original subject—his application of visual tradition to new and unfamiliar scenery—I know very well that his services to the field of art history and to teaching extend beyond the writing of this book'; and later, 'I [have] continued to be impressed by the range of his interests, his common sense and his openness to ideas.'[7] Gombrich also accepted Bernard's coinage 'the Formalesque', suggesting it might be 'a psychological obstacle for your colleagues in accepting a term they have not invented . . . I have no such inhibitions'.[8] This approval, as far as Bernard was concerned, was sacrosanct.

It is not surprising then that Bernard dedicated his second volume of autobiography *A Pavane for Another Time* (2002) to Ernst Gombrich, or that he used Poussin's allegorical painting of restrained simplicity, *A dance to the music of time* (1634–36), on the cover (fig. 53). Painted during Poussin's transition to his mature style, it served to convey Bernard's own maturing as a scholar in Britain during 1949 and 1950 when Anthony Blunt, the Poussin expert, had sent him to study under the eminent scholars at the Warburg Institute. That was Bernard's golden period and, as Michael Ann Holly suggests, 'The yearning for the past that poets and painters often evince is also latent in the longings of scholars who have devoted their intellectual lives to history writing, in invoking that which came before but no longer is.'[9]

The painting's iconographic complexity suited Bernard's enjoyment of mythic symbols as interpretative vehicles, especially the allegory of the 'Wheel of Fortune'. The dancers represent poverty, labour, wealth and pleasure, which translates as a poor man who works hard can gain wealth—an ethos Bernard aspired to, at least intellectually rather than materially. But it is Father Time, often referred to as Chronos and who, as legend has it, devoured his children, that operates metaphorically for Bernard's relationship with his own intellectual children. Erwin Panofsky, the art historian and contemporary friend of Gombrich, wrote that 'Kronos', also known as 'Saturn', signified the 'sharp-toothed' Time who 'devours whatever he has created', and Nietzsche in *Thus Spake Zarathustra* (1883) similarly refers to Father Time as 'that law of time that must devour its children'.[10] Such readings refer to the generational disputes that take place between a father and his sons and daughters and, as the father of Australian art history, Bernard had spent decades combating his postmodern progeny. John T. Irwin effectively captures these regenerative battles as 'the endless displacement of the generator by the generated . . . the castration of the present [by] the past [which] convicts the present of inadequacy . . . to come after is to be fated to repeat the life of another.'[11]

Poussin's painting also expressed some of the important aspects Bernard ascribed to his marriage with Kate, in particular how she had transformed his provincial identity through her cultivated modes of communication, art, craft and music. Furthermore, as Father Time sits and observes the cyclic passage of the seasons he plays his lyre, another oblique reference to Gombrich and Kate, both of whom were skilled musicians; Gombrich played the violin, Kate the cello—a small detail, but worthy of note.

Not long before Bernard's *The Boy Adeodatus* was published in 1984 he wrote that through 'memory, sensation and expectation' he was able to develop a 'possessable' past and an awareness of his identity, adding that 'though my memory selects and distorts the things remembered, and also forgets, it is the only direct access to the past I possess'.[12] While memory is an important revisionist tool, Bernard's admission was not entirely true. As a compulsive collector of letters received and sent, diaries and journals for every year of his adult life, books, exhibition catalogues, articles and pamphlets amassed and annotated, Bernard's scholarly identity mattered, and he used his meticulously compiled archive to record historical events as much as to preserve and locate the self. After all, he had written in *Modernism's History* that 'The human memory is stored as the archival records of its experiences, in the form of language and art.'[13]

This second autobiographical volume, begun while Kate was alive, relied heavily on their correspondence to one another during the 1940s and his travel journals. He had also encouraged Kate to write about her youth and meeting and marrying him, and he used that substantially unaltered; it gave the memoir an acutely personal tone, making it as much Kate's autobiography as his own. At the time of Kate's death the book was unfinished, for when Bernard met and married Maggi Forster it was put aside. Kate had also convinced her family that Cuthbert Adeney's diaries should be given to the Royal College of Surgeons in London, so when Bernard resumed writing *A Pavane*, he asked his London researcher Emma Hicks to investigate those. They contained highly sensitive and potentially inflammatory material, but also resolved some of the mystery surrounding the strange relationship Cuthbert had formed with Kate during her childhood and later with Bernard in 1948.[14] Cuthbert, who had displayed all the 'self-confidence of the *haute bourgeoisie*', as Bernard put it, had disliked him for having won Kate, but also because of Bernard's class and nationality. In one extract Cuthbert wrote, 'I must confess, I have not the true socialist spirit. I do not believe in raising the status of the working man . . . The most important men in this country at present . . . are those who direct and control the working man'.[15] Such elitism was anathema to Bernard who used the diaries with intended revenge.

Cuthbert had also recorded his sexual obsessions; as Jaynie Anderson noted in her review of *A Pavane*, 'He was a surgeon of many passions, with too keen a love for children.'[16] Bernard also wanted to wait until Elizabeth Edmunds, Hilda and Cuthbert Adeney's biological daughter, had died before returning to the memoir, so that he could include sensitive extracts without unduly embarrassing family members.[17] When his relationship with Maggi began deteriorating he resumed writing the memoir and devoted more than 40 pages to Cuthbert's sexually tortured life, his guilt and the rivalry that existed between him and Bernard. It was Bernard's way of avenging Kate and himself and, as with most of his adversaries, it was a battle waged and won on the page; another example of his wielding 'the [literary] whip with the velvet thorn'.

While he was reliving the 1940s Bernard's engagement with the contemporary art world continued as vigorously as ever, albeit a bit slower. In his review of Gary Catalano's monograph *The Solitary Watcher: Rick Amor and His Art* (2001), he wrote that 'Amor's art might be viewed as flotsam from the Enlightenment washed onto an Antipodean beachhead . . . [he] is a disenchanted *flaneur* in search of Melbourne's voids and menacing silences.'[18] Those poetic lines dredged up the silt of the past, with Bernard claiming that Amor was 'heir to the Antipodeans', those figural expressionists such as Brack, Boyd, Blackman and Pugh and the Angry Penguins, and it revived the old argument about figuration, cultural identity and the relationship of centre and periphery:

> In 1959, the Antipodean Manifesto *theorised* a position that was already in practice since the 1940s. But, in Australia, most art historians (and those Nescafé historians known as curators) have convinced themselves that all art theory proceeds from Europe (or occasionally from America). It is an area of our culture that continues to suffer from chronic (if not endemic) cultural cringe.[19]

Australian art, whatever the period, had to stand alone and proudly proclaim its cultural differences, not 'twist on the eternal merry-go-round of avant-garde art'.[20] Amor's sombre figurative realism had also led Bernard to think about the more concrete substance of life and human emotions, what Hegel referred to as ideas that 'appear only when actuality is . . . cut and dried' and the 'shape of life grown old'.[21]

The unclothed object

'The portrait (above all the self-portrait), the diary and the biography (especially the auto-biography) reveal heightened perceptions of individuality, the proud ego vaunting and flaunting his own being', wrote Roy Porter.[22] Each of those genres were important to Bernard; he had painted his own portrait, been painted by others (fig. 54), was a fastidious diarist and, by 2002, had written two accounts of his own life story up to 1950. Since retirement, his conspicuous auto-referencing in essays, articles and lectures was as much about establishing his historical inclusivity and retaining his visibility as it was about reflecting on all he had done and achieved. But old age also offered a greater freedom of expression without having to worry too much about what came after.

When the Melbourne artist Carmel O'Connor approached Bernard to paint his portrait for the 2002 Archibald Prize he initially refused. O'Connor persisted, and after thinking about the stagnant state of portraiture in Australia Bernard capitulated on condition that she paint him naked (fig. 55). Being portrayed naked would be his final sacrifice for art history—the Archibald being one of the most accessible public forums available for a broader appreciation—as well as provide, one last time, an opportunity to revive his activism in the contemporary art world. He also had other motives: he intended to address ageism and sexism.

'The power of controversy is a very extraordinary one', Plato wrote,[23] and who better to transgress the limits of respectability than the outsider. By using himself as the object/subject and manipulating or making complicit the artist's role, Bernard hoped he might move the viewer into a stronger aesthetic response to figurative art, painting and portraiture. Devising a symbolic construction for his outer and inner psychological and human condition was important, but equally he had always believed in unadorned reality: whether a gardener or a god-professor, men are made of the same material and form—it is privilege and politics that separates them. Bernard's friend, the art historian Margaret Rose, has suggested that the unexpected can provoke laughter, but parody is also loaded with a subverted afterlife and in this respect Bernard's Archibald portrait is a parodic, allegorical riposte of the emperor with no clothes, the bridegroom stripped bare, and the father of art history giving his last inescapable lesson aimed at the crisis of representation and identity in the postmodern age.[24]

At the time O'Connor was preparing to paint him, Bernard was reading extensively on the subject of nudity. Beat Wyss's *Hegel's Art History and the Critique of Modernity* (1999) contains a segment on the 'costume debate'—to be clothed or not to be clothed, a moral argument that typified the puritan values of the nineteenth century in which 'the uninhibited . . . innocence of the classical age had vanished . . . indignation, embarrassed chuckles or vulgar ridicule were the only reactions the heroic nude could now expect'.[25] Looking to the classical age to embellish his argument about the poverty of postmodernist painting, Bernard took the classical as the 'final stage beyond which the tool can no longer be perfected', its tradition 'contrasted the idea of perfection with the dangers of corruption and denounced any striving for outward show that pandered to the senses'.[26] But Bernard wanted to introduce the sensual on his terms. Underlined in his copy of Freud's *Totem and Taboo* (1913) is the passage 'To a certain extent man remains narcissistic, even after he has found outer subjects for his libido, and the objects on which he bestows it represent, as it were, emanations of the libido which remain his ego and which can be withdrawn into it.'[27] Certainly O'Connor was a cooperative recipient of those emanations, but Bernard was also calling into question his very own egocentric masculinity.[28] Further, the Platonic argument acknowledged male nudity as wholesomely permitted in society and in *The Republic* Socrates discusses how old men freely attend the gymnasia and exercise naked beside toned, young athletes.[29] The glorification of the body, though gendered, respected the elderly whose functioning bodies held the right of exposure and of participation. Moreover, Poussin's old Father Time sat playing the lyre naked, but in modern society the old were mute ghosts, out of sight and out of mind.

There were many artists Bernard admired who captured an essential human need for display—the simple, sensual depiction of Australian Aboriginal men and women by the 'Port Jackson Painter' (fig. 56) or the contemporary Indigenous artist Brook Andrew, whose *Sexy and dangerous* won the RAKA award in 1998 (fig. 57). William Dobell and Noel Counihan had marvelled at flesh and given it 'something of ancient ritual, the fertility rite, the worship of life itself—a function of the erotic, the biological and the aesthetic';[30] Arthur Boyd, Albert Tucker, Peter Booth, George Gittoes and Juan Davila depicted humanity's darker passions and primal intensity, while Lucien Freud's languid mountains of flesh, and Richard Larter's women—especially his wife—were captured in explicit poses. Bernard felt there was no reason why he could not be portrayed naked, and if 'the risk was worth taking', as he often said, it was justified.

Fantasy, free will and freedom of the self can, as Alex Potts points out, 'come to an end only with death or withdrawal into narcissistic isolation'.[31] Donald Kuspit sees, 'death [as] play[ing] a "positive role" in life, stimulating the creativity that defiantly produces the new as an indication that life has not become completely immobile, that the source of life has not dried up'.[32] In refusing to face death, Bernard saw the portrait as a way of announcing he was still very much part of the art world and its arguments. He failed to recognise, however, that he risked becoming what T. S. Eliot called a 'regionalist', someone who 'attempts to revive some language which is disappearing . . . to revive customs of a bygone age . . . or to obstruct the inevitable'. Eliot also pointed out that the outsider often 'misconceive[s] their own case' and, with Bernard's multifarious agenda, the end result was bound to be either misconceived by art historians or indecipherable to the lay viewer.[33]

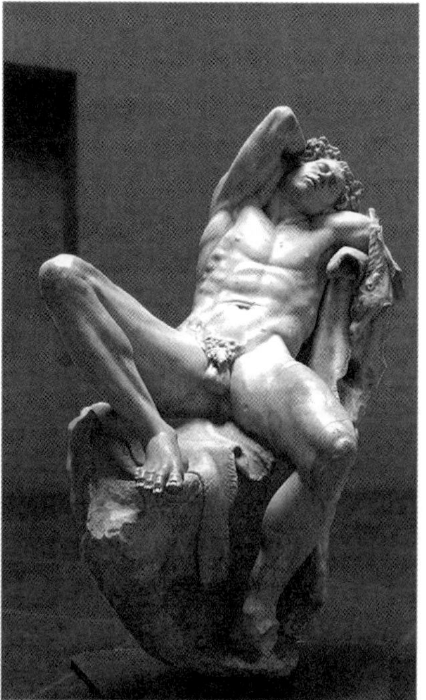

Fig. 58 Barbarini Faun, early second century BCE

Nakedness also presumes the sensationalised gaze and, while Bernard had based his pose on the homoerotic Hellenistic marble sculpture the *Barberini faun* (c. 230–200 BCE), sometimes referred to as the 'Sleeping satyr' (fig. 58), his nudity was also intended to challenge feminism and perceptions of ageism, and to shake bourgeois complacency. Bernard's antipathy towards women who challenged the system, or his system, was certainly one of his blind spots, and stemmed from his childhood model of women as nurturers. Most people, however, saw the portrait as a crude exposure of his vanity and his priapic propensity for display or, as one critic put it, 'an unbridled revealer [whose] mania for self-disclosure is of a piece with his "hatred of being regarded as an icon or a national treasure"'.[34] But, as Sol Yurick wrote, 'perhaps crudity is a necessary corrective'.[35]

It was Sigmund Freud who asked a critical question: how do we perceive ourselves, our identity, our bodies? It was a preoccupation Bernard found endlessly fascinating. There was vanity, of course, but our propensity to turn against ourselves seemed inherent: 'The fear of the image was the fear of the human', Bernard said.[36] Hegel inferred something similar when he wrote 'western modern man had alienated himself from his own body.'[37] In more recent times, feminist and psychoanalytical theory, gender studies and ideology critiques had reduced the public reception of the naked male body to a position of caricature, novelty or pornographic aesthetics. Art and the visual had been reduced to linguistic analysis and the act of looking had largely lost its sensual impact.[38] Bernard had reviewed Abigail Solomon-Godeau's book on masculinity *Male Trouble: A Crisis in Representation*, and it had confirmed for him this crisis in contemporary art. Her suggestion that 'there is . . . every reason to think that like capitalism, masculinity is always in crisis, but like the phoenix . . . it continually rises again, retooled and reconstructed for its next historical turn',[39] accorded with Hegel's belief that art was 'the spirit's act of reproduction', as well as Bernard's determination to be part of the ongoing dialogue with art and culture. Reflecting on the sheer pleasure of looking at art he told Humphrey McQueen:

the work [of art] has a presence and good art gives you a sense of pleasure, of fitness. Again it is a great problem to know just why

it happens, that is the beauty of it and the mystery of it and it is
related to our enjoyment of nature and our enjoyment of things
very well put together . . . There is a kind of eternal paradox here.
Perhaps Gombrich was right. There is only one norm and that
is the classical norm. He did not mean that we all have to draw
Greek statues but that when art changed it was deviation from the
norm [on which] progress in an aesthetic sense depended . . . in the
history of art, the Gothic, Baroque, Rococo, Neo-Classicism . . .
are deviation from an original.

And continued:

That said, I also believe [w]hat Mathew Arnold [said], that all art
is a criticism of society and so we have the problem of art being a
critique of society and yet giving us a kind of pleasure . . . Is it the
pleasure of art or the pleasure of criticism? I think the two things
are indubitably linked. All great art has this quality of criticism
and Guernica was the great example in the twentieth century.[40]

This encapsulated Bernard's sociocultural, aesthetic and political spirit.
But Bernard was also the respected, preeminent father of Australian
art history who had articulated the Antipodes as a mirror into which
Europeans peered in order to understand themselves. Casually draping
his academic gown over one elbow and resting his foot on three large
books, he may have evoked the posed theatrics of classicism, but it is the
scholar's determined gaze that suggests he is ruffling art history's robes to
remind us of the power of representation, especially at a time when many
were prescribing art's death. A Streetonesque landscape framed by the
rear window leads the eye into the long view of a golden summer, another
metaphor for Hegelian distance and history's inescapable lesson, or perhaps the pundit's provocative gesture to those neo-Marxist art historians.

Complex connections and mythical metaphors had always excited
Bernard and there was yet another agenda in his portrait program.
O'Connor's anatomical refashioning of Bernard's body to that of the
classical Roman model of the *Barberini faun* operated analogically as an

exploration of his paradoxical self, the primitive 'Other'. Alfred Kühn wrote that, 'primitive people think mythically'; the satyr or faun, with his peaked, furry ears—it is why Kate called Bernard 'Peach'—half-man, half-animal was Bernard's totemic other; it is another reason why he chose to pose like the *Barberini faun*. Friedrich Nietzsche wrote that the satyr 'expressed nature in a rude, uncultivated state', not in the primate sense, but rather as 'man's true prototype . . . an enthusiastic reveller . . . a compassionate companion . . . a prophet of wisdom . . . a symbol of the sexual omnipotence of nature. The satyr was sublime and divine' and a mythic messenger of humankind's origins.[41] In a drawing by Albrecht Dürer, titled the *Rape of Europa*, the continent of Europe stretches out across the foreground and Europa's arrival upon the great bull is greeted by a couple of satyrs that represent 'the inhabitants of an unpeopled land, an idea that has echoes of ancient geography and draws upon the satyr's most fundamental role: the personification of the wilderness'.[42] Bernard had preferred to operate at the edge of society or on the margins and had always perceived himself as the 'Other'; O'Connor's portrait was Bernard's 'identity performance' and a homily to his personification of the global antipodean.

In 2002 the painting went on display at the AGNSW before travelling to the Performing Arts Centre in Melbourne. Many viewers were astonished or shocked that a man of 86, and of his station, could allow himself to be shown in such an explicit fashion; nor would they have registered Bernard's encoded symbolism. But Emeritus Professor Bernard William Smith wanted no whimpering discourse about him in old age, declaring 'I am what I represent, a living, feeling embodiment of mind and matter, a real human being.'[43]

While he had heroically revealed himself naked for the public, privately Bernard's world was falling apart. His marriage to Maggi had dissolved in all but name and, alone again, old age gnawed away at him. With deafness, osteoporosis and his eyes dimming with macular degeneration, his dependency on women intensified. He had come full circle, a return to his childhood where a cluster of females satisfied his emotional, sexual and physical needs. His old friend and colleague Ursula Hoff, who lived not far away in Carlton, remained an intellectual comfort, but she too had announced some years earlier at the age of 90 that finally she was getting old (fig. 59). His daughter Elizabeth called by regularly, as did his son, John. Carmel O'Connor was in regular contact and the photographer Joyce Evans was called upon to photograph the old scholar in his decrepit, narcissistic nakedness, though he insisted that he be reconstituted in the 'classical norm'. Many others visited, but effectively women had become instruments for his posthumous reception.

His devoted granddaughter, Kate Challis, helped him organise his work and intellectual affairs and gradually Bernard began to put the egotistic bathos and his fixation with the naked 'I' behind him. As the Australian art world's éminence grise who once joked that he was neither eminent nor grey, Bernard approached his ninth decade with urgency, fuelling his days with a ferocious work regime and intent on preserving the role that he had so brilliantly carved out and created for himself. Like Aby Warburg, he was emphatic that 'the history of art matters and still matters', not as a strictly narrow accumulation of facts, but as a broad record of human development in all its suffering and triumphs.[44] While his posthumous reception was important, to provoke the younger generations into a responsible engagement with art and its history remained very much a priority.

A number of younger art historians had already begun reassessing Bernard's importance. Rex Butler considered him the pioneering figure in art historiographical discourse, especially as the originator of 'the great Australian idea', of antipodal inversion or 'reversal to the rest of the world'. Butler urged that 'we should turn to the true precursor [of] revisionism'[45] whose discourse in *European Vision and the South Pacific* had opened up a deep and rich quarry of conceptual resources that continued to feed art history and cultural studies. When Bernard embarked on his path as a cultural revisionist in the 1940s he felt compelled to legitimise Australia as a place and not as an appendage of the empire, and he had used art, geography and spatial distance as driving concepts for the development of Australian identity. He reset the compass, reinterpreted the relations of exchange and interchange between the north and south and located the rebounds and ruptures of a dominant colonial culture as it translated itself into a new hybrid society.

It had been Bernard's life's mission to understand what it was to be antipodean in the world, to think antipodean and to resituate it politically, culturally, aesthetically. His concepts of antipodality, cultural convergence and the use of interdisciplinary narratives on the colonial, postcolonial, modernist and postmodern have retained a crucial currency in the history of ideas, with many new art historians qualifying their art histories against or alongside Bernard's—to come after is to be fated to some degree of appropriation. The list was long, with a growing number of international and British art and cultural historians indebted to his scholarship. Terry Smith admitted that most of his work had been in response to Bernard's imperialist concept of centre and periphery—'he was the best thinker on metropolitan powers'.[46] Ian McLean referred to him as our 'Noble Modern'; and Jocelyn Hackforth-Jones, a former student of Bernard's at the Power Institute, while noting his conventional teaching method, had found his 'forensic approach' to the history of ideas engaged with humanity's critical sources, and that 'to ask the "why" question' was the key to understanding art.[47]

'To what, save pride of intellect or professional peerage, is the reviewer, the critic, the academic expert accountable?' wrote the literary critic George Steiner. For Bernard it was summed up in what the Renaissance humanist Giambattista Vico called 'logical proofs' and 'governing roots', where evidence is historically traced backwards to sources and to origins. That empirical rationalism partly explains Bernard's lack of spiritualism or his avoidance of the transcendental; as he said, 'humanity has learned from bitter experience to distrust its gods'. As an atheist, Bernard's mental skills were his salvation, for there was no god or epilogue in his world; there were origins but no 'transcendental full-stops'.[48]

The poet Chris Wallace-Crabbe has commented on the lack of spirituality in Bernard's thinking and his secular shaping of history, a secularism that many scholars found refreshing. The literary historian John Frow considered Bernard's writing had a 'wonderful clarity . . . the marshalling of a multitude of details within clear lines of argument, the lucid balance of logic and empirical evidence'.[49] Bernard's rejection of Christianity was put this way: 'I rejected the notion of humility before the Unknown. Before the Unknown one has a duty to enquire'.[50] For him, 'if a work of art or writing was great, it was because of human talents, imagination and the skills of the artist, craftsman or scholar, not because God is pulling strings, but because the origins of art are immanent not transcendent.'[51] It was this rationalist trope that drove him to substantiate his existence and to validate his worth, for to defer responsibility or accountability to a higher being was an admission of misguided attribution.

The final word as dusk falls

We speak because we need the other . . . we write because we want to be heard by many.
Bernard Smith[52]

Art is about seeing, but seeing is conditioned by knowing, and as Bernard's eyesight deteriorated both reading and writing became difficult. Abandoning his tools of trade should have been devastating, but typically he adapted to his circumstances. Blessed with an acute recall and photographic memory he could retrieve important conversations, slabs of literature or documents, and where memorisation became his staff, Hegel became his main guide: 'Art history . . . begins and ends with a philosopher', he wrote, 'Hegel has good claim to being the originator of art history as an academic discipline for he historicised the concepts of both form and content in his *Lectures in Fine Art* first published in 1835. And it was Hegel who prophesied that Fine Art would eventually dissolve into philosophy'.[53]

And there remained Bernard Smith's unfinished business. In 1945, while working on a paper called 'Art and Imperialism', he began to define and to conceptualise the rise and fall of artistic phases and the notion of modernism's periodisation. 'As a style becomes diffused over a greater portion of the world, that is . . . becomes more and more international, that style . . . approach[es] the end of its career as a world influence. In art the spirit of the place attends the birth of a new art as much as the spirit of the time.'[54] It was this principle that he wanted to impart one more time, in one last book, as a postscript to *Modernism's History*.

Again he contacted his London researcher Emma Hicks and

instructed her to search for images and, with the aid of a large magnifying glass, a computer, a young assistant, his granddaughter Kate, and the publisher Jenny Zimmer, Bernard embarked on the manuscript of *The Formalesque*. This was another attempt at canalising his coinage, another final argument about semantics and periodisation, and his last attempt at staking his flag and claiming authorship in renaming modernism, a term he believed could not hold. He had made the point so many times about distinguishing styles and the problem of separating 'modern' from 'contemporary' for, as he said, 'Both words cling tenaciously to the present and will continue to do so indefinitely.'[55] Modernism had to be renamed, but it was also a history lesson and a tribute to those great aestheticians and scholars who had made art history a discipline. 'For me art history is a kind of biography. Its infrastructure is aesthetic', he wrote. *The Formalesque* was a compendium of masters, a biographical lineage from Plato to Gombrich, to which he was immodestly adding himself. Bernard used the introduction to confirm his position within art history but also stated, 'historians cannot write contemporary art history *in a general sense* because they live in it. All they can do is take part in it and do what they can to affect its outcomes and valuations.'[56]

Like Gombrich's *The Story of Art* (1950), *The Formalesque* was also intended as a primer for students at a secondary and tertiary level. The lives of artists mattered just as much as the stylistic qualities that situated them in time and place; or as Gombrich famously put it, 'There really is no such thing as Art. There are only artists',[57] and art historians had to tell that story. Bernard's continuing tête-á-tête with Ernst Gombrich had been a critical link for him, but his reliance on Hegel at this stage of his life had a deeper resonance: 'Art invites us to intellectual consideration, and that not for the purpose of creating art again, but for *knowing philosophically* what art is.'[58]

Art history enabled Bernard to synthesise many philosophical, political and historical strands and to articulate a comprehensible evolution of culture. Ihab Hassan noted, '*The Formalesque* has the lucidity born of wide learning and deep reflection, and the critical will to clarify the achievements of painters who have shaped our vision to this day.'[59] The word 'Formalesque', however, was almost universally considered an unfortunate choice for its linguistic inflexibility and, as others noted, Bernard's delimiting it to the visual arts, was problematic. Charles Nodrum pointed out to him that 'modernism still retains its currency in other disciplines.'[60]

In the first chapter Bernard began with a glossary or etymology on meanings, beginning with 'Abstraction': 'the act of taking away'. 'Art' he explained, came from 'ars, artis . . . to put together, join, fit, skill as the result of knowledge and practice.' On 'Meaning': 'that which is or is intended to be expressed in a sentence, word, dream, symbol, action.'[61] A vital part of a teacher's job was to explain the past lucidly and the present as objectively as possible, to reveal the distance between the acts, between major periods of historical actuality even when they folded over into each other. On postmodernism, Bernard felt that we had 'just passed through what might be described as an angry decade . . . it seems now to have exhausted most of its fire and the term modernism is slithering back into place under the temporal carpet'.[62] If, as Richard Evans believes, 'The past does speak through the sources, and is recoverable through them', and that there is 'a qualitative difference between documents written in the past, by living people, for their own purposes, and interpretations advanced about the past by historians living at a later date',[63] Bernard then was an exemplary case, maintaining that 'It's in the record. I've been an empiricist all my life . . . and the crux of art history is how to explain how the "new" happens.' *The Formalesque*, as neatly packaged as it was on 'the aesthetic infrastructure of art history', was a didactic guide, a little road map 'through the visual paths of time'.[64] In creating his distance as an art historian from the postmodernist world, Bernard called for the art of the past 30 years, since 1970, to be called 'contemporary art' because he believed we did 'not possess enough temporal distance to see it steadily and to see it whole'. Hegel's apostle had taken his final flight and had left the argument open.

In October 2007 the director of the NGV, Gerard Vaughan, launched Bernard's swan song, *The Formalesque* (fig. 60). Magnificently illustrated, which testified to the power of the image and its potential to be more evocative than the word, Bernard insisted on using Picasso's iconic 'howl of political protest', *Guernica*, on the cover. The famous painting had been exhibited at the Spanish Pavilion in Paris in 1937, the year that politics found Bernard and when he became 'a creature of the Spanish Civil War'. Seventy years later *Guernica* symbolised Bernard's fight for the meaning of art in a world in which theoretical positions and historical processes mirrored the flux of displacement, unanchored alterities and new cyber atrocities.

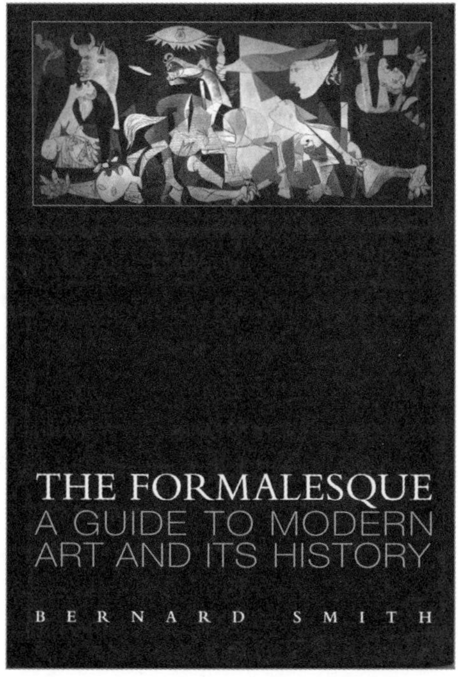

Fig. 60 Cover of *The Formalesque: A Guide to Modern Art and its History*

While he had been writing *The Formalesque* Bernard had also been reassessing his own past, especially his victories, tribulations and defeats. Consequently, he developed a plan to correct mistakes that he felt he had made, especially during his time as head of the Power Institute, a period which, with hindsight, he judged as a failure and one of his three great regrets. While the admission may have been an old man's melancholia, the result was an outline for an Institute of Art History, which he put to Gerard Vaughan: 'I have more experience in these matters than anyone else in Australia.'[65] Perturbed by the recent turn of academic events in which art history had fallen prey to economic rationalists and into a theoretical cul de sac, he proposed:

> the key to the development of an institute . . . lies in . . . the development of a powerful undergraduate course; and in the institute itself, though still part of the university, would lie in the development of post-graduate studies closely but not necessarily entirely related to the existing collections in the NGV.[66]

Bernard had also spoken to Jaynie Anderson, the *Herald* Professor of Fine Arts at the University of Melbourne, about establishing an institute and had sent her his draft. She told him that she had discussed it with the vice-chancellor who was very interested in the idea, but when he heard nothing further from her he took the matter up again with Vaughan. The institute's function, he said, should essentially be a postgraduate one and aligned to the 'existing strengths of the two NGV galleries' with 'new areas based upon the growing importance of Australia's near neighbours, e.g., India, China, Indonesia and Oceania'. He stressed that while it was important to 'remain in contact with our European origins, it would be wise also to keep in mind the realities of the twenty-first century'.[67] Unlike the Power Institute, Bernard believed the new institute should be built upon several benefactors, even international ones, such as India or China, and that ideally it should be situated close to the NGV with the State Library of Victoria and the university along the same tram tracks. While accepting Bernard's invitation to talk over the matter, Vaughan, who had also spoken to the vice-chancellor, warned him that 'the politics of the big cuts' to Arts at the university had temporarily put a hold on the issue and it would be a matter of waiting.[68]

Hegel's owl

Charles Mitchell, Bernard's supervisor at the Warburg Institute in 1948, told how Admiral Nelson often spoke of his 'most ambitious wish . . . to die in the fight'.[69] Bernard had also constructed his passage into old age as a vigilant battle, one in which he was determined to fight for art history until the end. In August 2008 he gave his final public lecture in the Clemenger Auditorium at the NGV. Assisted by his granddaughter Kate, his shuffling, feeble gait and physical decline obvious, his opening remarks were hesitant, but Bernard recovered and delivered his lecture. At 92 and still capable of precise memorisation he displayed his mettle and spoke of the discipline that had given his life form. It was an engaging history lesson about *The Formalesque* and he spoke to the audience as a teacher might speak to his class:

> I have never been a gallery guide, but you are all surely faced with something of a paradox when you use words to talk about drawings, paintings, fabrics etcetera . . . You are forced to give meanings, that is to say, you interpret what you see with words . . . There are only four chapters in my book . . . but the last chapter, 'On Meaning', goes far beyond the visual arts because meaning is relevant to all forms of human enquiry.[70]

The perplexing signs of the contemporary posed a similar question, he said, and that was why he coined a generic term 'the Formalesque' to describe the art of the twentieth century, now 'one of many past centuries'. Again he drew upon Hegel: '[the] art of the past cannot be recreated but only understood. [Hegel] was facing up to his own problem with the contemporary art of his time'; and 'it is only when time is no longer contemporary that we can see the past through a kind of rear vision mirror as we rush along into the future'.[71] As he said in *The Formalesque*, 'Distance is not a tyranny to a serious historian'.[72] Bernard was role-playing Minerva's owl, a timely masterpiece in which he had grown, in form and content into the greyest of greys, when 'a form of life has grown old . . . and cannot be rejuvenated but only understood'. Even if 'words slip and slide', as Bernard was fond of saying, his lesson was in accordance with Hegel's philosophy of the importance of events as reliable, quantifiable conditions of history's evolution:

> The teaching of the concept, which is also history's inescapable lesson, is that it is only when actuality is mature that the ideal first

appears . . . and that the ideal . . . builds for itself into the shape of an intellectual realm . . . The owl of Minerva spreads its wings only with the falling of the dusk.[73]

It was Bernard's way of turning his lecture to its final curtain call, of reflecting on all he had said, but it was the phrase, 'The Owl of Minerva takes flight only as the dusk falls' that stayed in people's minds. It was a clever device of image association, significant form and the lingering power of art's haunting beauty, all that he believed in.

As he was led from the auditorium women approached and congratulated him. In her coquettish and melodious accent the artist Mirka Mora said, 'You know Bernard, writers are better in bed than painters'.[74] Though apparently they were never lovers, he looked at her and smiled, her teasing compliment appreciated. While there was life in his limbs there were memories to unfold and to touch, and he remembered the beautiful Mirka of the 1950s, the dark-eyed rebel breaking open her bohemian basket of love and laughter.

In 2008 the NGA acquired Bernard's two paintings *Lot and his Brethren* and *Pompeii*, both painted in 1940. They had been included, along with his watercolour *Drought* (1940), in the large exhibition *Surrealism: Revolution by Night* in 1993; now they hung in a section devoted to his generation. Hanging beside the paintings of Arthur Boyd, James Gleeson, Albert Tucker, Herbert McClintock and Noel Counihan, Bernard the artist had finally found a place. Though unable to travel to Canberra to see his paintings, it was a crowning moment for the old art historian who boasted that they were two of the finest modernist paintings ever produced in Australia—it was a case of the old artist looking nostalgically back at his younger self with tenderness and egocentric pride.

But old age wore on and after a fall and hospitalisation in late 2008 Bernard was moved into an aged-care facility where he ruminated about his life and work; and waited. He heard nothing more about his great plan for an institute. He was aware that the wheels of academia often moved slowly, but he appeared unaware that Jaynie Anderson had made significant progress in developing his concept. Under her aegis, the university had provided seed funding to develop the Australian Institute of Art History and she was busy organising programs, visiting scholars and sponsorship. But as the initial driver of the concept, Bernard, it seemed, had been forgotten—out of sight, out of mind.[75] One day he said 'I am a communist, in so much as a utopian communist, I believe in the future—the hope is in the waiting.' This reflected his belief that 'the perfectibility of human institutions by the measured application of reason,' was achievable. It was why he never gave up on an idea.[76]

During his final months admirers visited and paid homage. Some came out of gratitude, some out of guilt, but one thing remained undisputed: all agreed that he had not only altered the course of Australian art history, he had defined it—he was the benchmark. James Murdoch, the music impresario, considered him one of Australia's most significant icons. Ian McLean affectionately referred to him as his intellectual father—'I seem to always return to him, it is as if I am riding on his shoulders'; Peter Beilharz said Bernard had shown him a rich route, one that could be followed parallel to the sociological road.[77] For Terry Smith, Bernard was 'his measure' as much as 'our measure' and that 'only someone with [his] history, skills and bloody-minded determination could . . . do things . . . differently in ways that changed *for the better* how it is done, for everyone, everywhere, for ever'.[78] It was Bernard's insistence on Australia's artistic value, which he had consistently and defiantly positioned against 'the external value system', that had helped universalise Australia as a vital, relational place.[79] Bernard was one of art history's giants. From the outset his intellectual compass and sophisticated interdisciplinary praxis had incorporated a broad range of the humanities and his influence had emanated well beyond the discipline of art history. He had questioned the antipodean psyche and given it significant cultural form, insistently proclaiming its legitimate place within a globalised world. The ethnographer Greg Dening beautifully encapsulated him as a man who 'made us look at our own marginality in a positive way. Be Antipodeans, he told us'. In defining Bernard's epistemological spirit, Dening also suggested that 'in the margins is where his centre is.'[80] The German art historian, curator and Bernard's close colleague and friend Rüdiger Joppien defined him as 'an embodiment of Australia's development into a modern, learned nation . . . a foundation layer in every respect'.[81] Bernard, though, was much more than a foundation layer; he was a pioneering revisionist in the history of ideas. As Charles Nodrum observed of *European Vision and the South Pacific* '[it was] one of those mind-changing works which truly extend not just knowledge but the framework in which to place that knowledge'.[82] For 70 years Bernard's conscientious criticism had clarified the role of artists in society and his cogent discourse and colossal body of published work on art and on cultural identity had substantiated it as a discipline. Based on exacting scholarship, a deep commitment to empirical inquiry and an accessible rationalism, he was an inescapable presence and a magnificent intellectual. It was not fame that Bernard sought; it was hard-earned posterity.

One day he quietly said, 'I am looking into the eye of death'; he was standing at the final door of anonymity, but looked at it with calm inevitability. On 2 September, the eve of the 2011 RAKA, Bernard William Smith passed quietly through that door. At first his death was a muted affair and his funeral attended only by family and closest friends. The Jesuit poet Peter Steele, himself gravely ill, officiated in the chapel at Newman College; Bernard had asked that it be held there, even though he insisted he was still an atheist. Consistent with his double agendas or multiple motives, it was in part a tribute to his mother's religion, but also because there was a tradition of funerals for deceased academics being held at Newman College and Bernard felt he belonged to that tradition and was deserving of such official status. Yet, in death the economy of his mind prevailed, having insisted that his coffin be as inexpensive as possible. What he got was a plain, unstained wooden casket that evoked the functionalism befitting his beloved Arts and Crafts Movement.

During the next twelve months many tributes appeared in journals and a magnificent memorial service was held in the Great Hall of the NGV, an honour reserved for those whose contribution to the arts of Australia was of the highest order. Filled to capacity with people from all walks of life, it was, as one historian said, the end of an era in so many aspects of Australian intellectual life. Bernard Smith was one of the last of the great postwar intellectuals who had steered Australia's cultural history and its identity into a global space, while never neglecting his roots or local responsibilities. Bronwyn Hughes of the National Trust of Australia's Public Art Committee has said:

> It was the passing of a legend . . . with the death of Bernard Smith and I was reminded by others, older and wiser, of [his] involvement in the formation of the National Trust's Public Art Committee. When the Karl Duldig mural was destroyed in St. Kilda road, he not only wrote a damning letter to the press, but was instrumental in convincing Arts Victoria to offer support for the original Public Art committee [and] the cause for protection and preservation. It may be only one achievement within his lifetime of great art historical achievement, but it has helped maintain Melbourne's distinctive cultural and physical landscape.[83]

In 2012 Rex Butler organised a symposium in honour of Bernard Smith at the University of Queensland; another symposium, the 'Legacies of Bernard Smith', was held at the University of Melbourne and jointly between the Power Institute at the University of Sydney and the AGNSW in September and November 2012; and the AAANZ conference in Wellington, New Zealand, in December 2012 was dedicated to him. He was, as Peter Beilharz said, 'an exemplary intellectual [who] . . . at the end of the day, to the end of his life . . . was a Marxist'.[84]

Finally, at Bernard's request his family drove with his ashes to Govetts Leap in the Blue Mountains and cast them into the antipodean forest and deep valley of geological time. It was where he had run through the bush as a boy; where he had taken Kate on their first romantic weekend; and where he had occasionally taken their children during school holidays, instructing them on evolution, nature and survival—after all, Charles Darwin had stood there in 1836. It was also where Vere Gordon Childe fell to his death in 1957. This final resting place, with its long, haunting view, was perhaps the most unencumbered space Bernard had known, the closest he could be to his universal origins.

NOTES

In preparation for this biography, the author interviewed and held regular conversations with Bernard Smith over a period of three years. Where remarks are quoted and no reference is provided, they have been recalled from these conversations. Where BSP NLA MS 8680 is given alone, these papers have recently been lodged at the National Library of Australia:

The following abbreviations have been used:

    BSP – Papers of Bernard Smith, 1912–2008, National Library of Australia, MS 8680

    BWSP – Bernard William Smith Papers, Mitchell Library, State Library of New South Wales, MSS 5202

Introduction

1   Olwyn Hughes, quoted in Janet Malcolm, *The Silent Woman: Sylvia Plath and Ted Hughes*, Picador, London, 1994, p. 45.

2   Bernard Smith, 'Coleridge's *Ancient Mariner* and Cook's second voyage', *Journal of the Warburg and Courtauld Institutes*, vol. XIX, nos 1–2, London, 1956, p. 117.

3   George Kubler, *The Shape of Time: Remarks on the History of Things*, Yale University Press, New Haven, CT, and London, 1962, p. 29.

4   Bernard Smith, *Place, Taste and Tradition: A Study of Australian Art Since 1788*, 2nd edn, Oxford University Press, Melbourne, 1979, p. 23.

5   Ihab Hassan, *Dismemberment of Orpheus: Towards a Postmodern Literature*, 2nd edn, University of Wisconsin Press, Madison, WI, 1982, p. 8.

6   Robin W. Winks, *The Imperial Revolution: Yesterday and Tomorrow*, Oxford University Press, New York, NY, 1994, pp. 8–9.

7   Bernard Smith, interview with the author, 7 June 2001.

8   Joan Kerr, 'Bernard has been there, done that', *Sydney Morning Herald*, 6 February 1988.

9   G. W. F. Hegel, *Hegel's Philosophy of Right*, T. M. Knox (trans.), Oxford University Press, London, 1979, p. 13.

10   James Robert Goetsch, *Vico's Axioms: The Geometry of the Human World*, Yale University Press, New Haven, CT, 1995, p. 7.

Chapter One: Origins

1   Bernard Smith, 'On Being Antipodean', BSP, NLA, MS 8680, Box 7/54/141.

2   Rose Anne Tierney, letter to Bernard Smith, n.d., c. 1936, BWSP, ML, MSS 5202, Box 1.

3   ibid.

4   Margaret Mattar, Charles Smith's granddaughter, in conversation with the author, April 2013.

5   Rose Anne Tierney, letter to Bernard Smith, 4 March 1936, BWSP, ML, MSS 5202, Box 1.

6   It was 20 years later that Bernard had to obtain a statutory declaration from the Child Welfare Department confirming that 'Bernard William Smith' was the same person as 'Patrick William Smith'. This may have been when he registered on the electoral role.

7   Mrs Tierney, letter to Rose Anne Tierney, 8 April 1918, BWSP, ML, MSS 5202, Box 1.

8   Hassan, *Dismemberment of Orpheus*, p. 8.

9   Oliver MacDonagh, 'The Irish in Australia: A General View', in Oliver MacDonagh and W. F. Mandle (eds), *Ireland and Irish-Australia: Studies in Cultural and Political History*, Croom Helm, London and Sydney, 1986, p. 156.

10 Rose Anne Tierney, letter to Bernard Smith, 4 March 1936, BWSP, ML, MSS 5202, Box 1.

11 Jacques Derrida, *Specters of Marx: The State of the Debt, the Work of Mourning and the New International*, Peggy Kamuf (trans.), Routledge, New York, NY, and London, 2006, p. 7.

12 Freud, quoted in Peter Osborne, *The Politics of Time: Modernity and Avant Garde*, Verso, London and New York, NY, 1995, p. 91.

13 For an interesting analysis of identification, recognition and oedipalism, see Peter Osborne, *The Politics of Time: Modernity and Avant-Garde*, pp. 69–104.

14 Derrida, *Specters of Marx*. See Derrida's interpretation of Marxism as a haunting product of the origins and genealogy of modern Europe.

15 Bernard Smith, *The Boy Adeodatus: The Portrait of a Lucky Young Bastard*, Penguin, Melbourne, 1984, p. 267.

16 Smith, letter to Vincent Buckley, 8 December 1984 (copy), BSP, NLA, Acc. 10.088, Box 66.

17 Bertha Keen, letter to Rose Anne Tierney, 19 November 1919, BWSP, ML, MSS 5202, Box 1.

18 Mrs Keen was part of an enterprise, the Boarding-out Society of New South Wales, begun in the suburb of Newtown in the 1880s by Marian Jefferis, who relocated to the suburb of Burwood in 1885 and established a system of cottages in which she installed elderly couples to take in illegitimate or orphaned children. See Walter Phillips, *James Jefferis: Prophet of Federation*, Australian Scholarly

Publishing, Melbourne, 1993, pp. 115–19. See also Jenny Teichman, *Illegitimacy: A Philosophical Examination*, Blackwell, Oxford, UK, 1982, p. 2.

19   Smith, *The Boy Adeodatus*, p. 4.

20   Smith, interview with the author, 8 July 2009, for the NLA Oral History Program, TRC 6111.

21   Glyndwr Williams, conversation with the author, April 2012.

22   Bernard Smith, *Modernism's History: A Study in Twentieth-Century Art and Ideas*, UNSW Press, Sydney, 1998, p. 21.

23   Chris Wallace-Crabbe, 'Hey Robin', unpublished manuscript, courtesy of Wallace-Crabbe.

24   Walter Benjamin, cited in Smith, *Modernism's History*, p. 21.

25   Smith, interview with Neville Meaney, 6 November 1986, for the NLA Oral History Program, TRC 2053/17.

26   Smith, *The Boy Adeodatus*, p. 166.

27   Noel Pearson, Gough Whitlam memorial service, 5 November 2014.

28   Smith, interview with Neville Meaney, 6 November 1986, for the NLA Oral History Program, TRC 2053/17, p. 30.

29   Smith, *The Boy Adeodatus*, p. 129.

30   ibid., p. 139.

31   Julia Kristeva, *Strangers to Ourselves*, Leon S. Roudiez (trans.), Columbia University Press, New York, NY, 1991, p. 21; Smith, *The Boy Adeodatus*, p. 140.

32   Smith, *The Boy Adeodatus*, p. 140.

33   J. Y. A. Thompson to Bertha Chivers, 10 January 1934, BWSP, ML, MSS 5202, Box 1.

34   Smith, *The Boy Adeodatus*, p. 149.

35   ibid., p. 149.

36   ibid., p.154.

37   ibid., p.159.

38   Smith, 1937 journal, BSP, NLA, MS Acc. 10.64, Box 5.

39   Smith, *The Boy Adeodatus*, p.165.

40   ibid., p. 180.

41   Lou Klepac, *James Gleeson: Landscape out of Nature*, The Beagle Press, Sydney, 1987, p. 13.

42   Smith, *The Boy Adeodatus*, p. 190.

43   Smith, letter to Rose Anne Tierney, 21 November 1935, BWSP, ML, MSS 5202, Box 1.

44   Smith, *The Boy Adeodatus*, p. 151.

45   Murraguldrie was registered in the *Geographical Encyclopaedia* as being in the Parish of Murraguldrie and County Wynyard.

46   Smith, *The Boy Adeodatus*, p. 183.

Chapter Two: New Tremors

1   Smith, letter to Vincent Buckley, 8 December 1984, BSP, NLA, MS 8680, Acc. 10.088, Box 66.

2   Charles Darwin, *Voyage of the Beagle*, Janet Browne and Michael Neve (eds), abridged with an introduction, Penguin, London, 1989, p. 50.

3   Smith, 'Murraguldrie Pastorale I', *Poems 1938–1993*, *Meanjin*, Melbourne, 1996, p. 1.

4   Oswald Spengler, *Man and Technics: A Contribution to a Philosophy of Life*, Allen and Unwin, Sydney, 1932, pp. 40, 8.

5   W. H. Auden, 'Spain 1937', in *Another Time*, Faber & Faber, London, 1940, p. 106.

6   Smith, diary, 17 August 1937, BSP, NLA, MS Acc. 10.64, Box 5.

7   ibid., 3 March 1937.

8   Smith, *The Boy Adeodatus*, p. 255.

9   ibid., p. 236.

10 Smith, conversation with the author, 2008.

11 Sigmund Freud, *Civilization and its Discontents*, Penguin Books, London, 2002, p. 28.

12 Smith, diary, 4 February 1937, BSP, NLA, MS Acc. 10.64, Box 5. For a full account of Bernard's religious struggles, see Smith, *The Boy Adeodatus*, pp. 228–31.

13 Smith, diary, 4 February 1937, BSP, NLA, MS Acc. 10.64, Box 5.

14 ibid., 16 May 1937.

15 ibid., 11 December 1938.

16 Marx, 'A Contribution to the Critique of Political Economy', 1859, preface, in Lewis S. Feuer (ed.), *Basic Writings on Politics and Philosophy: Karl Marx and Friedrich Engels*, Anchor Doubleday, New York, NY, 1959, p. 43.

17 Smith, letter to Rose Anne Tierney, 1937, BWSP, ML, MSS 5202, Box 1.

18 H. G. Wells, *Experiment in Autobiography*, Penguin, London, 1934, pp. 206–7.

19 Smith, diary, 28 September 1938, BSP, NLA, MS Acc. 10.64, Box 5.

20 ibid., 4 February 1937.

21 Smith, *The Boy Adeodatus*, p. 263.

22 Smith, letter to Rose Anne Tierney, n.d., BSP, NLA, MS 8680.

23 Derrida, *The Specters of Marx*, p. 14.

24 Rose Anne Tierney, letter to Smith, 16 May 1937, BWSP, ML, MSS 5202, Box 1.

25 Mikhail Lifshitz, *The Philosophy of Art of Karl Marx*, Ralph B Winn (trans.), Critics Group, New York, NY, 1938, p. 21; Mark Bahnisch, 'Full Marx: The Legacy of the Great German Philosopher and Economist Still Reverberates', *Australian Literary Review*, 4 May 2011, p. 22.

26 Smith, interview with Neville Meaney, 6 November 1986, for the NLA Oral History Program, TRC 2053/17.

27 Smith, *The Boy Adeodatus*, p. 236.

28 Alexis Carrel, quoted in the inaugural catalogue of the 'First Exhibition of the Teachers' College Art Club', August 1938, BSP, NLA, MS 8680, Box 1.

29 William Morris, quoted in the second Teachers Federation Art Society exhibition catalogue, 1939, BSP, NLA, MS 8680.

30 Bernard Smith, 'The Function of the Club', in Teachers' College Art Club exhibition catalogue, 1938, BSP, NLA, MS 8680, Box 1.

31 Bernard Smith, 'Retrospect', Teachers' College Art Club Exhibition Catalogue, 1939, BSP, NLA, MS 8680.

32 Andrew Causey, 'Herbert Read and Contemporary Art', in David Goodway (ed.), *Herbert Read Reassessed*, Liverpool University Press, Liverpool, UK, 1998, p. 125.

33 F. B. Smith, 'H. G. Wells in Australia', *Australian Book Review*, October 2001, p. 32.

34 Melvin Rader, *No Compromise: The Conflict Between Two Worlds*, Macmillan, New York, NY, 1939, p. 3.

35 Smith, diary, 23 February 1939, BSP, NLA, MS Acc. 10.64, Box 5.

36 Smith, 'The New Realism in Australian Art', *Meanjin*, vol. 3, no. 1, Melbourne, 1944, p. 7.

37 Smith, diary, 11 December 1938, BSP, NLA, MS Acc. 10.64, Box 5.

38 Smith, letter to Lindsay Gordon, 6 November 1938 (copy), BWSP, ML, MSS 5202, Box 1.

39 Herbert Read, *Surrealism*, Faber & Faber, London, 1936, p. 22.

40 André Breton, *What is Surrealism?*, Faber & Faber, London, 1924.

41 Read, *Surrealism*, p. 19.

42 Herbert Read, quoted in Smith, diary, 1938, BSP, NLA, MS Acc. 10.64; and also underlined in Smith's copy of Herbert Read, *Surrealism*, p. 26.

43 Smith, interview with the author, 29 July 2009.

44 For a discussion of Smith's own expressionist surreal paintings of 1940 see *Art & Text*, spring 1982, pp. 34–47.

45 Smith, diary, 11 December 1938, BSP, NLA, MS Acc. 10.64, Box 5.

46 ibid.

47 Smith, diary, c. 1939, BSP, NLA, MS Acc. 10.64, Box 5.

48 ibid.

49 For a fuller description of Bernard's sexual rite of passage, see Smith, *The Boy Adeodatus*, pp. 270–4.

50 Paul Edwards (ed.), *Wyndham Lewis: Creatures of Habit and Creatures of Change: Essays on Art, Literature and Society 1914–1956*, Black Sparrow Press, Santa Rosa, CA, 1989, p. 16.

51 See Stuart MacIntyre, *The Reds: The Communist Party of Australia from Origins to Illegality*, Allen and Unwin, Sydney, 1998, pp. 319–21; Smith, *The Boy Adeodatus*, p. 288.

52 Smith, *The Boy Adeodatus*, p. 280.

53 ibid., pp. 256, 288; Smith, diary, 21 December 1939, BSP, NLA, MS Acc. 10.64, Box 4.

54 Smith, diary, 1939, BSP, NLA, MS Acc. 10.64, Box 4

55 Smith, *The Boy Adeodatus*, p. 276.

56 Smith, diary, 11 November 1939, BSP, MS Acc. 10.64, Box 4; see also Smith, *The Boy Adeodatus*, p. 285.

57 Smith, diary, 11 November 1939, BSP, MS Acc. 10.64, Box 4.

58 Smith, *The Boy Adeodatus*, pp. 285–6.

59 Richard Haese, *Rebels and Precursors: The Revolutionary Years of Australian Art*, Penguin, Melbourne, 1988, p. 61.

60 Smith, *The Boy Adeodatus*, p. 286.

61 ibid., p. 284.

62 Margaret A. Rose, *Marx's Lost Aesthetic*, Cambridge University Press, Cambridge, UK, 1984, p. 125.

63 Smith, *Modernism's History*, p. 22.

64 Smith, 'Tendencies in Modern English Verse', BSP, NLA, MS 8680, Box 1.

65 Sunil Khilnani, *Arguing Revolution: The Intellectual Left in Postwar France*, Yale University Press, New Haven, CT, and London, 1993, p. 7.

66 Smith, 'Tendencies in Modern English Verse', p. 8.

67 Brian Lukacher, 'Nature Historicized: Constable, Turner, and Romantic Landscape Painting', in Stephen F. Eisenman (ed.), *Nineteenth Century Art: A Critical History*, Thames and Hudson, London, 1994, p. 115.

68 W. J. T. Mitchell, 'Imperial Landscape', in Mitchell (ed.), *Landscape and Power*, University of Chicago Press, Chicago, IL, and London, 1994, p. 18.

69 Smith, 'Tendencies in Modern English Verse', p. 8.

70 ibid., p. 6.

71 Karl Marx, 'A Contribution to the Critique of Political Economy', p. 43.

72 Smith, 'Tendencies in Modern English Verse', p. 13.

73 See Edgar Allan Poe, 'The Philosophy of Composition', in R. Brimley Johnson (ed.), *The Complete Poetical Works of Edgar Allan Poe*, Oxford University Press, London, 1909, pp. 243–82.

74 Smith, letter to Rose Anne Tierney, 5 February 1940, BWSP, ML, MSS 5202, Box 1.

75 For a lengthy explanation of Smith's two paintings, see Smith, 'Lot and Pompeii' in *Art & Text*, Melbourne, spring 1982, pp. 34–47.

76 W. B. Yeats, quoted in Smith, diary, c. 1938, BSP, NLA, MS Acc. 10.64, Box 5.

77 Smith, *Lot* (1940), *Poems 1938–1993*, Meanjin, Melbourne, 1996, p. 8.

78 Smith, diary, c. 1939, BSP, NLA, MS Acc. 10.64, Box 5.

79 E. H. Gombrich, *Meditations on a Hobby Horse: And Other Essays on the Theory of Art*, Phaidon, London and New York, NY, 1963, p. 21.

80 Smith, *The Boy Adeodatus*, p. 293.

81 ibid.

82 ibid., p. 294.

83 Smith, *A Pavane for Another Time*, Macmillan, Melbourne, 2002, p. 44.

84 ibid., p. 296.

85 Smith, 'Surrealism', 16 October 1940, BSP, NLA, MS 8680, Box 1.

86 ibid.

87 ibid.

88 Louis MacNeice, 'Aubade', *Poems 1925–1940*, Random House, New York, NY, 1940, p. 40.

Chapter Three: Cultural Crossings

1 Karl Marx, letter to his father, 10 November [1837], quoted in Lifshitz, p. 23, and used by Smith in his lecture to the Teachers Federation Art Society entitled 'Reversion and Growth in Art', 16 September 1942, BSP, NLA, MS 8680, Box 1/5.

2 See Smith's review of Miranda Carter, 'Anthony Blunt', in *Art Monthly*, no. 147, Canberra, March 2002, p. 32.

3 Fredric Jameson, *Marxism and Form: Twentieth Century Dialectical Theories of Literature*, Princeton University Press, Princeton, NJ, 1971, pp. ix, xi.

4 Ian McLean, 'Bernard Smith: Noble Modern', *Art and Australia*, vol. 27, no. 4, 1990, p. 565.

5 Jameson, *Marxism and Form*, p. ix.

6 Smith, 'Communism and the Visual Arts in the 1900s', *Age*, 'Monthly Review', 5 October 1981, p. 2.

7 Smith, *The Boy Adeodatus*, p. 297.

8 MacNeice, 'Refugees' in *Poems 1925–1940*, p. 291.

9 Smith, interview with the author, 29 July 2009, for the NLA Oral History Program, TRC 6111.

10 Ernst Gombrich, 'An Autobiographical Sketch', in Richard Woodfield (ed.), *The Essential Gombrich: Selected Writings on Art and Culture*, Phaidon, London, 1996, p. 24.

11 Edwin Lachnit, 'Strzygowski', in Jane Turner (ed.), *The Dictionary of Art*, Grove, New York, NY, 1996, p. 795.

12 Smith, 'On Writing Art History in Australia', *Thesis Eleven*, no. 82, Melbourne, August 2005, p. 6.

13 Smith, notes for 'The New Realism in Australian Contemporary Art', 1943, BSP, NLA, MS 8680, Box 2/12, p. 4.

14 ibid.

15 For a description of the conflict between the conservatives and the moderns, see Haese, *Rebels and Precursors*, , pp. 38–41.

16   Norman Macgeorge, *Australian Art Annual 1939*, Ure Smith, Sydney, 1939, p. 10.

17   Published later in J. S. MacDonald, *Australian Painting Desiderata*, Lothian
     Publishing, Melbourne, 1958, p. 135. For an excellent study of the complexities of
     this debate between the traditionalists and moderns see Eileen Chanin and Steven
     Miller (eds), *Degenerates and Perverts: The 1939 Herald Exhibition of French and
     British Contemporary Art*, Miegunyah Press, Melbourne, 2005.

18   Lionel Lindsay, *Sydney Morning Herald*, 15 October 1940.

19   Smith, 'History as Criticism', in Bain Attwood (ed.), *Boundaries of the Past*, The
     History Institute of Victoria, Melbourne, 1990, p. 3.

20   Smith, 'Development of Australian Painting', lecture notes, BSP, NLA, MS 8680,
     Box 1.

21   Smith, letter to Keith Murdoch, 18 October 1945 (copy), BSP, NLA, MS 8680.

22   Smith, 'A Reply to My Critics', *Art Monthly*, no. 33, Canberra, August 1990,
     p. 4; T. J. Clark, *Farewell to an Idea: Episodes from a History of Modernism*, Yale
     University Press, New Haven, CT, and London, 1999, p. 21.

23   For a history of the movement, see Ann Stephen, Andrew McNamara and Philip
     Goad, *Modernism and Australia*, Miegunyah Press, Melbourne, 2006.

24   Bernard Smith, *A Pavane for Another Time*, Macmillan, Melbourne, 2002,
     pp. 43–4.

25   Smith, 'Foreword' to the Teachers Federation Art Society exhibition catalogue,
     1940, BSP, NLA, MS 8680.

26   ibid.

27   Marcus Bullock and Michael W. Jennings (eds), *Selected Writings/Walter
     Benjamin: Volume I, 1913–1926*, Belknap Press, Cambridge, MA, 1996, p. 201.

28   Smith, *A Pavane for Another Time*, p. 9.

29   Peter Craven, 'Watercolour Memories', *Australian Book Review*, no. 246,
     November 2002, p. 9.

30   Smith, letter to Rose Anne Tierney, January 1941, BSP, NLA, MS 8680.

31   Smith, 'Sonnet', diary, 1940, BSP, NLA, MS Acc. 10.64, Box 5.

32   ibid.

33   Smith, letter to Kate, 30 December 1940, BSP, NLA, MS 8680.

34   ibid, n.d.

35   Smith, letter to Rose Anne Tierney, 1941, BSP, NLA, MS 8680.

36   Smith, 'Dry Dock', *Australian New Writing*, no. 1, 1943, p. 23.

37   Kate, letter to 'P' (Clare Pepler), not dated, BSP, NLA, MS 8680.

38   Karl Marx and Friedrich Engels, *The German Ideology: Parts 1 and 111*, Lawrence
     and Wishart, Marxist-Leninist Library, London, 1940, p. 18.

39   Cuthbert Adeney, letter to Smith, 29 August 1942, BSP, NLA, MS 8680.

40   Smith, letter to Lindsay Gordon, 1942, on the birth of Bernard's daughter,
     Elizabeth, BSP, NLA, MS 8680.

41   Deidre Cable, letter to Smith, 30 July 1945 (copy), BSP, NLA, MS 8680.

42 Friedrich Nietzsche, 'Human, all too Human', in *A Nietzsche Reader*, R. J. Hollingdale (selected and trans. with an introduction), Penguin, London, 1977, p. 153.

43 Smith, 'History as Criticism', BSP, NLA, MS 8680, Box 6/42/53, p. 10.

44 Smith's lecture at the Cultural Conference, Sydney, November 1941, published in *Soviet Culture*, NSW Aid Russia Committee, pp. 57–63.

45 Smith, 'Reversion and Growth in Art', lecture notes, 16 September 1942, BSP, NLA, MS 8680, Box 1/5.

46 Fredric Jameson, *Marxism and Form*, Princeton University Press, Princeton, NJ, 1971, p. 53.

47 Smith, letter to George Farwell, 28 February 1943, (copy) BSP, NLA, 8680.

48 ibid.

49 Clem Christesen, letter to Smith, 20 February 1943, (copy) BSP, NLA, 8680.

50 *Australian New Writing*, vol. 2, March 1944, p. 4.

51 Noel Counihan, letter to Smith, 9 May 1943 (copy), BSP, NLA, 8680.

52 Smith, 'Counihan and Painting', BSP, NLA, MS 8680, Box 7/51/118.

53 Noel Counihan, letter to Smith, 26 January 1944 (copy), BSP, NLA, 8680.

54 Bernard Smith, *Place, Taste and Tradition: A Study of Australian Art Since 1788* 2nd edn., p. 235.

55 Geoffrey Dutton, *The Innovators: The Sydney Alternatives in the Rise of Modern Art, Literature and Ideas*, Macmillan, Melbourne, 1986, p. 61.

56 For a full evaluation of Smith and Ure Smith's relationship, see Nancy Underhill, *Making Australian Art 1916–49: Sydney Ure Smith Patron and Publisher*, Oxford University Press, Melbourne, 1991.

57 Sydney Ure Smith, 'Bringing Art to the Australian People', The Society of Artists Book 143, Society of Artists, Sydney, pp. 65–7.

58 ibid.

59 Steven Miller, 'Contingency as the Guard Dog of History: Bernard Smith at the Art Gallery of New South Wales, 1944–48', paper given at the Legacies of Bernard Smith symposium, University of Sydney, 10 November 2012, courtesy of the author.

60 Melissa Boyde, 'Making it Accessible: Mary Alice Evatt and Australian Modernist Art', http://evatt.org.au/publications/papers/217.html, accessed August 2010.

61 See Smith, *A Pavane for Another Time*, pp. 111–13; National Art Gallery of New South Wales Board Minutes, 25 September 1942, p. 2449 in Miller, 'Contingency as the Guard Dog of History'.

62 Smith, Art Gallery of New South Wales Education File 83.12.04.

63 Smith, quoted in Miller, 'Contingency as the Guard Dog of History'.

64 Smith, 'Taking Art to the Country: How it Began', in *Cultivating the Country: Living with the Arts in Regional Australia*, 1988, p. 42.

65 Smith, 'Canberra 1944', *Poems 1938–1993*, Meanjin, Melbourne, 1996, p. 29.

66 Smith, interview with Neville Meaney, 6 November 1986, for the NLA Oral History Program, TRC 2053/17.

67 Boyde, 'Making it Accessible'; Smith, 'Taking Art to the Country', pp. 33–6, 40.

68 Lionel Lindsay, letter to Daryl Lindsay, 8 July 1948, Lindsay Papers, State Library of Victoria, MS 9242, Box 2003/1434–1468; Lionel Lindsay, letter to J. R. McGregor, 10 April 1948, Mitchell Library, Lindsay Papers, ML, MSS 1969/5, Correspondence, 1946–1953.

69 Smith, letter to Harry Gould, 26 June 1944, National Archives of Australia, Item 09/686901/Series A 6126 (A6126/XMI).

70 Smith names Yosl Bergner, Noel Counihan, Vic O'Connor, Herbert McClintock, Roy Dalgarno, James Cant and Harry MacDonald as his chosen realists. See 'Realists Challenge Surrealists', *Tribune*, 1944, Newspaper Scrapbook, BSP, NLA, MS 8680.

71 Item 09/6869/ Series A6126 (A6/126/XM1), Item 86, National Archives of Australia. See *Communist Review*, vol. 58, June 1946, pp. 182–4; July 1946, pp. 215–17, written under the pseudonym 'Goya'.

72 Smith, 'History as Criticism', p. 3.

73 Smith, notes, 'History as Criticism', BSP, NLA, MS 8680, Box 6/42/53, p. 6.

74 Smith, letter to Lindsay Gordon, n.d., c. 1943, BSP, NLA, MS 8680.

75 Smith, letter to Ihab Hassan, 6 January 2001 (copy) BSP, NLA, MS 8680.

76 Smith, 'Is there a Radical Tradition in Australian Art?', paper given at the Canberra School of Art, 4 April 1984, BSP, NLA, MS 8680, Box 6/42, p. 10.

77 Rex Ingamells and Victor Kennedy, *The Flaunted Banners*, Economy Press, Adelaide, 1941.

78 Smith, interview with Hazel De Berg, NLA, TRC 2053–17, Tape 1, p. 43.

79 Russell Drysdale, letter to Smith, 6 June 1944 (copy), BSP, NLA, MS 8680.

80 Smith, 'Dobell and Drysdale', unpublished notes, BSP, NLA MS 8680, Box 2.

81 Smith, letter to David Cunningham, 8 March 1977, BWSP, ML, MSS 5202, add on 2039, Box 2; Robert Hughes, 'Painting in Australia', *London Magazine*, November 1963, p. 66.

82 Nettie Palmer, letter to Smith, 3 September 1945 (copy), BSP, NLA, MS 8680.

83 Margaret Preston, letter to Smith, 20 July 1945 (copy), BSP, NLA, MS 8680.

84 John Reed, letter to Smith, 16 February 1944 (copy), BSP, NLA, MS 8680.

85 C. R. Badger, *Australian Quarterly*, vol. XVII, no. 3, Sydney, September 1945, pp. 122–4.

86 Smith, letter to Kate Smith, 11 August 1945, BSP, NLA, MS 8680. The letter is reproduced in full in Smith, *A Pavane for Another Time*, p. 135.

87 Smith, letter to Kate Smith, 9 August 1945, BSP, NLA, MS 8680.

88 Smith, letter to Kate Smith, 11 August 1945, BSP, NLA, MS 8680.

89 Ihab Hassan, *Out of Egypt: Scenes and Arguments of an Autobiography*, Southern Illinois Press, Carbondale, IL, and Edwardsville, IL, 1986, p. 19.

90   Smith, 'Reflections of the 1940s', BSP, NLA, MS 8680, Box 6/44/72, p. 4.

91   Smith, 'The Dark Years', 29 August 1997, BSP, NLA, MS 8680, Box 57/62, p. 3.

92   Laurie Hergenham, 'Grattan, Clinton Hartley (1902–1980)', *Australian Dictionary of Biography*, vol. 14, Melbourne University Press, Melbourne, 1996, pp. 308–9.

93   ibid.

94   Smith, 'Australian Art and the War', BSP, NLA, MS 8680, Box 2/12/65.

95   Trendall had worked as a cryptologist in Melbourne during the war and had made a crucial code breakthrough during the Japanese invasion; it became known as the Trencode. See R. S. Merrillees, 'Professor A.D. Trendall and his band of Classical Cryptographers', working paper no. 355, Strategic and Defence Studies Centre, Australian National University, Canberra, 1999.

96   A. D. Trendall, quoted in 'Obituary for A. D. Trendall', *Times*, 4 December 1995.

97   Ian McPhee, 'Arthur Dale Trendall 1909–1995', in *1997 Lectures and Memoirs: Proceedings of the British Academy*, vol. 9, 1998, pp. 501–17.

98   Smith, 'Studio of Realist Art', in *Meanjin Papers*, Melbourne, winter 1945, p. 42.

99   *SORA Bulletin*, March 1945, cited in Andrew Reeves, *The Tapestry of Australia: The Sydney Wharfies Mural*, Waterside Workers Federation, Sydney, 1992, p. 26.

100   Donald Friend, diary entry of 18 October, 1946, *The Diaries of Donald Friend*, Paul Hetherington (ed.), National Library of Australia, Canberra, 2003, vol. 2, p. 425.

101   Lindsay Gordon, letter to Smith, 9 April 1949, BSP, NLA, MS 8680, Acc. 10.088, Box 19.

102   Roderick Shaw, interview with Barbara Blackman for the NLA Oral History Program, TRC 1749, p. 135.

103   'Strange Boosters', in *Things I hear*, series 95, 23 August 1948.

104   Smith, letter to Sir Keith Murdoch, 9 November, 1946 (copy), BSP, NLA, MS 8680; NGV Trustees Minutes, 18 December 1946, NGV, Shaw Research Library, accessed 17 April 2000.

105   Lionel Lindsay, letter to James McGregor, 10 April 1948, Lindsay Family Papers, ML, MSS 1969/5.

106   Smith, correspondence between Lilian Somerville, head of Fine Arts, Courtauld Institute, and Professor Bodkin of the Barber Institute, 25 October 1948, BSP, NLA, MS 8680.

107   Smith, letter to Clem Christesen, 31 May 1948, *Meanjin* Papers, 2005.0004, University of Melbourne Archives.

108   Lindsay Gordon, letter to Smith, 7 September 1948, BSP, NLA, MS 8680, Acc 10.088, Box 19.

Chapter Four: The Black Swan

1   Noel McLachlan, 'Godzone: The Australian Intellectual', *Meanjin*, vol. 26, no. 1, Melbourne, 1967, p. 6.

2   Smith, quoted in 'Interview with Bernard Smith' in Rex Butler (ed.), *Radical Revisionism: An Anthology of Writings on Australian Art*, Institute of Modern Art, Brisbane, 2005, p. 76.

3   Peter Kidson, quoted in Miranda Carter, *Anthony Blunt: His Lives*, Macmillan, London, 2001, p. 360.

4   Anthony Blunt, quoted in Smith, *A Pavane for Another Time*, p. 237.

5   Anthony Blunt, letter to John Summerson, 19 October 1949, BSP, MS 8680, Acc. 10.088, Box 33.

6   See Sheridan Palmer, *Centre of the Periphery: Three European Art Historians in Melbourne*, Australian Scholarly Publishing, Melbourne, pp. 5, 19–21, 40–2.

7   See Silvina P. Vidal's article, 'Rethinking the Warburgian Tradition in the 21st Century', *Journal of Art Historiography*, no. 1, December 2009, pp. 1–12.

8   T. J. Clark, *Lowry and the Painting of Modern Life*, Tate Publishing, London, 2013, p. 16.

9   Smith, *A Pavane for Another Time*, p. 247.

10   Carter, *Anthony Blunt*, p. 210.

11   ibid., pp. 209–10; and Palmer, *Centre of the Periphery*, p. 49.

12   I am grateful to John Mitchell for information about his father and the Warburg circle of scholars; see Craven, 'Watercolour Memories', *Australian Book Review*, no. 246, September 2002, p. 9.

13   Charles Mitchell, letter to Joseph Burke, 'Good Friday' [4 April] 1947, Joseph Burke Papers, University of Melbourne Archives.

14   Smith, 'On Being Antipodean', BSP, NLA, MS 8680, Box 7/54.

15   See David Bindman, *Ape to Apollo: Aesthetics and the Idea of Race in the 18th Century*, Reaktion Books and the Paul Mellon Centre for Studies in British Art, London, 2002, p. 17.

16   ibid.

17   Bronwen Price (ed.), *Francis Bacon's New Atlantis: New Interdisciplinary Essays*, Manchester University Press, Manchester, UK, and New York, NY, 2002, pp. 1–3, 15–16.

18   Smith, *A Pavane for Another Time*, p. 246.

19   ibid., p. 250.

20   Jack Lindsay, *Crisis in Marxism*, Moonraker Press, New York, NY, 1981, p. 1.

21   Jim Allen, 'Childe, Vere Gordon (1892–1957)', *Australian Dictionary of Biography*, National Centre of Biography, Australian National University, Canberra, http://adb.anu.edu.au/biography/childe-vere-gordon-5580/text9521. See also Kenneth Maddock, 'Prehistory, Power and Pessimism' in Peter Gathercole, T. H. Irving and Gregory Melleuish (eds), *Childe and Australia: Archaeology, Politics and Ideas*, University of Queensland Press, Brisbane, 1995, p. 110.

22   Childe, quoted in Peter Gathercole, 'The Relationship Between Vere Gordon Childe's Political and Academic Thought and Practice', in ibid., pp. 95–7; and see Tim Murray, 'Vere Gordon Childe: Archaeological Records and Rethinking the

Archaeologist's Project', in ibid., p. 19.

23 Neil Falkner, 'Gordon Childe and Marxist Archaeology', *International Socialism*, issue 116, pp. 1–17.

24 Smith, *A Pavane for Another Time*, p. 250.

25 Smith, *Modernism's History*, p. 86.

26 Press release 1948 and Herbert Read, draft preface, September 1948, Institute of Contemporary Art Papers, Tate Gallery Archives 955.1.12.10.

27 ibid.

28 Smith, notes for 'Art and Imperialism', BSP, NLA, MS 8680, Box 1/9.

29 Smith, *The Boy Adeodatus*, p. 295.

30 Later published as Smith, 'Henry Moore', in Bernard Smith, *The Antipodean Manifesto: Essays in Art and History*, Oxford University Press, Melbourne, 1976, p. 16.

31 ibid., p. 17.

32 Smith, diary, 1948, BSP, NLA, MS Acc. 10.64.

33 Smith, interview with Neville Meaney, 6 November 1986, for the NLA Oral History Program, TRC 2053/17, p. 30.

34 Wyndham Lewis, quoted in David Goodway, 'The Politics of Herbert Read', in *Herbert Read Reassessed*, p. 179.

35 Smith, 'Sir Herbert Read and the Power Bequest', in *The Antipodean Manifesto*, p. 70.

36 James Gleeson, letter to Smith, 11 February 2001, BSP, NLA, MS 8680.

37 Smith, diary, 11 March 1949, BSP, NLA, MS Acc. 10.64, Box 5; see also Smith *A Pavane for Another Time*, p. 293.

38 I am grateful to Jane Eckett for sharing her research on The Abbey.

39 James Gleeson, letter to Smith, 11 February 2001, BSP, NLA, MS 8680.

40 Perry Anderson quoted in Lesley Johnson, *The Cultural Critics: From Mathew Arnold to Raymond Williams*, Routledge & Kegan Paul, London, 1972, p. 12.

41 Smith, journal, 1948, BSP, NLA, MS Acc. 10.64, Box 5.

42 ibid.

43 Smith, Correspondence, BWSP, ML, MSS 5202.

44 Sali Herman, letter to Smith, 26 February 1949 (copy), BSP, NLA, MS 8680.

45 Clem Christesen, letter to Smith, 17 May 1949 (copy), BSP, NLA, MS 8680.

46 See Smith's account of Cuthbert Adeney in *A Pavane for Another Time*, pp. 193–233.

47 Smith, letter to Douglas Peplar, 1948, BSP, NLA, MS 8680.

48 Smith, diary 1949, BSP, NLA, MS Acc. 10.64.

49 Smith, 'Istalyfera', 1949, in *Poems 1938–1993*, Meanjin, Melbourne, 1996, p. 35.

50 Doris Lessing, *In Pursuit of the English*, Simon and Schuster, New York, NY, 1961, pp. 17, 75.

51 'Durer: Innesbruck, 1495', in *Ern Malley's Poems: With an Introduction by Max*

Harris, Lansdowne Press, Melbourne, 1966, p. 25.

52 Smith, unpublished notes, 'The Angel Sings', n.d., BSP., NLA, MS 8680, Box 2/10.

53 Smith, unpublished notes, BSP, MS 8680, Box 7/55/155.

54 Smith, letter to Gordon Lindsay, 16 June 1949 (copy), BSP, NLA, MS 8680.

55 Smith, journal 1948, BSP, NLA, MS Acc. 10.64, Box 5.

56 Smith, in Joppien Rudiger and Bernard Smith, *The Art of Captain Cook's Voyages: Volume One: The Voyage of the Endeavour 1768–1771*, Oxford University Press in association with the Australian Academy of the Humanities, Melbourne, 1985, p. ix.

57 Emanuel Levinas, quoted in Peter Osborne, *The Politics of Time: Modernity and Avant-Garde*, Verso, London and New York, NY, 1995, p. 123.

58 Smith, *European Vision and the South Pacific*, p. 4.

59 Greg Dening, 'Ethnography on My Mind', in Attwood (ed.), *Boundaries of the Past*, p. 15.

60 Bernard Smith, *Imagining the Pacific: In the Wake of Cook's Voyages*, Miegunyah Press, Melbourne, 1992, p. xi.

61 Ernst Cassirer, *The Question of Jean Jacques Rousseau*, Indiana University Press, Bloomington, IN, and London, 1963, p. 49.

62 George Steiner, *Language and Silence: Essays, 1958–1966*, Faber & Faber, London, 1967, p. 268.

63 Hakluyt Society, 'Revised plan February 1949', BSP, NLA, MS 8680.

64 Smith, letter to Doug Munro, 6 April 2000, copy provided by Doug Munro.

65 Anthony Blunt, quoted in Smith, *A Pavane for Another Time*, p. 283.

66 J. C. Beaglehole, letter to Smith, 6 April 1950, BSP, NLA, MS 8680.

67 Smith, 'On Writing Art History in Australia', *Thesis Eleven*, no. 82, Melbourne, August 2005, p. 7.

68 For a detailed examination of the painting, see Michelle Hetherington, 'John Hamilton Mortimer and the Discovery of Captain Cook', *British Art Journal*, vol. 4, no. 1, London, spring 2003, p. 70.

69 Alan Frost, 'The Planting of New South Wales: Sir Joseph Banks and the Creation of an Antipodean Europe', in R. E. R. Banks et al. (eds), *Sir Joseph Banks: A Global Perspective*, Royal Botanic Gardens Kew, Richmond, 1994, p. 137.

70 Smith, *A Pavane for Another Time*, p. 277.

71 Alwyne Wheeler, letter to Smith, 3 April 1987, BWSP, ML, MSS 5202, add on 2039, Box 1. Certainly, Sawyer used it in his 1971 catalogue of the museum's collection of manuscripts and drawings of the First Fleet, on which he had been working for a long period.

72 Smith, notes 'The First Australian Artist', BSP, NLA, MS 8680.

73 The full title is *An Account of the Voyages Undertaken by the Order of His Present Majesty, For Making Discoveries in the Southern Hemisphere. Vol. I.*

74 David Bindman, *Ape to Apollo*, p. 133–34.

75 Smith, 'William Hodges and English *Plein-air* Painting', *Art History*, vol. 6, no. 2,

London, June 1983, p. 144.

76   Smith, 'Cook's Voyage: Vision of the South Pacific', lecture, 11 June 1989, BSP, NLA, MS 8680, Box 7/50/102, p. 8.

77   Laurence Simmons, *Tuhituhi: William Hodges, Cook's Painter in the South Pacific*, Otago University Press, Dunedin, NZ, 2011.

78   See Hodges' descriptive catalogue to his exhibition of 'The Effects of Peace' and 'The Consequence of War', in 'Appendix', in Geoff Quilley and John Bonehill (eds), *William Hodges 1744–1797: The Art of Exploration*, Yale University Press and National Maritime Museum, Greenwich, London, 2004, p. 203.

79   Smith, 'On Writing Art History in Australia', p. 8.

80   Smith, letter to Kenneth Clark, n.d., Tate Gallery Archives, MSS 8812.1.2.6064.

81   Rex Nan Kivell, letter to Smith, 26 October 1948, Rex Nan Kivell Papers, NLA, MS 4000, Box 1/3.

82   Sheridan Palmer, 'Men Who Make their Own Histories: The Legacies of Bernard Smith and Rex Nan Kivell', Harold White Lecture, 27 July 2010, National Library of Australia, Canberra.

83   Michelle Hetherington, conversation with author, 19 May 2010.

84   Nan Kivell, letter to Major John P. Page, 28 December 1938, Rex Nan Kivell Papers, NLA, MS 4000, Box 1/1.

85   Smith, letter to Nan Kivell, 10 July 1954, ibid., Box 2/11; and Smith, letter to Nan Kivell, 26 November 1959, ibid., Box 3/26. For a more extensive examination of Rex Nan Kivell's life and career see Sheridan Palmer, 'Men Who Make their Own History: The Legacies of Bernard Smith and Rex Nan Kivell', *National Library Magazine*, NLA, March 2011, pp. 12–15.

86   Smith, journal, 1948, BSP, NLA, MS Acc. 10.64, Box 5.

87   Jim Davidson, 'Sir William Keith Hancock (1898–1988)', *Australian Dictionary of Biography*, National Centre for Biography, vol. 17, Melbourne University Press, Melbourne, 2007, pp. 482–85.

88   Smith, journal, 1948, BSP, NLA, MS Acc. 10.64, Box 5.

89   Smith, letter to Kenneth Clark, 1 November 1949, Tate Gallery Archives, KCP/MSS 8812.1.2.6059.

90   Smith, letter to Kenneth Clark, 14 May 1950, Tate Gallery Archives, MSS 8812.1.2.6063.

91   Smith, letter to Kate, n.d., BSP, NLA, MS 8680.

92   ibid.

93   ibid.

94   Smith, *A Pavane for Another Time*, p. 306.

95   Benjamin, *Selected Writings, Volume I*, p. 14.

96   Smith, *A Pavane for Another Time*, p. 341–42.

97   ibid., p. 338.

98   Smith, letter to Rose Anne Tierney, 1 September 1949, BSP, NLA, MS 8680.

99   Inge King, conversation with the author, 14 October 2013.

100 ibid.

101 Bienchen Ohly, conversation with the author, 17 September 2013.

102 Smith, letter to Rose Anne Tierney 19 June 1949, BSP, NLA, MS 8680.

103 See Barrett Reid and Nancy Underhill (eds), *Letters of John Reed: Defining Australian Cultural Life 1920–1981*, Viking, Melbourne, 2001, pp. 126–7.

104 Kate, letter to Smith, n.d. (c. January 1950), BSP, NLA, MS 8680.

105 Rod Shaw, letter to Smith, n. d. (c. 1950), BWSP, ML, MSS 5202, Correspondence, 1950.

106 Charles Mitchell, letter to Smith, 6 January 1950 (copy), BSP, NLA, MS 8680.

107 Smith, *European Vision and the South Pacific: A Study in the History of Ideas*, Oxford University Press, London, 1960, p. 12.

108 See Smith, *European Vision and the South Pacific*, pp. 10–14.

109 R. A. Skelton, letter to Smith, 7 April 1950 (copy), BSP, NLA, MS 8680.

110 Smith, diary 1949, BSP, NLA, MS Acc. 10.64, Box 5.

111 ibid.

112 ibid.

113 Smith, *A Pavane for Another Time*, p. 444.

114 Venice Biennale catalogue, annotated by Smith, State Library of Victoria, p. 395. Smith's private library is now held at the State Library of Victoria.

115 Fernand Windels, *The Lascaux Cave Paintings*, Faber & Faber, London, 1949, frontispiece.

116 ibid., p. 82.

117 Georges Bataille, *The Cradle of Humanity: Prehistoric Art and Culture*, introduced by Stuart Kendall (ed.), Zone, New York, NY, 2009, p. 22.

118 Thomas Hobbes, quoted in Hal Foster, 'I am the Decider', *London Review of Books*, 17 March 2011, p. 31.

119 Smith, 'Who is the Port Jackson Painter?' BSP, NLA, MS 8680, Box 6/43/65, p. 5.

120 Anthony Blunt, letter to Smith, 20 September 1950 (copy), BSP, NLA, MS 8680.

121 Smith, 'Sir Russell Drysdale (1912–1981) A Memoir', *Art Monthly*, no. 110, June 1998, p. 28.

Chapter Five: The Lone Antipodean

1   Bernard Smith, *Australian Painting Today*, University of Queensland Press, Brisbane, 1962, p. 10.

2   Smith, letter to Charles Lloyd Jones, 5 January 1951, BWSP, ML, MSS 5202, Box 2.

3   I am grateful to Jane Eckett for information concerning exhibitions in London and sources. See John and Sunday Reed Papers, State Library of Victoria, MS 13186, Box 5/13.3 (2 of 2), 2 December 1954, and Box 5/13.3 (2 of 2),

11 August 1955. See also Simon Pierse, *Australian Art and Artists in London, 1950–1965: An Antipodean Summer*, Ashgate, Farnham, UK, 2012, pp. 84–5.

4 Smith's ABC talk was published as 'Fifty Years of Painting in Australia', *Meanjin*, vol. 10, no. 4, summer 1951, pp. 354–8.

5 Smith, letter to the Editor, *Sydney Morning Herald*, 16 January 1951 (copy), BWSP, ML, MSS 5202, Box 2.

6 Giovanni Ponti, letter to Smith, 30 January 1951, BWSP, ML, MSS 5202, Box 2.

7 Smith, letter to James McGregor, 15 February 1951, BWSP, ML, MSS 5202, Box 2.

8 ibid.

9 Peter Bellew (ed.), *Aboriginal Paintings–Arnhem Land*, New York Graphic Society and UNESCO, New York, NY, 1959. For a review of the title, see Alan McCulloch, 'Arnhem Land Paintings', *Meanjin*, vol. 2, 1955, p. 237.

10 Nancy Underhill, *Making Australian Art 1916–49: Sydney Ure Smith, Patron and Publisher*, Oxford University Press, Melbourne, 1991, p. 130.

11 Smith, letter to Alan McCulloch, 25 June 1951, *Meanjin* Papers, MS 2005.0004, University of Melbourne Archives, Box 306.

12 Noel Counihan, letter to Smith, 30 December 1951 (copy), BSP, NLA, MS 8680.

13 Joseph Burke, letter to James W. Davidson, 5 October 1953 (copy), University of Melbourne Archives, Burke Papers, 1992.0004, Box 1.

14 Smith, letter to Joseph Burke, 28 May 1953, ibid.

15 Joseph Burke, letter to Smith, 8 June 1953 (copy), BSP, NLA, MS 8680.

16 Smith, 'Canberra', *Poems 1938–1993*, Meanjin, Melbourne, 1996, p. 29.

17 Oskar Spate, 'Early Days at ANU: An Anecdotage', O. H. K. Spate Papers, NLA, MS 7886, Box 7/3/2/2.

18 ibid.

19 E. G. Waterhouse, letter to Smith, 1 January 1954, BWSP, ML, MSS 5202, Box 3, General Correspondence, 1954.

20 Franz Philipp, letter to Smith, 9 February 1954 (copy), BSP, NLA, MS 8680.

21 Joseph Burke, letter to Rex Nan Kivell, 1 March 1955, Rex Nan Kivell Papers, NLA, MS 4000, Box 2/12.

22 Bernard Smith, 'The Interpretation of Nature During the Nineteenth Century', BA Hons thesis, Department of English, University of Sydney, 1952, BSP, NLA, MS 8680, Box 3/17/1, p. 78.

23 ibid., pp. 23, 78.

24 Smith, 'Is there a Radical Tradition in Australian Art?', BSP, NLA, MS 8680, Box 7/54.

25 Peter Beilharz, *Imagining the Antipodes: Culture, Theory and the Visual in the Work of Bernard Smith*, Cambridge University Press, Cambridge, UK, 1997, p. 76.

26 Ihab Hassan, 'Bernard Smith, Global Antipodean: The Language of Trust', *Art Monthly*, no. 144, October 2001, pp. 16–21.

27 John Smith, conversation with the author, 3 February 2010.

28 Elizabeth Heathcote, interview with the author, 26 February 2010.

29 Edmund Blunden, quoted in Smith, 'Coleridge's Ancient Mariner and Cook's Second Voyage', in the *Journal of the Warburg and Courtauld Institutes*, vol. XIX, nos. 1–2, London, 1956, p. 121, and in Smith, *Imagining the Pacific*, p. 135.

30 Charles Mitchell, letter to Frances Yates, 2 March 1955, Warburg Institute Archives, General Correspondence, 1953–56.

31 Smith, 'Coleridge's Ancient Mariner and Cook's Second Voyage', pp. 131 and 117.

32 Gertrud Bing, letter to Smith, 9 March 1955, BWSP, ML, MSS 5202, Box 3.

33 Erwin Panofsky, quoted in Michael Ann Holly, *Panofsky and the Foundations of Art History*, Cornell University Press, Ithaca, NY, and London, 1984, p. 192.

34 The AHRC was created in 1954 as 'a body to speak for and look after the interests of the humanities', see *The Australian Quarterly*, vol. 32, no. 2, Sydney, June 1960, p. 112.

35 Chris Wallace-Crabbe, 'A Day with Bernard Smith', Thesis Eleven symposium, La Trobe University, Melbourne, 23 April 2003.

36 *Herald*, Melbourne, 12 February 1955.

37 Robert Gollan, letter to Smith, 18 January 1956, BWSP, MSS 5202, Box 3.

38 Peter Bellew, quoted in Dutton, *The Innovators*, p. 70.

39 Kenneth Clark, *The Other Half: A Self Portrait*, Harper and Row, New York, NY, 1977, p. 151.

40 Chris Wallace-Crabbe, 'The Other Melbourne', *Meanjin*, no. 3, 1966, p. 333.

41 Chris Wallace-Crabbe, conversation with the author, 25 November 2014.

42 'The Twenty Club, 1957–2011: The First 600 Meetings', compiled by F. G. Nicholls from notes written by Dean Bunney with minor addition by Robert Newton, unpublished (privately held).

43 *University of Melbourne Catalogue of Works of Art*, University of Melbourne, 1971, p. xiv.

44 Kate Challis, 'The Marxist Collector: The Art Collection of Bernard and Kate Smith', paper given at the Legacies of Bernard Smith symposium, University of Melbourne, 20 September 2012.

45 June Stewart, interview with the author, 21 June 2001.

46 Peter Tomory, interview with the author, 14 August 2001.

47 For a detailed study of Hoff's early life and career up to 1960, see Palmer, *Centre of the Periphery*.

48 The historian Margaret Kiddle also sought Bernard's scholarship and advice on Australian architecture for her book *Men of Yesterday: A Social History of the Western District of Victoria 1834–1890*, Melbourne University Press, Melbourne, 1962.

49 Much of this material was deposited in the State Library of Victoria, AAA file.

50 Anita Aarons, letter to Smith, 22 October 1956, BSP, NLA, MS 8680.

51 June Stewart, telephone conversation with the author, 15 October 2008.

52 D. J. Mulvaney, in Peter Gathercole, T. H. Irving and Gregory Melleuish (eds),

Childe and Australia: Archaeology, Politics and Ideas, University of Queensland Press, Brisbane, 1995. p. 213.

53   Chris Wallace-Crabbe, 'Going Up to the Shop', unpublished manuscript, n.d., courtesy of Wallace-Crabbe.

54   Bernard Smith, *The Formalesque: A Guide to Modern Art and its History*, Macmillan, Melbourne, 2007, p. 29.

55   Helen Brack, conversation with the author, 2009.

56   June Stewart, conversation with the author, 4 October 2010.

57   Elwyn Lynn, letter to Smith, 12 March 1961, BWSP, ML, MSS 5202, Box 4.

58   Rosalie Horner, interview with the author, 21 September 2013.

59   Patrick McCaughey, *The Bright Shapes and the True Names: A Memoir*, Text Publishing, Melbourne, 2003, p. 61.

60   Lucy Ellem, conversation with the author, 29 May 2013.

61   John Mulvaney, conversation with the author, 27 October 2011.

62   Smith, letter to Robin Boyd, 22 September 1957 (copy), BSP, NLA, MS 8680.

63   Clifton Pugh, letter to Smith, 26 September 1984 (copy), BSP, NLA, MS 8680.

64   Smith, letter to Sidney Nolan, 1 February 1960 (copy), BSP, NLA, MS 8680.

65   Smith, letter to Kim Bonython, 21 February 1959 (copy), BWSP, ML, MSS 5202, Box 4.

66   Friedrich Nietzsche, *The Birth of Tragedy and the Genealogy of Morals*, Francis Golfing (trans.), Doubleday, New York, NY, 1956, p. 137.

67   Smith, 'The Antipodean Intervention 1959', in *The Critic as Advocate: Selected Essays 1948–1988*, Oxford University Press, Melbourne, 1989, p. 137.

68   Smith, *The Antipodean Manifesto*.

69   Peter Beilharz, 'A Day with Bernard Smith', La Trobe University *Thesis Eleven* symposium, Melbourne, 23 April 2003.

70   Smith, notes for a speech given at the annual dinner of the Fellowship of Australian Writers, Society Restaurant, 1 September 1959, BSP, NLA, MS 8680, Box 20/24. Smith later published a significantly revised version of events, 'The Truth about the Antipodeans', in his *The Death of the Artist as Hero: Essays in History and Culture*, Oxford University Press, Melbourne, 1988.

71   John Brack, the Antipodean Minute Book, BSP, NLA, MS 8680.

72   Smith, 'The Antipodean Manifesto', in *The Antipodean Manifesto: Essays in Art and History*, Oxford University Press, Melbourne, 1976, p. 166.

73   John Brack, letter to Smith, 26 February 1959, BWSP, ML, MSS 5202, add on 2039.

74   Charles and Barbara Blackman, letter to Smith (copy), BSP, NLA, MS 8680.

75   Smith, *The Antipodean Manifesto*.

76   Franz Philipp, 'Antipodeans Aweigh', *Nation*, issue 29, August 1959, p. 18.

77   Smith, cited in Beilharz, *Imagining the Antipodes*, p. 117.

78   David Boyd, interview with the author, 2010, NLA, TRC 6111/2.

79 John Reed, letter to Elwyn Lynn, 1961 (copy), BWSP, ML, MSS 5202, Box 4.

80 Georges Mora, Contemporary Art Society Broadsheet, March 1959, p. 3.

81 Sali Herman, letter to Smith, 19 August 1959, BWSP, ML, MSS 5202, Box 4.

82 I am indebted to Helen Brack for her astute observations about the *Antipodeans* exhibition.

83 Barbara Blackman, 'The Antipodean Affair', *Art and Australia*, vol. 5, no. 4, March 1968, pp. 607–16.

84 Smith, 'The Antipodeans', speech given at the annual dinner of the Fellowship of Australian Writers, Society Restaurant, 1 September 1959, BSP, NLA, MS 8680, Box 3/20/24.

85 Stephen Murray-Smith, letter to Smith, 2 September 1959, BSP, NLA, MS 8680, Box 3/20/24. Murray-Smith was the editor of the literary journal *Overland*.

86 Smith to Albert Tucker, 1 February 1960 (copy), BWSP, ML, MSS 5202, Box 4.

87 See 'Two Art Systems', *Meanjin*, vol. 40, no. 1, April 1981, p. 31. Also published in Smith, *The Death of the Artist as Hero*, p. 269, and in Jim Davidson (ed.), *The Sydney–Melbourne Book*, Allen and Unwin, Sydney, 1985, p. 174.

88 See 'Concerning "Impression in Painting"', in Bernard Smith (ed.), *Documents on Art and Taste in Australia 1770–1914*, Oxford University Press, Melbourne, 1975, pp. 206–8.

89 Smith, notes on Fred Williams, BSP, NLA, MS 8680, Box 6/45/79.

90 Smith, letter to Ursula Hoff, 3 November 1959 (copy), BSP, NLA, MS 8680.

91 Smith, letter to Kenneth Clark, 9 December 1959 (copy), BSP, NLA, MS 8680.

92 Hal Missingham, letter to John Henshaw, 25 February 1958, BSP, NLA, MS 8680. Missingham also invited Bryan Robertson in late March 1959 to act as the Art Gallery's London buyer, replacing David Blaxandall, see Bryan Robertson Papers, Whitechapel Archives, WAG/DIR/13/10.

93 Smith, 'The Myth of Isolation', *Australian Painting Today*, University of Queensland Press, Brisbane, 1962, p. 16.

94 Bryan Robertson, conversation with the author, 13 May 2002.

95 Bryan Robertson, 'An Artist in Our Time', *Listener*, 22 June 1961, p. 1079.

96 Bryan Robertson, letter to Hal Missingham, 22 June 1961 (copy), BSP, NLA, MS 8680.

97 ibid.

98 Bryan Robertson, in *Recent Australian Painting*, Whitechapel Art Gallery exhibition catalogue, 1961.

99 ibid.

100 Robert Hughes, in *Recent Australian Painting*, Whitechapel Art Gallery exhibition catalogue, 1961, p. 13.

101 ibid., pp. 19–20.

102 Smith, 'Sir Russell Drysdale (1912–1981): A Memoir', *Art Monthly*, no. 110, June 1998, p. 29.

103 John Douglas Pringle, 'The Australian Painter', *Observer*, London, 4 June 1961. Pringle was a well-informed and brilliant editor. He lived and worked in Australia during the 1950s and 1960s as editor of the *Sydney Morning Herald*.

104 'The Rebirth of Australian Painting', the John Murtagh Macrossan Lecture, 1961, in Smith, *Australian Painting Today*, University of Queensland Press, Brisbane, p. 31.

105 Daniel Thomas, 'The Margins Fight Back', *Art and Australia*, vol. 26, no. 1, 1988, pp. 60–71.

106 Smith, opening address at the S. H. Ervin Gallery for the exhibition *Aspects of Australian Figurative Painting 1942–1962: Dreams, Fears and Desires*, 16 April 1984 (copy), BSP, NLA, MS 8680.

107 Smith, letter to Vincent Buckley, 8 December 1984 (copy), BSP, NLA, MS Acc. 10.088, Box 66.

Chapter Six: The 1960s

1   J. C. Beaglehole, letter to Smith, 14 January 1963, BSP, NLA, MS 8680.

2   Smith, letter to William Dobell, 22 October 1962 (copy), BWSP, ML, MSS 5202, Box 4.

3   Smith, letter to Brian Johnstone, 24 October 1961 (copy), BWSP, ML, MSS 5202, add on 2039, Box 2; and Smith, letter to G. D. Richardson, 4 July 1961 (copy), ibid.

4   Smith, letter to Daniel Thomas, 14 June 1960 (copy), BWSP, ML, MSS 5202, Box 4.

5   Smith, letter to Neville Wran, 28 February 1983 (copy), BSP, NLA, MS 8680.

6   Ursula Hoff, 'Consistent View of History', *Art and Australia*, vol. 1, no. 2, 1963, pp. 119–20.

7   Elwyn Lynn, 'A History of Australian Painting', *Meanjin*, vol. 22, no. 2, 1963, pp. 229–35.

8   John Brack, 'Critic or Historian', *Australian Book Review*, December 1962, p. 26.

9   Julie and Klaus Friedeberger, conversation with the author, London, 2013.

10 Alan McCulloch, 'Shake-out is Needed at the Tate Show', *Herald*, Melbourne, 28 March 1962, Tate Gallery Archives, 92/172/1.

11 Smith, notes for the opening of the *Antipodeans* exhibition, 29 August 1959, BSP, NLA, MS 8680.

12 John Brack, letter to Smith, 20 May 1962, BSP, NLA, MS 8680.

13 Quentin Bell, 'The Received Image', *Listener*, London, 28 February 1963.

14 George Butcher, *Guardian*, London, 24 January 1963, p. 11.

15 For the more scathing reviews, see Waldemar Januszczak's review, *Sunday Times*, 22 September 2013; Brian Sewell's review, *London Evening Standard*, 23 September 2013; and Adrian Serle's review, *Guardian*, 17 September 2013.

16   Smith, draft, 'The Five Foot Gap', BSP, NLA, MS 8680.

17   Eric Westbrook, quoted in Christopher Marshall, 'Mind the Gap! Bernard Smith versus the Museum, 1961–95', paper delivered at the Legacies of Bernard Smith symposium, University of Sydney, 9–10 November 2012.

18   Smith, 'The Five Foot Gap: A Cultural Centre for Potential Connoisseurs or Potential Convicts', notes, BSP, NLA, MS Acc. 10.088, Box 39, and 'Design for Vandals: More Protests Against the Five-Foot Gap', *Nation*, no. 66, 8 April 1961, pp.17–18.

19   Smith, typed statement on the Cultural Centre Plans, 1960, BSP, NLA, MS 8680.

20   Daniel Thomas, letter to Smith, 16 January 1962, BWSP, ML, MSS 5202, Box 4.

21   Franz Philipp, letter to Smith, 14 January 1962, BWSP, ML, MSS 5202, Box 4.

22   John Perceval, letter to Smith, 29 May 1962 (copy), BSP, NLA, MS 8680.

23   Ursula Hoff, with an introduction by T. G. Rosenthal, *The Art of Arthur Boyd*, Andre Deutsch, London, 1986, p. 53.

24   Franz Philipp, *Arthur Boyd*, Thames and Hudson, London, 1967, pp. 100–6.

25   Smith, lecture notes on 'Nolan's Iconomorphic Form', May 1962, BSP, NLA, MS 8680.

26   See *Listener*, London, 19 July 1962, pp. 93–5 and republished in Smith, *The Antipodean Manifesto*, pp. 41–6.

27   Damian Smith, conversation with the author, 23 April 2014.

28   Smith, diary, 1962, BSP, NLA, MS Acc. 10.64, Box 1.

29   L. J. Ray, letter to Smith, 1 March 1962 (copy), BSP, NLA, MS 8680.

30   Smith, notes on Courbet, BSP, NLA, MS Acc. 10.088, Box 14.

31   Joseph Burke, letter to Smith, 24 April 1962, BWSP.

32   June Stewart, conversations with the author, 21 June 2001 and June Philipp, conversation with the author, 24 June 2003.

33   Sidney Nolan, interview with Bernard Smith, 1962, transcript, BSP, NLA, MS 8680.

34   Joseph Burke, letter to Alfred Barr Jr, 22 June 1962 (copy), BSP, NLA, MS 8680.

35   Alfred Barr Jr, letter to Smith, ibid.

36   Smith, 'Braudel's Long View', *Scripsi*, vol. 6, no. 1, Melbourne, 1990, p. 173.

37   Smith, diary, 1962, BSP, NLA, MS Acc. 10.64, Box 1; see Roland Pullen, 'How he Found "Lost" Paintings', *Herald*, Melbourne, 15 February 1965.

38   Ursula Hoff, letter to Smith, 30 August 1962, BSP, NLA, MS 8680. For the Lehmann article, see *Honi Soit*, 31 July 1962, p. 12.

39   Smith, diary, 1962, BSP, NLA, MS Acc. 10.64, Box 1.

40   ibid.

41   Ursula Hoff, letter to Smith, 15 October 1962, BWSP, ML, MSS 5202, Box 4.

42   Smith, letter to Clem Christesen, 1962, BWSP, ML MSS 5202, Box 4.

43   Ursula Hoff, letter to Smith, September 1962, BWSP, ML, MSS 5202, Box 4.

44   Smith, letter to Ursula Hoff, 24 November 1962, Hoff Papers, University of

Melbourne Archives MS 85/59, Box 10/1/57.

45 Sybil Gordon Kantor, *Alfred H. Barr Jr. and the Intellectual Origins of the Museum of Modern Art*, MIT Press, Cambridge, MA, 2002, pp. 365–6.

46 Smith, diary, 1962, BSP, NLA, MS Acc. 10.64, Box 1.

47 Joseph Smith, *The Cold War, 1945–1965*, Blackwell, Oxford, UK, 1989, pp. 40–1.

48 Ursula Hoff, letter to Smith, 8 November 1962 (copy), BSP, NLA, MS 8680.

49 Smith, letter to Ursula Hoff, 24 November 1962 (copy), BSP, NLA, MS 8680.

50 Christopher Heathcote, *A Quiet Revolution: The Rise of Australian Art, 1946–1968*, Text Publishing, Melbourne, 1995, p. 156–7.

51 Robert Hughes, 'Dog Eats Dog', *Nation*, Sydney, 26 January 1963, p. 19.

52 Smith, letter to Ursula Hoff, 21 August 1963, Hoff Papers, University of Melbourne Archives, Box 10/1/57.

53 See Palmer, *Centre of the Periphery*, pp. 223–7; and also Peter Tomory, interview with the author, 14 August 2001.

54 Smith, 'Great Display of Recent British Sculpture', *Age*, 27 July 1963.

55 Smith, 'The French Art Exhibition', *Meanjin*, vol. XII, no. 2, 1953, p. 165.

56 Smith, 'Extravagant Claim not Realised', *Age*, 18 December 1963.

57 Smith, 'Wither Painting', in *The Critic as Advocate: Selected Essays, 1941–1988*, Oxford University Press, Melbourne, 1989, p. 238.

58 Smith, 'Monthly Review', *Age*, March 1982.

59 Smith, notebook, 1964, BSP, NLA, MS 10.064, Box 1.

60 See A. D. S. Donaldson and Ann Stephen, *J. W. Power Abstraction–Création Paris 1934*, with contributions by Virginia Spate and Gladys Fabre, Power Publications, Sydney, 2012, p. 14.

61 Bernice Murphy, *Museum of Contemporary Art: Vision and Context*, Museum of Contemporary Art, Sydney, 1993, p. 40.

62 Smith, letter to Ralph Farrell, 23 July 1966 (copy), BSP, NLA, MS 8680.

63 Smith, letter to John White, 22 June 1964 (copy), BSP, NLA, MS 8680.

64 See Richard Haese, *Permanent Revolution: Mike Brown and the Australian Avant-Garde 1953–1997*, Miegunyah Press, Melbourne, 2011, p. 104.

65 Smith, 'Brown's Show Most Original for Year', *Age*, 14 October 1964.

66 Joseph Brown, interview with the author, 24 July 2008.

67 See *The Joseph Brown Collection: At NGV Australia*, National Gallery of Victoria, Melbourne, 2004; and Brown, interview with the author, 24 July 2008.

68 Oscar Edwards, letter to Alan Gamble, 14 June 1964 (copy), BSP, NLA, MS 8680. Oscar Edwards was a rare type of collector in Australia, whose eclectic collection consisted of works by major European, British, Asian and modernist artists, ranging from Asian art to Dubuffet, Fautrier, Naum Gabo, Picasso, Paolozzi, Soulages, Rodin, Chagall, Matisse and Alfred Wallis, see *Art and Australia*, vol. 7, no. 2, September 1969, pp. 132–43.

69 Ursula Hoff, 'To the Editor', in *Art and Australia*, vol. 1, no. 4, Sydney, winter

1964, p. 276.

70   Herbert Read, 'The Power Bequest: A Reply', *Meanjin*, vol. 3, 1964, p. 320.

71   Smith, letter to David Boyd, 12 December 1964, David Boyd Papers (privately held).

72   Robert Hughes, *Things I Didn't Know: A Memoir*, Random House, New York, NY, and Sydney, 2006, p. 272.

73   Andrew Riemer, *Hughes*, Duffy and Snellgrove, Sydney, 2001, p. 35; Hughes, *Things I Didn't Know: A Memoir*, pp. 272–3.

74   Riemer, *Hughes*, p.36.

75   Robert Hughes, 'Painting in Australia', *London Magazine*, November 1963, pp. 66–7.

76   Smith, letter to the editor of *Nation*, Sydney, 28 August 1963 (copy), BSP, NLA, MS 8680.

77   Smith, notes, BSP, NLA, MS 8680, Box 5.

78   Smith, diary, 28 March and 8 April 1987, BSP, NLA, MS Acc. 10.64, Box 3.

79   Smith, 'Changing Posture', *Australian Book Review*, no. 199, April 1998, p. 8.

80   Smith's *Age* review was republished in his book, *The Critic as Advocate*, p. 193.

81   For an extensive revision of McCahon's response to William Hodges, see Simmons, *Tuhituhi*, pp. 128, 288.

82   Smith, notebook, 1966, BSP, NLA, MS Acc. 10.64, Box 1.

83   I am grateful to Rodney James for information on McCulloch and permission to quote from an extract of his forthcoming biography, *Letters to a Critic: Alan McCulloch's World of Art*.

84   Smith, 'Jack Lindsay's Biographies of Artists', in Bernard Smith (ed.), *Culture and History: Essays Presented to Jack Lindsay*, Hale and Iremonger, Sydney, 1984, p. 294.

85   T. J. Clark wrote *Image of the People: Gustav Courbet and the Second French Republic 1848–1851*, Thames and Hudson, Melbourne, which was published in 1973, and Jack Lindsay's biography, *Gustave Courbet: His Life and Art*, Adams and Dart, London, was also published in 1973.

86   Smith, diary, 1966, BSP, NLA, MS Acc. 10.64, Box 1.

87   Patrick McCaughey, letter to Smith, 16 December 2008 (copy), BSP, NLA, MS 8680.

Chapter Seven: The Construction of Power

1   See Peter Kennedy and Janine Burke, 'Australian Art Scene in the 1970s', *Art and Australia*, vol. 18, no. 12, 1980, pp. 133–6.

2   John Kavanagh, '15 Years On: The Power Institute in Review', *Art Network*, vol. 8, Sydney, 1983, p. 15.

3   Oscar Edwards, *Sydney Morning Herald*, 14 January 1967.

4   Kavanagh, '15 Years On', p. 14.

5   Hughes, 'Bequest and Behest: Keeping Faith with John Wardell Power', *Nation*, 28 July 1962, p. 16.

6   ibid.

7   Herbert Read, 'Art in an Australian University', *Art and Australia,* vol. 1, no. 3, Sydney, 1963, p. 175.

8   Ann Stephen, in roundtable conversation at the Legacies of Bernard Smith symposium, 10 November 2012, Art Gallery of New South Wales, Sydney.

9   Smith, interview with the author, 1 August 2008.

10   Rudolf Arnheim, *The Split and the Structure*, University of California Press, Oakland, CA, 1996, p. 6.

11   'The Implementation of the Power Bequest', in *Dr John Power and the Power Bequest, the Power Institute and the Power Foundation: An Illustrated Survey*, the Power Institute of Fine Arts, University of Sydney, Sydney, c. 1976, p. 8.

12   Clement Greenberg, *Avant-Garde Attitudes: New Art in the Sixties*, Power Institute of Fine Arts, University of Sydney, Sydney, 1969, p. 2.

13   Smith, 'Sir Herbert Read and the Power Bequest', first published in *Meanjin*, vol. 23, no. 1, 1964, and later in *The Antipodean Manifesto: Essays in Art and History*, Oxford University Press, Melbourne, 1976, p. 83.

14   John Kaldor, 29 May 1968, unknown source.

15   Smith, 'The Power Bequest Exhibition 1968', in *Art and Australia*, vol. 5, no. 4, 1968, p. 630.

16   Phillip Knightley, 'Freedom's Necessary Lies', *Australian Review of Books, The Australian*, September 1999, p. 3. During World War II Joseph Burke had been seconded into MI5 in Britain and had been privy to high-security information, including meetings with the Americans on atomic bomb research. He had also been very close to Wilmarth S. Lewis, a key American intelligence figure before and during the war. It is possible that Burke could have had an alliance with a joint CIA and British Intelligence organisation, and much speculation circulated about Burke's cultural–political connections. Clem Christesen, as Cassandra Pybus notes, was deeply suspicious of the Australian Association of Cultural Freedom's financial backing and Christesen revealed in his editorial of 1954 that the Congress of Cultural Freedom was funded by the CIA. This created hostility between him and Burke, and *Meanjin's* existence at the university was precarious for some time. If Christesen was aware of the CIA funding, it is only reasonable to assume that so was Bernard Smith. See Cassandra Pybus, 'The CIA as Culture Vultures', *Australian Book Review*, August 2000, pp. 29–31.

17   Patrick McCaughey, quoted in Richard Haese, *Permanent Revolution*, p. 143.

18   Both McCulloch and Lynn knew and admired Greenberg, but the formal invitation would have come from Bernard Smith.

19   Patrick McCaughey, 'After Greenberg: New Bearings or Old Directions?'

Meanjin, vol. 4, 1968, pp. 480–5.

20 Terry Smith, 'The Style of the Sixties', *Quadrant*, Sydney, March–April 1969, pp. 49–53.

21 Greenberg, 'Avant-Garde Attitudes', p. 9.

22 Herbert Read, *Art Now*, Faber & Faber, London, 1933, p. 9.

23 Ronald Millar, interview with the author, 17 March 2009.

24 Smith, paper on surrealism, 16 October 1940, BSP, NLA, MS 8680, Box 1/5, p. 2.

25 Elwyn Lynn, 'Clement Greenberg sees Australia', *Art and Australia*, vol. 6, no. 2, September 1968, p. 152.

26 Elwyn Lynn, letter to Smith, 20 April 1968 (copy), in which he quotes Margaret Rose, BSP, NLA, MS 8680.

27 Daniel Thomas, telephone interview with the author, 7 February 2011.

28 Elwyn Lynn, 'Clement Greenberg sees Australia', pp. 150–2.

29 David Saunders, letter to Smith, 25 June 1968, Bernard Smith Papers, Fisher Library, University of Sydney Archives, MS G 35, Box 3.

30 Gordon Thomson, interview with the author, 18 June 2008.

31 Smith, letter to Bruce Williams, 18 March 1968, Fisher Library, University of Sydney, MS G 35/3, .

32 Smith, notebook, 1966–68, BSP, NLA, MS Acc. 10.64, Box 1.

33 ibid.

34 Smith, 'The Role of an Institute of Fine Arts in the University of Sydney', Power Lecture, Sydney University Arts Association, *Arts: The Journal of the Sydney University Arts Association*, vol. 6, Sydney, 1969, p. 5.

35 Jill Montgomery, 'Defense d'afficher: loi du 29 juillet 1881 . . . Paris May 1968', *Art & Text*, Melbourne and New York, NY, no. 16, 1984/85, p. 37.

36 Greenberg, quoted in Smith, 'Some Northern Critics of Southern Art', in *The Death of the Artist as Hero*, p. 276.

37 Smith, 'The Role of an Institute of Fine Arts in the University of Sydney', p. 5.

38 ibid., p. 7.

39 ibid., p. 14.

40 ibid., pp. 14–15.

41 Alexis Carrel, quoted in the inaugural catalogue of the *First Exhibition of the Teachers' College Art Club*, August 1938, BSP, NLA, MS 8680, Box 1.

42 Smith, 'The Role of an Institute of Fine Arts in the University of Sydney', p. 17.

43 Richard Larter, conversation with the author, 26 July 2010.

44 Smith, draft introduction for Christo, BSP, NLA, MS 8680, Box 3/75.

45 Donald Brook, 'The Undoing of Art History (Part I)', *Artlink*, vol. 21, no. 4, 2001, p. 68.

46 Gary Willis, in *Tony Woods: Archive*, Art Information, Melbourne, 2013, p. 43.

47 Daniel Thomas, 'Empathy and Understanding', *Artlink*, vol. 26, no. 4, 2006,

p. 29; and Thomas, interview with the author, 10 February 2011.

48   Peter Beilharz, *Postmodern Socialism: Romanticism, City and State*, Melbourne University Press, Melbourne, 1994, p. 73.

49   George Gittoes, interview with the author, 16 March 2015.

50   Robyn Ravlich, 'Art Works: Vale Bernard Smith', ABC Radio National, 18 September 2011.

51   Power Institute of Fine Arts, Fisher Library, University of Sydney Archives, G 35/3.

52   Donald Brook, in Therese Kenyon, *Under a Hot Tin Roof: Art, Passion and Politics at the Tin Sheds Art Workshop*, State Library of NSW Press, Sydney, pp. 10, 89.

53   Marr Grounds, quoted in ibid., p. 12.

54   ibid., p. 13.

55   Smith, 'Wither Painting', p. 243.

56   See Smith, 'Concerning Donald Brook's "New Theory of Art"', *Meanjin*, vol. 47, no. 1, 1988, pp. 5–10.

57   Donald Brook, 'From the Margin', paper delivered at 200 Gertrude Street, Melbourne, May 1988, for the Australian Bicentennial Contemporary Art Spaces Project 'STOP LOOK LISTEN: The Present and Past in Australian Art and Criticism'.

58   Smith, 'Elwyn Lynn on Sidney Nolan', in *The Critic as Advocate*, p. 145.

59   Lily Lynn, conversation with the author, 24 February 2013.

60   Patrick McCaughey, 'Signs of a Power Struggle for the Fine Arts in Australia', *Age*, Melbourne, 29 January 1972.

61   Smith, 'A Magisterial Work', *Australian Book Review*, no. 170, 1995, p. 57.

62   Smith, 'Reflections of the 1940s', BSP, NLA, MS 8680, Box 6/44/72, p. 5.

63   George Steiner, 'Ice-Cold in Arcadia', review of Miranda Carter's *Anthony Blunt*, *Times Literary Supplement*, 2 November 2011, p. 3.

64   Donald Brook, in conversation with the author, 1 December 2010.

65   Donald Brook, letter to Joseph Burke, Joseph Burke Papers, University of Melbourne Archives, 78/39/ 1/92.

66   Joseph Burke, character reference for Brook, ibid.

67   John Passmore, character reference for Donald Brook, 30 April 1973, ibid.

68   Donald Brook, '1968', *Art Monthly Australia*, no. 195, 2006, p. 30. See Heather Barker and Charles Green, 'Flight from the Object: Donald Brook, Inhibrodress and the Emergence of Post-Studio Art in Early 1970s Sydney', *emaj*, issue 4, 2009, p. 1, *melbourneartjournal.unimelb.edu.au/E-MAJ*.

69   Smith, 'Making the Future', September 1973, BSP, NLA, MS 8680, Box 3/22.

70   For an account of the new art imperatives of the 1970s, see Charles Green's *Peripheral Vision: Contemporary Australian Art, 1970–1994*, Craftsman House, Sydney, 1995.

71   Joanna Mendelssohn, 'The Yellow House: A Brief History', *Art and Australia*, vol.

27, no. 4, Sydney, 1990, p. 570.

72 Speech by Bernard Smith for the 25th Anniversary of the Glebe Society, c. 1994, BSP, NLA, MS 8680.

73 Max Solling, 'Bernard Smith as Activist', paper given at the Legacies of Bernard Smith symposium, Art Gallery of New South Wales, Sydney, 10 November 2012.

74 John Smith, eulogy at Bernard Smith's funeral service, 7 September 2011.

75 Smith, speech at the exhibition *Vietnam*, 3 March 1968 (copy), BSP, NLA, MS Acc. 10.088, Box 39.

76 ibid.

77 Neil Clerehan, letter to Smith, 26 June 1974, BWSP, ML, MSS 5202, add on 2039, Box 2; and Smith, letter to Clerehan, 5 July 1974 (copy), ibid.

78 Smith, 'On Writing Art History in Australia', p. 15.

79 Smith, 'The New Commonwealth Patronage and the Arts', c. 1973, BSP, NLA, MS 8680, Box 4/28/19.

80 The Ruth Adeney Koori Award (RAKA) was established as an Indigenous award in memory of Bernard's wife Kate, who died in 1989.

81 Smith, 'The New Commonwealth Patronage and the Arts'.

82 Kate Smith, diary entry, 1974, BSP, NLA, MS Acc. 10.64, Box 6.

83 ibid.

84 Terry Smith, letter to Joseph Burke, 16 August 1973, Joseph Burke Papers, University of Melbourne Archives, 78/39.

85 Smith, travel diary, 6 October 1973, BSP, NLA, MS 10.064, Box 1.

86 Smith, 'Art and Industry: A Systematic Approach', *Studio International, Journal of Modern Art*, vol. 187, no. 965, London, April 1974, p. 158.

87 ibid., p. 158.

88 Published in *Australian and International Art Monthly*, no. 5, October 1987, pp. 2–4 and no. 6, November 1987, pp. 3–6; Smith, 'On Writing Art History in Australia', p. 8.

89 Christine Harris, correspondence with the author, 16 May 2003.

90 Humphrey McQueen, conversation with the author, 9 November 2010.

91 Smith, letter to Paul McGillick, unpublished letter, n.d., courtesy of Paul McGillick.

92 Jim Davidson, 'Mr Whitlam's Cultural Revolution', *Journal of Australian Studies*, May 1987, La Trobe University Press, Melbourne, p. 83.

93 Smith, 'The Australian Government and the Visual Arts: Is it a Labor Policy?', BSP, NLA, MS 8680, Box 4/37.

94 Jacques Derrida, 'The Truth in Painting', in Andreas C. Papadakis (ed.), *The New Modernism: Deconstructionist Tendencies in Art*, Academy Group, London, 1988, pp. 19, 24.

95 Smith, 'The Australian Government and the Visual Arts'.

96 Smith, 'Notes on Abstract Art', BSP, NLA, MS 8680, Box 6/42/59.

97 Kate Smith, diary entry, 1974, BSP, NLA, MS Acc. 10.64, Box 6.

98 Smith, 'Notes on Abstract Art', p. 4.

99 Smith, interview with Paul McGillick and unpublished notes, n.d., courtesy of Paul McGillick.

100 Kate Smith, diary entry, 9 March 1974, BSP, NLA, MS 10.064, Box 6.

101 T. S. Eliot, *Burnt Norton*, *Four Quartets*, Faber & Faber, London, 1959, pp. 13–14.

102 Smith, letter to Ernst Gombrich, 21 April 1974, Warburg Institute Archives, correspondence, 1953–56.

103 Ian Donaldson, conversation with the author, 21 September 2012.

104 Smith, letter to Bruce Williams, 15 November 1971 (copy), BSP, NLA, MS 8680.

105 See Kenneth Clark, *Provincialism*, The English Association, London, 1962.

106 Smith, letter to Frank Eyre, 18 February 1975 (copy), BWSP, ML, MSS 5202, add on 2039, Box 2.

107 Michael Rosenthal, interview with the author, 15 May 2013.

108 Terry Smith, interview with the author, 2 September 2014.

Chapter Eight: The Constant Revisionist

1 Smith, 'History as Criticism', in Attwood (ed.), *Boundaries of the Past*, p. 1.

2 Jim Davidson, interview with the author, 8 August 2014.

3 Kate Challis, 'The Marxist Collector: The Art Collection of Bernard and Kate Smith', unpublished manuscript.

4 ibid.

5 *Journals of Captain James Cook*, vol. III, p. ccxxiii, quoted in Bernard Smith, *Imagining the Pacific*, p. 197.

6 Smith, diary, 15 April 1978, BSP, NLA, MS Acc. 10.64, Box 2.

7 *Journals of Captain James Cook*, vol. 2, p. 119, quoted in Bernard Smith, *Imagining the Pacific*, p. 120.

8 I am grateful to Glyndar Williams for alerting me to Bernard's importance in the revision of Beaglehole's authority.

9 Smith, 'Cook's Posthumous Reputation', in Robin Fisher and Hugh Johnston, *Captain James Cook and his Times*, ANU Press, Canberra, 1979, p. 185.

10 Pierre-Édouard Lémontey, quoted in Bernard Smith, 'Lémontey Lecture', in *Post Scripts: The 1988 Boyer Lectures*, ABC, Sydney, 1989.

11 Smith, 'Depicting Pacific Peoples', BSP, NLA, MS 8680, Box 6/54/77, p. 22.

12 'William Hodges and English *Plein-air* Painting', in Smith, *Imagining the Pacific*, p. 132.

13 Smith, proposal to Yale University Press 1978, BWSP, ML, MSS 5202, add on 2022, Box 2.

14 Smith, letter to Ursula Hoff, 14 November 1980, Hoff Papers, University of

Melbourne Archives, MS 85/59; 85/68, Box 10/1/57.

15 Janine Burke, interview with the author, October 2014.

16 Smith, quoted in Peter Fuller, *The Australian Scapegoat: Towards an Antipodean Aesthetic*, University of Western Australia Press, Perth, 1986, p. x.

17 Anthony Bradley and Terry Smith (eds), *Australian Art and Architecture: Essays Presented to Bernard Smith*, Oxford University Press, Melbourne, 1980, p. vii.

18 Virginia Spate, letter to Smith, 25 June 1979, BSP, NLA, MS Acc. 10.088, Box 39.

19 Joseph Burke, quoted in Smith's diary, 14 June 1978, BSP, NLA, MS Acc. 10.64, Box 2.

20 Janet Malcolm, 'Thoughts on Autobiography from an Abandoned Autobiography', *New York Review of Books*, vol. 47, no. 7, 29 April – 12 May 2010, p. 16.

21 Smith, letter to Jack Lindsay, 26 November 1982 (copy), BSP, NLA, MS 8680, Box 1/1.

22 Jack Lindsay, letter to Smith, 1 December 1982 (copy), ibid.

23 Vincent Buckley, quoted in John McLaren, *Journey Without Arrival: The Life and Writing of Vincent Buckley*, Australian Scholarly Publishing, Melbourne, 2009, p. 5.

24 Terry Smith, video address for Bernard Smith's Tribute at the National Gallery of Victoria, 2011.

25 Smith, letter to Brian Johns, 10 March 1983, BWSP, ML, MSS 5202, add on 2022, Box 2.

26 Smith, quoted in 'Four Decades Later, a Festival Premiere', *Age*, Melbourne, 10 March 1986.

27 Ihab Hassan, letter to Smith, 8 November, 1996, BWSP, ML, MSS 5202, add on 2210, Box 1.

28 Smith, diary, 26 May 1987, BSP, NLA, MS Acc. 10.64, Box 3.

29 Smith, 'Art and the NGV', BSP, NLA, MS 8680, Box 8/56/163.

30 Benjamin, *Selected Writings, Vol. 1, 1913–1926*, p. 14.

31 Daniel Thomas, 'Aboriginal Art as Art: Who was Interested', paper given at New Visions: Histories of Art in Australia, NGV International, 3 June 2006.

32 Smith, *The Spectre of Truganini*, 1980 Boyer Lectures, ABC, Sydney, 1981, p. 10.

33 ibid., p. 14.

34 Smith, 'History as Criticism', p. 1.

35 Heinrich Wölfflin, *Principles of Art History: The Problem of the Development of Style in Later Art*, M. D. Hottinger (trans.), Dover Publications, New York, NY, 1950, p. 11.

36 See David Hansen, 'Seeing Truganini', *Australian Book Review*, no. 321, May 2010, pp. 45–53, and Gareth Knapman, 'The Pacificator: Discovering the Lost Bust of George Augustus Robinson', *La Trobe Journal*, State of Library of Victoria, Melbourne, no. 86, December 2010, pp. 37–52.

37 C. P. Mountford, *Australian Aboriginal Art*, exhibition catalogue, The Berkeley Galleries, London, 1950.

38 Smith, *Australian Painting 1788–1970*, 2nd edn, Oxford University Press, Melbourne, p. 223–4.

39 See R. and C. Berndt 'Aboriginal Art in Central-Western Northern Territory', *Meanjin*, vol. 9, no. 3, Melbourne, 1950, p. 183.

40 Smith, 'Notes for the Opening of Red Letter Press Exhibition', 27 November 1986, BSP, NLA, MS 8680, Box 6/43/67.

41 Fred Myers, 'Unsettled Business: Acrylic Painting, Tradition, and Indigenous Being', paper given at the Australian Institute of Aboriginal and Torres Strait Islander Studies Conference, September 2001, BSP, NLA, MS 8680.

42 Smith, *The Spectre of Truganini*, pp. 12, 20.

43 ibid, p. 52

44 Jack Lindsay, letter to Smith, 30 May 1981, BSP, NLA, MS 8680, Box 1/1.

45 Patricia Rolfe, *Bulletin*, 5 June 1984, p. 91.

46 Jack Lindsay, letter to Smith, 23 October 1979 (copy), BSP, NLA, MS 8680, Box 1/1.

47 John Arnold, paper given at the Legacies of Bernard Smith symposium, Art Gallery of New South Wales, Sydney, 10 November 2012.

48 Jack Lindsay, 'The Alienated Australian Intellectual', *Meanjin*, vol. 22, no. 92, no. 1, 1963, p. 48.

49 Kate Challis (granddaughter), 'A Personal Tribute', NGV memorial service for Bernard Smith, 15 December 2011.

50 Patrick McCaughey, *The Bright Shape and the True Names*, Text Publishing, Melbourne, 2003, p. 61.

51 Janine Burke, interview with the author, 25 September 2014; Geoff Hogg, interview with the author, 25 September 2014.

52 Tim Bonyhady, 'The Uncritical Culture', *Eureka Street*, October 1997.

53 See Paul Taylor, 'Clement Greenberg and Post Modernism, an Interview', *Art and Australia*, vol. 18, no.2, Sydney, 1980, pp. 141–4.

54 See Heather Barker and Charles Green, 'Provincialism No More: *Art & Text*', in *Impresario: Paul Taylor, The Melbourne Years, 1981–1984*, Surplus and Monash University Museum of Art, Melbourne, 2013, p. 113.

55 Green, *Peripheral Vision*, pp. 67, 73.

56 Paul Taylor, *Popism*, exhibition catalogue, National Gallery of Victoria, Melbourne, 1982.

57 Smith, letter to Jack Lindsay, 3 October 1984 (copy), BWSP, ML, MSS 5202, add on 3039, Box 2.

58 Geoff Hogg, conversation with the author, 25 September 2014.

59 Humphrey McQueen, 'Our Smith of Smiths', *24 Hours*, ABC Radio, August 1996, p. 60.

60 Oskar Spate, typeset copy of review of Smith's *European Vision and the South*

Pacific for *Age*, Melbourne, BWSP, ML, MSS 5202, add on 2039, Box 3.

61 Philip Morrissey, Legacies of Bernard Smith symposium, University of Melbourne, 21 September 2012.

62 Smith, letter to David Hanlon, 27 November 1985, BWSP, ML, MSS 5202, add on 2039, Box 3.

63 Greg Dening, 'Disembodied Artifacts: Edward Said's Culture and Imperialism', *Scripsi*, vol. 9, no. 1, 9 September 1993, p. 80.

64 Smith, 'Angry Penguins. . .', BSP, NLA, MS 8680, Box 7, p. 16.

65 Smith, 'The Dark Years', BSP, NLA, MS 8680, Box 8/57/62, p. 3.

66 Smith, 'Counihan and Painting', BSP, NLA, MS 8680, Box 7/51/118.

67 Smith, letter to Pat Counihan, 30 May 1986, Counihan Papers, NLA, MS 9107/7.

68 Richard Haese, 'Permanently Red', *Meridian*, vol. 13, no. 1, 1994, p. 66.

69 Smith, diary, 5 January 1982, BSP, NLA, MS Acc. 10.64, Box 3.

70 Smith to Manning Clark, 15 March 1990, Manning Clark Papers, NLA, MS 7550, Series I, Box 19/158.

71 Sara Kelly, telephone conversation with the author, 2 November 2014.

72 Michael Davie, 'Penguins Sighted on South Bank', *Age*, 21 May 1988.

73 Max Harris, *Angry Penguins and Realist Painting in Melbourne in the 1940s*, exhibition catalogue, Southbank Centre, London, 1988, pp. 15–17.

74 Smith, 'Reds, and Other Colours', 'Monthly Review', *Age*, vol. 1, no. 6, October 1981, pp. 7–8.

75 Smith, notes for opening address of 'Aspects of Australian Painting 1942–1962: Dreams, Fears and Desires', or 'What Did You Do in the Cold War Daddy?' BSP, NLA, MS 8680, Box 5/38/35.

76 Smith, 'Art and Industry: A Systematic Approach', *Studio International*, vol. 187, no. 985, London, April 1974, republished in *The Death of the Artist as Hero*, p. 35.

77 Smith, 'Australian Art in England', *Modern Painters*, vol. 1, no. 4, 1988/89, pp. 86–9.

78 Smith, diary, 6 May 1988, BSP, NLA, MS Acc. 10.64, Box 3.

79 These included Manning Clark, H. C. Coombs, Sir Zelman Cowen, Shirley Hazzard, Bob Hawke, Dame Roma Mitchell and Hugh Stretton.

80 See Smith, 'Lémontey Lecture', in *Post Scripts: The 1988 Boyer Lectures*, ABC, Sydney, 1989. Later in the 1990s Bernard became a member of the Australian Republican Movement.

81 Peter Sutton (ed.), *Dreamings: The Art of Aboriginal Australia* (1st edn), George Braziller, New York, NY, 1988, p. 3.

82 Smith, diary, 7 January 1989, BSP, NLA, MS Acc. 10.64, Box 3.

83 Smith, diary, 14 January 1989, BSP, ibid.

84 Mary Gilmore, 'Never Admit Pain', in Kate Smith's 1976 diary, BSP, NLA, MS Acc. 10.64, Box 6.

85 Manning Clark, letter to Smith, 12 February 1989, BSP, NLA, MS 8680.

86   Smith, diary, 7 January 1989, BSP, NLA, MS Acc. 10.64.

87   Kate Smith, *Tales from Sydney Cove*, Bernard Smith (ed.), Helicon Press, Melbourne, 2000, p. 12.

88   ibid., p. 104.

89   Jim Davidson, *Meanjin*, vol. 36, no. 4, December 1977, p. 419.

90   Tamsin Donaldson, conversation with the author, 2010.

91   Kate Challis, 'The Marxist Collector'.

92   Jim Davidson, interview with the author, 8 August 2014.

93   Smith, BSP, NLA, MS 8680, Box 7/49/97; and 'Peter Fuller's Impulse to Destroy', *Australian Society*, March 1989, p. 41.

94   Smith, diary, 1990, BSP, NLA, MS Acc. 10.64, Box 3.

95   Kate Challis, 'A Personal Tribute'; and Kate Challis, conversation with the author, December 2014.

96   Smith, undated letter, c. 1996, BWSP, ML, MSS 5202, add on 2210, Box 2.

97   Ian McLean, 'False Messenger: Visual Culture, Visual Studies and the New Art History', paper delivered at the Art Association of Australia annual conference, 1999.

98   Rex Butler, *Radical Revisionism: An Anthology of Writings on Australian Art*, Institute of Modern Art, Brisbane, 2005, p. 22.

99   ibid.

100 Geoffrey Batchen in Ian Burn, *Dialogue: Writings in Art History*, Allen and Unwin, Sydney, p. xviii.

101 Smith, notes for review of T. J. Clark, *Farewell to an Idea*, July 1999, BSP, NLA, MS 8680, Box 8, 57/176.

102 John Brack, 'Critic or Historian?' *Australian Book Review*, December 1962, p. 26.

103 Leon Paroissien, 'Reworking Australian Art History', *Art and Australia*, vol. 27, no. 2, Sydney, 1989, p. 252.

104 Smith, 'A Reply to My Critics', *Art Monthly*, no. 33, August 1990, p. 4.

105 Richard Haese, 'Cultural Deregulation', *Art Monthly*, no. 43, August/September 1991, p. 25. This fourth edition (2001) includes additional chapters by Terry Smith and Christopher Heathcote, and updates the survey to 2000.

106 David McNeill, 'The Necessity of Australian Art', *Art and Australia*, vol. 27, no. 2, Sydney, 1989, pp. 253–4.

107 Smith, letter to Maggi Forster, 25 April 1992, BWSP, ML, MSS 5202, add on 2039, Box 5.

108 Gary Willis, conversation with the author, 17 February 2010.

109 Smith, letter to Yvonne Boyd, 7 April 1992, BWSP, ML, MS 5202, add on 2039, Box 5.

110 Ken Wach, letter to the author, 27 March 2013.

111 Fay Brauer, 'Berlin-Berlin: The Art of Post-Unification Exchange', *Art Monthly*, no. 55, November 1992, p. 12.

112 ibid.

113 Smith, letter to Rüdiger Joppien, 30 July 1992 (copy), BWSP, ML, MSS 5202, add on 2039, Box 5.

114 Kemp shared an interest in art and science with Bernard, and later launched *Modernism's History*.

115 Peter Beilharz, *Imagining the Antipodes*, p. vii; Peter Beilharz, *Thesis Eleven: Bernard Smith—Antipodean Dialectics, Sage*, no. 82, London, August 2005, p. 3.

116 Beilharz, *Imagining the Antipodes*, p. 74.

117 Dinah Dysart, 'Reimagining the Pacific', *Art and Australia*, vol. 34, no. 3, 1997, p. 325.

118 Diane Losche, conversation with the author, February 2015.

119 Smith, letter to J. B. Potter, Registrar of the University of Melbourne, *Herald* Chair of Fine Arts reference for Jaynie Anderson, 30 November 1996, BSP.

120 Martin Kemp, in Bernard Smith's taped lecture on 'Modernism's History', at the Tate Gallery, 23 August, 1998, Tate Gallery Archives, TAV 2025A.

121 Smith, 23 August 1998, 'Modernism's History', tape recording, Tate Gallery Archives. The lecture was published as 'The Misplaced Apostrophe of Modernism's History', *Art Monthly Australia*, no. 119, May 1999, p. 24.

122 Smith, 'Modernism and Post-Modernism: Neo-Colonial Viewpoint—Concerning the Sources of Modernism and Post-Modernism in the Visual Arts', *Thesis Eleven*, no. 38, 1994, p. 104.

123 Claude Lévi-Strauss, *The Savage Mind*, University of Chicago Press, Chicago, IL, 1972, p. 258.

124 Smith, 'Intellectual Currents in Australia, 1930–1940', BSP, NLA, MS 8680, Box 7/52/121, p. 11.

125 Smith, 'Is There a Radical Tradition in Australian Art?', BSP, NLA, MS 8680, Box 6/42/54, p. 10.

126 See *Shorter Oxford English Dictionary*, 1993, quoted in Bernard Smith's *The Formalesque*, p. 20. In *Art since 1900*, the authors (Benjamin Buchloh, Hal Foster, Rosalind Krauss and Yve-Alain Bois) quote Clement Greenberg's misgivings about the term 'formalism'; 'Whatever its connotations in Russian, the term has acquired ineradicably vulgar ones in English', or more pertinent to Bernard Smith's argument as Roland Barthes put it, 'a little formalism turns one away from History, but that a lot brings one back to it' (p. 33).

127 Roger Kimball, 'The Treason of the Intellectuals and "The Undoing of Thought"', *New Criterion*, vol. 11, New York, NY, December 1992.

128 Ihab Hassan, *The Postmodern Turn: Essays in Postmodern Theory and Culture*, Ohio State University Press, Columbus, OH, 1987, p. 88.

129 ibid., p. 84.

130 Hal Foster, *The Anti–Aesthetic: Essays on Postmodern Culture*, Bay Press, Seattle, WA, 1983, p. xv.

131 Smith, *Modernism's History*, p. 11.

132 Fredric Jameson introduced the term in 'The Vanishing Mediator: Narrative Structure in Max Weber', *New German Critique*, vol. 1, Durham, winter 1973, pp. 52–89. For their use of 'Vanishing mediator', see Rex Butler and Susan Rothnie, 'Paul Taylor's '70s', *Impresario: Paul Taylor*, p. 188. Virginia Spate, conversation with the author, 2009.

133 Smith, *Modernism's History*, p. 5.

134 Smith to John Nicol, 7 November 1996, BSP, NLA, MS Acc 10.088, Box 42.

135 Friedrich Nietzsche, *The Birth of Tragedy*, pp. 209–10. The copy belonging to Bernard Smith is extensively annotated.

136 Smith to Margaret Rose, 9 September 1999, BSP, NLA, MS Acc 10.088, Box 42.

137 Smith, draft manuscript for 'Modernity and the Formalesque', BSP, NLA, MS 8680, 57/180.

138 Perry Anderson, *The Origins of Postmodernity*, Verso, London, 1988, p. 4.

139 Smith, 'On Modernism and Postmodernism', unpublished paper, c. 1992.

140 ibid.

141 Juliette Peers, 'The Practice of Australian Art', *In/Stead*, issue 1, Canterbury, spring 2005, doubledialogues.com/in_stead/in_stead_iss01/peers.html, accessed 17 October 2008.

142 Smith, letter to John Nicol, 7 November 1996, BSP, NLA, Acc. 10.088, Box 42.

143 Smith, letter to Kate Challis, 28 July 1994, BWSP, ML, MSS 5202, add on 2099, Box 1.

144 Terry Smith, letter to Bernard Smith, 3 August 1994, BWSP, ibid. Bernard gave several papers, such as 'Two Meanings of Art' and 'Modernity and the Formalesque', at numerous universities, including Witwatersrand University in Johannesburg and at the Revisions: Art History, Modernity and Visual Cultures symposium in October 1994 at the Power Institute, Sydney.

145 James Malpas, 'Self-critiquism . . . An Exploration of the Meaning of Modernism', *Art Newspaper*, 1 January 1999.

146 Smith, letter to John Nicol, 7 November 1996, BSP, NLA, MS Acc. 10.088, Box 42.

147 Smith, interview with Humphrey McQueen, 22 July 2000, for the article 'Portrait of the Artist as Critic, *Bulletin*, 12 September 2000, pp. 82–4.

148 See E. H. Gombrich, *Tributes: Interpreters of Our Cultural Tradition*, Phaidon, Oxford, UK, 1984, p. 31.

149 Bernard Smith, letter to Terry Smith, 11 December 1993, BWSP, ML, MSS 5202, add on 2099, Box 1.

150 Fay Brauer, 'Hegelian History, Wölfflinean Periodisation and "Smithesque Modernism"', *Art History*, London, 2001, p. 449.

151 Ian McLean, 'Scholarly Ironies: Hassan on Smith on Modernism and New Art History', *Third Text*, vol. 16, no. 1, Southampton, UK, 2002, p. 81.

152 Patrick McCaughey, 'From a Distance', *Australian Review of Books*, August 1998, p. 19.

153 Bernard's *Australian Review of Books* reply titled 'Dialogue: Patricidal Tendencies', no. 3, September 1998, p. 6, was followed with another reproachful attack in *Art Monthly*, titled 'McCaughey's Malapropos', no. 114, October 1998, pp. 26–7.

Chapter Nine: Permissible Limits

1 Oskar Spate, 'Early Days at ANU: An Anecdote', O. H. K. Spate papers, NLA, MS 7886, Box 7, Series 3/2/2.

2 Ross Woodrow, letter to author, 24 April 2013.

3 ibid.

4 ibid.

5 Gombrich, 'G. W. F. Hegel. The Father of Art History', *Tributes: Interpreters of Our Cultural Tradition*, Phaidon, London, 1984, p. 62.

6 Ernst Gombrich, letter to Smith, 20 December 1998, BSP, NLA, MS 8680.

7 Ernst Gombrich, letter to Johnstone, Registrar of the University of Melbourne, 15 July 1963; Gombrich, reference letter for Smith, 21 April 1974, Warburg Institute Archives, General Correspondence.

8 Ernst Gombrich, letter to Smith, 7 March 2000, BSP, NLA, MS 8680.

9 Michael Ann Holly, 'Mourning and Method', *Art Bulletin*, vol. 84, no. 4, College Art Association, New York, NY, December 2002, p. 661.

10 For an extensive analysis of Father Time, see Erwin Panofsky, *Studies in Iconology Humanistic Themes in the Art of the Renaissance*, Harper Torchbooks, New York, NY, 1967, pp. 69–93. See Friedrich Neitzsche, *Thus Spake Zarathustra: A Book for Everyone and No One*, 1883, R. J. Hollingdale (trans.), Penguin Books, UK, 1961, p. 162.

11 John T. Irwin, 'The Dead Father in Falkner', in Robert Con Davis (ed.), *The Fictional Father: Lacanian Readings of Text*, University of Massachusetts Press, Amhurst, MA, 1981, p. 148.

12 Smith, 'Art Objects and Historical Usage', Isabel McBryde (ed.), *Who Owns the Past? Papers from the Annual Symposium of the Australian Academy of Humanities*, Oxford University Press, Melbourne, 1985, p. 74.

13 Smith, *Modernism's History*, p. 278.

14 Emma Hicks had known Bernard since 1975 and was a trusted researcher who worked on most of his major books from the mid-1980s through to *The Formalesque.*

15 Smith, *A Pavane for Another Time*, pp. 201–2.

16 Jaynie Anderson, Review of *A Pavane for Another Time*, in *Australian and New Zealand Journal of Art*, vol. 3, no. 2, 2002, p. 117.

17 Ric Edelmann, conversation with the author, September 2013.

18   Smith, 'The Urban Uncanny', *Australian Book Review*, no. 234, September 2001, p. 33.

19   ibid.

20   ibid.

21   Hegel, *Hegel's Philosophy of Right*, pp. 12–13.

22   Roy Porter, *Flesh in the Age of Reason*, Allen Lane, London, 2003, p. 5.

23   Plato, *The Republic of Plato*, Book V, John Llewelyn Davies and David James Vaughan (trans.), Macmillan, London, 1943, p. 159.

24   See Margaret A. Rose, *Parody: Ancient, Modern, and Post-Modern*, Cambridge University Press, Melbourne, 1993, pp. 34–5.

25   See Beat Wyss, *Hegel's Art History and the Critique of Modernity*, Caroline Dobson Saltzwedel (trans.), Cambridge University Press, Cambridge, UK, 1999, pp. 18–20.

26   J. Trapp, 'E. H. Gombrich: The Debate on Primitivism in Ancient Rhetoric', *Journal of the Warburg and Courtauld Institutes*, vol. 29, London, 1966, pp. 24–38.

27   Sigmund Freud, *Totem and Taboo: Resemblances Between the Psychic Lives of Savages and Neurotics*, A. A. Brill (trans., with an introduction), Pelican, Middlesex, UK, 1942, p. 94.

28   See Georges Bataille, *Eroticism* [1957], Mary Dalwood (trans.), Marion Boyars, London, 2006, p. 31.

29   Plato, *The Republic of Plato*, p. 157.

30   Noel Counihan, quoted in Smith, 'Counihan and Painting', BSP, NLA, MS 8680, Box 7, 51/118.

31   See Alex Potts, *Flesh and the Ideal: Winckelmann and the Origins of Art History*, Yale University Press, New Haven, CT, and London, 1994, pp. 4–5.

32   See Donald Kuspit discusses Eugene Minkowski's thesis, 'Lived Time, Phenomenological and Psychopathological Studies' in *The Dialectic of Decadence Between Advance and Decline in Art*, Allworth Press, New York, NY, 2000, p. 65.

33   T. S. Eliot, *Notes Towards the Definition of Culture*, Faber & Faber, London, 1948, p. 52.

34   Luke Slattery, Higher Education Supplement, *Australian*, 21 August 2002.

35   Sol Yurick in Christopher Caudwell, *Studies and Further Studies in a Dying Culture*, Monthly Review Press, New York, NY, 1971, p. 19.

36   Smith, 'Notes on Abstract Art', *The Death of the Artist as Hero*, 1988, p. 189.

37   Wyss, *Hegel's Art History*, p. 20.

38   ibid.

39   Abigail Solomon-Godeau, *Male Trouble: A Crisis in Representation*, Thames and Hudson, London, 1997, p. 40.

40   Humphrey McQueen, interview with Bernard Smith, *Bulletin*, 22 July 2000.

41   Nietzsche, *The Birth of Tragedy*, p. 52.

42   Lynn Frier Kaufmann, *The Noble Savage: Satyrs and Satyr Families in Renaissance Art*, University of Michigan Research Press, Michigan, 1984, p. 45.

43 Joyce Evans, conversation with the author, 12 June 2009.

44 See Margaret Iversen, 'Aby Warburg and the New Art History', in Horst Bredekamp, Michael Diers and Charlotte Schoell–Glass (eds), *Aby Warburg: Akten des internationalen Symposions Hamburg 1990*, Hamburg Universität, Hamburg, 1991, pp. 281–3.

45 Butler, *Radical Revisionism*, p. 12.

46 Terry Smith, interview with the author, 2014.

47 Jocelyn Hackforth-Jones, interview with the author, 23 April 2012.

48 Smith, review of George Steiner's *Real Presences*, BSP, NLA, MS 8680, Box 7/49/99, p. 5.

49 John Frow, review of Peter Beilharz, *Imagining the Antipodes: Culture, Theory and the Visual in the Work of Bernard Smith*, BSP, NLA, Acc. 10.088, Box 65.

50 Smith quoted in Peter Fuller 'Art History in a Slim Volume', *Independent Monthly*, October 1989, p. 42.

51 Smith, review of George Steiner's *Real Presences*, BSP, NLA, MS 8680, Box 7/49/99.

52 ibid.

53 Smith, 'In Defence of Art History', *Art Monthly*, no. 1, July 2000, pp. 5, 130.

54 Smith, notes for 'Art and Imperialism', BSP, NLA, MS 8680, Box 1/9.

55 Smith, 'Modern c. 1920 – c. 1960, Or Shall We Say: The Formalesque?', in *Two Centuries of Australian Art: The National Gallery of Victoria*, Thames and Hudson, Melbourne, 2003, p. 86.

56 Smith, *The Formalesque*, p. 13.

57 E. H. Gombrich, *The Story of Art*, 3rd edn, Phaidon, London, 1950 p. 5.

58 Hegel, *Aesthetik I*, cited in Wyss, *Hegel's Art History*, p. 100.

59 See Ihab Hassan, review of Smith's *The Formalesque*, in *Georgia Review*, vol. 62, no. 2, summer 2008, pp. 439–41.

60 Charles Nodrum, 'Bernard Smith and the Formalesque', unpublished article, courtesy of Charles Nodrum.

61 Smith, *The Formalesque*, pp. 17, 21.

62 Smith, 'The Formalesque', final public lecture at the NGV, August 2008, notes, BSP.

63 Richard Evans, *In Defence of History*, Granta Books, London, 1997, p. 126.

64 Smith, 'On Writing Art History in Australia', *Thesis Eleven*, no. 82, 2005, p. 13.

65 Smith, letter to Gerard Vaughan, 28 May 2008 (copy), BSP, NLA, MS 8680.

66 ibid.

67 Smith, draft plan for an Institute of Art History (copy), BSP, NLA, MS 8680.

68 Gerard Vaughan, letter to Smith, 26 June 2008 (copy), BSP, NLA, MS 8680.

69 See Charles Mitchell, 'Benjamin West's *Death of Nelson*', Douglas Fraser, Howard Hibbard and Milton J. Lewine (eds), *Essays in the History of Art Presented to Rudolf Wittkower*, Phaidon, London, 1967, p. 265.

70   Smith, final lecture notes, BSP.

71   ibid.

72   Bernard Smith, *The Formalesque*, p. 40.

73   Hegel, *Hegel's Philosophy of Right*, pp. 12–13.

74   The author was present when Mora spoke to Bernard.

75   Apart from conversations with Gerard Vaughan, a number of key individuals were unavailable for comment about the Australian Institute of Art History.

76   R. B. Rose, 'Utopias and the Enlightenment', Eugene Kamenka (ed.), *Utopias*, Oxford University Press, Melbourne, 1987, p. 35.

77   James Murdoch, conversation with the author, 2010; Ian McLean, conversation with the author, 2011; Peter Beilharz, conversation with the author, 2014.

78   Terry Smith, 'Our Measure', memorial speech given at the National Gallery of Victoria, 28 November 2011.

79   ibid.

80   Greg Dening, *Readings/Writings*, Melbourne University Press, Melbourne, 1998, p. 142.

81   Rüdiger Joppien, 'Tribute', memorial speech given at the National Gallery of Victoria, 28 November 2011.

82   Nodrum, 'Bernard Smith and the Formalesque'.

83   Bronwyn Hughes, email to the author, 21 November 2011.

84   Peter Beilharz, 'Marxism and Politics', memorial speech given at the National Gallery of Victoria, 28 November 2011.

BIBLIOGRAPHY

MANUSCRIPT SOURCES

Papers of Bernard Smith, National Library of Australia (BSP) (NLA)

Bernard William Smith Papers, Mitchell Library, State Library of New South Wales (BWSP) (ML)

Bernard Smith Library, State Library of Victoria

Power Institute Papers, Fisher Library, University of Sydney

Ursula Hoff Papers, University of Melbourne Archives

Ursula Hoff Diaries, in possession of Graham Ryles

Joseph Burke Papers, University of Melbourne Archives

June Stewart Papers, in possession of Sheridan Palmer

Meanjin Papers, University of Melbourne Archives

Noel Counihan Papers, National Library of Australia

Rex Nan Kivell Papers, National Library of Australia

Jack Lindsay Papers, National Library of Australia

Manning Clark Papers, National Library of Australia

Lionel Lindsay Papers, State Library of Victoria

Lindsay Family Papers, Mitchell Library, State Library of New South Wales

Institute of Contemporary Art Papers, Tate Gallery Archives, London

Kenneth Clark Papers, Tate Gallery Archives, London

Warburg Institute Archives, University of London

Bryan Robertson Papers, Whitechapel Gallery Archives, London

National Archives, Kew, London

Natural History Museum Archives, London

SELECTED WORKS BY BERNARD SMITH

Books

Place, Taste and Tradition: A Study of Australian Art Since 1788, Ure Smith, Sydney, 1945.

European Vision and the South Pacific, Oxford University Press, London, 1960.

Australian Painting Today, The John Murtagh Macrossan Lectures, University of Queensland Press, Brisbane, 1962.

Australian Painting 1788–2000, with Terry Smith and Christopher Heathcote, Oxford University Press, Melbourne, 1962, 2001.

Concerning Contemporary Art: The Power Lectures 1968–1973, Bernard Smith (ed.), Clarendon Press, Oxford, 1975.

Documents on Art and Taste in Australia 1770–1914, Oxford University Press, Melbourne, 1975.

The Antipodean Manifesto: Essays in Art and History, Oxford University Press, Melbourne, 1976.

Art as Information: Reflections on the Art from Captain Cook's Voyages, vols 1 & 2, Sydney University Press for the Australian Academy of the Humanities, Sydney, 1978.

The Spectre of Truganini, 1980 Boyer Lectures, ABC, Sydney, 1981.

The Boy Adeodatus, Penguin, Melbourne, 1984.

The Art of Captain Cook's Voyages: The Voyages of the Endeavour, Vol. 1, with Rüdiger Joppien, Oxford University Press and the Australian Academy of the Humanities, Melbourne, 1985.

The Death of the Artist as Hero: Essays in History and Culture, Oxford University Press, Melbourne, 1988.

The Architectural Character of Glebe, Sydney, with Kate Smith, Sydney University Press, Sydney, 1973, 1989.

The Critic as Advocate: Selected Essays 1948–1988, Oxford University Press, Melbourne, 1989.

Imagining the Pacific: In the Wake of Cook's Voyages, Miegunyah Press, Melbourne, 1992.

Noel Counihan: Artist and Revolutionary, Oxford University Press, Melbourne, 1993.

Poems 1938–1993, Meanjin, Melbourne, 1996.

Modernism's History: A Study in Twentieth-Century Art and Ideas, Yale University Press, New Haven and London, 1998.

A Pavane for Another Time, Macmillan, Melbourne, 2002.

Two Centuries of Australian Art: The National Gallery of Victoria, Thames and Hudson, Melbourne, 2003.

The Formalesque: A Guide to Modern Art and its History, Macmillan, Melbourne, 2007.

Articles

'European Vision and the South Pacific', *Journal of the Warburg and Courtauld Institutes*, vol. 13, London, 1950, pp. 65–100.

'Coleridge's Ancient Mariner and Cook's Second Voyage', *Journal of the Warburg and Courtald Institutes*, vol. 19, nos 1–2, London, 1956, pp. 117–54.

The Antipodeans 4th–15th August 1959, exhibition catalogue accompanying 'The Antipodean Manifesto', August 1959.

'Sir Herbert Read and the Power Bequest', *Meanjin*, vol. 1, Melbourne, 1964, pp. 37–50.

'The Role of an Institute of Fine Arts in the University of Sydney', *Journal of the Sydney University Arts Association*, vol. 6, Sydney, 1969, pp. 5–17.

'Art and Industry: A Systematic Approach', *Studio International Journal of Modern Art*, vol. 187, no. 965, London, April 1974, pp. 158–63.

'Art Marketing in Sydney 1970–1975', in Peter Quatermaine (ed.), *Readings in Australian Arts: Papers from the 1976 Exeter Symposium*, University of Exeter, 1978, pp. 74–83.

'Cook's Posthumous Reputation', in Fisher, Robin and Hugh Johnstone (eds), *Captain James Cook and His Times*, Douglas and McIntyre, Vancouver, and Croom Helm, London, 1979.

'Reds, and Other Colours', *Age*, 'Monthly Review', vol. 1, no. 6, Melbourne, October 1981, pp. 7–8.

'*Lot* and *Pompeii*—Two paintings from 1940', in *Art & Text*, no. 7, Melbourne, 1982, pp. 34–47.

'William Hodges and English *Plein-Air* Painting', *Art History*, vol. 6, no. 2, London, June 1983, pp. 143–52.

'Marx and Aesthetic Value: Part Two', *Art Monthly*, no. 6, Canberra, November 1987, pp. 3–6.

Post Scripts, 1988 Boyer Lecture, ABC, Sydney, 1988.

'Australian Art in England', *Modern Painters*, vol. 1, no. 4, London, 1988/9, pp. 86–9.

'Taking Art to the Country: How it All Began', in *Cultivating the Country: Living With the Arts in Regional Australia*, Peter Timms and Robyn Christie (eds) Oxford University Press, Melbourne, 1988, pp. 33–46.

'Concerning Donald Brook's "New Theory of Art"', *Meanjin*, vol. 47, no. 1, Melbourne, 1988, pp. 5–10.

'Wither Painting', in *The Critic as Advocate*, Oxford University Press, Melbourne, 1989, pp. 235–44.

'History as Criticism', in Bain Attwood (ed.), *Boundaries of the Past*, The History Institute of Victoria, Melbourne, 1990, pp. 1–7.

'Braudel's Long View', *Scripsi*, vol. 6, no. 1, Melbourne, 1990, pp. 171–7.

'A Reply to My Critics', *Art Monthly*, no. 33, Canberra, August 1990, pp. 3–5.

'Changing Posture', *Australian Book Review*, no. 199, Melbourne and Adelaide, April 1998, pp. 7–8.

'McCaughey's Malapropos', *Art Monthly*, no, 114, Canberra, October 1998, pp. 26–7.

'The Misplaced Apostrophe of Modernism's History' in *Art Monthly*, no. 119, Canberra, May 1999, pp. 24–7.
'In Defence of Art History', in *Art Monthly*, no. 130, Canberra, July 2000, pp. 5–7.
'In Defence of Art History, Part II', in *Art Monthly*, no. 132, Canberra, August 2000, pp. 5– 7.
'On Writing Art History in Australia', *Thesis Eleven*, no. 82, Melbourne, August 2005, p. 7.

INTERVIEWS

John Arnold, 27 October 2012, Venus Bay
Tim Beaglehole, 6 December 2011, New Zealand
Peter Beilharz, 27 August 2014, Melbourne
David Bindman,, 21 August 2013, London
Barbara Blackman, 21 May 2009, Canberra
David Boyd, 29 May 2009, Sydney
Helen Brack, 26 May 2011 and 1 August 2013, Melbourne
Donald Brook, 1 December 2010, Adelaide
Joseph Brown, 24 July 2008, Melbourne
Janine Burke, 25 September 2014, Melbourne
Kate Challis, 23 February 2011 and 19 July 2012, Melbourne
Josephine Collier, 14 August, 29 September 2013, England (via email)
Oliver Crimmen, 20 September 2013, London
Ann Datta, 20 September 2013, London
Jim Davidson, 8 August 2014, Melbourne
Catherine de Lorenzo, 23 February 2013, Sydney
Mary Eagle, 28 October 2011, Canberra
Ric Edelmann, 7–8 September 2013, Suffolk
Lucy Ellem, 29 May 2013, Melbourne
Ralph Elliot, 11 May 2009, Canberra
Joyce Evans, 12 June 2009, 28 February 2013, Melbourne
James Fairfax, 10 December 2009, Melbourne
Christine France, 23 February 2013, Sydney
George Gittoes, 16 March 2015, Melbourne
Ronald Greenaway, 27 September 2012, Melbourne
Jocelyn Hackforth-Jones, 23 April 2012, London
Richard Haese, 23 May 2012, Melbourne
Peter Haynes, 6 May 2011, Canberra
Elizabeth Heathcote, 26 February 2010, Melbourne

Michelle Hetherington, 19 May 2010, Canberra
Emma Hicks, 20 April 2012, London
Ursula Hoff, 15 August 2001 and 28 November 2001, Melbourne
Geoff Hogg, 25 September 2014, Melbourne
Rosalie Horner, 19 September 2013, London
Nigel Hughes, 7–8 September 2013, Suffolk
Clytie Jessop, 13 April 2012, London
Sara Kelly, 3 November 2014, Canberra (via telephone)
Inge King, 14 October 2013, Melbourne
Richard Larter, 26 July 2010, Canberra
Lily Lynn, 24 February 2013, Sydney
Margaret Manion, 13 May 2009, Melbourne
Jennifer Marshall, 12 February 2000, Venus Bay
Margaret Mattar, 10 April 2013, Sydney
Paul McGillick, 22 June 2010, Sydney
Joyce McGrath, 27 March 2001, 17 November 2011, 27 September 2012, Melbourne
Humphrey McQueen, 9 November 2010, Canberra
Ronald Millar, 17 March 2009, Melbourne
John Mitchell, 17 August 2013, England
Neil Moore, 23 February 2013, Sydney
Mirka Mora, 17 October 2011, Melbourne
D. J. Mulvaney, 20 July 2010, Canberra
Doug Munroe, 6 December 2011, New Zealand
Mary, Lady Nolan, 16 April 2012, Wales
Carmel O'Connor, 29 May 2010, Melbourne
Bienchen Ohly, 17 September 2013, England
June Philipp, 24 June 2003, Melbourne
Peter Quartermaine, 10 August 2013, London
Francis Reiss, 26 May 2011, Melbourne
Bryan Robertson, 13 May 2002, London
Michael Rosenthal, 12 September 2013, London
Bernard Smith, 7 and 14 June 2001, 13 April 2003, 8 September 2008 and multiple conversations between 2008 and 2011, Melbourne
F. B. Smith, 2 September 2009, Canberra
John Smith, 14 February 2010, Melbourne
Margaret (Maggi) Smith, 24 March 2009, Melbourne
Robert Smith, 11 February 2010, Geelong
Sarah Smith, 2 December 2008, London
Terry Smith, 16 December 2009, Sydney, and 2 September 2014, Melbourne
Virginia Spate, 18 December 2009, Canberra

Noel Stannard, 14 August 2013, London (via email)

June Stewart, 15 October 2008 and 4 October 2010, Melbourne

Lillianne Teboul, 27 March 2012, Nice, France

Martin Terry, 27 June 2009, Canberra

Daniel Thomas, 2 and 7 February 2011 (via telephone)

David Thomas, 2 March 2010, Melbourne

Gordon Thomson, 20 July 2001 and 2 July 2003, Melbourne, and 18 June 2008, Castlemaine

Peter Tomory, 14 August 2001 and 25 June 2002, Poole, England

Ken Wach, 27 March 2013, Melbourne

Chris Wallace-Crabbe, 25 November 2013, Melbourne

Guy Warren, 19 July 2011 (via telephone)

Glyndwr Williams, 11 April 2012, London

Gary Willis, 17 February 2010, Melbourne

Richard Woodfield, 15 March 2012, London

Ruth Zubans, 29 June 2011, Melbourne

Other interviews

Bernard Smith, interviewed by Neville Meaney, 6 November 1986, NLA, Oral History Program, TRC 2053/17.

Bernard Smith, interviewed by Hazel De Berg, 20 November 1975, including NLA tape 888.

Bernard Smith, interviewed by Sheridan Palmer, 2009, NLA, Oral History Program, TRC 6111.

David Boyd, interviewed by Sheridan Palmer, 2009, NLA Oral History Program, TRC 6111/2.

Jean Langley, interviewed by Sheridan Palmer, 2013, NLA, Oral history Program, TRC 6111/7.

FURTHER READING

Ades, Dawn (ed.), *Art and Power: Europe Under the Dictators, 1930–45*, Thames and Hudson, London, 1995.

Adorno, Theodor W., *Negative Dialectics*, E. B. Ashton (trans.), Routledge, London, 1973.

Anderson, Jaynie, Obituary of Charles Mitchell, *Independent*, 31 October 1995.

Anderson, Jaynie, Review of Bernard Smith, *A Pavane for Another Time*, in *Australian and New Zealand Journal of Art*, vol. 3, no. 2, Melbourne, 2002, pp. 117–20.

Anderson, Perry, *The Origins of Postmodernity*, Verso, London, 1998.

Anderson, Perry, *In the Tracks of Historical Materialism*, University of Chicago

Press, Chicago, 1983.

Arnheim, Rudolf, *The Split and the Structure*, University of California Press, California, 1996.

Bhabha, Homi K., *The Location of Culture*, Routledge, London and New York, 1994.

Barker, Heather and Charles Green, 'Flight from the Object: Donald Brook, Inhibodress and the Emergence of Post-Studio Art in Early 1970s Sydney', *emaj*, iss. 4, 2009, melbourneartjournal.unimelb.edu.au/E-MAJ.

Barker, Heather and Charles Green, 'Provincialism No More: *Art & Text*, in Helen Hughes and Nicholas Croggan (eds), *Impresario: Paul Taylor, The Melbourne Years, 1981–1984*, Surplus/Monash University Museum of Art, Melbourne, 2013, pp. 104–39.

Barker, Heather and Charles Green, 'Cold War Warrior', in *Thesis Eleven*, no. 82, Melbourne, August 2005, pp. 38–53.

Bataille, Georges, *Eroticism: Death and Sensuality*, Mary Dalwood (trans.), Marion Boyars, London, 2006.

Bataille, Georges, *The Absence of Myth: Writings on Surrealism*, Michael Richardson (ed.), Verso, London, 1994.

Bataille, Georges, *The Cradle of Humanity: Prehistoric Art and Culture*, Michelle Kendall and Stuart Kendall (ed. and trans.) Zone Books, New York, 2009.

Beilharz, Peter, *Imagining the Antipodes. Culture, Theory and the Visual in the Work of Bernard Smith*, Cambridge University Press, Cambridge, UK, 1997.

Beilharz, Peter, *Postmodern Socialism: Romanticism, City and State*, Melbourne University Press, Melbourne, 1994.

Beilharz, Peter, 'Imagining the Antipodes', in Rex Butler (ed.), *Radical Revisionism: An Anthology of Writings on Australian Art*, Institute of Modern Art, Brisbane, 2005, pp. 67–72.

Benjamin, Walter, *Selected Writings, Vol. 1, 1913–1926*, Marcus Bullock and Michael W. Jennings (eds), ,The Belknap Press of Harvard University Press, Cambridge, Mass., and London, 1996.

Bindman, David, *Ape to Apollo: Aesthetics and the Idea of Race in the Eighteenth Century*, Reaktion Books and the Paul Mellon Centre, London, 2002.

Blackman, Barbara, 'The Antipodean Affair', *Art and Australia*, vol. 5, no. 4, Sydney, March 1968, pp. 607–16.

Bonyhady, Tim, 'The Uncritical Culture', *Eureka Street*, October 1997, pp. 24–32.

Bourdieu, Pierre, *Distinction. A Social Critique of the Judgement of Taste*, Richard Nice (trans.), Harvard University Press, Cambridge, Mass., 1984.

Boyd, Robin, *The Australian Ugliness*, Cheshire, Melbourne, 1960.

Boyde, Melissa, 'Making it Accessible: Mary Alice Evatt & Australian modernist

Art', evatt.org.au/publications/papers/217.html.

Bradley, Anthony and Terry Smith, *Australian Art and Architecture: Essays Presented to Bernard Smith*, Oxford University Press, Melbourne, 1980.

Brauer, Fay, 'Hegelian History, Wolfflinean periodisation and "Smithesque Modernism"', *Art History*, vol. 24, iss. 3, London, June 2001, p. 449.

Breton, André, 'Limits Not Frontiers of Surrealism?' in Herbert Read (ed.), *Surrealism*, pp. 95–116.

Breton, André, *What is Surrealism?*, Faber & Faber, London, 1936.

Brook, Donald, 'Theory and Criticism', *Art and Australia*, vol. 5, no. 1, Sydney, June 1967, pp. 390–2.

Brook, Donald, *ARE: Art, Representation, Education*, Perth Institute of Contemporary Art, Perth, 1992.

Brook, Donald, 'The Undoing of Art History (Part I)', in *Artlink*, vol. 21, no. 4, Adelaide, 2001, pp. 68–9.

Brook, Donald, '1968', *Art Monthly*, no. 195, Canberra, 2006, pp. 30–5.

Burke, Janine, *Australian Gothic: A Life of Albert Tucker*, Knopf, Sydney, 2002.

Burn, Ian, Nigel Lendon, Charles Merewether and Ann Stephen, *The Necessity of Australian Art: An Essay About Interpretation*, Power Publications, Sydney, 1988.

Butler, Rex (ed.), *Radical Revisionism: An Anthology of Writings on Australian Art*, Institute of Modern Art, Brisbane, 2005.

Butler, Rex and Susan Rothnie, 'Paul Taylor's "70s"', in Helen Hughes and Nicholas Croggon (eds), *Impresario: Paul Taylor, The Melbourne Years 1981–1984*, Surplus/Monash University Museum of Art, Melbourne, 2013, pp. 186– 97.

Callinicos, Alex, *Is there a Future for Marxism?* Macmillan, London, 1982.

Carrel, Alexis, *Man, the Unknown*, Hamish Hamilton, London, 1936.

Carter, Miranda, *Anthony Blunt: His Lives*, Macmillan, London, 2001.

Cassirer, Ernst, *The Question of Jean Jacques Rousseau*, Indiana University Press, Bloomington and London, 1963.

Caudwell, Christopher, *Illusion and Reality: A Study of the Sources of Poetry*, Macmillan, London, 1937.

Caudwell, Christopher, *Studies and Further Studies in a Dying Culture*, Monthly Review Press, New York, 1971.

Challis, Kate, 'The Marxist Collector: The Art Collection of Bernard and Kate Smith', paper delivered, 'The Legacy of Bernard Smith' Symposium, 2012.

Clark, Kenneth, *Provincialism*, The English Association, London, 1962.

Clark, Kenneth, *The Other Half: A Self Portrait*, Harper & Row, New York, 1977.

Clark, T. J., 'In Defence of Abstract Expressionism', *October*, no. 69, 1994, pp. 23–48.

Clark, T. J., *Farewell to an Idea: Episodes from a History of Modernism*, Yale University Press, New Haven and London, 1999.

Clark, T. J., *The Absolute Bourgeois: Artists and Politics in France 1848–1851*, Thames and Hudson, London, 1982.

Clark, T. J., *Lowry and the Painting of Modern Life*, Tate Publishing, London, 2013.

Craven, Peter, 'Watercolour Memories', in *Australian Book Review*, no. 246, Melbourne and Adelaide, November 2002, pp. 9–10.

Curthoys, Ann and John Merritt (eds), *Australia's First Cold War 1945–1953: Society, Communism and Culture*, vol. 1, Allen and Unwin, Sydney, 1984.

Darwin, Charles, *Voyage of the Beagle*, Janet Browne and Michael Neve (eds), abridged, Penguin, London, 1989.

Dening, Greg, 'Disembodied Artifacts: Edward Said's *Culture and Imperialism*', *Scripsi*, vol. 9, no. 1, Melbourne, 1993, pp. 79–83.

Derrida, Jacques, *Specters of Marx: The State of the Debt, the Work of Mourning and the New International*, Peggy Kamuf (trans.), Routledge, New York and London, 2006.

Donaldson, A. D. S, and Ann Stephen, *J. W. Power: Abstraction-Création, Paris 1934*, with contributions by Virginia Spate and Gladys Fabre, Power Publications, Sydney, 2012.

Dutton, Geoffrey, *The Innovators*, Macmillan, Melbourne, 1986.

Eagleton, Terry and Drew Milne (eds), *Marxist Literary Theory: A Reader*, Blackwell, Oxford, 1996.

Eagleton, Terry, *The Ideology of the Aesthetic*, Blackwell, Oxford, 1990.

Ebury, Sue, *The Many Lives of Kenneth Myer*, Miegunyah Press, Melbourne, 2008.

Eisenman, Stephen F. (ed.), *Nineteenth-Century Art: A Critical History*, Thames and Hudson, London, 1994.

Eliot, T. S., *Four Quartets*, Faber & Faber, London, 1959.

Eliot, T. S., *Notes Towards the Definition of Culture*, Faber & Faber, London, 1948.

Ellis, Havelock, *Kanga Creek*, Thomas Nelson, Melbourne, 1970.

Engels, Friedrich, *Ludwig Feuerbach and the End of Classical German Philosophy*, Progress Publishers, Moscow, 1976.

Evans, Richard, *In Defence of History*, Granta Books, London, 1997.

Fausett, David, *Images of the Antipodes in the Eighteenth Century: A Study in Stereotyping*, Rodopi, Amsterdam, 1995.

Foster, Hal (ed.) *The Anti-Aesthetic: Essays on Postmodern Culture*, Bay Press, Seattle, 1983.

Foster, Hal, *The Return of the Real: The Avant-Garde at the End of the Century*, MIT Press, Cambridge, Mass., 1996.

Foster, Hal, Rosalind Krauss, Yve-Alain Bois, Benjamin H. Buchloh, *Art Since*

1900: Modernism, Antimodernism, Postmodernism, Thames and Hudson, London, 2004.

Foucault, Michel, *This is Not a Pipe*, James Harkness (trans.), California Press, Berkeley, California, 1983.

Freud, Sigmund, *Civilization and its Discontents*, David McLintock (trans.), Penguin, London, 2002.

Freud, Sigmund, *Totem and Taboo*, Penguin, London, 1938.

Fuller, Peter, *The Australian Scapegoat: Towards an Antipodean Aesthetic*, University of Western Australia Press, Perth, 1986.

Gathercole, Peter, T. H. Irving and Gregory Melleuish, *Childe and Australia: Archaeology, Politics and Ideas*, University of Queensland Press, Brisbane, 1995.

Goetsch, James Robert, Jr, *Vico's Axioms: The Geometry of the Human World*, Yale University Press, New Haven, 1995.

Gombrich, Ernst, *Tributes: Interpreters of our Cultural Tradition*, Phaidon, London, 1984.

Gombrich, Ernst, *The Essential Gombrich: Selected Writings on Art and Culture*, Richard Woodfield (ed.), Phaidon, London, 1996.

Goodway, David (ed.), *Herbert Read Reassessed*, Liverpool University Press, Liverpool, 1998.

Green, Charles, *Peripheral Vision: Contemporary Australian Art, 1970–1994*, Craftsman House, Sydney, 1995.

Greenberg, Clement, *Avant-Garde Attitudes: New Art in the Sixties*, Power Institute of Fine Arts, University of Sydney, 1969.

Grosz, Elizabeth, *In the Nick of Time: Politics, Evolution and the Untimely*, Allen and Unwin, Sydney, 2004.

Haese, Richard, *Permanent Revolution: Mike Brown and the Australian Avant-Garde, 1953–1997*, Miegunyah Press, Melbourne, 2011.

Haese, Richard, *Rebels and Precursors: The Revolutionary Years of Australian Art*, Penguin, Melbourne 1988.

Hansen, David, 'Seeing Truganini', *Australian Book Review*, no. 321, May 2010, pp. 45–57.

Hassan, Ihab, *The Dismemberment of Orpheus*, Oxford University Press, New York, 1971.

Hassan, Ihab, *The Postmodern Turn: Essays in Postmodern Theory and Culture*, Ohio University Press, Columbus, 1987.

Hassan, Ihab, 'Bernard Smith, Global Antipodean: The Language of Trust', *Art Monthly*, no. 144, Canberra, October 2001, pp. 16–21.

Heathcote, Christopher, *A Quiet Revolution: The Rise of Australian Art, 1946–1968*, Text Publishing, Melbourne, 1995.

Hetherington Michelle, 'John Hamilton Mortimer and the Discovery of Captain Cook', *British Art Journal*, vol. 4, no. 1, London, spring 2003, pp. 69–77.

Hegel's Philosophy of Right, T. M. Knox (trans.), Oxford University Press, London, 1967.

Hoff, Ursula, 'Consistent View of History', in *Art and Australia*, vol. 1, no. 3, spring 1963, pp. 119–20.

Hoff, Ursula, 'To the Editor', in *Art and Australia*, vol. 1, no. 4, summer 1964, p. 276.

Hughes, Helen and Nicholas Croggan, *Impresario: Paul Taylor, The Melbourne Years, 1981–1984*, Surplus/Monash University of Modern Art, Melbourne, 2013.

Hughes, Robert, *The Art of Australia*, Pelican, London and Melbourne, 1966.

Hughes, Robert, 'The Meaning of Herbert Read', in *Nation*, Sydney, 13 July 1963, pp. 12–13.

Huxley, Aldous, *Brave New World*, Penguin, London, 1974.

Hynes, Samuel, *The Auden Generation; Literature and Politics in England in the 1930s*, Faber & Faber, London, 1976.

Irwin, John T., 'The Dead Father in Faulkner', in Robert Con Davis (ed.), *The Fictional Father: Lacanian Readings of Text*, University of Massachusetts Press, Amhurst, 1981.

Jameson, Fredric, *Marxism and Form. Twentieth Century Dialectical Theories of Literature*, Princeton University Press, Princeton, New Jersey, 1971.

Johnson, Lesley, The *Cultural Critics: From Matthew Arnold to Raymond Williams*, Routledge, London, 1979.

Johnson, R. Brimley (ed.), *The Complete Poetical Works of Edgar Allan Poe*, Oxford University Press, London, 1909.

Kantor, Sybil Gordon, *Alfred H. Barr, Jr. and the Intellectual Origins of the Museum of Modern Art*, MIT Press, Cambridge, Mass., and London, 2002.

Kaufmann, Lynn Frier, *The Noble Savage: Satyrs and Satyr Families in Renaissance Art*, UMI Research Press, Ann Arbor, Michigan, 1984.

Kavanagh, John, '15 Years On—The Power Institute in Review', *Art Network*, vol. 8, Sydney, summer 1983, pp. 14–16.

Kenyon, Therese, *Under a Hot Tin Roof: Art, Passion, and Politics at the Tin Sheds Art Workshop*, State Library of NSW Press, Sydney, 1995.

Khilnani, Sunil, *Arguing Revolution: The Intellectual Left in Postwar France*, Yale University Press, New Haven and London, 1993.

Klepac, Lou, *James Gleeson: Landscape Out of Nature*, Beagle Press, Sydney, 1987.

Knapman, Gareth, 'The Pacificator: Discovering the Lost Bust of George Augustus Robinson', *La Trobe Journal*, no. 86, State Library of Victoria, Melbourne, 2010, pp. 37–52, slv.vic.gov.au/latrobejournal/issue/latrobe-86/t1-g-t4.html, accessed on 11 August 2014.

Kristeva, Julia, *Strangers to Ourselves*, Leon S. Roudiez (trans.), Columbia University Press, New York, 1991, Columbia University Press, New York and Oxford, 1991.

Kubler, George, *The Shape of Time: Remarks on the History of Things*, Yale University Press, New Haven and London, 1962.

Kuspit, Donald, *The Dialectic of Decadence Between Advance and Decline in Art*, Allworth Press, New York, 2000.

Lessing, Doris, *In Pursuit of the English*, Simon and Schuster, New Haven and London, 1961.

Lévi-Strauss, Claude, *The Savage Mind*, University of Chicago Press, Chicago, 1966.

Lévi-Strauss, Claude, *Totemism*, Rodney Needham (trans.), Beacon Press, Boston, 1962.

Lewis, Wyndham, *Creatures of Habit and Creatures of Change: Essays on Art, Literature and Society, 1914–1956*, Paul Edwards (ed.), Black Sparrow Press, Santa Rosa, 1989.

Lifshitz, Mikhail, *The Philosophy of Art of Karl Marx*, Ralph B. Winn (trans.), Critics Group, New York, 1938.

Lindsay, Jack, *A Short History of Culture*, Victor Gollancz, London, 1939.

Lindsay, Jack, *Gustave Courbet: His Life and Art*, Adams and Dart, Bath, 1973.

Lowish, Susan, 'European Vision and Aboriginal Art: Blindness and Insight in the Work of Bernard Smith', in *Thesis Eleven*, no. 82, Melbourne, August 2005, pp. 62–72.

Lynn, Elwyn, 'Clement Greenberg sees Australia', *Art and Australia*, vol. 6, no. 2, Sydney, spring 1968, pp. 150–2.

Lysaght, A. M., 'Banks's Artists and his Endeavour Collections', in *Captain Cook and the South Pacific, The British Museum Yearbook 3*, published for the Trustees of the British Museum by the British Museum Publications, London, 1979, pp. 9–50.

MacDonagh, Oliver and W. F. Mandle (eds), *Ireland and Irish-Australia: Studies in Cultural and Political History*, Croom Helm, London, 1986.

MacIntyre, Stuart, *The Reds: The Communist Party of Australia from Origins to Illegality*, Allen and Unwin, Sydney, 1998.

MacNeice, Louis, *Poems 1925–1940*, Random House, New York, 1940.

Malcolm, Janet, *The Silent Woman: Sylvia Plath and Ted Hughes*, Picador, London, 1994.

Marshall, Christopher, 'Mind the Gap: Bernard Smith Versus the Museum', paper delivered at the Legacies of Bernard Smith symposium, University of Sydney, 9–10 November 2012.

Marx, Karl, 'The Eighteenth Brumaire of Louis Bonaparte', in Lewis S. Feuer (ed.), *Marx & Engels: Basic Writings on Politics & Philosophy*, Doubleday Anchor, New York, 1959.

Matthiessen, F. O., *The Achievements of T. S. Elliot*, Oxford University Press, London, 1958.

McCalman, Iain, *Darwin's Armada: Four Voyages and the Battle for the Theory of Evolution*, Penguin, Melbourne, 2009.

McCaughey, Patrick, 'After Greenberg: New Bearings or Old Directions?' *Meanjin*, vol. 27, no 4, Melbourne, 1968, pp. 480–5.

McCaughey, Patrick, 'From a Distance', *Australian's Review of Books*, vol. 3, no. 5, August 1998, pp. 18–19.

McCaughey, Patrick, *The Bright Shapes and the True Names: A Memoir*, Text Publishing, Melbourne, 2003.

McLaren, John, *Journey Without Arrival: The Life and Writing of Vincent Buckley*, Australian Scholarly Publishing, Melbourne, 2009.

McLean, Ian, 'Bernard Smith: Noble Modern', *Art and Australia*, vol. 27, no. 4, Sydney, 1990, pp. 565–6.

McLean, Ian, 'Hegel or Darwin? The Role of Tendencies in Bernard Smith's Historiography', *Thesis Eleven*, no. 82, Melbourne, August 2005, pp. 54–61.

Miller, Steven, 'Contingency as the Guard Dog of History: Bernard Smith at the Art Gallery of New South Wales, 1944–48', paper given at the Legacies of Bernard Smith symposium, University of Sydney, 9–10 November 2012.

Missingham, Hal, *They'll Kill You in the End*, Angus and Robertson, Sydney, 1973.

Mitchell, Charles 'Benjamin West's *Death of Nelson*', in Douglas Fraser, Howard Hibbard and Milton J. Lewine (eds), *Essays in the History of Art Presented to Rudolf Wittkower*, Phaidon, London, 1967.

Mitchell, W. J. T. (ed.), *Landscape and Power*, University of Chicago Press, Chicago and London, 1994.

Murdoch, Iris, *The Sovereignty of Good*, Routledge & Kegan Paul, London, 1970.

Murphy, Bernice, '"Provincialism Refigured" or Culture Disfigured', in Peter Townsend (ed.), *Australian and International Art Monthly*, no. 15, October 1988, pp. 1–3.

Murphy, Bernice, *Museum of Contemporary Art: Vision and Context*, Museum of Contemporary Art, Sydney, 1993.

Paradise Possessed: The Rex Nan Kivell Collection, National Library of Australia, Canberra, 1998.

Nietzsche, Friedrich, *A Nietzsche Reader*, R. J. Hollingdale (selected and trans.), Penguin, London, 1977.

Nietzsche, Friedrich, *The Birth of Tragedy and the Genealogy of Morals*, Doubleday Anchor Books, New York, 1956.

Osborne, Peter (ed.), *A Critical Sense: Interviews with Intellectuals*, London, Routledge, 1996.

Osborne, Peter, *The Politics of Time: Modernity and Avant-Garde*, Verso, London, 1995.

Palmer, Sheridan, 'Bernard Smith, 1916–2011', in *Australian and New Zealand Journal of Art*, vol. 12, 2012, pp. 17–23.

Palmer, Sheridan, 'The Importance of *Leitmotifs* and Distance in the Biography of Bernard Smith', in *Australian Historical Studies*, vol. 43, no. 1, Melbourne, March 2012, pp. 28–44.

Palmer, Sheridan, 'The Lone Antipodean: Bernard Smith's Post-War Modernism', in *Eyeline*, no. 78/79, Kelvin Grove, autumn/winter 2013, pp. 52–8.

Palmer, Sheridan, *Centre of the Periphery: Three European Art Historians in Melbourne*, Australian Scholarly Publishing, Melbourne, 2008.

Phillips, Walter, *James Jefferis: Prophet of Federation*, Australian Scholarly Publishing, Melbourne, 1993.

Porter, Roy, *Flesh in the Age of Reason*, Allen Lane, London, 2003.

Postmodernism: ICA Documents 4 and 5, Institute of Contemporary Art, London, 1986.

Potts, Alex, *Flesh and the Ideal: Winckelmann and the Origins of Art History*, Yale University Press, New Haven and London, 1994.

Price, Bronwen (ed.), *Francis Bacon's New Atlantis: New Interdisciplinary Essays*, Manchester University Press, Manchester, 2002.

Pybus, Cassandra, 'The CIA as Culture Vultures', *Australian Book Review*, no. 223, Melbourne and Adelaide, August 2000.

Pyle, Forest, 'Raymond Williams and the Inhuman Limits of Culture', in Dennis L. Dworkin and Leslie G. Roman (eds), *Views Beyond the Border Country: Raymond Williams and Cultural Politics*, Routledge, New York, 1993.

Quilley, Geoff and John Bonehill (eds), *William Hodges, 1744–1797: The Art of Exploration*, Yale University Press, New Haven and London, 2004.

Rader, Melvin, *No Compromise: The Conflict Between Two Worlds*, Macmillan, New York, 1939.

Read, Herbert (ed.), *Surrealism*, Faber & Faber, London, 1936.

Read, Herbert, 'Art in an Australian University', in *Art and Australia*, vol. 1, no. 3, Sydney, November 1963, pp. 174–5.

Read, Herbert, *Art and Society*, Faber & Faber, London, 1936.

Read, Herbert, *Art Now: An Introduction to the Theory of Modern Painting and Sculpture*, Faber & Faber, London, 1933.

Reid, Barrett and Nancy Underhill (eds), *Letters of John Reed: Defining Australian Cultural Life, 1920–1981*, Viking, Melbourne, 2001.

Riemer, Andrew, *Hughes*, Duffy and Snellgrove, Sydney, 2001.

Rose, Margaret A., *Marx's Lost Aesthetic*, Cambridge University Press, Cambridge, UK, 1984.

Rose, Margaret A., *Parody: Ancient, Modern, and Post-Modern*, Cambridge University Press, Melbourne, 1993.

Ryan, Tom, 'Revisioning the Pacific: Bernard Smith in the South Seas', in *Thesis Eleven*, no. 82, Melbourne, 2005, pp. 16–28.

Seitler, Dana, *Atavistic Tendencies: The Culture and Science of American Modernity*, University of Minnesota Press, Minneapolis, 2008.

Shute, Neville, *On the Beach*, Pan Books, London, 1966.

Simmel, Georg, *Simmel on Culture: Selected Writings*, David Frisby and Mike Featherstone (eds), Sage Publications, London, 1997.

Simmons, Laurence, *Tuhituhi: William Hodges, Cook's painter in the South Pacific*, Otago University Press, Dunedin, 2011.

Smith, Barry, 'H. G. Wells in Australia', in *Australian Book Review*, no. 235, Melbourne and Adelaide, October 2001, pp. 32–6.

Smith, Joseph, *The Cold War, 1945–1965*, Blackwell, Oxford, 1989.

Smith, Terry, 'The Style of the Sixties', *Quadrant*, vol. 13, iss. 2, Sydney, March–April 1969, pp. 49–53.

Smith, Terry, 'Provincialism Refigured', in Peter Townsend (ed.), *Australian and International Art Monthly*, 1988, pp. 4–6.

Solomon-Godeau, Abigail, *Male Trouble: A Crisis in Representation*, Thames and Hudson, London, 1997.

Spate, O. H. K., *Australia*, Lothian, Melbourne, 1968.

Spencer, John and Peter Wright (eds), *The Writings of Bernard Smith: Bibliography 1938–1998*, Power Publications, Sydney, 2000.

Stanner, W. E. H., 'The Boyer Lectures: After the Dreaming', in Robert Manne (ed.), *W. E. H. Stanner: The Dreaming and Other Essays*, Black Inc. Agenda, Melbourne, 2009.

Steiner, George, *Language and Silence: Essays, 1958–1966*, Faber & Faber, London, 1967.

Stephen, Ann, Andrew McNamara and Philip Goad (eds), *Modernism and Australia: Documents on Art, Design and Architecture, 1919–1967*, Miegunyah Press, Melbourne, 2006.

Sutton, Peter (ed.), *Dreamings: The Art of Aboriginal Australia*, George Braziller, New York, 1988.

Taylor, Paul (ed.), *Anything Goes: Art in Australia, 1970–1980*, Art & Text, Melbourne, 1984.

Taylor, Paul, 'Clement Greenberg and Post Modernism: An Interview', *Art and Australia*, vol. 18, no.2, Sydney, summer 1980, pp. 141–4.

Teichman, Jenny, *Illegitimacy: A Philosophical Examination*, Blackwell, Oxford, 1982.

Thomas, Daniel, 'The Margins Fight Back', *Art and Australia*, vol. 26, no. 1, Sydney, autumn 1988, pp. 60–71.

Thomas, Daniel 'Aboriginal Art as Art: Who was Interested?', paper given at *New Visions: Histories of Art in Australia*, National Gallery of Victoria International, 3 June 2006.

Thomas, Nicholas and Diane Losche (eds), *Double Vision: Art Histories and*

Colonial Histories in the Pacific, Cambridge University Press, Cambridge, UK, 1999.

Thompson, Duncan, *Pessimism of the Intellect: A History of the* New Left Review, Merlin Press, Wales, 2007.

Trapp, Joseph, 'E. H. Gombrich: The Debate on Primitivism in Ancient Rhetoric', *Journal of the Warburg and Courtauld Institutes*, vol. 29, London, 1966, pp. 24–38.

Underhill, Nancy, *Making Australian Art 1916–49: Sydney Ure Smith, Patron and Publisher*, Oxford University Press, Melbourne, 1991.

Ure Smith, Sydney, 'Bringing Art to the Australian People', in *Society of Artists Book 1943*, Ure Smith, Sydney, pp. 65–7.

Wells, H. G., *Experiment in Autobiography*, Penguin, London, 1934.

Wells, H. G., *The Rights of Man*, Penguin, London, 1934.

Williams, Glyndwr, 'Explorers and Geographers: An Uneasy Alliance in the Eighteenth-Century Exploration of the Pacific', in Donna Merrick (ed.), *Dangerous Liaisons: Essays in Honour of Greg Dening*, Department of History, University of Melbourne, 1994, pp. 95–114.

Windels, Fernand, *The Lascaux Cave Paintings*, Faber & Faber, London, 1949.

Winks, Robin, *The Imperial Revolution: Yesterday and Tomorrow*, Oxford University Press, Oxford, 1994.

Woodfield, Richard, *The Essential Gombrich: Selected Writings on Art and Culture*, Phaidon, London, 1996.

Wyss, Beat, *Hegel's Art History and the Critique of Modernity*, Caroline Dobson Saltzwedel (trans.), Cambridge University Press, Cambridge, UK, 1999.

Young, Blamire, *The Proverbs of Goya*, Jonathan Cape, London, 1923.

CATALOGUES

Australian Aboriginal Art, The Berkeley Galleries, London, 1950, C. P. Mountford (introduction).

Paul Taylor, *Popism*, National Gallery of Victoria, Melbourne, 1982.

Christine Dixon and Terry Smith with an introduction by Virginia Spate, *Aspects of Australian Figurative Painting 1942–1962: Dreams, Fears and Desires*, The Power Institute of Fine Arts, University of Sydney and the Biennale of Sydney, 1984.

Angry Penguins and Realist Painting in Melbourne in the 1940s, Hayward Gallery, London, Southbank Centre, 1988.

Surrealism, Revolution by Night, National Gallery of Australia, Canberra, 1993.

Art and Power: Europe Under the Dictators 1930–45, Council of Europe exhibition, Hayward Gallery, London, 1996.

Achim Borchardt-Hume (ed.), *Malevich*, Tate Publishing, London, 2014.

ACKNOWLEDGEMENTS

Like his contemporary Manning Clark, Bernard Smith was intent on 'documenting the self, as [much as] documenting Australia's past'.[1] This compulsion to collect and file papers, correspondence, diaries and personal ephemera was no doubt in preparation for their posthumous reception, but it is to their credit that they did so, for without such material, history and lives cannot be reconstructed. Such archives connect with other people and places, and open extraordinary dialogues across time and place. An archive, though, is also the interface between a researcher and institutions. The National Library of Australia, where the majority of Smith's archive is housed, became the locus of my research and I am particularly grateful to Dr Marie-Louise Ayers, Margy Burn, Robyn Holmes, Lee Christofis and their wonderful staff for providing me with unending assistance and friendship. I also wish to thank Des Cowley of the State Library of Victoria; Steven Miller of the Edmund and Joanna Capon Research Library at the Art Gallery of New South Wales; Stephen Coppel, Curator of Prints and Drawings at the British Museum; Nicholas Keyzer, John Spencer and Peter Wright of the Schaeffer Fine Arts Library at the Power Institute; Jane Brown of the Visual Culture Resource Centre at the University of Melbourne; and the photographer David Loram. Thanks also to the librarians at the Mitchell Library in Sydney, the Baillieu Library at the University of Melbourne, the Fisher Library at the University of Sydney, and to those at the Warburg Institute Archives at the University of London. Also in London, to Paul Martyn Cooper and Lisa Di Tommaso at the Natural History Museum Library and Archives, the Royal Botanical Gardens Library, Kew, the

Tate Gallery Archives, and The Whitechapel Gallery Research Library I extend my thanks. I am also grateful to Carl Bridge and Ian Henderson of the Menzies Centre for Australian Studies at the University of London, the staff of Anglesea Abbey, and the Paul Mellon Centre for Studies in British Art, London, whose support has been enormously appreciated. During the course of writing this biography I wish to acknowledge the assistance I have received from the University of Melbourne and La Trobe University where I hold Honorary Fellow positions.

This biography of Bernard Smith could not have been written without the sponsorship received from the late Dame Elisabeth Murdoch, the late Dr Joseph Brown, James Fairfax AO, the late Emmanuel Hirsh, Dawn Palmer and Nola Oliver. Funding from a Manning Clark House/CAL Fellowship, a Sidney Myer Fund grant, a Harold White Fellowship and a grant from the Paul Mellon Centre for Studies in British Art enabled me to maintain a consistent pace through many years and in various locations, and I am grateful to the Australian Academy of the Humanities for their Publication Subsidy Award. I must also thank my friends who accommodated me in England, Canberra and Sydney, especially Bill and Alison Church, Allan and Hazel Hayhurst, Mary and Boyd Hilton, Michael and Trish Bull, Mark and Liz White, Rosalie Horner, Chris and Riteke Chenowith, Diane Kirkby and Sue Pedley.

Peter Osborne considers interviews are 'children of opportunity'; I consider interviews part of a dialogic relationship in understanding the subject, providing key words that inflect the tone, colour or shape of a person, a period or an anecdote, whether past or present. The spontaneity of a conversation retrieves and revises a memory, giving both explanation and reflection; I am deeply indebted to the very large number of people who agreed to be interviewed by me. They are listed in the bibliography.

In particular I want to thank Kate Challis, Bernard Smith's granddaughter, for her unwavering support and friendship. Her measured insight into the complexities of her grandfather's life as a scholar and his relationships with people, intimate, casual and official, was invaluable. There are many others who helped me to understand Bernard Smith, each and every one adding to the character of a complex, difficult but admirable man—in particular his daughter, Elizabeth Heathcote, and son, John Smith, Bernard's nephew Ric Edelman, Nigel Hughes, Helen Brack, Joan Beck, Catherine de Lorenzo, Rodney James, Bruno Leti, Joanna Mendelssohn, Donald Brook and Gary Willis. In addition, I would like to thank those who have assisted me in my research for this book: Bronwen Douglas, Diane Kirkby, Doug Munro and Ken Wach. I also wish to thank Mark Ledbury, the Director of the Power Institute, for placing faith in me to write the biography of this remarkable historian and father of Australian art history; also Marni Williams of Power Publications, Robin Appleton, my copy editor, and Paige Amor the proof reader for helping to bring the work to fruition. Finally, I wish to thank my family, Philip, Alexandra and Lily, for their great patience and tolerance towards an often-absent partner and mother—in particular to Philip for his consistent support and invaluable advice.

1   Mark McKenna, *Notes from the Underground: Writing the Biography of Manning Clark*, University of Melbourne, Melbourne, 2007, p. 26.

INDEX